# THE HAND
## THAT HELD
# THE GUN

CLARE
BOOKS

# THE HAND
## THAT HELD
# THE GUN

## UNTOLD STORIES OF THE WAR OF
## INDEPENDENCE IN WEST CLARE

## EOIN SHANAHAN

CLAREBOOKS

Published by Eoin Shanahan with the support of ClareBooks
Ennis
County Clare
Republic of Ireland

www.clarebooks.ie
info@clarebooks.ie

ISBN 13: 9781999611637
ISBN 10: 1999611632

Cover & book design and image enhancement by Niall Allsop; niallsop@mac.com
Body text in Adobe Garamond Pro: cover titles in CelticHand
Printed and bound in the EU

For my four best friends, Catherine, Neil, Vera and Mary.

# Contents

# Acknowledgements

To say that this book could never have been written without the friendship and support of Geoff Simmons would be a gross understatement. For many years he trawled through archives in London and in Northern Ireland in search of the pieces of a very complex jigsaw that he shared with me in countless emails and text messages.

More than anybody else, Geoff has contributed to this publication and I will be forever grateful to him for that.

Niall Allsop of ClareBooks, himself an accomplished author, is more than just a publisher. He has played a major role in bringing this work to fruition as copy editor, graphic designer, proofreader, project manager, publicist and motivator.

To each of these roles he brings skill and meticulous attention to detail that go beyond the level of professionalism. Curiously, the only time our joint collaboration came to a full stop was when we argued about the use of a capital letter. Niall was magnanimous in victory.

I have been most fortunate to have had the benefit of the wisdom and scholarly support of Professor Kevin Whelan, Michael Smurfit Director of the Keough Naughton Notre Dame Centre in Dublin.

I first experienced Kevin as a '1798 man' in the 1970s when I used video recordings of his contributions to TV documentaries to support my teaching. He brought history alive for me and for my students and his enthusiasm was infectious.

More recently, Kevin has been my trusted scholarly advisor and I am grateful to him for that.

Grateful thanks also to 'everybody's cousin', Paddy Waldron, whose expertise in genealogy has solved many a puzzle during the writing of this book.

Who else could have made the fascinating discovery that Geoff Simmons and I are ninth cousins?

On a personal level, I acknowledge my many great teachers, the first of whom were my parents, John and Kitty Shanahan, who imbued me with a thirst for knowledge and a love of learning.

I was fortunate to have attended St Flannan's College, Ennis, where the tutors were second to none and where my interest in history was fostered by inspiring teachers Tim Kelly and Liam Ashe. Later, St Patrick's Training College and Dublin City University were the settings for some of my most profound academic learning experiences.

Thanks to the staffs of the National Library of Ireland and the National Archives, Lisa Dolan of the Military Archives, Cathal Brugha Barracks, Dublin, Kirsty McHugh of the National Library of Scotland, Patricia Marsh of the Public Record Office of Northern Ireland, Ken Bergin and staff, Special Collections, Glucksman Library, University of Limerick, Michael Lynch, Archivist, Kerry Library, Neil Cobbett and Paul Johnson, National Archives of the UK.

Thanks also to Liz Parker, Research Assistant, Archives of the Society of Jesus, Melbourne, Australia for taking the time and trouble to scan and share the papers and photographs of Fr Willie Hackett.

Historian Dr Pádraig Ó Ruairc has been more than generous with his time and knowledge.

# ACKNOWLEDGEMENTS

Special thanks to Murt McInerney for his research on Willie Shanahan and Michael McNamara through the decades. The pageantry of Murt's Easter Sunday commemorations at the Republican Plot in Doonbeg is etched in my memory.

Thanks to John and Joe Daly (Kilmurry Ibrickane), Berna Kirwan, Michael Russell, Peadar Falsey, Rob McFadden, Jim Tubridy (Kilrush), Mick Honan (Leadmore), Jimmy O'Higgins, James Stephens, Brendan and Paul Daly, Paul O'Looney, Joe and Patsy O'Connor, Pat Kirby, Bríd Talty, Nora Meade, Pádraig De Barra, Jim Tubridy (Cooraclare), Paul Markham, Martin Quealy, Dympna Bonfield, Captain Donal Buckley, Patricia and Christy McCarthy, Tomás Ó Flaithearta, Carmel O'Callaghan, Michael Neenan, Morgan O'Connell (Cranny), Conor Nyhan, Paddy and Dolores Murrihy, Michael McCarthy, Eddie Cotter, Seán Keane, Tim and Patrick Kelly (Cloonagarnaun), Paddy Killeen, Mikie Whelan, Bill McNamara, Pat Sullivan, Michael Flanagan, Frank Considine (Clohanmore), Bernadette Considine (Dunboyne), Noel Bermingham, Martina Cotter, Joe Lineen, Michael Shannon (Moyasta), Mary McNamara, Gerard Morrissey, Mary Keane, Greg Fitzpatrick, Annelen Madigan (New York), Rev Patricia Hanna, Fr Joe Haugh and Fr Gerry Kenny, Kathleen Haugh, Cindy Wood, Jake Boland, Francie Killeen, Martin O'Halloran, Mary Flanagan, Maureen Kelly (Sale, Cheshire), Sheila Haugh, Mary Hamilton, Aidan Carroll, Brian Carroll, Peter Shanley, Paul Turnell, the Fennell family (Carrigaholt), Peter McGoldrick, Ronan Kelly (RTÉ) and Mick O'Connor, Colette and James McAlpine, Kevin O'Connor, Leasandra Lynch, Mary Dillon and Dympna Mulkerrin.

Raymond and Martina Coughlan are to be greatly commended for preserving in its original state the IRA dugout on their land at Greygrove, Kilmihil and for facilitating its refurbishment. Together with Martin Keane, they have preserved a very important part of the history of west Clare. My visits there have been among the most profoundly evocative experiences of my research.

Mary Driver has shared some unique photographs and material relating to her uncle, Michael Fahy.

Thanks to my special friends in Chicago, the Neylon family, Jimmy, Chris, Bill and of course Máirín Ní Níalláin. Getting to know them has been one of the great highlights of the last ten years.

I acknowledge the contribution of the late Mathún Mac Fheorais, who left some valuable accounts of interviews that he conducted in the 1970s. Regrettably, others too have passed on, including Danny Garry, Michael Howard, Michael Studdert, John Shanahan, Gerry Neenan, John Quealy, Siney Talty, Vera Shanley, Peadar McNamara, Éamonn Burke, Matthew Bermingham, Martin O'Halloran, Francie Killeen, Liam Haugh (Jnr), Mary Margaret Shanahan, Bridget Brew, Mícheál Ó Catháin, John Kelly (Clonina), James Cahill, Phyllis Winslow and Paul Daly.

Parts of four chapters of this book have been previously published as 'Telling Tales: the story of the burial alive and drowning of a Clare RM in 1920', *History Ireland,* Volume 18, No 1, 2010; 'The Blackened Tans' in *The Clare Champion*, 1 November 2013; 'The Shooting of Tom Shannon, forgotten hero of the War of Independence in West Clare' in *Clare Association Yearbook, 2016* and 'Kilmihil's Bloody Sunday' *Clare Association Yearbook, 2018.*

The publication of these articles was made possible by Tommy Graham, Editor, *History Ireland* and Patricia Molony and the Committee of the Clare Association.

I owe a huge debt of gratitude to all of the people who helped me with my research over the last decade. In the likely event that I omit some, I hope that they will accept this as an acknowledgement of their role.

Thanks to my brothers and sisters for their encouragement and especially to Martha for her hospitality on my visits to Clare.

# ACKNOWLEDGEMENTS

Special thanks to my wife and children, Catherine, Neil, Vera and Mary, for their enduring patience and their unfailing confidence in me.

*Deirtear gur ar scáth a chéile a mhaireann na daoine, rud a thuigtear dom go maith tar éis breis agus deich mbliana a chaitheamh ar an taighde seo. Gabhaim buíochas ó chroí leo siúd a maireann agus leosan nach maireann as ucht a gcabhrach agus a dtacaíochta chun an beart oibre seo a chur i gcrích.*

# Abbreviations

### In text

| | |
|---|---|
| ASU | Active Service Unit |
| CC | Catholic Curate |
| CI | County Inspector |
| CO | Commanding Officer |
| DC | Divisional Commissioner |
| DI | District Inspector |
| DIG | Deputy Inspector General |
| GAA | Gaelic Athletic Association |
| HQ | Headquarters |
| IRA | Irish Republican Army |
| JP | Justice of the Peace |
| LGB | Legitimate Government Body |
| MP | Member of Parliament |
| NT | National Teacher |
| OC | Officer Commanding |
| PP | Parish priest |
| RAMC | Royal Army Medical Corps |
| RIC | Royal Irish Constabulary |
| RIP | Rest in Peace |
| RM | Resident Magistrate |
| RMS | Royal Mail Ship |
| TB | Tuberculosis |
| US | United States |

### Captions

| | |
|---|---|
| MA | Military Archives |
| MSPC | Military Service Pensions Collection |
| NAUK | National Archives of the United Kingdom |
| NLS MS | National Library of Scotland, Manuscript Collections. |
| PRONI | Public Record Office Northern Ireland |

### Archives

| | |
|---|---|
| BMH | Bureau of Military History |
| CO | Colonial Office |
| CSORP | Chief Secretary's Office Registered Papers |
| HO | Home Office |
| IWM | Imperial War Museum |
| MA | Military Archives |
| MSP | Military Service Pensions |
| MSPC | Military Service Pensions Collection |
| NAI | National Archives of Ireland |
| NAUK | National Archives of the United Kingdom |
| NLS MS | National Library of Scotland, Manuscript Collections. |
| PRONI | Public Record Office Northern Ireland |
| REF | Referee |
| UCDA | University College Dublin Archives |
| WO | War Office |
| WS | Witness Statement |

# Introduction

On a summer's day in 2008, a young London-based graphic designer arrived in McInerney's shop in Mountrivers, Doonbeg, County Clare.

He introduced himself to shopkeeper Rita McInerney:

"My name is Geoff Simmons," he began, "and I'm the great-nephew of a Resident Magistrate who was ambushed and killed near here in 1920. I'm trying to learn more about him. His name was Alan Lendrum. Have you heard of him?"

Rita had some knowledge of the Lendrum ambush, enough to know that the daughter of one of the ambush participants was actually in the shop. Ever the diplomat, she directed her visitor to Caherfeenick, where the ambush had happened, about a mile away. Rita's father, Murt, was hot on Geoff's heels and their subsequent interaction led to the collaboration between Geoff and myself that has resulted in this publication.

The Lendrum ambush had taken place not far from my family home and I knew that my uncle, Willie Shanahan, had driven the magistrate's car from the scene.

Every now and again I would thumb through the pages of an old book in my father's library to find and read a chilling account of the incident. Describing Lendrum's killing as 'an act of insensate savagery' the book stated that the poor man had been buried to his neck on a nearby beach and left to drown in the incoming tide:

> The Volunteers returned the next day to find the victim still alive. They dug him out and buried him again farther down the beach, where he could watch the next tide advance, to put him slowly out of his long agony.

By this time similar accounts had begun to proliferate on the internet and I was initially a little reticent about making contact with this relative of a man who had been widely reported as having been the victim of a rather brutal IRA atrocity.

Indeed, it was only when I accessed Lendrum's death certificate – which disproved the drowning myth – that I plucked up the courage to approach Geoff Simmons.

Following an exchange of emails, we met for the first time in Kilskeery, County Tyrone in August 2009.

It was the beginning of a collaborative research effort that turned the drowning myth on its head and that led to mutual understandings and lasting friendship. Significantly, it was also the beginning of the journey that has led to the publication of this record of revolutionary times in west Clare.

There were some unforgettable moments along this research journey:

A trip to Kilkee to view and handle what was believed to be Alan Lendrum's briefcase; a rainy evening search of Doolough Lake for Lendrum's car; a wild New Year's Day quest in Rockmount bog for the unmarked grave of a soldier who was shot and buried there in 1921.

Seeing and handling the blood-stained back-brace that saved Éamon Fennell from serious injury recalled the tragic consequences of the Carrigaholt bayonet charge in 1918.

My memorable visits to the home of the late Francis Dooley in Cloonagarnaun brought to life the scene of a police and military raid that took place there on 6 December 1920.

# INTRODUCTION

The IRA dugout at Greygrove, Kilmihil is a special place and my visits there have been among the most profoundly evocative experiences of my research.

The research effort has uncovered many images that had not previously been part of the photographic record of the War of Independence. Although the passage of time has not been kind to some, their inclusion is warranted and worthwhile.

When General Peter Strickland, the General Officer commanding the British Army in Munster, visited Clare in March 1920, he found what he described as '… the hotbed of republican activity'.

Strickland thought he had the solution to the problem …

Believing that the majority of the population were opposed to the armed struggle, he urged his local contacts to set up unarmed community-based vigilante police patrols in the towns and villages.

However, Strickland greatly underestimated the strength of character, the resolve and the determination of the members of the East Clare, Mid Clare and West Clare Brigades.

This is the story of the West Clare Brigade. It is the story of ordinary men and women who did extraordinary things in extraordinary times.

**Eoin Shanahan**
October 2019

## Note for the reader

The spellings and punctuation in primary sources quoted in this book retain their original status. Otherwise, the spellings of place names are those that are common in current usage. They may vary from the conventions of a century ago when, for example, Kilmihil was spelled Kilmihill and Miltown Malbay was spelled Milltown Malbay.

The spellings of people's names usually reflect the spellings that were used by the people themselves and their families. For example, the name Darcy was spelled D'arcy in many official documents. The name Michael is incorrectly shortened to Micko in a number of referenced documents and in these cases the correct spelling Micho is used.

# Drilling for Ireland

In the Kilrush area, the National Volunteers were formed in 1913 by Charlie Glynn, a member of a well-known, local merchant-family who had loyalist leanings.[1]

Known as the Redmondite Volunteers, the organisation's membership quickly grew and many boys as young as 15 joined up. At the time, the town was home to many British Army Reserve men of the Munster Fusiliers and the British Navy, who took up leadership positions. Not surprising therefore, that training was often provided by ex-British soldiers.[2]

When, on 3 August 1914, John Redmond pledged Volunteer support for the British in the Great War in return for a promise of Home Rule, he caused a split in the ranks. In Clare, the effects of the split were mixed; the Kilrush Volunteers had mostly sided with Redmond while, in nearby Tullycrine, Art O'Donnell's men remained staunchly loyal to their founding principles and forged links with other west Clare companies that had been established in Carrigaholt and Cranny.[3]

Prior to 1916, the Limerick Volunteers held training camps at the GAA sports field at George's Head near Kilkee. Camp bell tents and a marquee were erected there and participants paid a fixed fee for board and lodging. The police turned a blind eye to these 'holiday camps', despite the fact that arms, including Mauser-type rifles and revolvers, were carried openly. Departing

Volunteers were seen off at the railway station by their comrades, who lined the platform and fired a volley of shots as the train departed.[4]

The RIC, who were seen by many as the eyes and ears of the British Government, also turned a blind eye and never more so than when an area was under military rule. After all, while RIC personnel were never stationed in the county of their birth or the county of birth of their spouse, nearly all were Irish, most were Catholic and some were long-time residents of west Clare.

With a force that numbered 11,000, there was an RIC station in every single parish, so the local constable was acquainted with local revolutionaries and had intimate knowledge of his area.[5] Indeed, RIC efforts to uphold law and order had enjoyed the tacit support of their local communities prior to revolutionary times.

RIC personnel carried out many of the functions that would normally be associated with Civil Servants in Britain.[6] Many west Clare census returns, for example, bear the names of local constables. Some were less diligent than others, which endeared them to most, and in west Clare, one such law officer was about to end his career in Doonbeg without a single enemy in the locality.

This was a significant achievement for a policeman, but there was a sting in the tail. For, since he had never had a single prosecution, he would have to retire on a reduced pension. Had he been prepared to lose friends, securing the necessary indictment would have been easy, but that would tarnish his unblemished record. Instead, the resourceful policeman persuaded his local drinking buddy to turn his pig out onto the road in order to facilitate a Court Summons. The case was duly heard at Kilkee Petty Sessions Court, where the defendant was found guilty as charged and he was fined one shilling. This obliging friend collected his reward in the local pub when the retiree cashed his first pension payment.[7]

~

Kerry-born Constable Michael Monaghan, who was based in Kilkee, had chalked up an impressive record of successful prosecutions prior to the outbreak of the War of Independence. He is immortalised in local lore, all because his accent merged two pairs of phonemes. The first pair – /hw/ and /f/ – affected his pronunciation of a relatively small number of words. For Constable Monaghan, the phenomenon was most notable when he asked questions, something constables were no strangers to. Thus, he was regularly heard to ask 'Fere are oo going?' and 'Fot are oo doing?' And in common with many west of Ireland accents, Monaghan's speech also merged the /i/ and the /e/ vowel phonemes (a phenomenon known as the pin/pen merger), which resulted in pronunciations of the 'pincil' variety.

Now, in his pursuit of justice, Monaghan had occasion to summons members of the Hodges and McCarthy families for having a donkey and a white jennet grazing the long acre.[8] When the case came to court there was some amusement when the phonologically-challenged constable referred a couple of times to the offending hybrid as the 'Fite Jinnet'. From that day forward, Monaghan was known in west Clare as the 'Fite Jinnet'.

Sometime later, Monaghan summonsed old Paddy Keane for having an unlicensed dog.

When Paddy claimed that the dog was not his, the Court Chairman asked him, "Whose dog was it so?"

When Paddy replied that it was his son Francie's dog and that Francie was in France, the judge asked, "Well, why did you not tell somebody?"

To the great amusement of all present, save one, Paddy replied, "I told the 'Fite Jinnet'."

On another occasion, Tommy Kelly, who had fought in the Great War, was being beaten up by the Tans near the Stella Maris Hotel. Spotting Constable Monaghan nearby, Kelly pleaded, "Oh, 'Fite Jinnet', save me!"[9]

≈

Prior to 1917, the whole of Clare had been part of the Limerick Brigade,

Following Michael Brennan's release from Frongoch in December 1916, discussions took place with a view to the establishment of a Clare Brigade and this came to pass in January 1917.

Paddy Brennan was appointed Brigade Commandant, Frank and Joe Barrett became Vice-Commandant and Adjutant respectively and Éamon Waldron, a teacher at St Flannan's College in Ennis, took on the role of Brigade Quartermaster.[10]

Limerick and Clare were divided into eight battalion areas and the eighth battalion constituted what would later become the West Clare Brigade. Éamon Fennell, from Carrigaholt, was appointed OC and Michael Keane, from Kilbaha, became Vice-OC.[11] Towards the end of 1918, the county was divided into three Brigade areas, East Clare, Mid Clare and West Clare.[12]

West Clare Brigade was then comprised of five battalions:

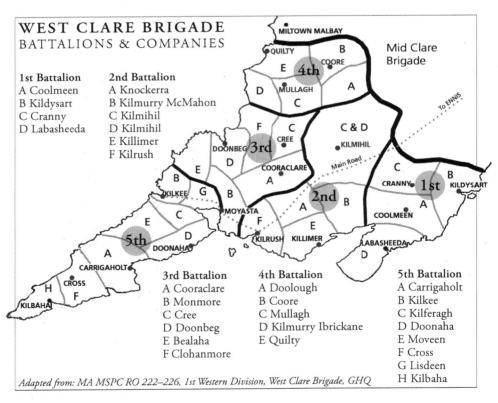

**WEST CLARE BRIGADE**
BATTALIONS & COMPANIES

**1st Battalion**
A Coolmeen
B Kildysart
C Cranny
D Labasheeda

**2nd Battalion**
A Knockerra
B Kilmurry McMahon
C Kilmihil
D Kilmihil
E Killimer
F Kilrush

**3rd Battalion**
A Cooraclare
B Monmore
C Cree
D Doonbeg
E Bealaha
F Clohanmore

**4th Battalion**
A Doolough
B Coore
C Mullagh
D Kilmurry Ibrickane
E Quilty

**5th Battalion**
A Carrigaholt
B Kilkee
C Kilferagh
D Doonaha
E Moveen
F Cross
G Lisdeen
H Kilbaha

*Adapted from: MA MSPC RO 222–226, 1st Western Division, West Clare Brigade, GHQ*

There was a remarkable upsurge in expressions of nationalist sentiment and pride among the population as a whole and west Clare was no exception.

These expressions were most noticeably manifest in the re-establishment of Gaelic League branches, the flying of Sinn Féin flags, the organising of parades of Volunteers and Na Fianna Boy Scouts, the singing of Republican songs and in the swelling of the membership of Sinn Féin Clubs and the Volunteers.[13] By the middle of 1917 there were Sinn Féin Clubs in practically every parish in west Clare.[14]

For special occasions, an old Parnellite custom of wearing an ivy leaf on one's lapel in memory of the uncrowned king was reinvented as a symbol of belonging to the Irish Volunteers (IV).[15] On Sundays after Mass and on some weekday evenings, Volunteers were drilled on roadways and in fields, where they marched in military formation with wooden guns, hurleys or long sticks on their shoulders. Training in military manoeuvres and in the use of weapons was provided by those with military experience, however limited, and, in their absence, by Volunteer officers using training manuals. For the most part, training was regarded as effective, though one enthusiastic military instructor raised a few eyebrows when he cautioned his charges ...

"The enemy that's nearer to you than you are to him is the most dangerous enemy of all."

Ever watchful, the Constabulary made regular arrests and convicted offenders would serve prison sentences. Following an arrest, crowds (often numbering hundreds) would assemble outside the police barracks singing rebel songs (*The Soldier's Song* and *The Felons of our Land* were favourites) and shouting slogans like 'Up the Republic' and 'Our day will come'. At Sinn Féin concerts, nationalist pride was nurtured by rousing choruses like:

Shoulder high your hurleys, boys,
Keep your rifles tight,
The mangy bulldog only barks,
He has no teeth to bite.[16]

On one such occasion, a Volunteer Captain had just been arrested by police and military and had been lodged in Kilrush's Toler Street Barracks. A hostile crowd had gathered outside, singing and chanting, and police had warned of a baton charge if they failed to disperse.

Local priest Fr O'Gorman saw the commotion on his way to the nearby church and began telling the crowd to go home. He was admonished by a more patriotic Christian Brother named Walshe:

"There is enough of these fellows here in black to do that dirty work besides you doing it."

Spotting the developing clerical dispute, an RIC man came forward and grabbed Walshe by the shoulder, whereupon the Christian Brother levelled him with an uppercut.

There were some tense moments and fiery exchanges.

Walshe later ruminated, "No, I would not have struck Father O'Gorman, but that cad. To think that he laid a hand on the cloth I wear."[17]

≈

Recruitment wasn't all plain sailing for the Republican movement in Kilrush. Thanks to local businessman and controller of recruiting, Charlie Glynn, Kilrush was unique in Clare (if not in Ireland) for its contribution to the Great War effort with the result that 70% of the male population had served with the colours.[18]

The wives of these men became known as 'separation women' and, being in receipt of a regular separation allowance from the British Government, they were largely unsympathetic and often openly hostile to active Republicanism.

It was around this time that teacher Brian Mac Lua set up a branch of Fianna Éireann in Kilrush. One evening, having first drilled in the schoolyard, his group went marching in the streets in military formation, waving a Sinn Féin flag. However, their public expression of nationalism was interrupted when they were attacked by a stone-throwing group of separation women.[19]

In Kilrush, early on Sunday morning 6 May, a police patrol discovered and removed Sinn Féin flags hanging from the Manchester Martyrs monument, the Courthouse, the Post Office and the Provincial Bank.

In Kilmihil, a few brazen local Volunteers attached three flags to the chimneys of the RIC Barracks.[20] Mary Hayes, a Kilkee publican, Anne O'Neill and Martin McCarthy were charged with similar offences at Kilkee Petty Sessions Court in August. Mrs Hayes was fined £2, mitigated by the court to 10s, for hanging two Sinn Féin tricolours from her premises.[21] She was warned that she would lose her licence if she re-offended.

Many similar cases were reported throughout Clare,[22] while in west Clare a groundswell of support for self-determination was steadily developing with hundreds of Volunteers being recruited in every parish.

∽

Attitudes to the eyes and ears of the British Government in Clare had hardened considerably, so much so that, by December 1917, the RIC were regarded as enemies of the people.[23]

A Kerry-born policeman's use of his eyes and ears was beginning to make some enemies for him in the Kilrush district. Known to locals as 'Hanley', even to the present day, Constable John Hanlon had been first stationed in Cork in 1909, where he met and married Cork native Hannah Nyhan.[24]

In keeping with RIC protocol, he could not serve in the county of birth of his spouse and so he was posted to the detective unit in Kilrush in December 1915.[25] There, he established something of a reputation for himself as an active (some would say overly zealous) member of the detective department.

On Sunday 5 August 1917, Hanlon arrested Richard Behan of Tarmon at Knockerra. Behan had been drilling a company of 68 men on the public road near Knockerra Chapel with the usual commands, 'fall in ... form fours ... number ... quick march ... right ... as ye were.'

When Hanlon attempted to interview his target, Behan waved him away, saying, 'Never ming [sic] you until I finish."

Back in Toler Street RIC Barracks, the constable wrote his report:

... after he dismissed them he asked me what I had to say to him. I then asked him was he aware that he was committing an illegal act by drilling and he replied that he did not know; wern't [sic] they drilling in England. He asked me the following questions "whathire [sic] per week had I; what was my name, was I an Irishman."[26]

Behan appeared at Kilrush Petty Sessions Court on other similar charges, but the cases against him were dismissed when he gave and honoured undertakings not to engage in further drilling exercises.[27]

Monmore Captain Martin Chambers fell foul of Constable Michael Hurley when he drilled his men openly in front of Doonbeg RIC Barracks in July or August 1917. Chambers was forced to go on the run when the 'officious' constable reported him to the RIC district HQ in Kilrush.[28]

Meanwhile, in the 5th Battalion area, all companies were actively drilling with dummy rifles at this time. In Kilferagh, by contrast, Simon McInerney, Tom Lillis and members of C-Company were busy making slugs for real guns.

A daring plan was hatched to attack and disarm a military party at Moveen.

Michael Fahy, OC of Fianna Éireann in Kilkee learned from a local garage owner that the military had hired three cars to bring them and their arms from Kilkee to Carrigaholt. Fahy contacted Éamon Fennell and a plan of action was drafted.

The driver of the first car was to stop at a pre-arranged location under the guise of doing some running repairs. Having brought all three cars to a halt, the military would be ambushed and relieved of their weaponry which would be transferred to a fourth car at the back carrying Fahy and Jim Talty. Unfortunately, the driver of the first car misunderstood his instructions and stopped the car at the wrong place.[29]

On 7 June 1917 Willie Redmond, MP for East Clare and brother of John Redmond, died at the Battle of Messines in Belgium. Éamon de Valera was selected as the Sinn Féin candidate in the ensuing by-election.

During the campaign, Volunteers appeared on the streets in full uniform and carrying sticks, for the first time since the 1916 Rising.[30] Significantly, Kilrush Urban Council unanimously passed a resolution in support of de Valera's opponent, Patrick Lynch. The motion was proposed by Thomas Nagle and seconded by Michael Crotty. The chairman, Batt Culligan JP (Justice of the Peace), said that the least the electorate of East Clare could do as a compliment to Willie Redmond was to elect his friend.[31]

In the heel of the hunt it was a landslide victory for de Valera, whose follow-up visit to west Clare was a huge morale boost for Republicans.

~

Art O'Donnell from Tullycrine and Seán Liddy from Danganelly quickly emerged as two of the most talented leaders and organisers in the west Clare district.

O'Donnell, whose mother was a first cousin of executed 1916 leader Con Colbert, had been arrested in Kilrush on 29 May 1916 and had been interned in Frongoch Prison until his release on 22 July. In common with his fellow prisoners, his reception in his native Clare was notably less hostile than the send-off he had been given following his post-Rising arrest.

He was arrested again on 14 August 1917 and brought to Ennis Barracks on a charge of illegal drilling. In order to avoid the crowds that usually turned up to cheer the departing prisoners, he and his fellow inmates were ferried to Clarecastle. Not to be outdone, the Ennis crowd boarded the train and travelled there to give the men a rousing send-off.[32]

On 28 and 29 August 1917, O'Donnell, together with Bertie Hunt (Corofin), James Madigan, James Griffey (Ennis) and Michael O'Brien (Ruan) were charged with illegal drilling of men at various locations and at various dates. Each of the prisoners was asked if he objected to being tried by any member of the court and Hunt, in refusing to recognise the court, responded with the memorable line, "It is a matter of perfect indifference to me."

O'Donnell, whose offences were alleged to have been committed on 22

July, 3 August and 12 August, objected to being described on the charge sheet as a 'civilian' when he was, in fact, a soldier of the Irish Republican Army. Evidence was given by Sergeants John Daly and William Reilly and Constables Hayes, Donovan, Sullivan and Gleeson. Sergeant Reilly had informed O'Donnell and his men that drilling was illegal and ordered them to stop. O'Donnell addressed the Volunteers:

This is British law and we recognise no laws except those made by the Irish people. The constable tells you it is illegal, but that is why we are doing it. You should break every law made by the British Government – Defence of the Realm Acts, Coercion Acts and every other law. I don't blame the police for doing their duty; that is what they are paid for; but what do we care about their laws? It would be better for you, as Irishmen, to rot in prison than be driven from home by British laws which will not give you an existence in your

Volunteers outside Frawley's Pub, Cooraclare.
(*Courtesy Jim Tubridy*)

own country … I would like if you would pay tribute to Roger Casement's memory and the best tribute you could pay is to bestir yourselves. Drill as much as you can and don't mind the Defence of the Realm or any other law.

Constable Donovan deposed that, when he asked the prisoner if he knew that drilling was illegal, O'Donnell replied that he did, but that English Law had no moral or legal standing in Ireland.

In a statement to the court, he went on to compliment the accuracy of the policemens' recall of his military instructions to the parading Volunteers and suggested that the same policemen might be more useful to the British Government training the American or Russian armies.

In the event that he would be detained further, he demanded that he be treated as a prisoner of war in accordance with International Law.[33]

Newspapers reported that all were sentenced to one year's imprisonment without hard labour, save O'Brien, who got six months without hard labour and these figures are confirmed in official reports.[34]

However, O'Donnell's detailed account of the court-martial and subsequent incarceration not only specifies that the sentences included hard labour, but also outlines the tasks that prisoners had to perform.[35]

Following sentencing, the prisoners were taken to Mountjoy, where they met with Seán Treacy and fellow Claremen, Peadar O'Loughlin and the brothers Austin, Michael and Paddy Brennan, as well as the prisoner in cell no. 34 – Thomas Ashe.[36] Following his release from prison, Ashe, whose cousin Pádraig Ashe was teaching at Doonbeg National School, had met and addressed local Volunteers in the Doughmore sandhills.[37] The Clare contingent in Mountjoy would shortly be joined by five neighbours from Cooraclare.

~

Seán Liddy, a 26-year-old farmer's son from Danganelly, Cooraclare was beginning to make a name for himself as an aspiring young leader – albeit under the watchful eye of the RIC.

Patrick (Sonny) Burke had earlier abandoned his secondary school education at Kilrush Christian Brothers School to play his part in the national struggle and now held the rank of Company Quartermaster.[38]

On 13 August 1917, together with brothers Joseph and William Breen, Patrick Burke and James Callinan, all from Cooraclare, Liddy appeared before Kilrush Petty Sessions Court. They were charged with having organised a church-gate collection for the de Valera Fund without a permit.

All five refused to pay the token fine of one penny and costs of one shilling, before leaving the court to be greeted outside by a large cheering crowd.

The group fell into processional formation and marched to Toler Street waving flags and singing *The Soldier's Song*. At the RIC Barracks, they offered themselves for arrest, but the police declined.

All the men paid up in the coming weeks.[39]

Liddy's activities were closely monitored thereafter and he was arrested by Sergeant O'Reilly on 25 August 1917 and charged with offences under the Defence of the Realm Act. The case was heard at a District Court-martial in Cork Barracks on 5 September 1917. Liddy, who declined to plead, was charged with practising men in movements of a military nature on 12, 15 and 20 August 1917.

Sergeant Ed Michael Sullivan told the court that he had witnessed Liddy drilling about 100 men on the night of 12 August 1917 and that at Cree on 15 August, he saw the defendant drilling about 80 men before they marched towards Cooraclare. Constables Martyn and Costigan gave supporting evidence and Costigan deposed that he had seen Liddy drilling 32 men at Danganelly Cross on 20 August 1917. In all cases, the men had marched at Liddy's command in military formation.

Liddy told the court that as a soldier of the Irish Republican Army he had no regrets and that he would happily do the same again for his oppressed country. He stated that, in the event that he would be detained in custody, he wished to be treated as a prisoner of war.[40]

Seán Treacy from Soloheadbeg, William McNamara from Ennis, John

Minihan from Ballykinacurra and Michael Murray from Newmarket-on-Fergus were all tried on similar offences. All were found guilty and sentenced to one year's imprisonment with hard labour.[41]

~

The reaction around the country to these and other arrests was phenomenal, with well-attended protest marches, demonstrations and meetings being organised throughout the four provinces.[42]

Countess Markievicz later recalled meeting Liddy and Thomas Browne while they were under arrest at Limerick Station. Realising that both were resolutely intent on hunger striking, she tried in vain to dissuade them, but they responded:

> We are soldiers pledged to Ireland, and we can fight in jail as well as out, and die in jail as well as out, and it is up to us to do it.[43]

The prisoners' first days were spent in solitary confinement stitching sacks. Complaints were made to the Governor and free association was demanded, after which the men were brought out to the prison yard, splitting wood in open fronted cubicles.

Liddy prepared a memo with a list of demands, which was sent to the governor and signed, 'J J Liddy, Clare Brigade, Irish Republican Army.' The prisoners were threatening that they would go on hunger strike if the demands in prisoner Liddy's letter were not granted.[44]

When prison staff failed to accede to their demands, about 40 prisoners began to ignore regulations, which resulted in an even stricter regime.

Matters came to a head when the protesters began ringing their bells incessantly and breaking the glass in their cell windows. The authorities responded by removing beds, bedclothes and boots from the cells.

On 20 September, the prisoners began to refuse all food[45] and, two days later, forcible feeding began.

The prisoners were tied with straps and a mixture of milk and eggs was pumped twice daily via a rubber tube into their stomachs. On Tuesday morning 25 September, Art O'Donnell was taken out to be forcibly fed:

A new doctor named Dr Lowe was in the cell where the food was forcibly administered and he proceeded to insert the tube, which I thought hurt more than usual, and on the first stroke of the pump I coughed violently. Dr Lowe withdrew the tube, re-inserted it after the fit of coughing had ceased and then completed the operation ... after I was taken back to my cell I saw Tom Ashe going to be forcibly fed.

Ashe also coughed violently and became so ill that he was removed to the Mater Hospital, where he died a few hours later. The remaining prisoners continued to be forcibly fed until Saturday night, 29 September, when the prison authorities agreed to treat the men as prisoners of war.[46]

Mountjoy hunger-strikers, October 1919.
Tom Howard, Lisladeen, is on the back row, second from left.
*(Courtesy Tom Howard Jnr)*

Ashe's death provoked a national outcry ... not since the funeral of O'Donovan Rossa had the streets of Dublin been so thronged in honouring a dead patriot. And when the protracted inquest returned a verdict that included the words 'inhuman treatment', public emotions ran high.[47]

Those emotions were keenly felt in west Clare and were given public expression on Saturday and Sunday, 6 and 7 October, when de Valera visited Kilrush. He arrived in the town on Saturday and a suitable platform had been erected in the Square which a number of men with hurleys had guarded overnight.[48]

It was a truly memorable occasion and, from early that morning, huge numbers of people converged on the town from every town and village in west Clare. Mickey Tubridy (an O'Donovan Rossa lookalike from Dromelihy) led at least 100 men on horseback through the town behind the Kilkee Band.

De Valera was met on the Ennis Road by a guard of honour of Volunteers holding aloft on their hayforks blazing sods of turf that had been dipped in paraffin.[49] Such was the throng that the square couldn't hold everybody. De Valera had to ask those in Frances Street to move back ten paces in order to accommodate the people who were approaching via Henry Street.[50] The event was marshalled by Peadar Clancy and Matthew Bermingham was appointed *aide-de-camp* to de Valera for the duration of his visit to west Clare, where he also visited Kilkee and Carrigaholt.

Following de Valera's visit Volunteer levels of engagement increased and numbers swelled significantly.[51]


The Mountjoy hunger strike was over by the time Cooraclare's Joseph Breen was imprisoned there. He had been arrested once again on 19 September 1917 on a charge of illegal drilling.

Sergeant William Reilly, Constable Costigan, Constable Hayes and Constable Cuniffe testified that Breen had been seen drilling a total of 159 men at Danganelly over a period of three consecutive Sundays beginning on 2 September 1917.

Breen was tried and found guilty by District Court-Martial in Cork on

2 October 1917, where he refused to recognise the Court in similar fashion to Liddy and was sentenced to two years with hard labour. The hard labour element and one year were later remitted.[52]

Breen began his prison term in Mountjoy in the company of Thomas Browne of Toonavoher, who had been found guilty of similar charges. On 13 November they were transferred to Dundalk Gaol together with Liddy, Art O'Donnell and the other Republican prisoners, many of them Claremen.[53]

After the death of Thomas Ashe, Dublin Lord Mayor, Alderman Laurence O'Neill, had secured a verbal agreement that the prisoners would enjoy political status. However, following their transfer to Dundalk, the authorities served up ordinary prison fare and locked the cell doors earlier than the agreed time.

Under the leadership of Austin Stack, the prisoners went on hunger strike again before being released on 'temporary discharge for ill health' on 16 and 17 November under the Cat and Mouse Act.

The terms of their discharge stipulated that they were to return to complete their sentences on the 5 and 6 December. Released prisoners were warned that, 'While you are at large under this order the currency of your sentence is suspended.'[54]

# Hunger for Land

Towards the end of 1917 and in early 1918, agrarian strife, which had been experienced for decades, escalated significantly in the rural west, and Clare was no exception.

During the Great War, the British Government had put an embargo on emigration, which increased the population of landless and uneconomic small-holders. At a time when land values had soared due to high prices of agricultural produce, these people had limited or no means of growing crops to feed their families.[1]

The British Government had stalled the process of land division that had begun a few decades earlier and those who had nothing often found themselves living next door to those who had much. That was bad enough, but on the other side were those who had benefited from earlier Land Acts.[2]

The British Government was advocating for more tillage, but was not inclined to enforce the appropriate percentage of tillage; the big ranches were being grazed by cattle and sheep and owners were reluctant to part with land in a time of boom for produce. Matters were further exacerbated by the failure of government to relieve congestion through the promotion of land settlement.[3]

Throughout the west of Ireland, the have-nots began to take over the land of the have-a-lots, and even of the have-mores. Cattle and sheep were driven from targeted farms and sections of the land were immediately ploughed with a view to tillage.[4]

~

There was considerable turbulence in east Clare, where police baton-charged groups of cattle drivers and 21 men who were arrested, and held pending trial, went on hunger strike.

Pandemonium broke out in Ennis on the day of the trial. A convoy of cars drove through the streets to the station to welcome the prisoners on their arrival from Limerick. There was much cheering, flag-waving and singing of Republican songs.

In the courtroom, the cheering continued, leaving the judge little option but to abandon the sitting. His order to clear the court, however, was taken literally by the prisoners, who made a rush for the door and escaped, before

Laying claim to Ireland. A regular sight in west Clare during the War of Independence.
*(Courtesy Mary Driver)*

marching through the streets shouting slogans like, 'Up the Cattle Drivers' and 'The Land for the People.'[5]

This complete disregard for the courts was matched by open hostility towards the police.

On 17 January a group of Volunteers carrying sticks and hurleys organised a cattle drive near Kinloe, marching in fours and singing *The Soldiers Song*. When they were confronted by police they shouted, "Mind your own business. Your day is done."

It was the beginning of the end of the British justice system in Clare. In late January, 50 extra police were drafted into the county and were deployed at key police stations.[6]

In east Clare, the unrest reached crisis point when John Ryan lost his life at Castlefergus, having been shot by police at a cattle drive on 24 February.

The incident aroused further widespread ill-feeling towards police, as evidenced in Cooraclare some days later. There, a group of Volunteers were drilling when a combined force of RIC and military ordered them to disperse. The leaders of the drilling party made it clear that they would obey the orders of the military but would have no truck with the police.[7]

Conflicting claims were made about whether or not Sinn Féin were responsible for the dramatic increase in land agitation during the early months of 1918. In response, the Sinn Féin Executive issued a statement outlining its position, while ruling that members' involvement in land agitation should only happen with official sanction.[8]

Bishop Fogarty decried the attempts by 'the hostile press' to lay the blame at the door of Sinn Féin, describing the unrest as '… a revolt of the poorer peasants against the economic scandal of dead ranches …'[9]

Indeed, the unrest was a bottom-up, economically-driven phenomenon and the fact that many of the have-nots were members of Sinn Féin and of the Volunteers was merely coincidental. However, as time went on, Sinn Féin and the Volunteers in east Clare saw the political expediency of 'cashing in' by involving volunteers.[10]

~

Organised Sinn Féin-sponsored agrarian unrest was practically unheard of in west Clare during 1918. Brigade Headquarters had issued orders early in March 1918 that Volunteers in west Clare were not to take any active part in cattle drives and Brigade Officers were not to be seen at them.[11]

In fact, much of the land-related conflict in west Clare during this period took place in 1919 and after, and was characterised by a proliferation of historical land disputes and opportunistic land-grabbing.[12]

Consequently, throughout this turbulent period, West Clare Sinn Féin and Volunteers played a very different role to their east Clare counterparts, a role that would extend in 1919 and 1920 to policing and arbitration. In west Clare, officers who attended cattle drives were far more likely to be there for the purpose of preventing them than of organising them.

Of the historical land disputes, the Kilballyowen case, involving William Jonas Studdert, was the most complex and the most difficult to resolve. Studdert, a wealthy landowner and JP for the county, had acquired the land about ten years previously and was being blackguarded at the time by people who wanted to take his land from him.[13]

The Brigade officers held Studdert in some regard, since he had been well disposed towards them. When Studdert had come into possession of a large number of drums of much-valued petrol that had been washed ashore in 1917, he had given a share to the Brigade.[14]

Part of this land was tenanted and, although the ancestors of a number of the tenants had been evicted many years previously, Studdert had lived harmoniously with his neighbours prior to August 1919. But from that time on, he was subjected to a campaign of intimidation that included cattle drives with a view to forcing him off part of the large farm. At the root of the problem was a claim by the cattle drivers that an Officer of the Land

Commission had promised that the land would be divided.

On Monday 18 August 1919, Studdert was returning home to Kilballyowen from a funeral in Carrigaholt when he met a party of local men – mostly farmers' sons – who had just driven 28 of his milch cows, four of his heifers, two jennets and a bull off his land.

With the aid of the RIC, Studdert got his stock back and on 29 August twelve men were charged with unlawful assembly and driving of stock. A pacifist by nature, Studdert had no wish to see his tormentors punished and the trial had to be adjourned when he and his farmhand didn't turn up in court.

But neither was Studdert a fan of the *lámh láidir*[15] approach; he was prepared, he said, to submit the case for arbitration to the Chair of the Congested Districts Board, Canon Glynn, or to any other tribunal.

Eleven of the twelve were found guilty and John Hedderman of Cross, John Brennan of Oughterard and Patrick Haugh Jnr of Kilballyowen were each sentenced to two months in Limerick Prison with hard labour and four months without hard labour in default of bail. The remaining eight were imprisoned until the rising of the court on condition that they entered recognisances.

All eleven immediately lodged an Appeal, which was heard by Judge Bodkin in Ennistymon on 3 October 1919. There, it was claimed on behalf of the appellants that, in 1910 when Studdert acquired the land from a Mr Scott, the latter had stated that the untenanted land would be divided among the uneconomic occupiers in the area. The cause of the disturbances was because this had not happened.

Judge Bodkin stated that he had much sympathy with the aggressors in terms of their cause, but he cautioned against their methods. Further agitation, he felt, would do nothing to advance their cause. He offered to accept personal guarantees from the men that there would be no repetition of the offence.

Brennan, Hedderman and Haugh refused bail and were gaoled. The remaining eight all gave the required undertakings except for Thomas Mahoney. When Bodkin appealed to his better judgment, Mahoney simply replied, "I have no land sir and I want to get a bit."

The judge said that he had no option but to affirm the decision of the earlier court and Mahoney was sentenced to four months in prison.[16]

Studdert, fearing further trouble from his neighbours, applied unsuccessfully for an injunction to prevent the men and their cohorts from interfering with him and his property.[17]

On Sunday night 19 October 1919, the next phase of his troubles began, when shots were fired into the home of his herdsman, Thomas Slattery, who had been one of the prosecution witnesses at the trial.[18]

The agitation would continue ...

# Bayonet Charge in Carrigaholt

Through the early months of 1918, the regulations on illegal drilling were for the most part enforced but, throughout west Clare, they were ignored by the Volunteer movement. Sinn Féin clubs were in existence in every parish in the county and drilling after Sunday morning Mass was common.

On Sunday morning 24 March 1918, the Carrigaholt Volunteers paraded as usual under the direction of Michael Keane. Later, a meeting of over 40 members of the Seán Heuston Sinn Féin Club was held in the village Reading Room.[1]

One of the attendees was a 21-year-old national teacher from Ballyferriter in Kerry named Thomas Russell. Russell had recently qualified from Waterford's De La Salle College and had taken up a position as an Irish teacher in the village.

Meanwhile, unknown to the Volunteers, 20 soldiers of the Fife and Forfarshire Yeomanry, under the command of Captain William Mervyn Glass, were in the grounds of Carrigaholt Castle, having travelled from Kilrush to the village by patrol boat that morning with the expressed purpose of preventing drilling.[2]

At about 2.00pm, the RIC's Sergeant Moynihan alerted them to the drilling exercise that had taken place and 15 minutes later Glass arrived in the village with two carloads of soldiers and sent Moynihan to the Reading Room to fetch the man in charge of the drilling: he returned with Michael Keane.

When Keane refused to give an undertaking not to engage in future drilling, Glass had him arrested, but the prisoner was allowed to go home to eat after he gave his word in Fr Vaughan's presence that he would not abscond.[3] There, he planned to make good his escape, but his father insisted that he honour his word.[4]

Glass then banged on the door of the hall and it was opened by Éamon Fennell. Glass ordered Fennell to disperse the meeting but Fennell responded that this was a Sinn Féin Club meeting that was discussing the distribution of land and that it would be over in a minute or two.

On the Captain's order to clear the room, Sergeant Duff shouted 'Charge' and rushed into the hall with Lance Corporal Bremner and Privates Tate,

ABOVE: The blood-spattered back brace that was worn by Éamon Fennell in Carrigaholt on 24 March 1918 when he was stabbed by British soldiers at a Sinn Féin meeting in the village's reading room.
BELOW: Detail from the brace highlighting the bayonet hole. Fennell believed that the brace had possibly saved his life.
LEFT: Éamon Fennell with shotgun.
(Courtesy Fennell family)

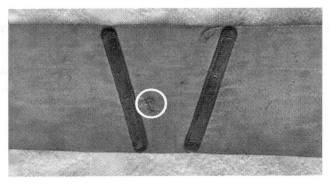

Hutton, Kenny, Robb and Lumsden. Somebody shouted, "Clear out you bastards!" and some of the soldiers proceeded to jab at the men with their bayonets as they moved towards the exits.[5]

Six men were named as having been stabbed: Éamon Fennell, Patrick Keating, Denis Ginnane, John Blake, a man named Corbett and Thomas Russell. It quickly became apparent that Russell's injury was serious and he was brought to Molly Behan's Hotel, where he said that he believed he was 'done for'.

Outside, a crowd, that included a significant number of young women, had gathered in the street and there were angry scenes when other military personnel arrived. There were shouts of 'Up the rebels', 'Wait until the Germans come' and 'Up Sinn Féin' and accusations that the military were murderers.

A military officer even misinterpreted a shout of 'Up de Valera' as 'Up the devil', one of the few amusing vignettes in an otherwise tragic episode.[6] Several baton charges took place before the hostile crowd dispersed.[7]

Dr Studdert examined Russell and noted a flesh wound in the right buttock and when he visited him later that night the patient was in agony. The following day Russell was brought to Kilrush Hospital where he died at about 6.30pm on Wednesday 27 March.

The nature and extent of the injury only became known at the post-mortem: the bayonet had penetrated the wall of both the rectum and the bladder and the consequences for the young teacher were catastrophic.

The Inquest into the death of Thomas Russell was opened in the schoolroom at Kilrush Workhouse on Thursday 28 March and a jury of 18 was empanelled under the stewardship of Luke O'Brien.[8]

There was notable conflict between the evidence of the medical witness Dr Richard Moynihan, on behalf of the Russell family, and that of the other doctors who were present at the post-mortem. Drs Counihan, Callinan and Captain Scales, RAMC, suggested that minimal force would have been required to inflict the wound on Russell that reached a depth of six inches and claimed that the wound could have been caused by accident.

Dr Moynihan disagreed on almost every significant detail, stating his opinion that the stabbing was deliberate and that considerable force would have been necessary.[9] Furthermore, Moynihan noted that Dr Counihan had objected to his presence at the preliminary meeting subsequent to Russell's death. He was, after all, representing Russell's next of kin, in line with professional etiquette.[10]

Military witnesses supported the accident theory, while repudiating suggestions that the soldiers had effected a bayonet charge on as many as 40 unarmed men who were attempting to exit the hall, which measured 23ft by 13ft. They even tried to claim that, in the panic to get out the door, the victims had reversed into the bayonets.[11]

But there was compelling evidence to the contrary.

Thomas Keane Jnr stated that the soldiers were thrusting their bayonets in every direction and that he saw one soldier deliberately stabbing Éamon Fennell in the back. Witnesses John Quinlan, Denis Ginnane and Stephen Hanrahan heard Sergeant Duff shout the order to charge and Club Secretary Tim Haier gave evidence that Private Tait and other soldiers were jabbing and lunging at the men.

The evidence of Denis Ginnane and Stephen Hanrahan gave the lie to military assertions that the men were moving backwards when they were stabbed. Both men testified that the order was given to '... charge and clear them out'.

Ginnane's perspective on the bayoneting of Russell was from within the hall, while Hanrahan witnessed it from without. Ginnane was exiting the door with Russell when he heard Russell give a long, loud groan, while Hanrahan observed Russell jerking upwards as he came out the door.[12]

Private Hutton, who had been blamed for stabbing Russell, admitted that his bayonet had stabbed a man, but claimed that the wound was caused by backward pressure from a swaying crowd, that it would have been only two inches deep and that it was high up on the hip. He said that he didn't report the matter as the wound had been caused by the crowd pressing backwards, though he was forced to acknowledge that his bayonet had not been in the correct position.[13]

The Inquest concluded on 9 April with the unequivocal verdict of the jury:

> We find that Thomas Russell met his death by a deliberate bayonet thrust, received from one of the four following soldiers – Sergt. Duff, Privates Hutton, Tait and Kenny, in the Reading Room, Carrigaholt, on Sunday, 24th March.[14]

Sergeant Sweeney for the military quickly retorted that the verdict had no legal standing whatsoever, but the same wording did feature in a legal document – Russell's death certificate.[15]

Predictably, the funeral was a huge affair on both sides of the Shannon. A military presence on the approach roads to Kilrush prevented many from attending.[16] The remains were brought to Cappa Pier and from there they were brought by boat to Ballylongford accompanied by Matthew Bermingham and Marty McNamara.[17]

~

The outrage was widely reported in both the local and national press.

Eva Gore-Booth, younger sister of Countess Markievicz, noted in a letter to the editor of the *Manchester Guardian* '… a man cannot put his back against a vertical bayonet if he is standing on the floor.'[18]

Kerry newspapers in particular included significant detail in their accounts of the Inquest. Predictably, the *Irish Times*, as ever the mouthpiece of Dublin Castle, was sparse with the facts and easy on the culprits. On Saturday 30 March, six days after the stabbings in Carrigaholt and three days after the death of Thomas Russell, the paper lived up to its reputation when it reported:

> The particulars available are of a meagre character … The military, with fixed

bayonets, proceeded to clear the hall, when it is reported that four young men received bayonet wounds in the resistance that was offered.[19]

On the same day, the *Clare Champion* published a public appeal for donations to a fund for the families of men who had been imprisoned following recent cattle drives, together with an advertisement for a proclaimed concert.

News reports stated that in consequence, the paper's offices were taken over by a party of police and military on the following Tuesday and its critical machinery components were removed in two lorries.[20]

The matter was the subject of a formal protest in the House of Commons by Arthur Lynch MP, himself no fan of the publication. Lynch noted that a recent edition of the paper had repudiated pro-Germanism and argued against rebellion.[21]

The *Clare Champion* would remain under suppression for six months. In his first post-suppression editorial, Sarsfield Maguire was unrepentant:

> ... if the freedom of the press is to be trampled upon, the last line of defence between the people and unrestricted tyranny will be swept away forever ... We need not say that where we stood previous to our enforced silence we stand to-day.[22]

≈

The incident that resulted in the death of Thomas Russell was to be one of a litany of outrages that were visited upon the people of Clare over the next three years by British army regiments that had significant Scottish membership.

As the senior officer, Captain Glass, himself a Scotsman, stated that the soldiers had not been authorised to use their bayonets.[23] However, when challenged by Tim Haier at Molly Behan's about the indiscipline of his soldiers, Glass said that he would stand by his soldiers regardless of the rights and wrongs of their behaviours.[24]

Glass went on to make a name for himself as an artist with a talent for coastal scenes that were more tranquil than the one he created in Carrigaholt on Palm Sunday 1918.

The killing of Russell provoked widespread revulsion throughout Clare and beyond and it served to strengthen support for Sinn Féin in the advent of the conscription crisis that was about to unfold. The incident also cemented the bond between Sinn Féin and the clergy, the latter having maintained a conspicuous, and at times vocal, presence at the Inquest. Bishop Fogarty weighed in with a letter to Ennis Sinn Féin Club, where he wrote:

The self-control maintained by the young people of Ireland, and especially of Clare, in spite of the callous provocation to which they are being subjected, is beyond all praise. Everything truly Irish is being oppressed with a tyranny both brutal and scandalous. Young men, the flower of the country, are being arrested wholesale, degraded, insulted, imprisoned, shot or bayoneted like poor Thomas Russell, of Carrigaholt, the killing of whom is, in all its circumstances, one of the most horrid and atrocious things I ever heard of. Were these things done in Belgium how the world would be made to ring with the cry of German atrocities.[25]

# Gaoled for Ireland

Following the death of Thomas Russell, attitudes hardened towards the police and locals boycotted them by refusing to sell them turf.[1]

Michael Keane was tried on a charge of unlawful assembly at a court of summary jurisdiction in Ennis on 29 March 1918. He was sentenced to four months in Limerick Prison with hard labour and an extra two months in default of sureties after having steadfastly refused to give any undertakings or to recognise any proclamations.[2]

At the same court, Christy McCarthy of Clounlaheen was convicted on a charge of unlawful assembly with 100 others at Coore West on 3 March 1918. He had been arrested on 24 March, after which he was brought first to Mullagh, where he was presented to the young men of the village as an example of the consequences of Republican activity. He was later prodded with bayonets while being transported to Ennistymon.[3]

McCarthy was sentenced to six months at the same gaol with hard labour and an extra three months in default of sureties.[4] Like most of his fellow Republicans, McCarthy defiantly stated that he would do the same again and that he was a soldier of the Irish Republic who gave no recognition to British Law in Ireland.[5]

In Carrigaholt, Sergeant Moynihan was equally determined that men like

McCarthy would not do the same again. He arrested Mick Greene of Kilbaha on 14 April 1918 and charged him with unlawful assembly. Greene was remanded in custody until 5 July when he was sentenced at Ennis Courthouse to two months in Limerick Prison with hard labour, and a further three months in default of recognisances.[6]

At 9.15pm on 28 June 1918, a military motor-lorry arrived at Carrigaholt RIC Barracks, where Sergeant Moynihan had Greene in custody, to take the prisoner to Kilkee. A crowd of about 150 had gathered in the street in a show of support for Greene. There were cries of 'Up the rebels', 'Our day will come yet', 'Up Sinn Féin' and 'Up the Irish Republican Army', each followed by loud cheers. There were also shouts of support for Greene, 'You are going to jail for a good cause.'

After the prisoner had been taken away under heavy escort, Patrick Keating NT (Carrigaholt), his namesake, also from Carrigaholt, and Thomas McGrath NT (Kilbaha) were arrested and charged with unlawful assembly.[7] Their court case in Ennis on 26 July 1918 heard evidence that the men had waved their caps while taking part in an unlawful assembly '... and being so assembled did there and then make a great noise to the terror of the people.'

All three were sentenced to one month with hard labour.[8]

Sergeant Moynihan followed up by arresting Patrick O'Shea and Martin Collins NT (both Carrigaholt), in connection with the same demonstration. They too were sentenced to one month with hard labour and three months in default of bails at Ennis Petty Sessions Court on 11 October 1918.[9]

Feeling that they had been unjustly treated, the pair brought an appeal before County Court Judge Matthias Bodkin at Ennis Quarter Sessions on 21 January 1919.

Ever the pragmatist, Bodkin declared that there was no evidence that the young men had done anything on the evening in question, either by action or by dissent. They were simply meeting on the street as young men in Carrigaholt did almost every evening of the week. Bodkin reminded the court that the practice of drilling had, for long periods in the past, been tolerated and even applauded by the authorities. He went on to famously describe drilling as:

> ... pure 'tomfoolery' – little 'garsúns' playing on the streets with tin swords.
> It was mere tomfoolery to be going about drilling as they could not fight
> the British Government, even if they wanted to do it. So all this drilling,
> marching and pretending to fight only made fools of the people engaged in it.
> It was mere stupid folly, and there was no use in sympathising with it.

Bodkin was unequivocal in his judgment on O'Shea's and Collins's appeal:

> I consider that sentence to be a most unjust, vindictive and unreasonable one.
> I express that opinion clearly and strongly and I have no hesitation whatever
> in reversing the magistrates' decision.[10]

∽

On the night of 28 June, following the Carrigaholt demonstration, Greene
had been brought before a special court at the Barracks in Kilkee. During the
sitting, which began at 10.30pm, a crowd of between 200 and 400 gathered
outside. They sang *Wrap the Green Flag* and *The Soldier's Song* and shouted
'Up the rebels', 'Up the Kaiser', 'To hell with John Bull, the bulldog breed'
and 'Down with King George'. There was booing and prolonged chanting of
'Ho, ho, ho, ho'. (Sergeant Corduff attributed the turnout to the fact that it
was easy to gather a crowd in Kilkee, since there were people there who had
nothing to do.)

Fianna Éireann members repeatedly blew their whistles and, after stones
were thrown, the crowd was dispersed by a police baton charge.[11]

Many similar arrests and incarcerations were effected throughout the county
and this aggressive approach by the authorities at such an early stage was later
credited by the authorities for Clare's unexpected timidity (in contrast with
the experience in Cork and Kerry) during the War of Independence.[12]

In Labasheeda, Vice Commandant of the 1st Battalion, Michael Falahee, was arrested and charged with illegal drilling of 50 Volunteers on 7 April 1918. During an attempt to free him, his brother Patrick was injured by a bayonet thrust.

That evening a demonstration was held in the village, as a result of which Charles Callinan and James Corbett were arrested at their homes in the middle of the night. They were charged with unlawful assembly at a special court in Knock and when they refused bail, were gaoled in Limerick. They were later released when friends signed bails for them.[13]

Michael Falahee was sentenced to two months with hard labour, and to a further three months without hard labour when he failed to enter into recognisances, all to be served in Limerick.[14]

The authorities were less fortunate in apprehending 18-year-old Company Quartermaster Patrick (Sonny) Burke at his home in Carhue, near Cooraclare on Sunday evening 21 April 1918.

There, a passing soldier, peering through the window of the Burke home, thought he saw somebody in possession of a rifle. The matter was duly reported to the RIC sergeant in the village who promptly arrived at the scene accompanied by two policemen and a dozen soldiers.

Burke was arrested in a nearby field and escorted to his parents' home. There, it was discovered that what the soldier had actually seen was a wooden imitation rifle, nevertheless the sergeant ordered that the youth be brought to the barracks.

Burke, who was 6ft 2½in tall, weighed almost 14 stone and was powerfully built, wrestled himself free of his captors, upended the Sergeant and made his escape through the back door before leading all 15 of them on a chase that extended for several miles before the posse was forced to abandon it.[15]

~

Kilkee was home to the 5th Battalion, and also to a young shopkeeper's son from O'Curry Street named Michael Fahy.

Born in 1900, Fahy would become one of the west Clare Republican movement's most determined and courageous members. As early as 1915, he set up a branch of Fianna Éireann in Kilkee, which was to become the most active and the most effective Boy Scout branch in west Clare.

Together with Fred Barry, Tom Prendergast (the Little Corporal), Jim O'Grady, Pat Behan, Joe Russell, David Conroy and Jim Talty, Fahy rented a small house in Kilkee's Corry's Lane and later in Grattan Street. They held regular meetings for the remainder of the year, before Fahy went to Cork to train and work as a wireless operator; he worked on a British ship between September 1916 and January 1917.[16]

The skills he acquired enabled him to train Fianna Éireann and Cumann na mBan members in First Aid as well as teaching them to read, send and receive signals. He and his friends would have fun reading the signals that were sent between the Coastguard Station and passing ships and Fahy was reputed to have tried unsuccessfully to make contact with Roger Casement on the German gunboat *Aud* as it moved south along the coast in April 1916.

His colleagues had scouted along the coastline but it later transpired that

Kilkee Coastguard Station after it was burnt down at the outbreak of the Civil War.
*(Courtesy Mary Driver)*

the ship had no signalling equipment on board. The uniformed band paraded the streets of Kilkee during Easter Week waving banners in support of the Easter Rising.

At that time, large numbers of barrels of petrol from torpedoed ships were being washed ashore along the west coast. A detachment of Marines stationed in the Coastguard Station at this time would keep watch seawards using a powerful telescope and had collected quite a few of the barrels. Fahy and his men managed to snatch both the telescope and some of the barrels in January 1917.

The petrol was used later in the run-up to the East Clare Election of July 1917. By this time, the Kilkee Company of Fianna Éireann was the only fully-functioning company in west Clare. Fahy and his men would regularly disrupt military and police movements by positioning broken glass and steel spikes at carefully-chosen locations across roads to puncture their tyres.

In July, Kilkee Company joined Ennis Company for a parade in full uniform with Countess Markievicz at the head.

When she visited Kilkee and Carrigaholt, she was accompanied at all her engagements by Fianna men, who did round-the-clock sentry duty for her.[17]

≈

On 26 May 1918, both groups organised a picnic at Dunlicky Castle, about four miles south-west of Kilkee, under the watchful eye of the police. As a result, an order was made for the arrest of Fahy, Jim Talty and Dan Brosnahan.

Fahy went on the run, while Talty and Brosnahan were arrested on 1 June 1918 and were tried at Kilkee by Military Court-martial on charges of unlawful assembly. When they failed to give bail, they were sentenced to two months in prison.[18]

Tom Marrinan was arrested on a charge of 'communicating with the enemy' and was transported to Cork for trial.[19] Short in stature and of stocky build, the Kilkee man was christened 'Nap' by his friends, who likened him to Napoleon.[20] Together with Michael Keane, Talty, Brosnahan and Marrinan were imprisoned in Belfast Gaol, where their term of incarceration coincided with a period of ongoing controversy surrounding the ill-treatment of inmates.[21]

The trouble began following the death of Thomas Ashe, after the Lord Mayor of Dublin had secured a commitment from the Prison Authorities to treat the Mountjoy hunger strikers as political prisoners. When the Governor of Belfast Gaol failed to keep his end of the bargain, about 70 prisoners, led by Austin Stack, caused serious disturbances and broke every prison rule.

It was only when Talty and Brosnahan were released that the full extent of the prisoners' ill-treatment became known. The men were brought to Fleming's Hotel in Dublin, where statements were taken from them. Brosnahan, a baker from Kilkee, outlined what happened after the prisoners had brought iron bars into their cells at lock-up time. Having barricaded the doors of their cells, they proceeded to bore holes in the walls and smashed water pipes:[22]

When the police arrived at the door of my cell, finding it barricaded, they got a fire hose and turned it on me. They then broke in the door. Four police entered the cell and rushed at me. I made no resistance, but was seized and handcuffed, my hands being manacled behind my back, and, when being dragged out of the cell, I got a stroke of a baton on the back. The Governor, Prison Doctor and Chief Warder were at the door of the cell looking on. I was brought by two police to a ground floor cell, which was dirty and badly ventilated, and locked in. After a time I lay as best I could on the bed but rolled off it onto the floor and was unable to rise for a considerable time, after which I spent the remainder of the night pacing up and down the cell. There was no water in the cell, and when I asked for it I was refused. There were no sanitary or other utensils in the cell, and in the course of the night I was obliged to relieve myself on the cell floor, which remained in that condition until I was removed to hospital on the following Sunday ... Both on Friday and Saturday I was very ill and vomited any food which I took. Owing to there being no utensils in the cell I was obliged to vomit on the cell floor, which was allowed to remain in that filthy condition, notwithstanding that I drew the warder's attention to it, and then asked to see the chief warder which was also refused.

Except at meal times the handcuffs were not removed ... Some of the men instead of being handcuffed were muffed – that is, pinioned by straps which fix their arms tightly by their sides. The men so pinioned had to be assisted before they could stand up from the altar rails. All the men presented a filthy appearance, as none had been able to wash themselves since Thursday night, and several bore marks of the violence to which they had been subjected ...[23]

Others gave similar accounts of ill-treatment, including Jim Talty who managed to strike one of the policemen with his iron bar:

Six or seven police entered (one in plain clothes), and the Governor, the Doctor and one warder remained outside. The police rushed at me, and even though I made no effort to resist, one of them caught me by the hair of the head and another by the back of the head and forced me forward until my head almost touched my knees. They then knocked me face forwards on the floor of the cell, one of them pressing his knee on the back of my neck and the other in the middle of the back, my mouth and nose were pressed against the floor of the cell, and my hands held behind my back. I was almost suffocated, and large beads of perspiration came out on me. In addition, my face was covered with dirt, mortar etc., which were on the floor. Whilst in this position my hands were handcuffed behind my back, and I was dragged down to the ground floor cells in 'C' Wing with great violence, although I did not at any time attempt to resist. I had no coat or vest on, and only cell slippers instead of boots, and in this condition I was thrust into a dirty and ill-ventilated cell on the ground floor. Owing to the position of my hands I found it impossible to lie down, and was obliged to walk up and down the cell floor all night dressed as above described, and suffered very much from cold as well as from the treatment I had received. There was no water in the cell, and although I repeatedly asked for it I did not get it.[24]

Talty was left with hands handcuffed behind his back for three days in an empty cell and on a diet of bread and water. The only rest he got was on the floor. His hands were then handcuffed to the front and he remained in the same cell for a further four days.[25]

～

At Doolin Harbour in north Clare on 12 April 1918, two fishermen on their way to check their nets spotted a man waving for help from the shore of nearby Crab Island. When the men reached the island the man told them that he had been on a ship that had been torpedoed and that he had made his way to the island on a collapsible boat.[26]

On the hustings in west Clare during the 1918 Election Campaign.
(*Courtesy Mary Driver*)

Back in Doolin he was spotted by police, who took him to the barracks for questioning. At first, he gave his name as James O'Brien, but inconsistencies in his story aroused suspicion and he was taken to London.

There, his real identity was established as Lance Corporal Joseph Dowling, who had travelled to the Clare coast on board a German submarine. As a German prisoner-of-war at Limburg, Dowling had collaborated with Roger Casement in the recruitment of fellow prisoners to The Irish Brigade. The British authorities alleged that Dowling's arrival and the manner of it were part of a Sinn Féin conspiracy with Germany to spark an armed insurrection in Ireland.

Dowling was tried, found guilty and sentenced to death, which was commuted to life imprisonment.[27] The British used what became known as 'The German Plot' as an excuse for the rounding up and imprisonment of Sinn Féin's main players. On the night of 16–17 May, 73 Sinn Féin leaders were arrested and deported to England. Among them were teachers Éamon Waldron and Brian O'Higgins.[28]

Waldron, from Cong, County Mayo, had been a Gaelic League organiser in Louth and, latterly, in Ennistymon. Operating primarily at the political end of the spectrum, he was interned subsequent to the 1916 Rising after being found in possession of a rifle and ammunition.

On his release from Frongoch Prison, following the general amnesty in December 1916, Waldron was appointed Mid Clare Brigade Quartermaster on the formation of an independent brigade in Clare.[29]

O'Higgins, a poet and author, who was Principal of O'Curry's Irish College in Carrigaholt, commanded '… an extraordinary degree of widespread popularity' throughout Ireland and among his fellow prisoners. He wrote for Republican-minded school magazines and religious periodicals using the nom de plume 'Will E Wagtail'.

The prison day began with breakfast at 7.30am, after which internees were allowed out into limited space of the prison yard. Dinner was at 12.30pm, tea was at 4.00pm and the cells were locked at 8.30pm.

The prisoners' only contact with home was by post, which was heavily censored by the prison authorities. They were offered one visit every three months, which they declined.[30] Inmates were expected to supplement the prison diet with food that would be delivered to them by friends and relatives.

Waldron flatly refused, claiming that "… it is the duty of the government that keeps us unlawfully in its prisons (even against all the canons of its own constitution) to feed us in proper manner …"

The consequences for his health were significant and by September 1918 he had been ill for two months. His diet was rice and milk. By December, there were concerns for his health and he was placed on a hospital diet and he was released on medical advice on 17 January 1919.[31]

Such was O'Higgins's popularity that, when candidates were being selected to contest the 1918 General Election, the constituencies of North Meath, South Louth and West Clare laid claim to his candidacy, each refusing to yield until O'Higgins himself declared for West Clare.[32]

He was still in prison in Birmingham when both he and de Valera were elected unopposed for West and East Clare respectively in the General Election. Though the results were not announced until 28 December, the messages of congratulations poured in before Christmas, one of them coming from as far away as India.[33]

Mrs O'Higgins wrote to her husband on 10 November 1918 asking, in coded language, for an election address that Fr James (Fr James Clancy, PP, Kilballyowen, Cross, president of the local Election Committee) would mediate to the electorate on his behalf. One week later, O'Higgins responded that he would be unable to get the address past the censors, but that his silence might be more effective than his words.[34]

On the day following the announcement of the landslide victory for Sinn Féin, O'Higgins's fellow-prisoner, Peter O'Hourihane, wrote of the election result to Rev T O'Molloy, a professor at St Flannan's College, Ennis:

It is better than we thought. It is wonderful news, and our mother's heart should be bounding with joy tonight. God's hand and the martyrs' prayers are in the work without doubt, and though it is good, we will have better news yet ...[35]

It was as momentous a defeat for the Irish Parliamentary Party as it was a victory for Sinn Féin. For the first time, all adult males and women over the age of 30 who were householders were entitled to vote. Significantly, 70% of those who voted had never voted before.[36]

Meanwhile, Brian O'Higgins played ducks and drakes with Birmingham Prison's censorship officials, who were busily trying to decode his cryptically worded letters. As well as 'Mr Wagtail', he traded under various sobriquets, such as 'Mary Forde', 'Barney Kileredan', 'Brian na Banba', 'Brendan Hughes', 'Barney Corcoran', plain 'Belinda' and 'Hugh O'Byrne' (in which case reversing the initials cracks the code).[37]

His befuddled custodians had some head-scratching moments, none more so than Mrs O'Higgins's 20 January 1919 coded description of a combined military and police search in Carrigaholt:

There was great excitement round here Thursday night. Hadn't we a travelling circus – five big lorries full of the grandest clowns and handy Andys ever you saw. They paraded lots of the roads and some of the clowns gave performances in the houses. It seems two or three acrobats who don't care for the life escaped from them and were being chased. It was very exciting while it lasted and mind you the acrobats were looking on part of the time unnoticed. You never saw anything like the conjuring tricks some of the little yellow clowns and handy-Andys did. Actually swung a big fat pig out of a sty into one of their waggons and charmed a £10 note out of a mattress and £4 out of some other place.[38]

The prying eyes of the censors were kept busy with teasers like this one, which they interpreted as a mobile patrol ('circus') of police and military ('clowns' and 'handy Andys') in hot pursuit of deserters ('acrobats'). Their interpretation was accurate except for the 'acrobats', which probably referred to Tim Haier and John 'Shang' Scanlon (so-named after he had joined the Shanghai Police Force), who had been actively sought.

(In fact, the word 'circus' was commonly used in Republican circles in reference to Active Service Units or Flying Columns).[39]

Following his release from prison, O'Higgins arrived in Kilkee by car on Tuesday evening 11 March to a hero's welcome. He was met on the outskirts of the town by the Kilkee Brass and Reed Band which led him through the town in procession, accompanied by large numbers of Volunteers and townspeople. After the speeches, he was again accompanied to Carrigaholt by the band.

The houses of Kilkee and Carrigaholt were illuminated for the occasion.[40]

# The conscription crisis

The spectre of conscription, having been rebuffed by John Redmond's Parliamentary Party when it was first mooted, had begun to feature once again in British newspaper columns in September 1917.[1]

West Clare was awake to the prospect and, while Volunteer membership was healthy, the movement set about preparing itself more fully.

Those who had no guns were encouraged to arm themselves with pikes, pointed, spear-like weapons forged from ribbon iron and then mounted on wooden shafts that measured between 7ft and 8ft.[2]

Clonderlaw blacksmith Pa Frawley charged £1.6s. per pike head.[3] In the Knockerra area, pike heads that were forged by George Russell, a Cooraclare farrier, were paid for out of company funds that came from levies on Volunteers.[4] Blacksmith John Pender made pike heads at a cost of 2s,6d each and wooden rifles (for drill practice) at a shilling for the Monmore men, each of whom paid for his own.

The Kilmurry Company pikes were made by John Harrisson from Clohanmore and they were paid for from the proceeds of house dances.[5] News of an upcoming house dance would spread quickly by word of mouth and Brews's of Ballykett was a favourite venue. People would still be arriving at the dance at two in the morning and funds were used on occasion for the purchase of arms and ammunition.[6]

Occasionally, dances were raided and broken up as happened at Knockerra School at around midnight on Sunday 9 November 1919 when the building was surrounded by a force of ten police and about 50 military with a motor-lorry in waiting half-a-mile away. The women were ordered outside and the men were searched, some as many as three times. As they were leaving, the men had to give their names and addresses.[7]

In the Second Battalion area, which was comprised of companies at Knockerra, Kilmurry McMahon, Kilrush, Killimer and Kilmihil (two companies), each Volunteer was required to subscribe weekly to an arms fund which was supplemented by funds raised through organised entertainments.[8]

Being prepared for the eventuality of conscription also involved the appropriation of arms which, in most cases, were freely handed over upon request. It was not all plain sailing for the raiding Volunteers, however.

On 25 January 1918, a series of planned raids for arms took place in the Kilrush area. In all cases, the raiders wore black cloth face masks and had their coats inside-out. The first raid happened at 8.15pm when five or six men visited the home of Martin J Costelloe, a civil engineer, at Ballykett, and took a revolver and a bayonet.

Less than half an hour later, four men called to the home of Mrs Henrietta Nolan and demanded her gun. When Mrs Nolan made a grab for the gun, which was over the door, one of the men shouted, "Shoot her" and a crisis was only averted when a young girl in the house restrained her.

The raid at the home of Thomas and Margaret Lyons of Moyadda took

Pike head from the time of the 1918 conscription crisis.
*(Courtesy Siney Talty)*

place at 8.45pm and yielded a double-barrelled shotgun. But here, John 'Folk' McNamara was recognised, a mishap which would later cost him his freedom. On his way to Kilrush RIC station to report the raid, Thomas Lyons came across four men, three of whom were disguised. He identified the fourth as William Moody.[9]

On the raid at the house of John Brews in Moyadda, McNamara gave armed cover while Matthew Bermingham and Martie Mulqueen conducted the raid. Brews quickly barricaded the door and refused to hand over his gun, whereupon the raiders gave him five minutes to reconsider his decision. After Brews's continued refusal to give up the weapon, McNamara lost his nerve and his gun went off, the bullet narrowly missing Bermingham and Mulqueen.[10]

Meanwhile, at about 9.00pm, Murty Tubridy led his group of raiders on an expedition to Leadmore, to the home of bedridden John Murphy whose son Tom was writing a letter in the kitchen.

The five raiders entered the house and ordered, "Hands up; we want your shotgun!"

Murphy, who was being covered by three guns, put his pen in his mouth and replied, "All right," as he reached for the gun that was hanging over the fireplace.

"Ye came to the wrong house, boys," he shouted as he turned the gun on the five and chased them out and through the fields.

When one of the men fired a revolver shot at him, he returned fire, wounding Johnny Mulqueen in the hip. Murphy quickly caught up with Mulqueen and overpowered him by striking him on the head with his gun, before returning home with his prisoner. There, he tied him first to a chair, then to the stairs and threatened him with the contents of the second barrel if Mulqueen didn't disclose the identities of his co-raiders.

Mulqueen wrote down the names Jimmy Connell, Michael Corry and Patrick Greene, none of whom took part in the raid.[11] Murphy's brother went for the police, who arrested Mulqueen.

When William Moody and the three named suspects were arrested and brought before him, Mulqueen denied that they had been involved, stating that he had only given those names under threat from Tom Murphy.[12] All were later gaoled save Corry, who was quickly released.

The prisoners' incarceration coincided with the Republican hunger strikes. Some simply refused prison food and accepted food that was delivered to them by Cumann na mBan members.

Greene, however, took the strike seriously and, as a consequence, was in a weakened state upon his release. When he and other released prisoners arrived back at the family pub in Vandeleur Street, a crowd gathered to welcome them home and they gave speeches from an upstairs window.

Mulqueen was admitted to Kilrush Hospital for treatment before being tried and sentenced. Tom Murphy was later tried by a Republican court, but was cleared of any wrongdoing.[13]

~

From 26 February 1918 County Clare was declared a Special Military Area

Military Pass used by Limerick Jesuit priest Fr Willie Hackett in June 1918.
*(Courtesy Archives of the Society of Jesus, Australia)*

in response to what was described as widespread lawlessness. Entry to and exit from the county was restricted for a period to those in possession of a Military Pass and movement within the county was curtailed.

Schoolgirls who needed to leave the county to attend school in Limerick were reportedly subjected to 'rude and insulting' behaviours on the part of RIC and Military.[14]

Drilling and the wearing of uniforms was prohibited, as well as unauthorised meetings and processions. Additionally, printed matter would be subject to censorship.[15] Communication between the West Clare Brigade and Headquarters was facilitated by boat from Coolmeen and Labasheeda on the Clare side of the Shannon to Foynes on the Limerick coast, despite the fact that RIC and Military patrolled the waters.[16]

Policemen were prime targets for anti-conscription Volunteers in search of quality firearms and ammunition. In one such attack in April 1918 two constables, on protection duty at a disputed farm near Cree were ambushed at Alva, near Cooraclare by Seán Liddy (having been recently been released from prison), together with members of Cooraclare Company – Paddy Lynch, Michael McMahon, Michael Cullinan, Martin Shannon, Michael Breen (Tom), James Callinan, Mick McGrath and Patrick 'Pa' Darcy.

They knocked the pair from their bicycles and Lynch gave a 'hammer' to one of them with whom he had a score to settle. They then wrenched the policemens' carbines from the straps that secured them to the bicycles and made good their escape.[17]

While there was no injury to the policemen, the incident signalled the beginning of a new chapter in the relationship between the community and the RIC and military authorities. Almost immediately, and as a direct consequence of the attack, an order was made by Colonel R L Owens, Commandant for the Clare area:

'... prohibiting processions, meetings or assemblies, including fairs and markets, and closing all licensed premises, except from 7 am to 7 pm., within a radius of two miles from the police barracks at Cooraclare …'[18]

Military outposts were established at Cooraclare, Danganelly and Dromelihy, the homes of suspects were raided and arrests were commonplace.[19]

On 8 August 1918 the RIC barracks at Cooraclare were closed down, in keeping with the emerging trend of moving police personnel into the larger towns for their safety. Some time later, local Volunteers painted Republican slogans with tar all over the outside of the building. Some of these graffiti messages encouraged locals to buy the Irish Loan Bonds in support of the National Loan, the first of three successful Bond issues, which Dáil Éireann launched during the War of Independence.[20]

One read 'Buy the Irish Loan Bond. Support the government elected by yourselves.' Cooraclare's messages to both Britain and Ireland were clear –

Anti-Conscription pledge that was taken at every church door on 21 April 1918.
*(Courtesy National Library of Ireland)*

'God save the Republic', 'Tell John Bull that Ireland must be free'. And there was even a message for Lord John French, appointed Lord Lieutenant for Ireland in May 1918 – 'John's French failed in France. He'll fail in Ireland too.'

Field Marshall Sir John French, a former Chief of Staff of the British Army, whose record in the Great War had been poor, became something of a hate figure to Republicans when he referred to them as vermin who must be exterminated. He had also advised the British Government that conscription could be enforced in Ireland.[21]

On 21 April 1918, on the direction of the Catholic Hierarchy, a Mass of intercession would be offered in every parish church in Ireland '... to avert the scourge of conscription with which Ireland is threatened.' Church-gate collections would be held at an early date for the funding of the anti-conscription effort. Furthermore, an anti-conscription pledge was administered in every parish, the wording of which left nobody in any doubt about the mood of the country:

> Denying the right of the British Government to enforce compulsory service in this country, we pledge ourselves solemnly to one another to resist conscription by the most effective means at our disposal.[22]

One of the first to sign the pledge in west Clare was the Protestant (and loyalist) Justice of the Peace, William Charles Doherty; he did so on a billiards table in a club next door to the Stella Maris Hotel in Kilkee.[23]

The pledge was administered by Bishop Fogarty in the thronged Ennis Cathedral following Mass on Sunday 21 April. Describing the Act as oppressive and inhuman, the pastor told his flock that they were entitled to resist it '... by every means consonant with the law of God.'

One of the first public demonstrations of resistance took place across Ireland on Tuesday 23 April, when there was a national work stoppage. With the exception of banks and post offices, all business establishments in Ennis shut down. Trains ceased to operate, resulting in the suspension of mail and newspaper deliveries.[24]

A rare quadripartite coalition had emerged, composed of moderate Irish nationalist opinion in the form of the Irish Parliamentary Party and separatist Sinn Féin, together with the Labour Movement and the Catholic Church. Their common aim was to thwart the looming menace of Conscription.

Huge numbers, including the elderly and those who had eligible sons, turned out in Kilrush for anti-conscription marches, which were believed to have been the brainchild of Ballykett native and Clare All-Ireland footballer Marty McNamara. The separation women hurled stones and abuse at the marchers in Moore Street and soldiers who were home on leave and ex-soldiers attempted to disrupt the ranks and started fistfights with them. The Volunteers would later find them and beat them up, which put an end to that practice.[25]

On one occasion, a stone thrown by one of the separation women struck Matthew Bermingham on the chest. When he gave chase, the culprit ran to Toler Street RIC barracks and had just reached the front door when Bermingham caught up with her and 'dealt' with her.[26]

The success of the Kilrush marches were thought to have inspired headquarters in Dublin to recommend them to Volunteer groups throughout the country.[27]

When the British Government quickly abandoned its planned conscription initiative, the real winners were Sinn Féin and the Irish Volunteers, both of which attracted significant numbers of new members during April and May 1918.[28]

# Michael Fahy

After he joined the Volunteers in 1918, Michael Fahy began drilling groups of Volunteers in and around Kilkee. In May 1918, he was caught drilling 20 men by Sergeant Corduff, a Donegal native who arrived at his home in early June to arrest him.

When cautioned, Fahy replied that the men would drill when and wherever they wished, that they did not recognise the British Government and they would fight when the time was right.

"I am not a member of the Sinn Féin organisation," he said, "it is too constitutional. I believe there is nothing to be gained except by the pike."[1]

Before he could be taken into custody, Fahy broke free and went on the run.

On 19 December 1918 Sergeant Corduff and Constable Sharkey finally caught up with him in the home of Margaret O'Reilly. Following an unsuccessful attempt to escape, Fahy was arrested and declared defiantly, "If I were arrested outside I would do a McNeillis on you."[2]

He was referring to the daring escape from Cork Prison of Denis McNeillis on 11 November 1918, a carefully-planned operation that had been described as the stuff of movies.[3]

In Fahy's bedroom they found a leather bandolier and belt and a Volunteer uniform hat hanging on the wall. On the dressing table were two service cartridges, Mark VII, and in an overcoat pocket was a six-chamber revolver that was not in good working order.

Sergeant Corduff asked if he had a permit.

"I have a permit but it's not the one you want," replied Fahy.

The prisoner was tried by District Court-martial in Cork on 14 January 1919, where he was found guilty on charges of possession of a revolver and ammunition. Sergeant Corduff described him as very hostile to the police and military and '… one of the worst young men in the County Clare'. That said, District Inspector Barrett was more circumspect with his depiction of the lad as '… a captain of the Irish Volunteers, but not otherwise of importance.'

Michael Fahy.
*(Courtesy Mary Driver)*

Fahy was sentenced to six months with hard labour and spent 13 weeks in solitary confinement in Cork Gaol before he was released on 13 May 1919 by direction of the prison doctor. [4]

On his return to Kilkee, Fahy resumed his role as captain of the Fianna Éireann Scouts and was appointed to the position of Company Captain. He was known to observe British soldiers drilling in Ennis in order to improve his own drill practices.[5] On one occasion, he cycled to Cork and back (a round trip of at least 200 miles) for a meeting.[6]

During a raid for a shotgun in the home of a civilian in July 1919, Fahy was recognised and he was reported to the police, who raided his home, forcing him to go on the run.[7]

Around 8 December 1919, on his way to meet with Jim Talty in Kilkee, his revolver discharged in his pocket, wounding him in the thigh. He was treated at Corry's Lane by Dr Hickie who recommended that he be taken to hospital. But the RIC got word that he had been shot and began searching for him.

The next day, he was brought by Tom Marrinan and Jim Talty to Moyasta station, where he boarded a train for Ennis with a view to catching an onward train to Limerick.[8] On arrival at Ennis, the policeman on duty at the station became suspicious and reported back to his barracks. After a phone call to Kilkee RIC Barracks, it was decided to arrest the men.

Fortunately, the IRA in Ennis alerted Fahy's party to the fact that a police van was on its way to apprehend them and they left on the westbound train just as the police arrived at the station. Knowing that the police would be waiting for them at Ennistymon, they left the train at Ruan and Talty and Marrinan took turns to shoulder their injured comrade across the fields to a friendly house where they remained for a couple of days.[9]

Michael Colivet, who had commanded the Limerick and East Clare Volunteers during the 1916 Rising, and who knew Fahy well from business and holiday visits to Kilkee, later wrote:

The young men with him had evidently got scared, and feared informing his mother or any superior officer. They thought it better to get him to a Limerick Hospital. But they knew no one in Limerick and hid him in Cratloe Woods whilst making contact with the IRA in Limerick. He got taken into some house later but these few days of medical inattention eventually cost him his life.

Colivet arranged for Dr Roberts from Barrington's Hospital in Limerick to collect Fahy from Cratloe on 12 December 1919 and drive him to the hospital in his car. He would spend the next 109 days in hospital and the RIC maintained a presence at the hospital when they learned of his whereabouts.[10]

Fahy underwent an operation but the bullet was not removed as it was deemed to be too risky. On 10 March 1920 he developed meningitis and died nine days later at the age of 19½.[11]

On Monday 22 March 1920, Michael Fahy's funeral procession passed by his home in O'Curry Street, Kilkee. His family decided not to inform his ailing grandmother. As she watched through her front window, she noted the huge turnout and remarked that this must have been a greatly loved young man.

Fahy's remains were shouldered by his comrades into Kilferagh Cemetery, where he was buried with full military honours. RIC and military warnings were ignored by the Battalion, which marched in formation, led by the Kilkee Brass Band playing the *Dead March*.[12]

Among the wreaths was one labelled 'Michael's Own', Kilkee Company.[13]

# Hear, Hear, Paddy

On Sunday 5 January 1919, Constable James Reynolds and a colleague cycled from Carrigaholt to Kilkee and onward to Kilrush with two other constables for duty at Toler Street Barracks.

On his return that evening, Reynolds was cycling alone from Kilkee to Carrigaholt. Waiting to ambush him at Furoor, about 2½ miles south of Kilkee, were Carrigaholt Company IRA members Tim Haier, Michael Keane, Pat Blake and Michael Kelly; Thomas Keane and D Collins were the scouts.

Thomas Keane, the 20-year-old son of a publican of the same name, was arrested and charged with the offence on 6 January by Sergeant Moynihan, who had arrested his brother Michael the day of the bayonet charge in Carrigaholt when Thomas Russell was fatally stabbed. Having given critical evidence at the inquest of Thomas Russell, Keane would neither expect nor receive any favours from the justice system. He was remanded to Limerick Prison for a week.

When the authorities became aware that the defence would consist of an alibi, it was decided that a jury trial was out of the question. Keane would be tried on a charge of assault of a police constable by General Court-martial at Victoria Barracks, Cork, on 13 February 1919 at 10.00am.[1]

On the night before the trial, a large and spirited group of relatives and supporters of the Sinn Féin prisoners gathered outside the prison. There followed a veritable hooley, with song-singing and cheers and the prisoners inside joined in. When a shout went up from outside enquiring for the welfare of a named prisoner, the response, 'He's alright' came back to loud cheers from the crowd.

Not everybody in Cork joined in the festivities, however. Some passing young women gave voice to their anti-Sinn Féin sentiments, whereupon they were pounced on and some of their hats and dresses were torn.[2]

The following morning in court, Constable Reynolds stated that he was cycling from Kilkee to Carrigaholt on the night of 5 January. At Furoor, a couple of miles from Kilkee, he met four men walking on the road towards him. As he was passing them, he claimed that John Scanlon knocked him from his bike, after which Haier grabbed his baton and struck him on the head, before grabbing him around the waist. He reached for his revolver, but Scanlon spotted the move and struck him with the baton on the hand. Thomas Keane then threw a cloth over the constable's head, after which he was knocked to the ground and bound hand and foot.

Reynolds maintained that Haier then kicked him and said, "Take that!" after which he was robbed of his revolver, baton, handcuffs and £6. He then stated that he was ducked repeatedly in a drain before being covered with his cape and was then thrown on his back in a nearby field.

Constable Reynolds freed himself after three hours and made his way to the home of local schoolteacher John Keane. Keane gave him a change of clothes and provided refreshments and drove him to Carrigaholt RIC station the following morning.

The constable said that the night was bright and that the men had made no effort to conceal their identities. He knew Thomas Keane, whose family pub was located only a few doors from Carrigaholt RIC Barracks. Haier and Scanlon were wanted for illegal drilling and had been on the run for some time.

The evidence of Dr John M Studdert, who attended the injured constable, brought an element of controversy to the proceedings.

Studdert stated that he knew Keane to be of quiet disposition and not one to be involved in activities like this. The character reference clearly brought him into conflict with Reynolds.

The doctor had met Constable Reynolds and a colleague in Limerick, but was rebuffed when he attempted to make conversation with them. One of them had threatened him that he would see him in court at the trial and said that Studdert '... carried a face under two hoods.'

Studdert had warned the constable that he 'would break his face' and added, to the amusement of the court 'and I meant it.'

There were numerous witnesses for the defence, all of whom stated that Thomas Keane was at a dance and that he had played cards on the night of the assault. Counsel for the prosecution remarked that, in cases from Clare, the defence was invariably an alibi and that the alibi was invariably a wedding, a wake or a dance.[3]

The court closed for the finding of the verdict which was to be promulgated in due course. Meanwhile, Keane's mother wrote to Brian O'Higgins in Birmingham Gaol, 'He had several witnesses to prove an alibi, but of course justice means anything at the present time'.[4]

Keane was found guilty and sentenced to two years hard labour, to be served in Cork Men's Gaol. His incarceration coincided with a period of controversy concerning the treatment of Sinn Féin prisoners in Cork Gaol who had been convicted under the Defence of the Realm Act. Conditions at the gaol at this time had been receiving much press attention and there was concern that Sinn Féin prisoners were being held in solitary confinement for long periods, had had their boots and furniture removed and were having to eat their meals off the floor.[5]

On 25 February 1919, a special meeting of the Cork Board of Guardians was convened at the request of three of its members to inquire into the treatment of Thomas Keane, who had been brought by ambulance on 20 February from gaol to the District Hospital, suffering from influenza. It had been brought to the attention of the three Board Members that a prison warder had accompanied Keane to the hospital and was remaining with him.

The members were concerned that this was not for the benefit of the patient but no action was taken when it was learned that the warder had been withdrawn.[6] The matter came up for consideration again a month later, when it became known that police were stationed in the hospital to watch him.

No action was taken when the Board Chairman revealed that he had visited the patient, who was content; there was a fear that if they complained Keane would be transferred to a Military Hospital, where conditions might not be so good.[7] Keane was stated to be suffering from the after effects of flu and he remained in hospital for almost three months.

To what extent his illness was precipitated or exacerbated by prison conditions while on remand in Limerick or while awaiting promulgation of his sentence in Cork is not known. What is known is that, on 6 March 1919, a visiting Justice of the Peace warned of the consequences for prisoners' health of the long periods of solitary confinement that they were being forced to endure. He added that six prisoners had been hospitalised.[8]

And what is also known is that of the seven west Clare prisoners who were in Cork Men's Gaol at this time, six were released on medical grounds within a couple of months of their incarceration. The first of these was Keane.

Michael Fahy, having spent 13 weeks in solitary confinement, was released on grounds of ill health on 13 May 1919 and Art O'Donnell, John Grogan, Mick Mahoney and Joe Sexton were all released on similar grounds at various dates over the next couple of months.[9]

On 11 April 1919, Thomas Keane was transferred from the District Hospital back to prison. The prison Medical Officer requested time to assess his preparedness for promulgation of his sentence, fearing for the effect it might have on his health. In the event, Keane had to be re-admitted to hospital.

In a somewhat remarkable development, the prison doctor, despite pressure from the Governor, refused to state – either verbally or in writing – whether Keane was or was not well enough to have his sentence promulgated. The patient was examined on 8 May by a Royal Army Medical Corps Officer, whose detailed and comprehensive report highlighted heart and lung issues with a suggestion of 'tubercular mischief'. The report concluded:

> I would advise his early and unconditional release – because if when his sentence is promulgated he thought it unfavable [sic] in any way to him the shock might do him [sic] irreparable mischief to his present condition.

Thomas Keane was discharged on 11 May 1919 following remission of the remainder of his sentence.[10]

In April, at Kilrush Quarter Sessions before Judge Bodkin, Constable Reynolds claimed £1000 in compensation for his injuries, together with £17 for damage to his bicycle. He was awarded £43.4s for his injuries, just over £13 in expenses and the full £17 in respect of his bicycle.[11]

In May 1919, the long arm of the law finally caught up with Éamon Fennell, who had taken over drilling of the Carrigaholt Volunteers after Michael Keane's arrest and imprisonment in March 1918.

Fennell had been targeted for arrest shortly after, but went on the run and avoided capture until he was arrested at his aunt's farmhouse early in May 1919. He was brought before a special court in Kilkee, where he was sentenced to four months in prison on a charge of unlawful assembly. But he was forced to go on the run again on his release, when an RIC sergeant told his brother that he would be shot on sight the next time he was caught.[12]

~

In Coolmeen, the RIC finally caught up with Paddy Clancy of Derryguiha – who had been on the run since St Patrick's Day 1918 – after Constable Boland had seen him drilling 40 men and boys.

Following several unsuccessful attempts to apprehend him, Constable Patrick Gleeson arrested Clancy at his home on 14 February. Clancy was brought before a court of summary jurisdiction in Ennis on 21 February 1919.[13]

Constable Boland deposed that on 17 March 1918 Clancy had drilled about 30 men and boys in a field across from the church in Coolmeen. Clancy had shouted various orders, such as, 'eyes front … form fours … odd numbers one pace forward … even numbers one pace to back … march … ranks right and left turn …' Presently, the troupe came back on to the road and marched up and down in front of the church before Clancy had dismissed them.

There was drama and hilarity in the courtroom, which was packed with the

Sinon Haugh (left) and Paddy Clancy in the colours of Coolmeen GAA Club.
During a Black and Tan raid on Haugh's home a set of the club's jerseys was burned.
*(Courtesy Tommy Haugh)*

prisoner's supporters, when the court Chairman, George McElroy, RM, gave Clancy leave to question Constable Gleeson. Clancy proceeded to address Gleeson in his native tongue. The Irish was very nice, remarked McElroy, but not relevant, since the Constable didn't know what the prisoner was saying.

"I suppose I am only talking to the horse and the horse asleep," responded Clancy, "I am a soldier of the Irish Republic and I do not have a dog's esteem for this court. I don't recognise English law and with the help of God I never will. It will take all the bayonets and rifles of the British Government to make me do so."

Following an eruption of spontaneous applause, he continued, "What can you do? The most you can do is murder me, and you have done that already to better Irishmen than me. But while I live I will be a Sinn Féiner and if there is any such thing as politics in the next world I will be a Sinn Féiner there also."

After another outburst of applause, the judge upbraided the police for allowing the court to descend to this level of farce and ordered the room to be cleared.

At this point, Constable Boland reported that Clancy's neighbour, John O'Brien, had shouted, 'Hear, hear, Paddy', during the prisoner's speech. The magistrates were less than impressed and charged him with contempt of court.

O'Brien, stomping his feet, emphasised that he was simply registering his approval of Clancy's statement, and he was not shouting but speaking loudly.

He was sentenced to seven days imprisonment in Limerick Prison.

Clancy's case proceeded with evidence from Constable Boland and the Chairman asked Clancy if he had any questions for the witness.

"Níl beann agam oraibh," (I am indifferent to you), said Clancy.

"Talk in English for a minute," exhorted the Chairman, "I don't know what you are saying."

Clancy turned to the constable, "Any chance you'd give us a few steps of a hornpipe?"

"Do you wish to ask this witness any questions, Mr Clancy?" There was no response from the defendant.

"Now, Mr Clancy, you can make your defence, any statement you wish or call witnesses."

"I have my defence made already," said Clancy.

"So you don't wish to say anything more?" enquired McElroy.

Clancy shook his head.

"Do you deny the charge?" pressed the Chairman.

"Don't ask me any more questions. I don't recognise you," Clancy answered.

"But you are in the unfortunate position of being here. Will you give bail that you won't repeat this offence?" asked McElroy.

"No indeed," answered Paddy as he turned to Constable Gleeson, "Any chance of a dance?"

Paddy Clancy was sentenced to two months imprisonment with hard labour and four months without hard labour was added on account of his refusal to enter recognisance.

"I care no more about six months than I do about six minutes," was Clancy's final, defiant retort before he was led away.[14]

~

After what he described as his 'short holiday', John O'Brien arrived in Kildysart on the evening of Thursday 6 March 1919 to a hero's welcome.

He was met by members of Coolmeen Volunteers and Cumann na mBan, holding aloft lighted torches and Republican banners. At the Square there was a rousing rendition of *Felons of Our Land,* before the assembled crowd headed for Coolmeen. On the way, the houses were lit up and there were bonfires on the hills.

O'Brien was shouldered high along the final stage of his homeward journey as far as Coolmeen Cross where he addressed the crowd amid exhortations of 'Up Clancy' and 'Up O'Brien.'[15]

It was typical of the rousing reception that was given throughout west Clare to returning prisoners.

# The Shooting of Pat Studdert

Fifty-five-year-old father of nine, Pat Studdert, was a farmer and a fisherman who lived at The Blocks, Kilkee. He is described in contemporary accounts as quiet, inoffensive and industrious. He was also deaf.

On 29 June 1919, Studdert was tending to his cows close to a military camp outside the town when he was shot in the head by a sentry from the nearby camp.

Having suffered a catastrophic injury to his head and brain, he was brought to Kilrush Hospital, where he died the following evening.

The Inquest into Pat Studdert's death was held at the schoolroom in Kilrush Workhouse on Wednesday 2 July 1919, where the body was identified by Mrs Studdert.

Drs Counihan and Callinan described a three-inch wound at the back of the head that resulted in loss of blood and of brain tissue. Together, they performed an operation to remove fragments of skull from the brain.

Captain Wewoller, 2nd Battalion, Scottish Horse, stated that orders had been received from Headquarters to treble the guard on that particular day and sentries were under orders to shoot to kill on the third challenge to trespassers.

Sergeant Wolesley, the soldier who fired the fatal shot, reportedly insisted on giving evidence, even though he had been cautioned against doing so.

Wolesley stated that a private drew his attention to the presence of a man on a nearby fence; he beckoned to the man to leave and he did. But the man returned again and Wolesley first took aim with a rifle and then beckoned to the man with the rifle to move away. When the man failed to do so, the soldier moved 40 yards closer and fired.

Lieutenant Cousins stated that he had heard shouts of warning, followed by shots. He saw a man stagger for twelve paces before dropping to the ground. The jury's verdict was read:

> … we find that in accordance with the medical testimony that Patrick Studdert died at the Kilrush Hospital on the 1st July from fracture of the skull from a bullet wound deliberately inflicted by Sergeant Wolesley and we strongly disapprove of the military orders given in this peaceful district and recommend the wife and family of the deceased for compensation from the military authorities for the great loss sustained by the death of their breadwinner and we tender to the family our sincere sympathy.

Captain Wewoller apologised on behalf of the military and promised support for Mrs Studdert.

Pat Studdert was buried in Farrihy Graveyard.[1]

His was the second needless killing of a civilian in about 15 months by a soldier from a Scottish regiment in west Clare.

# Saving hay and saving Ireland

On Sunday 13 April 1919, following Mass in Knockerra Church, a group of over 30 volunteers assembled for drill practice. Among their number was Ernie O'Malley, sent by Headquarters to provide training in military tactics and logistics for members of all companies.[1]

Sergeant Jeremiah O'Donoghue, Constable James McDermott and Constable John Hanlon had cycled the four miles from Kilrush to keep a watchful eye on events.

Battalion Commandant John Flanagan persuaded O'Malley that they should put their training to good use by disarming the RIC men and Flanagan proceeded with the customary drilling while O'Malley and Brigade OC Art O'Donnell retrieved their revolvers from the nearby Nolan home, where they had left them during Mass.

At this point, O'Malley instructed O'Donnell to play no part in the attack, possibly because O'Donnell was so easily identifiable.[2] As soon as O'Malley emerged from Nolan's with his revolver, Flanagan and Mick Ryan overpowered Hanlon and McDermott and their carbines were subsequently taken.[3] Shots were fired from the crowd and Sergeant O'Donoghue returned fire, causing the main body of men to scatter.

Spotting one of the men escaping with a cycle and a carbine, O'Donoghue fired again, forcing him to abandon his booty. Hanlon took the carbine and provided backup while O'Donoghue and McDermott pursued some men who had fled to Nolan's. Inside, they arrested Art O'Donnell and recovered the second carbine which had been hidden in a bed. John Grogan of Carrowfree ran from the house but was apprehended by the waiting Constable Hanlon.

By now, Thomas Howard, together with Mick Mahoney of Knockerra and Joe Sexton of Tarmon, all of whom had taken cover in an outhouse, realised that the game was up and they surrendered on McDermott's order.[4] All five were arrested and marched to Kilrush, together with a 16-year-old youth named Michael Kelly.[5]

Due to his age and the belief that his father was not a Sinn Féin sympathiser, Kelly was not tried, but was brought instead before an RM in Kilkee on 5 May 1919. There, he apologised to the court and said that he had not and would not interfere with the police. He was bound over to keep the peace.[6]

At their subsequent trial by court-martial in Cork's Victoria Barracks, on 8 May, all five refused to plead.[7] There was a tetchy exchange between O'Donnell and Sergeant McDermott during O'Donnell's cross-examination of the witness. McDermott stated that he was sure O'Donnell was present at the time of the attack and asserted that, while O'Donnell '... was otherwise well-behaved, (he) became abusive ... and declared that he had been in Nolan's house at the time. The outburst appeared a genuine one, but O'Donnell is a clever fellow.'

Despite the observation by the military that he was '... extremely debilitated with a strong suggestion of TB,' O'Donnell was later sentenced to two years imprisonment and his comrades to 18 months, all with hard labour, on a charge of illegal drilling and abetting an attack on police.[8]

In recognition of their bravery, Dublin Castle awarded Sergeant O'Donoghue the Constabulary Medal and promoted him to the rank of Head-Constable; Constables McDermott and Hanlon were also awarded the Constabulary Medal, a first-class favourable record and a grant of £10 from the Constabulary Force Fund.[9]

The five prisoners began their period of incarceration as Thomas Keane of Carrigaholt and Michael Fahy of Kilkee were about to end theirs. Four of the five would soon be released on grounds of ill health – O'Donnell on 28 May, Sexton on 3 June, Mahoney on 5 July and Grogan on 22 July.[10] Howard was less fortunate; he was transferred to Mountjoy Prison in Dublin on 28 September.[11]

Following his stint in prison, Howard's activities were closely monitored by Hanlon.

On his conditional release from Mountjoy on 20 October 1919 Howard's relative, a chemist from Kilrush, travelled to Dublin with a change of clothes for the freed prisoner. The Howards had intended to travel on third-class tickets until the chemist spotted Hanlon at the station. They avoided his attentions by travelling in a first-class carriage. It was only when he had disembarked at Kilrush station that Hanlon discovered that his prey had been on the train all along.

That night, to welcome the prisoner home, 200 marched from Knockerra to Kilrush, each holding aloft a two-pronged fork on top of which was spiked a sod of turf that was oiled and lit before Howard was shouldered in procession through the town.[12]

The striking image of the nocturnal hayfork parade gave added symbolic expression to historian David Fitzpatrick's memorable line 'Thousands who saved hay in the sunlight sought to save Ireland in the moonlight.'[13]

When Howard failed to honour the conditions under which he was released, he was greatly sought after and had to go on the run and featured in the *Hue and Cry* in the company of Tim Haier and John 'Shang' Scanlon.[14]

~

'Saving Ireland in the moonlight' involved tossing hay in the moonlight in Danganelly when a local publican and shopkeeper named Edmund Murphy, a member of the British recruiting organisation, began to billet the military.

When Murphy was found to have supplied the British forces with a list of local Republican activists, he was boycotted.

During the enforcement of the boycott, a watch was kept on the comings and goings at his pub and there was some consternation when a number of the most regular customers were noted to be fathers of prominent Volunteers.[15]

Nearby, the Callinan family had built a house that was unoccupied and military billeted there also, resulting in a boycott of both families.

When the time came for the Callinans to draw in their hay, their neighbours, Thomas Quealy and Paddy Mescall, joined the *meitheal* as they always did in order to help with the making of the rick and wind. It was what good neighbours did.

That evening, the IRA ordered that the rick and the wind were to be knocked, so Quealy dutifully played his part in the levelling. It was what good Volunteers did.

But as a good neighbour he felt obliged to help with the rebuilding the following day. It was twice the job, but if he hadn't helped with the rebuilding the Callinans would have known that he had been involved in the knocking of the hay.[16]

Both the Murphys and the Callinans availed of military and police protection but, nonetheless, endured four months of harassment by Liddy and his men.

Murphy's workers were fired on and on Sunday 26 October 1919, as Murphy was on his way to church with his daughter, he was held up by ten or twelve masked men, who forced him to return to his home and to hand over two guns and a revolver.[17]

Brigade Commandant Art O'Donnell was unhappy about the boycott, since he believed that Murphy was not a spy and that his only crime was that he was friendly with the military Commandant.

Following the intervention of a member of the clergy, O'Donnell met with Chief of Staff Richard Mulcahy, who agreed that steps should be taken to resolve the conflict and to end the boycott. O'Donnell arranged by letter to meet Murphy a short distance from Murphy's home, where the central issues were discussed. O'Donnell then drew up a list of terms, which were agreed by Murphy, and the boycott was ended.[18]

It was to be the first of three boycotts that were ended following intervention by O'Donnell, the second of which involved Shragh farmer Michael 'the Fenian' Whelan.[19] Shortly after, in February 1920, O'Donnell again ordered an end to a Carrigaholt boycott which resulted in his having to resign as Brigade Commandant.[20]

In Cahercullen, Cree, 'saving Ireland in the moonlight' meant spiking meadows in the moonlight. There, the loyalty of a different Callinan family to the British armed forces 'in the hour of need' would land them in trouble with local Volunteers.

Denis Callinan had answered the call to join the British Army in 1917, serving in France as a gunner while his sister managed his farm. On a visit home, by way of discouraging him from returning to France, his tunic was taken and burned. Undeterred, he walked across country to Ennis on the first leg of his journey back to his post.

After the War ended, Callinan was discharged on a pension of five shillings per week, but his wife Annie later detailed a catalogue of persecutions that were visited on the Callinan farm during the coming years.

Their land was grazed, their turf stolen and their hay couldn't be cut as the meadows had been spiked with steel bars. They were forced, she claimed, to seek assistance from the Southern Irish Loyalist Relief Association and the United Service Fund. She claimed that the intimidation had precipitated her husband's death at the age of 37 in 1927.[21]

~

Following the end of the Great War an international peace conference was held in Paris between the months of January and June 1919 for the purpose of agreeing post-war protocols.

During one of his trips to Paris, David Lloyd George – Britain's first Welsh Prime Minister – attended the boxing finals at the Inter-Allied Games between 22 June and 6 July. He and other dignitaries were in the company of General Pershing at the recently-constructed Pershing Stadium, named in his honour.

Doonbeg man Mick Killeen, who had served in the US Army during the war, represented the American military in one of the semi-finals. As he warmed up before the fight, the Doonbeg Dynamo spotted the Welsh Wizard at the ringside and his first thought was to jump the ropes, strike a blow for Irish freedom (on the Prime Minister's chin) and ask, "Why don't you give freedom to Ireland?"

Killeen lost the bout and later acknowledged the superiority of his opponent, "He beat me. He knew too much. But Lloyd George nearly got all I knew."[22]

Meanwhile, Killeen's brother Tim was being treated in The Curragh for devastating shrapnel wounds inflicted while fighting with The Irish Guards in the Great War. Mick arrived back in Doonbeg on 26 July 1919 and spent time with his brother before he passed away on 31 July.

Tim's remains were met by a huge crowd at Doonbeg Station and men jostled each other for a chance to carry the coffin at regular intervals along the 1½-mile route to Doonbeg Church. The funeral the next day was described by Mick Killeen in a letter to his sister in the United States:

> We had few military. One officer and 14 enlisted men from Kilkee paid military honours. Everything was done and done quietly and respectively [sic] ... The Union Jack or British Flag was not displayed nor wrapped around his coffin, this being his own request, and the military officer, being a gentleman, kindly consented to avoid everything that might cause friction or hurt feelings.[23]

≈

On 22 September 1919, at around 10.30am on a wet Monday, a three-man

RIC patrol led by an 'aggressive' Kilmihil-based sergeant was ambushed at Cahercanivan, near Kilmihil.[24]

Under the stewardship of Seán Liddy, the ambush party consisted of Patrick Burke, Mick Honan, Michael Browne, Tadhg Neenan, Denis McGrath, Michael Breen and John Morrissey.[25] The men took up positions on both sides of the road, with a view to engagement at close quarters, since they were only armed with shotguns.

However, when the approaching patrol was still 50 yards away, one of the Volunteers accidentally fired a shot, forcing Liddy and his men to break cover. The ensuing exchange lasted for about an hour and Mick Honan was wounded in the chest but, despite the RIC's superior weaponry, the ambush party were not apprehended.[26]

The police returned to the scene the following morning, where they found eleven topcoats, three or four caps, a number of assorted bullets and cartridges and a Bull Dog revolver. In a coat pocket (probably Honan's) they found a handkerchief saturated in blood.[27]

On 19 October 1919, five masked raiders got more than they had bargained for during a raid for arms at the home of a professional fowler named Lynch at Doonmore, between Doonbeg and Kilkee.

Lynch grabbed an iron bar and struck one of the raiders with it, knocking him over, while a relative struck another with a chair. And, no sooner had the fallen man struggled to his feet, than he was struck on the head with a stick.

Some of the raiders who were still unhurt headed for the kitchen, but all five retreated from the house when Lynch grabbed his fowling piece and chased them. Shots were fired by both parties but there were no casualties.[28] Lynch's two guns were later handed over to the police.[29]

Joseph Haugh, of Farrihy, was later charged in connection with the raid, but was released when no evidence was forthcoming.[30]

At about 5.15pm on 11 November 1919, a group of 14 volunteers were in Dromelihy to collect six shotguns that had been sourced for them by Jim

McGrath.[31] They were marching towards Cree in military formation in the charge of Michael Fitzmartin, 1st Lieutenant, Cree Coy.[32]

A Kilrush police patrol comprising Sergeant William Reilly, Constable John Horan and Constable Martin Gleeson, stopped them at Dromelihy Bridge and asked for their names.[33] All of the men complied except Jim Kelly, Michael Prendergast and Michael Fitzmartin.

Constable Gleeson had spotted Kelly throwing what he believed to be a revolver into a field but a search yielded nothing. But when the men were searched twelve sporting cartidges were found on Fitzmartin. Kelly eventually gave his name but Fitzmartin and Prendergast were arrested, handcuffed to each other and marched to Cooraclare.[34]

Cooraclare RIC Barracks after it was tarred with republican slogans on
26 October 1919.
(*Courtesy Tubridy's Bar, Cooraclare*)

The remaining twelve became hostile and followed the patrol to the village, where they demanded the release of the prisoners. The police took cover with their prisoners in the disused RIC Barracks, the walls of which had been extensively tarred with Republican slogans by local Volunteers on 26 October 1919.

When they discovered that the telephone lines to Kilrush had been cut, Constable Gleeson cycled the four miles to Toler Street Barracks for reinforcements. Meanwhile, Liddy had gathered about 20 men who launched an offensive on the barracks.

Following a prolonged and brisk exchange of fire, scouts reported that police reinforcements, led by Inspector Barrett and Head-Constable Sweeney, were approaching from Kilrush.[35] Liddy and his men withdrew, but the following night they returned to the Barracks and exploded two bombs in the men's kitchen and in the day-room, which burned out the building.[36]

It would be one of the first, if not the first, of many RIC Barracks to be destroyed throughout the country.[37]

Fitzmartin and Prendergast were brought forward for trial by court-martial in Limerick on 2 December, where they were charged with possession of ammunition and illegal drilling. Having pleaded guilty to possession of ammunition, Fitzmartin was sentenced to 84 days imprisonment without hard labour. Prendergast was sentenced to 28 days on the lesser charge of illegal drilling.[38]

## The drowning of Michael Darcy

By late 1919, due largely to the increasing number of attacks on rural outposts and patrolling policemen, two of the eleven police stations in West Clare Brigade's territory – those at Doonbeg and Cooraclare – had been closed.

Following the closure of the Cooraclare RIC barracks, Constable William Costigan had been moved to Kilmihil on 8 August 1919.[1] He had left his furniture at the Cooraclare lodgings, but had been given notice to quit by a 'Sinn Féin landlord'.

On Monday 19 January 1920 Constable Costigan and some police colleagues were moving his furniture to Knock by police motor-lorry.[2] The movement of the first lorry load had run smoothly, but 22-year-old Michael Darcy noted the activity and informed company Commander Seán Liddy.

Liddy immediately decided to ambush the lorry and he rounded up four IRA men – John Morrissey (Clonreddan), Patrick Burke (Carhue), Michael Campbell (Dromelihy) and Michael Breen, (Kilmacduane East).[3] Armed with some shotguns and a punt gun (a large shotgun), they took up positions on the west side of the road at Tiernaglohane, less than half a mile from the village.

Michael Darcy, acting as scout, was positioned closer to the village on the east side of the road and his task was to signal to the ambush party when the police van was coming.[4]

Darcy's first cousin, Company Lieutenant Michael Campbell loaded the punt gun with black powder, metal fragments and various types of shot.[5]

The lorry was driven by Constable James Irwin accompanied by Constable William Driscoll. At 1.45pm it climbed a steep incline just outside the village.[6]

When Darcy saw the police lorry he gave the agreed signal and, as it moved downhill on the other side, Campbell fired the punt gun, striking the bonnet.[7] The muzzle of the gun exploded, creating a cloud of black smoke and the recoil knocked Campbell over.[8] The only damage to the vehicle was shot marks on the bonnet and on the hood and several small shot were later found in the cab and in the stays of the hood.[9]

Irwin accelerated at speed and made it safely to the bottom of the hill as a volley of shots was fired from the furze bushes at the side of the road. Driscoll ran to the back of the lorry and fired two revolver shots uphill at the main party.[10]

What Liddy and his men had not known was that the vehicle was being escorted by a four-man police bicycle patrol under the command of Sergeant John Daly from Kilrush station. With him were Constables William Costigan, Patrick Nagle and James Mannion from Knock station. The patrol had fallen behind when the officers dismounted to walk their bicycles up the hill and they were unaware of the ambush until they caught up with the lorry at the foot of the hill.[11]

Meanwhile, when Darcy saw the patrol he had signalled again and the ambush party remained under cover.

While Costigan and Irwin guarded the lorry, the other policemen crossed the wall into a field at the eastern side. Then, for some unknown reason, one of the armed attackers crossed the road at this point and was spotted by Irwin, who fired at him.[12]

On seeing this, Darcy panicked and ran off eastward, closely followed by Sergeant Daly and Constables Nagle, Mannion and Driscoll. Being closer to him than to the other man, the police concentrated their fire on Darcy.[13]

Darcy's escape route brought him to the Doonbeg river which was in flood. A Miss Frawley spotted him first running towards the river at Poulmore from the opposite side to where she stood and then he was in the water.

Her shouts for help alerted John Brock who was quickly on the scene where he was joined by Thomas McGrath and Michael Browne.

Suddenly, McGrath spotted something in the water and said, "There he is down the river."

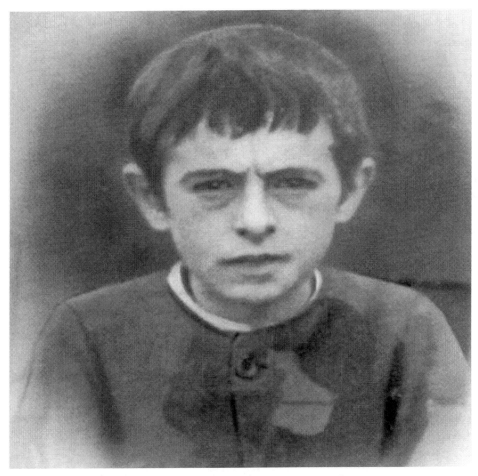

Michael Darcy.
(*Courtesy Paul Daly*)

As the men followed, Constable Mannion appeared on the opposite side and Brock shouted across, "The man is drowned and floating in the river."

Mannion then fired a shot which Brock took to be an alert for Mannion's colleagues, who were swiftly on the scene.

Sergeant Daly instructed the men to get back and gave the order to shoot. When a rifle was aimed at them the men retreated and Brock later deposed that he would have tried to save Darcy only for Sergeant Daly's order.[14]

A number of witnesses later gave their account of what they saw: when a Miss Reidy arrived on the scene, she saw Michael Darcy struggling in the water before going under and, once again, it was Sergeant Daly who warned her at gunpoint to get back.

It was another witness, a Mrs Lynch, who told Patrick O'Brien that a man was drowning in the river and he rushed to the scene where he encountered Michael Browne who had spotted Darcy's cap floating in the water. Both men followed the cap with a view to rescuing the lad but, yet again, the police warned them to get back before firing in their direction.[15]

Published accounts varied in the accuracy levels of reportage but the *Freeman's Journal* took first prize for exaggeration.

According to it, the attackers numbered 30; the police were attacked from both sides of the road; the lorry was moving slowly in order that the cycle patrol could keep up; police chased two men named Corry and Harrington across country for three or four miles and Darcy was the leader of the group.[16]

The two men the police followed across fields and randomly arrested were in fact two farmers' sons, 23-year-old Patrick Corry and 19-year-old Dan Harrington, at Tiernaglohane. The pair would probably have been charged with attempted murder were it not for the professionalism of Captain William C Gover who, having visited the scene with police witnesses, concluded that the evidence was not '... in any way convincing.'

Dan Harrington's only transgression appeared to be that he was wearing his waistcoat inside out and the police statement that he was seen 100 yards from the scene of the ambush was found to be a gross exaggeration.[17] The pair appeared at Kilkee Court on 11 February 1920, where they were bound over to the peace for a period of twelve calendar months.[18]

At the Inquest into the death of Michael Darcy at Cooraclare National School on 21 January 1920, Patrick O'Brien gave evidence of having recovered the body from the Pollmore at midday on the previous day. There was nothing in his pockets only an old pipe and some tobacco. The jury returned the following verdict:

> That the body of Michael Darcy was found drowned and we unanimously condemn the heartless action of the police in preventing his rescue.[19]

There was a large police and military presence at the funeral of Michael Darcy at Kilmacduane Cemetery, but they stopped short of entering the cemetery and, after the grave had been filled in, a volley of shots was fired.[20]

≁

The drowning of young Michael Darcy was to signal the beginning of bad feeling between the Darcy and Liddy families that would endure for decades.

Darcy's sister Margaret would later make sensational allegations about the manner in which Seán Liddy managed the immediate aftermath of her brother's death. At a sworn Inquiry during her application for a Service Medal with Bar for her late brother Patrick, Margaret Daly stated:

> The rumour went around to say that there was somebody in the river, somebody was drowned, and Mr Leddy [sic] sent a message to our place to say that all the party were safe and that my brother was with him, which was not true, and then he sent a message to some of his other Vols. To tell them to drag the river and find the body and to bury him and not to tell us at all about the matter – to bury him in a bog outside the village of Cooraclare, and some of them were in agreement with this and more of them were not, and

they then dragged the river but they didn't find the body that particular night and then the following morning they found the body.[21]

But Liddy's evidence to the same Inquiry was markedly different. Michael Darcy, he thought, was about 14-years-old, 'just a child; but that he might have been a bit older as he was 'a little fellow who didn't grow up'. (Darcy was 22-years-old).

Liddy stated that before the ambush he had told Darcy to '… clear away as quickly as you can and get away to a safe distance' after Darcy had followed the ambush party. These conflicting accounts of the events of 19 January 1920 both exemplified and typified the serious rift that had developed between two families that had once been friends.

Liddy, who had slept many nights in Darcy's house, was no longer welcome there and Paddy Lynch had reported to Liddy that Patrick Darcy had threatened revenge on account of what had happened to Michael.[22]

≁

On Easter Sunday 1928, a crowd estimated to number between 2000 and 3000 gathered at Kilmacduane graveyard to honour those who had died in the struggle for freedom. Following the recitation of the Rosary in Irish, Brian O'Higgins placed a large number of floral tributes on the grave of Michael Darcy. Two buglers sounded the *Last Post*.[23]

In 1933 Michael Darcy's mother was awarded a gratuity of £100 by the Army Pensions Board in respect of the loss of her son, on whom she was deemed to be partially dependant. In 1945 a Service Medal with Bar, engraved with the name of the deceased, was issued to her.[24]

≁

Liddy and his men caught up with Sergeant Daly and Constable Nagle while they were on cycle patrol on 1 March 1920.

Together with Sinon Haugh, Paddy Clancy, Denis Shannon, Art O'Donnell, Patrick (Sonny) Burke and Michael Kennedy, he staged an ambush on the pair at Clonross, between Knock and Labasheeda.

Daly was lucky to escape with his life, having been struck in the face by shotgun pellets. Nagle's rifle was taken and both men were forced to flee on foot. Following the incident, Colonel Murray White, who was in charge of police and military, visited the area and armoured car patrols became a regular feature.

A Clonross-based Irish teacher, Joseph O'Connor, who had been gaoled in 1915 for abusing police, was arrested on suspicion of involvement in the ambush after a paper in his possession appeared to outline the plan for it.[25]

# Republican Courts

The efficient functioning of the justice system was central to effective British rule in Ireland and the administration of justice depended on law officers and courts. Small wonder, therefore, that it was these very cogs in the wheels of justice that were targeted nationally and, perhaps most effectively, in west Clare.

In the decade preceding the setting up of the Sinn Féin Arbitration Courts, minor cases, both civil and criminal, were heard in Petty Sessions Court sittings. These cases typically included turbary disputes, assaults, public drunkenness, trespassing and rights of way.[1]

They were presided over by unsalaried Justices of the Peace, who were often well-to-do farmers or gentlemen. The Court Clerk recorded the details of each case as well as collecting fees that were due. Petty Sessions Courts sat as often as required by their case load. Cases requiring a jury were heard at Quarter Sessions and murder cases were dealt with at twice-yearly Assizes.

On occasion, two Resident Magistrates (RMs) presided at these sessions, but generally the bench comprised five members, including the local salaried RM or unsalaried JP, one of whom would normally sit in the Chair. The presence of three was required for a sitting to proceed and both civil and criminal cases were processed.

It was here that offences such as public disorder, drunkenness, common assault and damage to property were dealt with. Typically, these sessions would last for a couple of hours and upwards of ten cases might be heard.

On one memorable occasion in Kilrush in May 1918, Constable Sullivan summonsed Catherine Coughlan for not having a dog licence. The defendant arrived into court with her faithful mutt smartly festooned with the Sinn Féin colours. Coughlan's defence was that the king had her husband and she needed a dog; the Chairman reminded her that she also needed a licence and she was fined one penny.[2]

Amusing though it was, the presence of a political dog in court was symptomatic of exponential growth in indifference among local populations to the rule of British law. In fact, by this time, *ad hoc* tribunals had begun to be established in response to widespread land-grabbing in parts of the west of Ireland.[3]

They constituted a welcome and very necessary response to the threat to Republican unity that was posed by agrarian unrest in the region.[4] By early 1919 in west Clare, these tribunals had morphed into the more formal Republican Courts or Sinn Féin Courts.[5]

In late 1919, Sinn Féin Parish Courts and Circuit Courts were first set up and these courts were brought under the control of Dáil Éireann in mid-1920 before being formally constituted under the authority of Dáil Éireann's Department of Justice in 1921.[6]

In west Clare, the early courts materialised via the growth, maturation and adaptation of *ad hoc* interventions that were hastily convened in reaction to some local crisis. At a time of great respect for the priest's collar, and when the majority of west Clare priests and their Bishop were in sympathy with the independence movement, it was no surprise that these random intermediations were usually presided over by members of the local clergy.

However, clerical interventions were generally, but not universally, successful.

≈

In Quilty, where most relied on the sea for a living and had little or no land for growing crops, publican Michael Casey organised a mob to drive the cattle from the Seafield farm owned by a man named M S Brew who lived in Kilrush. In an effort to stop the cattle drive, Fr Michael McKenna – a former army chaplain who had taken up his appointment as curate in Mullagh in March 1919 – accompanied by Company Captain Joe Daly and a group of Volunteers from the Kilmurry Company, confronted Casey's men and pleaded with them to abandon the drive.[7]

In the ensuing standoff, stones were thrown, one of which struck Fr McKenna on the forehead, forcing the withdrawal of the cleric and his entourage. Shortly afterwards, Liddy and some of his men arrested Casey, who avoided extreme censure by giving certain undertakings and by paying a fine.[8]

Labasheeda curate, Fr P K Hayes would later participate in another memorable clerical intervention when he stout-heartedly defended his parishioners against Black and Tans and Auxiliaries.[9]

In Carrigaholt at this time, an intervention of a different kind was called for when a valuable plantation at the Burton estate came under threat of destruction by local elements who, presumably, would have preferred to divide the land. It was saved by the round-the-clock security that was provided by the IRA over a period of several months.[10]

The proliferation of similar agrarian issues, combined with an increased propensity for litigation among local populations, demanded more formal legal structures. In consequence, *ad hoc* mediations gradually morphed into locally-convened tribunals that became known as Arbitration Courts. The establishment of these local tribunals was a bottom-up spontaneous development that actually led the way for Dáil Éireann's decree of August 1919 that Arbitration Courts were to be instituted on a national basis. But, in the absence of agreed structures and procedures, that decree was aspirational.

In fact, it was west Clare that led the way in the establishment of formal Sinn Féin courts and it was west Clare that pioneered the structures and procedures that would later be adopted elsewhere throughout the country when the Dáil Éireann Courts came into being.[11]

Much of the credit for the establishment of those structures and procedures must go to Brian O'Higgins who convened a Representative Republican Conference which not only set up courts in each parish and a District Court but also drafted a formal constitution with the help of local legal people.

Rules were written and a scale of fees and fines was tabulated. It was these very structures that both led and showed the way for the rest of the country.[12]

A number of different parishes have been credited with the formation of the first 'formal' Arbitration Court. The home of Dan 'Dootsie' Grogan in Gowerhass was believed to have been the venue for the first Arbitration Court in that area while, in Kilmurry, the first one at parish level was convened at the suggestion of Rev John Canon Glynn, PP.[13]

Agreements between litigants were brokered by a local arbitrator and while this court functioned quite effectively throughout the parish, there was no means by which agreements could be enforced. This situation, coupled with the fact that the RIC had been withdrawn to the safety of the towns, had implications for law and order.

Again at the suggestion of Canon Glynn, a few Volunteers patrolled each townland at night on the lookout for wrongdoers who were taking advantage of lax policing. Later, this very basic approach to enforcement was formalised when an IRA Volunteer Police Force was established in each company, whereby a company sergeant and three Volunteers were given responsibility for law and order as well as the enforcement of Arbitration Court decisions. [14]

In Kilmihil, after a spate of robberies had been reported to John Breen, the imposing Kiltumper man assembled a group of about 30 men who kept watch by night. The culprits were swiftly arrested and brought to justice in the Sinn Féin Courts, where they admitted their guilt and subsequently made restitution to their victims.[15]

In the First Battalion area comprising Kildysart, Coolmeen, Cranny and

Labasheeda, the Volunteers had established control as early as 1918:

> ... since 1918 the volunteers had entire control of all administrative affairs in the area. Court orders were executed, volunteers enforced ordinary law, rates were collected and handed over to L.G. Offices of Dáil Éireann. The Dáil Loan was opened and contributions received by volunteers. In short alien law and alien Government Departments were ignored.[16]

In Kilkee, David Conroy was one of a number of local Volunteer policemen who were called upon to deal with a volatile situation involving a postman who was in the throes of a psychotic episode.

Conroy, Jim Talty and Joe Marrinan secured the use of a car and, having restrained their violent patient, brought him to the Mental Hospital in Ennis. The Medical Superintendent there agreed that the poor man needed to be taken in. But the rule book had no guidelines for the committal of patients who were referred by an *ad hoc* police force and he could be sued if he got it wrong. Finally, it was agreed to release the patient in the hospital grounds and protocol now allowed staff to have him forcibly admitted.

As they toured the hospital, the Kilkee Volunteers caused a bit of a stir and one of the patients teased Conroy, claiming to be a better Republican than he.

Conroy sought clarification, only to be told, 'I never kissed the king', though the exact words used were believed to have been, 'I never licked the king's arse.'

In mock indignation, Conroy denied ever having stooped so low whereupon his taunter triumphantly stuck out his tongue, gave his finger a lick and chortled, "Didn't you ever do that to a stamp?"

King George V's image was featured on the postage stamps of the day.[17]

Later still, a hierarchical structure was established when the same policing protocols were extended to battalion and brigade level.[18] The development was both warranted and timely for the absence of an RIC presence in all but the larger towns resulted in increasing lawlessness.

One notice that was posted near Doonbeg in January 1920 outlined pub opening hours and warned of stiff penalties for those who would flout the Licencing Laws:

Notices

*Public House Restrictions*

*By Competent Military Authority IRA*

To be enforced on and from 11th January (Sunday).

Closing hours on Sundays 2 o'clock pm. Holidays 4 pm.

1st October to 1st March Week Days 8 o'clock pm.

1st March to 1st October Week Days 10 o'clock pm.

Violation

In all cases of violation of above Laws the offenders will be summonsed before the Parish Court and the following fines imposed.

Offending Publicans 1st offence not less than £1 and not more than £5.

Simple Drunkeness [*sic*] Found on Licensed Premises minimum fine 5 shillings maximum fine £1. The previous fine will be doubled for every subsequent offence

Travellers limits 5 miles Irish by road.

Courts martial Trial for a Publican giving drink to a Volunteer after hours or when under the influence of drink.

*Signed Competent Military Authority IRA.*[19]

There was a conspicuous IRA police presence at public events such as race meetings and even the poteen makers were quickly brought to heel. In areas where the Licencing Laws were repeatedly broken, all of the public houses were closed for a period of time.[20]

The west Clare courts '... were policed and guarded by IRA and ... justice was dispensed on common-sense bases, and accepted by mutual agreement of the litigants.'[21] The business of the dispensing of justice was taken very seriously and a dim view was taken of those who were less than committed to the smooth operation of the courts.

When Martin Chambers of Monmore questioned a member of the Sinn Féin Court as to why he was absent from so many meetings the accused said that he had hay to save, to which Chambers replied, "We all have hay to save".

"Go away out of that", was the retort, "I let more hay go with the breeze than you will ever save."[22]

~

Throughout 1919 and for the first half of 1920, court sittings were held openly, often even in public buildings. From the middle of 1920, however, the courts nearly always sat in remote locations that would remain secret until shortly before they were held. This was due in part to the fact that so many Volunteer police were themselves on the run which was greatly resented by the RIC whose role they were fulfilling so effectively.

Scouts took up strategic positions on approach roads, often atop ricks of hay, and they would signal the arrival of police and military.

Courts were held at O'Donnell's of Tullycrine, Slattery's and Brew's of Ballykett, Dootsie Grogan's of Gower, Patrick Burke's of Carhue, Cooraclare, Joe Daly's of Kilmurry, McNamara's of Mountrivers and at a remote uninhabited farmhouse in Cloonagarnaun, between Doonbeg and Quilty.[23]

Further west, court sittings were held in the old courthouse in Carrigaholt, where their case load was mainly comprised of land disputes.[24] Among the magistrates were Kilrush Curate, Fr Moloney, Tom Shannon of Moyasta and Danny McMahon from Carnacalla.[25]

Further north, the officers of the Kilmurry Parish Court in the months before and after the Truce were Canon Glynn, PP, Tom Garry Burke, Jack Pyne, Michael Meade, Tot O'Connor and a man who was known by the sobriquet of Coco. Seosamh Mac Mathúna filled the role of Registrar from

May 1921 after the arrest and imprisonment of Fr Gaynor and Fr McKenna.[26]

In Carrigaholt, Éamon Fennell acted as Arbitrator in a number of cases in 1920 and 1921.[27]

Even after the establishment of formal Arbitration Courts, disputes were regularly mediated and, on occasion, summarily adjudicated by members of the clergy. In Mullagh, Peter Meade and some of his henchmen drove cattle from the land he had sold 20 years earlier to his cousin Michael Meade ('the straightest man in the parish'). Fr Gaynor organised some volunteers to reinstate the cattle and Peter was forced to pay 10s to each for the time they spent in the recovery operation.[28]

Elsewhere, a cattle drive on the lands of a Sinn Féin supporter was abandoned only after the intervention of a priest when the owner contributed £100 to de Valera's election fund.[29]

~

When the courts were reconstituted under the stewardship of Dáil Éireann in 1921, the model that had been employed so effectively in west Clare was adopted almost in its entirety. The Parish Court was composed of three members, none of whom was required to have legal experience and one of whom was almost invariably a priest. This court dealt with petty offences (claims of under £10) and had the power to take evidence in more serious cases as well as to refer certain cases for processing at District Court level. These later Parish Courts did not usually deal with land title issues.

At the next level, the District Court had five members, one of whom was likewise invariably a clergyman, three of whom could constitute a quorum. Again, legal training was not a requirement of membership. These courts would typically meet once a month and in west Clare much of their time was taken up with land disputes.

The first West Clare District Arbitration Court or Circuit Court was formally set up on 1 November 1919 at Cunningham's house in Cree at a well-attended meeting of the West Clare Sinn Féin Executive. The meeting had been convened by Brigade Commandant Art O'Donnell in his capacity as vice-Chair of the executive. Before the ordinary business of the meeting was discussed, O'Donnell addressed the delegates concerning the proliferation of land disputes that had occurred and their potential for division among members of the Republican movement.

In a spirited 'united we stand, divided we fall' speech, O'Donnell called for the setting up of a court that would adjudicate on contentious issues. Fr Charlie Culligan, presiding, said that O'Donnell had hit the nail on the head in terms of what was required and the delegates voted overwhelmingly in favour of the proposal.

Fr Culligan was elected President and the elected court members were James McInerney (Killard or Baltard), Patrick 'Soldier' Kelly (Clonina, Cree), Batt Crowley (Tullagower) and Brian O'Higgins of the O'Curry Irish College, Carrigaholt. Art O'Donnell was appointed Court Registrar and one of his duties was to ensure that disputing parties signed an agreement that they would abide by the decision of the court.

The first case that was heard was McGrath v Tubridy and McGrath.[30] The case concerned a farm that had earlier been sold to a man named Tubridy by the Estates Commissioners, a subsidiary of the Land Commission whose brief extended to facilitating land purchase by descendants of evicted tenants and ex-servicemen. The solicitor for McGrath, the plaintiff, argued that, even though he had not been the owner of the land when it was sold, he would nevertheless have been entitled to a share when his brother would marry and settle down. He was awarded £550.[31]

The courts dealt with a wide variety of cases, such as trespass, watercourses, boundary fences and breaches of warranty.[32] By mid-1920, such was the proliferation of land-related issues in the courts generally that the District courts were commonly referred to as Land Courts and such was their popularity that the Crown Courts were practically deserted.

At Kilrush Petty Sessions Court on 12 July, Resident Magistrate Alan

Lendrum heard the only case that had been processed in a month. When he asked if the complainant had any witnesses, he was told that he had, but that they were afraid to attend. The *Clare Champion* correspondent who reported on the court sitting attributed the slackness in business to '... the good order which prevails and is being preserved in Kilrush district.' The reality was that the local population had voted with its feet, deserting the Petty Court in favour of the Parish Court.[33]

The situation in Miltown Malbay was dramatic; for the first time in a century, not a single case had been listed for a whole month. Volunteers had been patrolling the area for the purpose of maintaining law and order and were bringing drunks to their homes to keep them out of trouble.[34] In fact, such was their effectiveness that in the first three months of 1919, not a single case of public drunkenness came before Miltown Malbay Petty Sessions Courts.[35]

The Irish Bar Council had ruled that participation in Sinn Féin Courts by its members was tantamount to unprofessional conduct. Yet, barristers and

Arbitration Court Sitting at Westport, County Mayo, summer 1920.
*(Source: Capuchin Annual 1970, p. 383)*

solicitors followed their clients (and their money) into these courts.

One solicitor justified this with the rhetorical question, 'Am I to throw away a practice that has taken me thirty years to build up?'[36] In west Clare, Kilrush-based solicitor Michael Killeen was regularly in attendance.

When Republicans appeared before Crown Courts, they invariably refused to recognise the court. In north Clare, one defendant who had been accused of larceny was brought before the local Sinn Féin Court.

"I refuse to recognise the authority of this court," he declared confidently.

"That being so", responded the Court President, "kindly inform us which court do you recognise and we shall be pleased to hand you over immediately."

Having considered the alternative, the defendant owned up to his misdemeanour and accepted his punishment.[37]

The very few who brought their cases to the official courts, thereby refusing to recognise the Sinn Féin Courts, were threatened and boycotted.

In October 1919, Michael 'the Fenian' Whelan of Shragh was in dispute with a neighbour over title. A party of Sinn Féin representatives visited him and suggested that he would submit his claim to the Sinn Féin Court (presumably the local Parish Court, since the District Court had not yet been set up). Whelan refused and instead took his dispute to the October Quarter Sessions in Kilrush, which found in his favour.

The Whelans, who were also believed to have sold turf to the local Resident Magistrate, were then subjected to boycott. Tradesmen refused to work for them, shops refused to serve them and shots were fired outside their Shragh home on the night of 19 October.

On 22 January 1920, at Kilrush Quarter Sessions, Nora Whelan lodged a £500-claim for permanent injury to her health 'through fright' as a result of shots being fired outside her home the previous November. Her husband Michael gave evidence that notices branding him as an informer, and signed by the Competent Military Authority, had been affixed to chapel gates in the area. These notices, one of which was produced in court, warned the public against having anything to do with Whelan. Sergeant Corduff stated that he had seen one of the notices as far away as Kilkee.

In support of her claim, Mrs Whelan stated that she had spent three weeks in bed following the fright that she had got. She was no longer able to work on the farm as she had done previously and even still she could only leave the bed for an hour or two each day. Nora Whelan was awarded £40 compensation, which was paid by the Local Authority. The boycott ended only after mediation by Art O'Donnell who, with the help of Conor Whelan, brokered a settlement between the warring parties.[38]

~

As the courts' popularity grew the complexity of the cases that came before them increased and it was not unusual for them to have to hear cases involving historical land disputes that dated back 40 or 50 years.[39]

One such case involved a publican named Bid O'Dwyer in Clonadrum, with whom a local farmer named Michael McNamara had, through fondness for drink, run up a large bill. Following his death in 1909, O'Dwyer had taken over his farm and knocked his house. As a result, Mrs McNamara was forced to live in a cottage on a separate five-acre parcel of land and the O'Dwyers were boycotted.[40]

Fr McKenna, sensing the potential for trouble, sent the case for hearing by the District Arbitration Court.[41] The case was heard over a period of two days in July 1920.

Mrs McNamara deposed that Mrs O'Dwyer had purchased the farm from her husband in lots over a period of time, without the consent of the plaintiff, who did not benefit from the proceeds since her husband had drunk them. The court ruled that Mrs McNamara was to be given back the farm on payment of £125.[42]

Mrs O'Dwyer had previously been married to an RIC man named O'Connor from Quilty and, when widowed, had married Denny O'Dwyer. During the McNamara-related boycott or a later one, local enforcers had fired shots into the pub from the bridge at Áth na gCaorach while Denny sat talking to Andrew Clancy, Bid's grandson from her first marriage. One of the bullets ricocheted off the stone wall and lodged in the chair that Denny was sitting on.[43]

For Mick Nash, from nearby Clohanmore, observing the boycott would have entailed cycling some distance for his pint of stout, so he continued to patronise the establishment.

Mick and his brother Jack were two bachelor brothers and also sworn enemies who never spoke to each other, despite the fact that they shared a farm and a home. Whenever one of them wished to give a message to the other he would relate the relevant information to the dog within his brother's hearing.

The local enforcers were displeased that Mick was not honouring the boycott and they decided to give him a fright. One night, as he was on his way home, he was peppered with shotgun pellets. The doctor was called and his wounds were attended to.

Next day, Jack met neighbour Mick Murrihy on the road and Mick sympathised with him over what had happened. Jack replied.

"If I caught the fecker who shot my brother I'd tear him limb from limb!"[44]

One of the most unusual cases to come before the west Clare courts involved a young, recently-married couple. Having tied the knot, the pair had moved in to the young woman's family home. But romance went out the window when, on the wedding night, the newly-weds discovered that the blushing bride would be sleeping with the mother, while the befuddled son-in-law was ordered to share a bed with the man of the house.

There was some legal argument when the case (one of the few to be held *in camera*) came before the Parish Court. The stalemate was resolved when armed and masked men visited the home and ordered a revision of the sleeping arrangements.[45]

≈

Court decisions were enforced by Brigade police and non-compliance was punished by various means, depending on the severity of the issue. At the lower end of the scale, one could be fined or sentenced to hard labour in the service of a local farmer thinning turnips for a period.[46]

Following a cattle drive, Tony Garry of Ballymacurtan and Jim Shea were fined. When Shea failed to pay the fine, a member of the Republican police called to collect the debt and introduced himself as a Sergeant. Shea, unimpressed by his visitor's recently-acquired title, asked him if he could even spell the word 'sergeant'.[47]

Garry also refused to pay his fine, and he was visited by IRA police members Matthew Bermingham, and Micho Tubridy, who planned to bring him before the court. Garry initially refused to go with them and his devout sister, Mary Kate, doused all three with holy water as she interceded with the saints whose names they bore – St Anthony, St Matthew and St Michael – for a peaceful resolution to the impasse.

Mary Kate's prayers were answered on the double when her brother not only agreed to his 'arrest' but gave his custodians a lift to the court.[48]

Elsewhere, a recalcitrant individual (who had not the benefit of prayerful intercession) refused to pay the fine that had been imposed by the court. He was duly arrested and brought to a graveyard, where he was handed a lighted candle before being ordered inside a vault where there were five coffins.

His captors suggested that he might revise his decision before the candle burned out. Having sealed the entrance they left him for 24 hours, after which he secured his release by agreeing to pay the fine.[49]

Banishment to Mutton Island for a period was a common enough penalty and Volunteers would deliver food supplies at regular intervals.[50]

When three west Clare men appeared before the court to answer a charge of having knocked a neighbour's wall, they were duly fined 30 shillings and ordered to rebuild the wall. When two of them refused, they were incarcerated on Mutton Island for three weeks.

On hearing of their plight, some RIC policemen arrived on the shore by boat to free the two prisoners. Having first been pelted with stones, the sergeant-in-charge shouted, 'We have come to rescue you'.

He was told in no uncertain terms that the police had no authority to release the prisoners, "We are citizens of the Irish Republic and we don't want your help."[51]

This incident was cited as evidence of the widespread acceptance and popular consent enjoyed by the Republican Courts.[52]

In the Coore district, 20 prisoners were held for a number of weeks during the enforcement of Republican Court Orders.[53] In rare cases of non-compliance, offenders were even deported to England, a practice which was condemned in the House of Commons due to the perception that England was being used as a convict settlement.[54]

~

The business of arbitration was complicated by the fact that Sinn Féin members and Volunteers were often to be found on both sides of the same dispute. But, while the workings of the west Clare courts have been held up as a model for the rest of the country, their reputation would come to be tarnished by Fr Gaynor's claims of mismanagement of two of the many land-grabbing cases that were dealt with between August and December 1920.[55]

The first of these involved a widow named O'Dea from Cooraclare, who had sold her land to a Mr Brown about 20 years previously. However, she later changed her mind and, when Brown insisted on holding on to what was legally his, she organised a boycott against him.

The dispute was resolved following the intervention of the parish priest, who brokered an agreement that Brown would give back the land that was legally his but would retain over three-quarters of an acre of cutaway bog. All was fine until Mrs O'Dea's daughter grew up and married a local man named Chambers, who sought to recover the bog through the Arbitration Court.

According to Gaynor, the case was heard by magistrates James McInerney (Doonbeg), Batt Crowley (Tullagower) and Patrick Kelly (Cree) in the absence of the District Court president, Fr Charlie Culligan, who said later that he had to attend a Confirmation dinner. The majority decision of Crowley and Kelly favoured Chambers, who was granted possession of the bog from November 1920. When Brown sought to appeal the court decision, Gaynor, in the absence of recourse to a Circuit Court, arranged via Fr McKenna for the dismissal of the District Court on grounds of incompetence.

Perhaps the appeal could and should have been heard by the recently-constituted High Land Commission Court of the Irish Republic, which was authorised by Dáil Éireann to inquire and adjudicate upon all disputes arising out of land.

Dáil Éireann's warrant had bestowed on this court '… final and absolute voice in all adjudications.'[56] But there is no definitive timeline for the transition from *ad hoc* tribunals to Sinn Féin Arbitration Courts and from the latter to Dáil Courts proper and in west Clare, at least, appeals were processed at local level.[57]

In fact, Brown's appeal was heard and upheld by a Convention that was assembled by Fr Gaynor, the composition of which included the new District Court, members of the West Clare Sinn Féin Executive and officers of the West Clare Brigade.

Gaynor was scathing in his criticism of Crowley, who, he suggested, had 'an itching palm' and 'Soldier' Kelly, who was 'amenable to influence'.[58]

The second blight on the great success of the west Clare courts resulted from a decision that was taken at the same court sitting from which Fr Culligan was absent.

Mr and Mrs Peter O'Brien, a childless farming couple from Mullagh, had reared their nephew Patrick Connors from Cooraclare. Connors would have inherited the farm, but he had been difficult and he had demanded and got payment for his work on the farm before going to Dublin as a teenager, where he became a policeman.

When Connors left the police force in 1920, he returned to west Clare that spring and demanded that the O'Briens hand over the farm. When they refused, he tried to intimidate them by word and deed.

After the District Court, on the majority vote of Justices Kelly and Crowley, had first ruled in favour of Chambers and then granted possession to Connors, Fr McKenna had the court dismissed.

Once again, the O'Briens' appeal was not referred to the High Land Commission Court. Instead, Mullagh curate and Volunteer Commandant Fr Michael McKenna had Connors arrested and brought before an *ad hoc* tribunal at his and Fr Gaynor's home, where Connors was court-martialled by Battalion officers.

Such was the arrogance of Connors, a trained boxer who scoffed at his confronters, that the curate at one point even boxed him in the face during the court-martial.[59] The recalcitrant prisoner was duly sentenced to one month's detention on Mutton Island. However, in an extraordinary *volte face*, Brigade Chief of Police, Willie Shanahan, gave Connors and a number of Volunteer supporters written authority to evict the O'Briens.

Connors now had two decisions in his favour and would have remained in possession of the farm except for the Convention that ruled on the Chambers-Brown case and which reversed the original District Court decision. Predictably enough, there was no queue to carry out the Tribunal's decision but Fr Gaynor was equal to the task and he knew just the man to complete it:

> I went alone to Peter O'Brien's house, informed Connors of the convention decision and asked him to leave for sake of peace. He laughed in my face. 'It will take more than a bloody Tipperary man to put me out', he said. I also laughed, 'The position for you, Connors, is very simple', I told him, 'I shall come back in half an hour, but not alone next time: you have to decide whether you will walk out or be carried out dead'.

> There was one man in the townland, Joe Daly (Canon Meade's nephew) whom I could trust and who had no fear of Connors, even though he was armed

with a revolver. I called on Joe Daly and bade him get his rifle (which he did on the instant). We brought McGannon with us, and another volunteer, to whom I gave my little toy pistol, for he had no weapon. I explained to them that I took legal and moral responsibility: that they were in a position similar to that of any organised armed forces in any country and were free, if necessary, to open fire on Connors without any qualm of conscience. We marched to the north door of the house at an easy pace, not in the least excited as far as I could observe, and, as we approached, Connors took to his heels by the southern door and raced away at high speed back to Cooraclare.

The O'Briens returned to their home and Gaynor heaved a sigh of relief that Connors had capitulated, as there were few hiding places for priests who had doubled up as executioners.

Though he held no rank in the Volunteers, following Shanahan's brutal killing, Gaynor assumed the role of Brigade Chief of Police in the belief that there was hardly a single man he could trust to carry out the duties of the role without fear or favour. Furthermore, he saw to it that future cases involving land disputes were excluded from the jurisdiction of the District Court.[60]

≈

The West Clare District Court that Gaynor had earlier dismissed was re-constituted under Dáil Éireann in Mullagh on Thursday 22 July 1920. Representing the Dáil was Éamon Waldron, a teacher at St Flannan's College in Ennis and Fr Charlie Culligan chaired the meeting.

Waldron informed the attendees that the working model that had been adopted by Dáil Éireann was almost identical to the one that had been in existence in west Clare for quite some time. This model was duly adopted by the meeting. Elections to this District Court were then held under the proportional representation system and Waldron explained that those who were elected would remain in office until January 1921.

The elected members were Kilmihil curate Fr Culligan, William Carroll and County Councillors Patrick 'Soldier' Kelly (Cree), Peadar O'Loughlin

(Liscannor) and Jack O'Dwyer (Kilrush).[61]

O'Dwyer's election was significant, since he was no favourite of the clergy. Described as an 'anti-cleric' whose patriotism '… was manifested only in talk', O'Dwyer had stopped attending Mass following a row with Kilrush priests over a proposed town water supply. O'Dwyer's persistence in selling the *Clare Champion* during the boycott caused some annoyance to Gaynor when the curate discovered that a humble Kilrush street-seller had observed the Sinn Féin embargo. And, if the cleric was critical of 'Soldier' Kelly's court performances, he was scathingly so of O'Dwyer who, he later wrote, '… was quite useless, so Fr Culligan told me, as a member of the District Court'.[62]

It would be early 1921 before the formal Circuit Courts were established throughout the country. After the first round of appointments, judges would be required to have at least six years legal experience. Circuit Court Judge Cahir Davitt, son of the legendary Michael Davitt presided at Circuit Court sittings in west Clare, one of which was held at Slattery's of Ballykett, during 1921.[63] Davitt explained the workings of these courts thus:

> Each (judge) was to go Circuit three times a year, holding a Circuit sitting of the District Court in each district on the Circuit chosen. At these Circuit sittings, the Circuit judge was to preside, and the Court could exercise both an original and an appellate jurisdiction. It could hear appeals from the Parish Court in criminal cases, and from the ordinary sittings of the District Court in all civil cases other that Parish Court appeals.[64]

The cases of Connors and Chambers were classic examples of what David Fitzpatrick described as the 'parochial pressures' that court officers and Republican police were subjected to during the period.[65]

For justices (who were entirely sympathetic to, if not active in, the Republican movement) and Volunteer Police (who were invariably active) were administering and enforcing justice in cases that involved their neighbours, their fellow Volunteers and Volunteers' friends. Notwithstanding these pressures, for the most part the IRA Police operated without fear or favour in the enforced absence from rural west Clare of the constabulary. Their duties, in addition to the serving of summonses and the enforcement of court orders, involved the enforcement of licencing laws. In the peninsula, these laws were seen to apply equally to ordinary citizens and prominent Sinn Féin/IRA personnel.[66]

While the Connors and Chambers cases undoubtedly affected public perceptions of the efficacy and probity of the Republican Courts in west Clare, it must be remembered, however, that these tribunals were organised, administered and policed by untrained and inexperienced court personnel and Volunteer Police, many of whom were on the run.[67] It must also be remembered that, following the withdrawal of the RIC from the rural districts, these transitionary institutions performed an essential role in the maintenance of law and order and the administration of justice:

> There were no police, no guardians of the civil law. Soon the law-breaker saw his chance, not solely the criminal, but the land-hungry, the cattle drivers, the faction fighters, every group with a grievance.[68]

~

The inherent threat to the stability and cohesion of the Republican movement was probably averted by the collaborative efforts of the Sinn Féin Courts and the IRA Police, supported by a strongly-worded Dail Éireann proclamation:

> That the present time when the Irish people are locked in a life and death struggle with their traditional enemy, is ill-chosen for the stirring up of strife amongst our fellow countrymen; and that all our energies must be directed towards clearing out – not the occupier of this or that piece of land – but the foreign invader of our country.[69]

Indeed, the achievements of the early courts were remarkable, given what Kotsonouris describes as:

'... the inexperience of bureaucratic disciplines in the men hastily thrown into the role of court clerks. They were expected to comply with procedures, schemes and regimens, regardless of the difficulties of putting the apparatus of legal proceedings together in the face of official suppression and retaliation.'[70]

Such retaliation took the form of police and military raids on court sittings, and the arrest and imprisonment of those who would have anything to do with them.

By the Spring of 1921, Joe Daly of Kilmurry was spending most of his time managing the affairs of the Republican Courts. In March, after he was found in possession of court documents, he was arrested near his home by British soldiers and lodged in Limerick Gaol. He was then tried by a military court, which found him guilty of having illegal documents on his person and he was sentenced to six months imprisonment.[71]

Young men were arrested and threatened with death if they would not reveal the name of the local Republican Police Officer (in west Clare the role was fulfilled by Willie Shanahan).[72]

One police and military raid resulted in the shooting and subsequent death of Tom Curtin at Cloonagarnaun on 6 December 1920. Then, three months later, came the shooting dead (by lottery according to anecdotal accounts) of a respected west Clare farmer and Sinn Féin magistrate named Tom Shannon.

The success of the Sinn Féin Courts in west Clare was achieved by earning the respect of the ordinary people. And this was achieved by the wisdom and humaneness of their magistrates, who endowed their courts with what one London newspaper described as, 'a distinguishing characteristic which is usually absent from our traditional temples of justice – they leave no bitterness behind them.'[73]

## Kilmihil's bloody Sunday

On Sunday 18 April 1920, John Breen breakfasted with his father and mother at the family home in Kiltumper, about three miles from Kilmihil.

The 21-year-old tied a holster and belt around his waist and placed in it his loaded Webley service revolver. In his left trouser pocket he had one spare revolver bullet and some lead that was later described as the tip of a bullet that had been cut off to make an expanding bullet, commonly known as dum dum.[1]

An only son, Breen worked on his father's farm on completion of his primary school education at Clonigulane National School. He took up the position of Section Commander shortly after he joined Kilmihil Company in 1917, with responsibility for drilling and training in the use of firearms.[2]

With Michael Killoury and Mick Honan, Breen was sentenced to three months hard labour in Limerick Gaol for his role in the drilling of 70 Volunteers during the anti-conscription demonstrations at Kilmihil on 10 March 1918.[3]

Following transfer to Dundalk Gaol, the three made the acquaintance of Dick McKee, Oscar Traynor, Frank Thornton and Seán Treacy as well as Ballykett native, Murty Tubridy, who had been sentenced at the same court on a similar charge.

They were joined a few days later by Peter Daffy of Cahuirgane, Mullagh, who had, with Michael Kelly of Knocknahila, been caught illegally drilling in Mullagh on 10 March 1918. Twelve days later, both had been sentenced at Ennis Courthouse to one month with hard labour and the customary three months without hard labour was added on when they refused to enter recognisance.[4]

Breen was appointed First Lieutenant of his Company after his release and later became Quartermaster of the 2nd Battalion in 1919.[5]

Together with John O'Dea, Knockalough and Peter McMahon (2nd Lieutenant, C Company) and Martin Melican, both of Clonigulane, John Clancy of Knockalough and Michael Killoury of Clonakilla, Breen had planned to stage an attack on an RIC escort after the 8.30am Mass at St Michael's Church, Kilmihil. Clancy failed to turn up and was later tried by court-martial.[6]

As the Breen family breakfasted, RIC Head-Constable Bernard Hoare, together with Sergeant Edmond Sullivan and Constables Edward Dooley, Jeremiah O'Callaghan, Patrick Neary and William Hayes were preparing to attend Mass. Each man took a grenade (commonly known as a bomb) and put it in his pocket.[7] As was customary in Kilmihil, these men were accompanied by an armed escort of policemen that consisted on this occasion of Constables Daniel Collins and Patrick Martyn and Sergeant Patrick Carroll.[8]

After Mass, Hoare and his men were met by their escort outside Michael McCarthy's hardware shop and they headed back to the barracks in pairs. They were followed, at a distance of some 30 yards, by Sergeant Carroll on the right, Constable Collins in the middle and Constable Martyn on the left.[9]

The plan was for Melican, O'Dea and McMahon to approach the three constables from behind and shoot them. They would then retreat and a covering party consisting of John Breen and Michael Killoury (1st Lieutenant, C Company) would recover the police guns and make good their escape. When the police patrol was about 50 yards from the church the attacking party approached from the rear. Melican, who was directly in front of Breen, fired at Sergeant Carroll, who fell forward on his face and died almost instantly. O'Dea felled Constable Collins with a bullet in the back. Twenty-eight year-old Collins from Macroom, who had been stationed in the town for two weeks, was able to walk from the scene and later recovered.[10]

McMahon's target was Constable Martyn and, had he been successful, the operation would have had a very different outcome. Father Pat Gaynor, the Mullagh Curate who was on the Supreme Council of Sinn Féin and who would later become Parish Priest of Kilmihil, explained what happened next:

Peter McMahon had seized the revolver of a Canadian soldier named Mungovan (home on leave), which was hidden on top of a wardrobe at Mungovan's house ... but his ammunition did not fit the revolver, with the result that the first bullet went wide; evidently he had not tried the weapon

CLARE.

Description of MICHAEL KILLOUGHREY, native of Killoughrey (Kilmihill) and MICHAEL HONAN, native of Leitrim (Cooraclare), who stand charged with having, on the 18th April, 1920, in the barony of Clonderlaw, parish of Kilmihill, murdered Sergt. P. G. Carroll, R.I.C.; dangerously wounded Const. D. Collins, R.I.C., Kilmihill, by revolver shots; and attempting to murder Const. Pat Martin, R.I.C.—1. Square shoulders, military appearance, Clare accent, clean shaven, (believed to be wounded), blue eyes, long nose, pale complexion, broad face, active make; approximate weight, 12 st. 8 lbs.; 5 feet 10½ in. high; about 27 years of age; fair hair, not bald; wore a dark cap, tweed coat, riding breeches and leggings, dark vest. Farmers' son. 2. Active military appearance, clean shaven, Clare accent; may be wounded; grey eyes, regular nose, pale complexion, thin face, medium make; approximate weight, 11 st. 10 lbs.; 5 ft. 7 in high; about 25 years of age; fair hair, not bald; wore a grey cap, dark coat, grey breeches, dark vest. Farmers' son.

Kilrush, 19th April, 1920. (78240c.—47963).

ABOVE: Wanted notice for Michael Killoury and Mick Honan in *The Police Gazette* or *Hue and Cry*, 12 March 1920. *(Source: Oireachtas Library)*

LEFT: Michael Killoury.

out in advance. The second bullet jammed in the revolver.[11]

As planned, McMahon, O'Dea and Melican turned and ran while Killoury (whose gun was less than adequate for the task)[12] and Breen covered Martyn, who reached for his revolver and turned. Constable Martyn's first bullet went through Breen's forehead just over the left eye.

Recognising Killoury, who stood behind Constable Collins, he fired several shots at him and one bullet went through Melican's coat sleeve.[13] Having emptied his revolver, he grabbed Breen's Webley from his hand and used it to warn the approaching crowd to stand back.[14]

On hearing the sound of shooting, Constable Hayes, who was about 35 yards ahead, took a grenade out of his pocket. Hayes pulled the pin, struck the grenade against the iron rim of a nearby cart wheel and threw it into the crowd.[15] The explosion caused a number of injuries and some of the casualties were later identified as Kilmihil shopkeeper John Carey, Greygrove farmer Michael Higgins, Thomas Breen, also a farmer, and twelve-year-old John McMahon from Shyan.

Constable Martyn had recognised Killoury, whose home was later searched. Martyn gave a good description of another attacker, whom he believed to be Mick Honan.[16] Killoury narrowly escaped capture as he was pursued by soldiers at Lacken by hiding under a culvert after he had discarded his boots to give the impression that he had run ahead barefoot. Both Honan and Killoury avoided capture but their names were still being published in the *Hue and Cry* in August 1921.[17]

When Michael Breen arrived at the scene he saw his son lying motionless on the road flat on his back about 50 yards from the church. He identified himself to police as the victim's father but was refused permission to see his son. He was told that if he didn't go away they would blow his brains out.[18] He retreated to Carey's yard.

Breen's body was brought to his uncle's house, where it was held overnight under armed guard. On Monday his remains were brought to Dr Peter Daly's house where a post-mortem was carried out by Drs Daly and Callinan. There it was determined that he had been shot through the forehead and a revolver service bullet was extracted from his brain.

That evening Breen's remains were brought to the church and his funeral took place the following day to Kilmihil cemetery. The funeral itself was a remarkable event. Many hundreds of Volunteers, under the instructions of John Flanagan, OC of the 2nd Battalion and Martin Chambers, paraded behind the coffin in rank formation.

As Volunteers lined up outside the church a Highland Light Infantry armoured car edged provocatively close to the front line in an effort to upset the formation but the men steadfastly refused to budge. The funeral passed without incident, but there was a heavy police and military presence in the village and at the graveyard, which prevented the firing of a volley of shots at the graveside.[19]

⤳

The Inquest into the death of 41-year-old Sergeant Carroll, who had been transferred to County Clare from Portadown on 29 October 1919, was held at Kilmihil National School. His father, Cornelius Carroll, himself a retired RIC Constable from Kells, County Meath, identified the body and Dr Callinan gave evidence that death was caused by a bullet through the heart.[20]

Sergeant Hanna, King's Counsel for the Police, instructed by Solicitor Mr Hickman of Ennis, asked the jury to decide that John Breen had fired the shot that killed Carroll. Constable Martyn's statement that when he turned around he saw Breen standing behind Carroll would seem to support this contention.

But the evidence of Thomas Normoyle was compelling. Normoyle, a farmer of Lack West, deposed that, after he left Mass that morning, he was walking about three yards behind some policemen in the direction of Kilmihil Barracks. A man passed him on his left and fired a revolver in the back of one of the policemen. He was certain that this man was not John Breen.[21]

The jury delivered as follows:

We find that Sergeant Carroll died from shock and haemorrhage as the result of bullet wounds inflicted by some person or persons unknown whilst bearing arms on behalf of an alien and enemy government.

The Inquest into the death of John Breen was held at the school on 12 May.

Fr Charlie Culligan CC, Kilmihil, who was chairman of the Sinn Féin Executive in west Clare and President of the District Court, nearly brought shame on Sinn Féin even before the inquest proceedings began.

Having decided to entertain Coroner Lynch and King's Counsel Hanna to dinner, Culligan phoned the RIC barracks and asked if a police vehicle could be despatched to deliver a suitable leg of mutton. Post Office proprietor Joe Daly immediately recognised the folly of this and persuaded Culligan to cancel the order.

Sinn Féin took the matter very seriously and held an informal court-martial at which Culligan blamed his gaffe on naivety and drink. He avoided disciplinary action by going on his knees and taking the pledge.[22]

The Inquest was told by the solicitor for the Breen family that he had difficulty in sourcing witnesses who were prepared to give evidence due to threats and intimidation by the military. Two civilians had been threatened by a soldier that they would be shot dead if they gave evidence.[23]

Fr Culligan caused something of a stir as the proceedings began when he informed the Coroner that he had received by letter a threatening message from 'The Brotherhood of Irish Avengers'. The chilling message consisted of a sketch of a coffin with a lighted candle on top and a skull at the side. The threat read:

The Brotherhood of Irish Avengers
An Eye for an Eye and a Tooth for a Tooth. To the Rev. Charles Culligan, CC. Take notice, you were tried at a court of this Brotherhood for complicity in the murder of Patrick Blake, and were condemned to death. It is not right that a man should meet his Maker without preparing his soul. Make ready. The arm of the Brotherhood is long. Remember Carey.[24]

John Breen.
*(Source:* The Banner *Claremen and Women's Patriotic, Benevolent and Social Association of New York, (New York 1963), p. 171)*

Following an hour of deliberation by the jury, foreman John Chambers recorded the following verdict:

> We find that John Breen died from shock and haemorrhage caused by a bullet wound inflicted by Constable Martyn while John Breen was fighting for the freedom of his country. From the evidence before us, we desire to say that the present system of government in Ireland is as barbarous and as uncivilised as the authority on which that government is founded was immoral and unjust, and that that government is, as it always has been, destructive of material prosperity and intellectual development, and the way, and the only way, to secure peace and prosperity to Ireland is to allow the Irish people to choose their own form of government. We respectfully ask the civilised nations of the world to aid us in this choice.

Amid sustained applause, Michael Breen exclaimed, "The bed of Heaven to him."[25]

~

Both the wisdom and the morality of the decision to attack policemen on a crowded street after Sunday Mass have been the subject of some discussion over the years.

The attack had been sanctioned by the Battalion Council, whose members offered support if required.[26] One memo by the DIG, Chief Secretary's Office, Dublin Castle spoke of '… the terribly malignant feeling against the police that pursues them even to the house of God.'[27]

But in Kilmihil the rationale for police attendance at Mass extended beyond devotion. Indeed, Sergeant Sullivan and other policemen would send extensive reports of Fr Culligan's fiery sermons to County Inspector Munro. In one celebrated outburst Culligan had urged women to use their hatpins against Crown forces[28] and there were references to '700 years of oppression … by an enemy government'.[29]

It is conceivable that IRA personnel were privy to the content of these police reports as a result of frequent raids on mail trains.

Fr Pat Gaynor noted Dáil Éireann's sanction of attacks on Crown forces '... at every opportunity ...' and that the Volunteers had acted '... under extreme provocation ...' He outlined a campaign of harassment that had been visited on the local population by Crown forces:

> For months the Tans had played havoc with the people, constantly looting shops, raiding houses and taking away farmers' wooden gates for fuel.[30]

The Adjutant of West Clare Brigade IRA, Bill Haugh, reported significant IRA animosity towards the RIC throughout the period.[31] Many village stations had been closed down and their occupants had moved to the safety of larger stations in the towns. On Saturday night, 3 April, just two weeks before Kilmihil's bloody Sunday, 14 RIC barracks had been destroyed in Clare.[32]

The Breen Inquest heard of a prolonged campaign of intimidation by police and military against the local population. John McMahon, a 25-year-old from Greygrove and Timothy Fitzpatrick, a carpenter, gave evidence of threats, misconduct and assaults by drunken soldiers. John Breen's uncle Denis, a publican, gave evidence that Constable Armstrong had told him about two months previously, 'The first chance I get at John Breen I will shoot him dead'.

Armstrong had ordered Breen to go home when the military were stopping a fair in the village and would have arrested him only for Sergeant Sullivan telling him to let the lad go about his business.[33]

Michael Connell had suffered an unprovoked assault at the hands of Constable Sloan [sic: Sloyan], who had since been transferred.

Delia Browne had been harassed in her own home late at night by two drunken constables named McGowan and Creavin. The 24-year-old dressmaker later reported the pair to the District Inspector after which she was subjected to prolonged harassment that included a threat to her life by an

RIC constable. She would later give sworn evidence that masked men, whom she believed to be police, held her at gunpoint, cut her hair and threatened to burn her house. They left a note in the house that read, 'Anti-Sinn Gang. Beware, your fate is sealed.'[34]

It is likely that tensions had been further heightened by an incident that took place four days earlier in Miltown Malbay when a crowd of well over 100 had gathered around a lighted tar barrel at Canada Cross to celebrate the release from Mountjoy Prison of a number of Republican prisoners.

Indiscriminate shooting by police and military had led to the deaths of three local men and several injuries. At the subsequent Inquest the jury recorded a verdict of murder by Crown forces.

Kilmihil's bloody Sunday generated unexpected tensions between the RIC and the Highland Light Infantry when RIC Reports indicated that the military, who were stationed less than 400 yards from the scene of the trouble, took an hour to deliver backup support.

Amid accusations and denials, Head-Constable Hoare, while fulsome in his praise of the officers, pointed towards the presence of '... a number of conscripts ... who are tired of military life and say they are stationed in this backward place for the police protection.'[35]

At Ennis Courthouse on 22 September 1920, the day of the Rineen Ambush and the ambush and killing of Kilkee-based Resident Magistrate Alan Lendrum, Judge Bodkin awarded compensation of £1000 to Sergeant Carroll's family.[36]

~

On Sunday 17 April 1927 John Breen was honoured locally when a monument to his memory was unveiled close to the spot where he died. The ceremony was presided over by Miltown Malbay's James D Kenny and a rousing speech was delivered by Brian O'Higgins.[37]

In June 1930, Kilrush Urban Council adopted a resolution that the town's

Large gathering commemorates John Breen in Kilmihil.
(*Courtesy Mary Driver*)

principal streets be renamed in memory of a number of west Clare patriots and Vandeleur Street became Breen Street. The required plebiscite was never held, however, and most of the streets, including Vandeleur Street, had reverted to their original names by 1981.[38]

Following the Kilmihil and Canada Cross Inquests and other similar verdicts from around the country, the British authorities suspended civilian inquests. From August 1920 under the Restoration of Order in Ireland Act these inquests were replaced by Military Courts of Inquiry, which facilitated widespread cover-up of atrocities committed by Crown forces.

# New Arrivals

On 11 February 1920 the 2nd Battalion Highland Light Infantry, arrived at North Wall Quay from Holyhead and proceeded to Ennis where they set up temporary Headquarters in Ordnance House. It was a development that nobody had wished for; in the words of one of their own:

> … we were sent to Ireland to be scattered to the four winds, and to meet the eye of every scowling Bolshevik with a bigger scowl. They don't want us here, we don't want to be here, but here we are and here we will stay, until we get sent abroad.[1]

Presently, ten detachments were formed and posted at Ennis, Gort, Ennistymon, Lisdoonvarna, Corofin, Miltown Malbay, Kilmihil, Kilrush, Carrigaholt and Scarriff.

Battalion Headquarters was at Ennistymon, while the Ennis detachment was billeted at the town's State Inebriates Home, which had been renamed the Gaol '… which it used to be, evidently because they would prefer being mistaken for criminals to being considered inebriates.'[2]

It would not be long before both the Inebriates Home and the Gaol might be considered appropriate billets for military who were stationed in Clare.

As the Highland Light Infantry were in the process of taking possession of their stations, General Strickland, the General Officer commanding the 6th Division, visited the ones at Ennis, Kilrush, Miltown Malbay, Lisdoonvarna, Ennistymon and Corofin, after which he claimed to have acquired information from '... persons of standing who are reliable and knowledgeable, and in some cases also in touch with Sinn Féin.'

Strickland's subsequent report was uncannily prophetic:

> ... it is possible that attacks on RIC and possibly military barracks & patrols – intimidation of loyalists – and attempted murder of prominent supporters and officials of government will take place.[3]

~

Two other men were also posted to west Clare during the early months of 1920. For very different reasons, each would become a central figure in the Republican struggle in the peninsula and one would become the stuff of legend.

Fr Pat Gaynor, a Tipperary man and Diocesan Examiner for the diocese of Killaloe since 1914, was appointed to the curacy of Mullagh parish.[4] Gaynor was a member of the Ard Chomhairle and Standing Committee of Sinn Féin.

Alan Lendrum, from Kilskeery, County Tyrone, was appointed Resident Magistrate for County Clare and set up residence at 4 Albert Place, Kilkee.[5]

Lendrum had distinguished himself in the Great War where he served with both the 16th (Irish) and 36th (Ulster) Divisions. His initial involvement in the conflict was in West Africa, before being sent to the Western Front in 1916.

He was wounded five times and was awarded a Military Cross after leading 300 Dublin Fusiliers in putting up wire under heavy fire on the first day of the Battle of Cambrai in France. In the last weeks of the War he was further decorated with a Bar as the Inniskilling Fusiliers helped liberate the Belgian village of Gullegem.

In 1917 he was court-martialled for refusing to take charge of the execution of Robert Hope, a young soldier from Sunderland who had been charged with desertion. Robert's wife was from Derry and Lendrum claimed that he knew the family. His demotion was overturned as a result of his subsequent bravery.

In 1919 he went to Archangel (Arkhangelsk) as part of the North Russian Expeditionary Force. His medals are on public display in the Enniskillings Museum in Enniskillen Castle.

By the time Lendrum arrived in Clare, the Parish and District Arbitration Courts were up and running and the local population were increasingly putting their trust in them. His tenure as Resident Magistrate had scarcely begun when one of his court venues, the Justice Room, together with the Police Station at Knock was burned down on Easter Sunday 4 April 1920.[6]

LEFT: Fr Patrick Gaynor, CC Mullagh.
(*Source: Éamonn Gaynor. Memoirs of a Tipperary Family: The Gaynors of Tyone 1887–2000*)
RIGHT: Resident Magistrate Alan Lendrum, a native of Kilskeery, County Tyrone.
(*Courtesy Geoff Simmons*)

The RIC had been withdrawn to the safety of towns like Kilrush where his friend and Inniskilling comrade Captain George Noblett had been appointed District Inspector, RIC the previous November.[7] The pair would meet regularly in the dwindling Petty Sessions Courts of Kilkee and Kilrush. Lendrum would also preside at Miltown Malbay Petty Sessions Courts, where he served on the bench with Dr Hillery and Craggaknock-based farmer and JP Christy Kelly.[8]

# Fall From grace

Following the Canada Cross shootings in Miltown Malbay and the shooting of John Breen in Kilmihil, there was even greater antipathy to the RIC, whose members found themselves increasingly alienated.

It was about this time that Art O'Donnell's third intervention in a locally sanctioned west Clare boycott ended his tenure as Brigade Commandant.

Two Carrigaholt publicans had failed to observe an IRA boycott on members of the local RIC. In consequence, Molly Behan and a man named Carmody, both of whom had been loyal to the Republican cause, were themselves subjected to boycott.

Art O'Donnell travelled west to investigate and, having consulted locally, ordered an end to the boycott, believing that the two publicans risked losing their licences if they supported it. As for boycotts on the RIC, he favoured attack '... on every possible opportunity.'

O'Donnell's ruling met with strong resistance from Battalion Commandant Éamon Fennell and Battalion staff member Tim Haier, who handed him a letter for Headquarters giving their version of events and calling for O'Donnell's court-martial.

When (through no fault of his own according to himself) O'Donnell delayed the delivery of the letter, he was summoned to Dublin, where he was ordered by Adjutant General Gearóid O'Sullivan to resign as head of the Brigade.

He was offered a position in the Dublin Brigade by Chief of Staff General Richard Mulcahy and Diarmuid O'Hegarty, but he declined, saying that he would prefer to serve even as a Private among his comrades in west Clare.[1]

In May 1920 Peadar Clancy was sent by general Headquarters to oversee the appointment of new Brigade staff and he called a meeting for this purpose which was held at O'Donnell's house in Tullycrine.[2] There was majority support for Art O'Donnell's re-appointment as Brigade Commandant, but Clancy made it clear that Headquarters would not sanction this under any circumstances – a new order was required.

Seán Liddy was appointed Brigade Commandant, Patrick Clancy became Vice-Commandant and Dan Sheedy and Patrick Burke were selected as Brigade Adjutant and Brigade Quartermaster respectively. During the second half of 1920, Conor Whelan was appointed Vice Commandant, Bill Haugh succeeded Dan Sheedy and, following his arrest and imprisonment, Patrick Burke was replaced by Tom Marrinan.[3]

Thus, while O'Donnell retained his popularity at ground level, his opposition to boycotts of RIC personnel brought him into conflict with Volunteer Headquarters, which issued an unequivocal instruction in June 1920:

ÓGLAIGH na h-ÉIREANN
General Orders
1920 (New Series).
General Headquarters,
4th. June, 1920.
No. 6.
Boycott of R.I.C.

Volunteers shall have no intercourse with the R.I.C., and shall stimulate and support in every way the boycott of this force ordered by the Dáil.

Those persons who associate with the R.I.C. shall be subjected to the same boycott, and the fact of their association with and toleration of this infamous force shall be kept public in every possible way. Definite lists of such persons in the area of his command, shall be prepared and retained by each Company, Battalion and Brigade Commander.

By Order.

Adjutant General.[4]

Art O'Donnell, Tullycrine.
*(Courtesy Paul Markham)*

# The Belfast Boycott

As early as February 1920, a number of trade unions had instructed their members to desist from handling or selling 'Belfast or Carsonite goods.'[1]

In August, in response to the widespread discrimination that was being endured by northern Catholics, Sinn Féin had imposed a boycott on Belfast goods and northern banks in a number of counties. During the following month, Dáil Éireann, where members initially had reservations, ratified the boycott.[2]

Under the boycott, cigarettes, tobacco, soap products, matches, candles and shoe polish were banned. IRA police enforced the ban and goods were confiscated from non-compliant shops to be sold locally at reduced prices. The proceeds were a welcome boost to Sinn Féin and IRA coffers.[3]

While Fr McKenna fully supported the boycott, Fr Gaynor had reservations, particularly in light of the effects the boycott would have on firms like Gallahers, a long-established tobacco company which employed large numbers of Belfast Catholics.

Nonetheless, Gaynor supported the initiative and even extended it to British goods in west Clare. Gallahers despatched a salesman to Ennis with cut-price offers, with which he wooed shopkeepers. The company also placed weekly advertisements in the *Clare Champion*, to the annoyance of the West Clare Sinn Féin Executive, which had expected the paper's support. When the

*Champion* refused to cease publication of the advertisements, the Executive declared a boycott which was largely ignored throughout the peninsula.[4]

In fact the same newspaper published a strongly-worded advertisement that encouraged the boycotting by consumers of Belfast goods:

BELFAST TRADE BOYCOTT
Do you approve of
Partition.
The killing of people who stand for political and religious freedom, and the destruction of their homes and businesses.
The attempted STARVATION OF 35,000 PEOPLE.
BRUTAL ORANGE ATTACKS on prisoners going to Ballykinlar.
If so buy Belfast goods.
IF NOT, WALK OUT OF ANY SHOP WHERE BELFAST GOODS ARE OFFERED FOR SALE.[5]

Micho McMahon was in charge of the enforcement of the Belfast Boycott in west Clare:

I appointed Volunteers at Kilrush and Kilkee railway stations who had access to the railway office and they inspected manifest sheets and invoices. I also appointed a Volunteer at the shipping offices, Kilrush, to keep check on manifests there relating to goods coming from Limerick. All goods coming from Belfast were held up and the consignee ordered to have them returned to the sender. This was done on all occasions. Once, when a steamer owned by Messrs Kelly, Belfast, arrived at Kilrush with a cargo of coal for the railway, I interviewed the Chairman and Secretary of the Irish Transport and Workers' Union and asked to have the discharge of this steamer held up until I reported to Brigade HQ. After three days, we allowed the vessel to be discharged following a conference with the firm's representative from Cork.[6]

McMahon and his men cautioned business people against accepting delivery of Belfast goods. With help from railway worker Paddy Vaughan and another mole who worked on the boats, they kept a close eye on the goods that were coming into the town.

Kilrush's drapers came under close scrutiny, since much of their business was with Belfast firms. Once, after they got information that a consignment had arrived at the port for a local draper, they visited him and advised him not to accept delivery. When they discovered that he had done so, McMahon and Jack Moody went to his shop, demanded the goods and burned them outside his front door as an example to all.[7]

At Kilkee Railway Station, armed IRA Volunteers under Jim Talty OC held railway officials at gunpoint while their comrades sorted through a large consignment of Belfast goods and distributed them among the IRA members.[8]

And when the coastal steamer *SS Glencloy* docked at Kildysart pier with a large consignment of boycotted goods, 15 Volunteers seized the goods and destroyed them.[9]

At a time when large numbers of people smoked, the boycott on tobacco affected every category of worker, every class and creed of individual and every shade of political opinion. Few were pleased when the only cigarettes being sold in the shops were of inferior quality.[10]

When it became known in December 1920 that the owner of Clarefield House was purchasing bed-linen from a Belfast firm and using it for laundry work, a number of armed IRA personnel visited the house and secured assurances that the practices would cease.[11]

# The Indian Mutiny

Fighting and dying for Ireland took on new meaning on 27 June 1920 when five young British Army Privates, all members of the 1st Battalion, Connaught Rangers, met in the canteen of Wellington Barracks at Jullundur, India.

The prisoners' mail had brought news of heavy-handed tactics by British soldiers in Ireland. Ringleader, Private Joseph Hawes, a native of Kilkeedy, Tubber and who would later have long associations with Kilrush, told his comrades of a visit to Clare prior to his 1919 posting in India.

It was at a time when all assemblies had been prohibited by military order and he had witnessed the military preventing, at bayonet point, a hurling match from taking place.

The five agreed that, as British soldiers, they were doing in India what the British military were doing in Ireland. At 7.45am the following day, four of the five proceeded to the guard room, where Hawes addressed the sergeant in charge.

"As a protest against British atrocities in Ireland we refuse to soldier any longer in the service of the King."[1]

Thus began a three-day mutiny that spread to another company in nearby Solon, involving a total of 250 soldiers. The Union Flag was torn down and replaced by a home-made tricolour and the mutineers, wearing Sinn Féin rosettes, shouted Republican slogans and sang rebel ballads into the night.[2]

Following the Jullundur Mutiny, which has been described as '... the only stand made for Irish freedom outside the island of Ireland,'[3] 69 soldiers who had been identified as ringleaders were tried by general court-martial. Of these, 62 were convicted, 14 of whom were sentenced to death, including Joseph Hawes.

His court-martial on 30 August 1920 was told that he was '... one of the two leading spirits in the mutiny ... His attitude to the CO was very insubordinate; smoked a cigarette while the CO was speaking to him.'[4]

After five weeks, Private Hawes's death sentence was commuted to life imprisonment, which was in turn reduced to two and a half years.[5]

Eleven others also had their death sentences commuted, but James Joseph Daly, the leader of the Solon mutiny, was shot by firing squad on 2 November 1920. Hawes's witness statement to the Bureau of Military History provides a graphic account of the mutiny and its aftermath and his description of Daly's execution is compelling.[6]

Hawes was to serve part of his sentence in Dagshai, before being transferred to Portland and thereafter to Maidstone and Shrewsbury Prisons. His insubordination extended to Maidstone Prison where he and his comrades were singled out for harsh treatment by the Prison Governor.

Ever-recalcitrant, he endured two hunger strikes and earned for himself a period of eleven months in solitary confinement.

Private Hawes was eventually released on 4 January 1923.

He joined the National Army on 26 April 1923, four days before the ceasefire was declared by Frank Aiken. He was discharged as medically unfit on 19 March 1924.[7]

Joseph Hawes lived for most of the remainder of his life in Moore Street, Kilrush and was buried in Old Shanakyle Cemetery following his death on 29 November 1972.[8]

## Staying loyal to the Royal

From early 1920, JPs throughout the country were encouraged to resign their commission of the peace.

Many of them did so willingly and national newspapers reported the resignations, which were accompanied by standard statements to the effect that the JP in question was resigning in protest at the campaign of murder that was being carried out by British forces against his fellow Irishmen.

In October 1920, Sir Hamar Greenwood acknowledged in the House of Commons that 1069 of the 5000 magistrates in Ireland had resigned their commissions.[1]

They were not accompanied by Christy Kelly JP, a prominent and well-to -do farmer who lived at Prospect Hill House in Craggaknock, Mullagh, with his wife Anne and their only son Josie.

An uncompromising loyalist, Christy had held a commission of the peace since about 1908, serving as a magistrate at Miltown Malbay Petty Sessions Court. As the West Clare Arbitration Courts grew in popularity, Christy's fortnightly Petty Sessions Courts went into decline and he found himself in conflict with the fledgling courts on a number of fronts.[2]

At the time of the conscription crisis in 1918, all shotguns in the Kilmurry Ibrickane area had been voluntarily handed to the Volunteers. All, that is, except the one that was held by Christy Kelly, who refused to part with his firearms.[3] Christy eventually co-operated after he was visited by a party of seven or eight men in the charge of Joe Daly, the then captain of Kilmurry Company.[4] Following the Daly raid, however, Christy claimed that £60 had been stolen, which infuriated the members of the raiding party.[5]

As the year progressed, relations between the JP farmer and his neighbours would deteriorate further.

Early in 1920, Christy had been repeatedly served with written notices to surrender his commission, but he steadfastly refused to resign.[6] On the night of 24 June, a group of seven Volunteers arrived at the Kelly home at Craggaknock to arrest him. Christy retreated within and, communicating through the kitchen window, refused to go with them.

All was quiet for an hour, but the men returned and banged repeatedly on the front door. Inside, Christy put out the lights and remained silent. Presently, a shot rang out, possibly an accidental discharge from a Volunteer's gun. Thinking that Christy had opened fire, members of the raiding party fired a number of shots, one of which came through the window and struck the kitchen door, dislodging a splinter that grazed Christy's face. Following an unsuccessful attempt to scamper up the chimney, his wife and son helped him to climb into the roof space via a trap door.

The following morning, when DI George Noblett arrived from Kilrush, Christy sought military protection. When Mrs Kelly reported that the house was being watched he again hid under the collar braces until the arrival of a detachment of Highland Light Infantry and the setting up of a military outpost on the Kelly land at Craggaknock.[7]

But the military presence in the area was accompanied by frequent raids on the homes of known Republican activists in the locality and Brigade headquarters were unimpressed. In order to teach Christy a lesson it was decided that his son Josie would be kidnapped and the task was given to Company Captain Patrick Clancy.[8]

On Friday 9 June Josie, with an escort of two soldiers, was sent to Michael

O'Looney's pub at Áth na gCaorach, to sell a firkin of butter. Josie entered the shop alone, but he was immediately grabbed and gagged by Clancy's men and taken away via the back door. After the soldiers became impatient, they entered the shop, only to find that the lad was gone.

When Anne Kelly saw the soldiers coming along the avenue without her son, she asked, "Where's Josie"?

One of them responded, "The Shinners pinched 'im."[9]

The 'Shinners' included Seán Mullins and Micho Pat Mickey Kelly and Josie was treated well in captivity, having given his solemn promise that he wouldn't attempt to escape.[10]

Anecdotal accounts suggest that Josie quite enjoyed his sojourn in Marrinans of Cooraclare, where he was held and it was said that on one occasion he even lay down on the floor to avoid being seen by his father as Christy was passing on his way to Kilrush.[11]

Meanwhile, news of the kidnapping of the 18-year-old was widely reported in the newspapers. (Most accounts incorrectly stated Josie's age as 16, while the Republican side said that he was about 20.)[12]

The ongoing situation at Craggaknock was not to anybody's liking or benefit. Local Republicans were unhappy about the frequency of military raids and the Kellys were warned that Josie would be shot if the raids didn't stop.[13]

The military, who were camped out under canvas in Kelly's fields, accidentally knocked two of Christy's gate piers. For the troops, their situation was far removed from the relative comfort of the barracks, which were close to the pubs and where there were opportunities to meet with young women.

Boredom quickly set in and there were fun and frolics at the expense of Christy's stock. The men would grab young calves by the ears and compete rodeo-style to see who could hold on the longest as the calves bucked and ducked around the field. They helped themselves to Christy's hens' eggs when rations were low and even the fowl began to disappear.[14]

During the period of the boycott the Kellys' servants, '… three men and a girly', failed to turn up for work and both stock and crops were neglected.[15] Then there was the embarrassment for the soldiers of having let Josie slip through their fingers and the fears of the Kellys for his wellbeing. It was those fears that prompted Josie's mother to throw herself on her knees at Fr Gaynor's house in Mullagh and beg him to intercede for her son's release, promising that Christy would agree to any conditions.[16]

Christy's cousin, Fr Glynn, the parish priest of Mullagh, secured an agreement from Lieutenant Beresford of the HLI that he would withdraw his men in the event of a guarantee of safety and protection for the Kellys and the release of Josie.

Gaynor consulted with Liddy, who agreed to release the youth subject to three conditions.

First, Christy would have to place himself under the protection of the Irish Republic, with attendant ramifications for his loyalist leanings. Second, he would resign as magistrate at Miltown Malbay Petty Sessions Court. Lastly, he would appear before a Sinn Féin court to answer a charge of trespass on the property of his neighbour, Tom Curtin.[17]

Gaynor passed the terms to Mrs Kelly when she visited him two days later and he explained to her that Sinn Féin would not be happy for Christy to commit himself to their protection whilst under military protection. Neither would the military withdraw until Sinn Féin guarantees were in place. He suggested that Christy would sign the forms at Fr Glynn's house, after which Fr Gaynor would guarantee the Kellys' safety for Lieutenant Beresford, who would then withdraw his troops.

Kelly agreed to sign, but refused to leave his home, his wife stating (falsely according to Gaynor) that the military forbade it.[18] In the end, Joe Daly met with Liddy at Gaynor's house in Mullagh and was given the task of clinching the deal with Kelly. That involved Kelly's written agreement to Liddy's three conditions and a signed guarantee of Kelly's safety by Fr Gaynor on behalf of the Volunteers. That guarantee read:

Mullagh, 10th July 1920

Christopher Kelly,

I am instructed by the responsible authorities of the Irish Republican Government to guarantee you adequate safety and protection, provided you forthwith renounce the protection of an Alien Government.

As a guarantee of good faith, you will be required to resign your commission of the peace, which requires an oath of allegiance to the Government of Great Britain, and to sign a formal declaration of allegiance to the duly elected and lawful Government of Ireland.

Your son will be permitted to return when you formally place yourself under the protection of the Irish Republican Government.

I am sending Joe Daley [sic] to facilitate you in carrying out these instructions. (Signed) E [sic] Gaynor, C.C.

When Daly arrived at Prospect Hill House on 10 July, he found Christy and Mrs Kelly in the kitchen with Captain Glass. Mrs Kelly became hysterical, thinking that Daly was there to deliver news that Josie had been shot. When Captain Glass heard that Christy had claimed that the military would not allow him to travel to Mullagh for the purpose of signing agreements, he said, "The man is a liar! He can go to hell for all we care."

Daly produced the three-part agreement, which read:

Craggaknock,

Co. Clare.

10th July 1920.

To the Lord Chancellor,

Dublin Castle.

Sir,

I hereby renounce my commission as a Justice of the Peace. I take this course in order to manifest my abhorrence of the entire brutal policy, and in particular for the campaign of organised assassination at present in being and carried

out by the agents of the British Government against my fellow countrymen.
I am, Yours faithfully,
Joe Daley [*sic*] (Signed) C. Kelly.[19]

Kelly signed the document and Daly handed Gaynor's guarantee to Captain Glass. Josie was duly released the following day, 11 July, none the worse for his experience of captivity and the military withdrawal to Kilrush shortly afterwards marked the end of their stay in what they referred to as *Mireland*.[20]

It was not only the Kellys and the Kilmurry Volunteers who were glad to see the departure of the Highland Light Infantry. In Miltown Malbay, the events of Canada Cross on 14 April were still fresh in the memory.

On the morning of Saturday 17 July, in preparation for withdrawal, the C and D Company detachments at Ennistymon and Ennis had loaded a large amount of kit bags, military luggage and equipment onto the 7.00am train from Ennis for onward transportation to Queenstown via Kilrush port.[21] Shortly before 9.00am the train was forced to stop when the driver spotted a stone wall on the tracks at Black Hill, a couple of miles from Miltown Malbay.

About 20 men, armed with rifles and revolvers, boarded the train and loaded all of the military supplies into two motor cars. Two soldiers, who had been accompanying the equipment, were relieved of their own kits and letters to RIC and military personnel were taken.[22]

During the operation, which lasted about 20 minutes, the train driver and the fireman calmly ate their lunches. The raiders, having completed their search, removed the stone wall and the train was able to continue its journey.[23]

This embarrassing incident delayed the departure of the troops by a number of days while transport was arranged, courtesy of the HLI Brigade.

A convoy of motor lorries set out from Miltown Malbay and headed for Ennistymon, where it picked up C Company. On Thursday night 22 July, their final road journey '… through the bog and the mireland' brought them via Miltown Malbay to Kilrush in the middle of a downpour. As the five motor lorries proceeded through Miltown Malbay, the soldiers aimed their rifles at the townspeople, all the while shouting and sneering. A Union Jack hung atop the leading lorry; a Sinn Féin flag trailed behind it in the gutter.[24]

Beginning on 20 July, the sloop *Heather* ferried the departing troops from Kilrush to Queenstown over the next four or five days.

As all of this was happening, their replacements, the 2nd Battalion, Royal Scots, were arriving and settling in, having taken over Miltown Malbay's Town Hall.

Meanwhile, Fr Gaynor personally posted Christy's letter of resignation to Dublin Castle, since experience had taught him that Christy was '… a slippery customer' who was not to be trusted. Christy lived up to his reputation by writing to the Castle to withdraw his resignation which, he claimed, he had tendered under duress.[25]

In his memoirs, Fr Gaynor detailed just how deceitful and how treacherous he believed Christy to be and, if Gaynor's suspicions were accurate, Christy was very fortunate to escape execution.

He had convinced Dr Hillery at the time of the kidnap that he was '… nearly utterly collapsed … unable to walk … unable to dress himself … unable to shave himself.' Dr Hillery had noted that Christy had gone from being a fine healthy man to a '… very dilapidated old man' in the space of a year.[26]

After Fr McKenna visited the Kellys to say Mass in the house, he described Christy as '… a gone man' whose hands were trembling. Yet, when Fr Gaynor visited shortly afterwards in a vain attempt to settle the dispute between Kelly and Tom Curtin, he was astounded at how Christy negotiated high ditches and deep, wide drains '… with the ease of a greyhound.'[27]

In the end, Curtin had moved to have the matter dealt with at the next sitting of the Arbitration Court, presided over by Fr Charles Culligan in a vacant and remote farmhouse in the townland of Cloonagarnaun, a short distance from the Kelly home on 6 December 1920. Conor Whelan was Court Registrar and Willie Shanahan attended in his capacity as Brigade Chief of Police.[28]

At about midday most of the attendees were standing around outside waiting for proceedings to begin. Fr Gaynor happened to be cycling west along the narrow road off which the venue was located when he heard the lorry-loads of military approaching at speed from behind him. He pedalled as fast as he could to the end of the laneway that led to the house and shouted to one of the scouts, who raised the alarm.

Shanahan grabbed the court papers and ran north across the fields towards Parkduff, together with other wanted men. Fr Culligan exhorted the others to stand their ground, but a number of men ran.[29] Within seconds, the police and military were on the lane.

Lieutenant A W Tuffield, 2nd Battalion, Royal Scots, who was in charge of the military, later stated that he had orders to carry out the raid for the purpose of apprehending wanted men, of whom he had a list.

Tuffield shouted at the dozen or so who were running to halt and then ordered his men to fire a volley over their heads. When the men kept running, Tuffield took careful aim and fired.[30] One bullet struck Tom Curtin in the back of the head as he mounted a boundary fence about 200 yards away. Another shattered the leg of Michael 'Bully' Crotty from Kilrush as he faced the pursuing soldiers with his hands in the air.[31]

Head-Constable Jim Treacy, together with two sergeants and a constable, surrounded the house before entering.[32] One of the five magistrates present was Patrick 'Soldier' Kelly, from Clonina, near Cree. Kelly had served in the Life Guards during the Second Boer War in South Africa between 1899 and 1901 and when he gave this information to Tuffield, the Lieutenant gave him charge of two soldiers for the recovery of casualties.[33]

Kelly and solicitor Michael Killeen, together with the soldiers, crossed the fields to where Tom Curtin lay seriously injured and brought him to the house on an improvised stretcher at about 12.30pm, where he and Crotty were laid on two tables, while Killeen telephoned for medical aid.[34] The police and military had left again by 12.45pm.

Fr Gaynor gave last rites to Curtin and Crotty, who were both unconscious at that time. The wounded were tended to first by Nurse Teresa (Tess)

McNamara, whose brother was one of the targets of the raid and Hannie McGrath.[35] Dr Healy then took over and later three doctors all agreed that Curtin's case was hopeless. He died at about 7.00pm, after which Nurse McNamara accompanied Michael Crotty to Kilrush Hospital.

It will be remembered that jury inquests had been suspended in favour of military inquiries which invariably favoured the military.

The military inquiry into the death of Thomas Curtin was held in Kilrush on 9 December 1920. Curtin's family refused to participate or to attend and the body was unavailable for inspection, as it had been buried in Clohanes Cemetery on the previous day.

Predictably, the court found that the bullet that killed Curtin was fired by the military in the execution of their duty, but that '… the military were in no way to blame.'[36]

The military came close to shooting Fr Gaynor as he walked the Parkduff road with his bicycle just before they departed the scene. In fact, it was only the intervention of Fr Culligan that saved him when he shouted, "Stop! That is a priest", after the troops had raised their rifles.[37]

The detail of the injuries of Tom Curtin was highlighted in the evidence that was given by Dr Richard Counihan, one of four doctors who attended to the victim. Counihan, who arrived at the scene at 3.00pm, stated that:

> I examined his head and I found a wound extending from the back of his skull to the top of his skull. It was about three to four and a half inches long. It had ripped up the skull, the coverings of the brain and the brain itself. The wound was about one inch wide.[38]

The hint of an inference that an expanding bullet had been used was not lost on the members of the Court of Inquiry who were at pains to record on the official record that '… an ordinary rifle bullet was used at about 500 yards range.'[39]

The police and military who raided the Cloonagarnaun Arbitration Court had very specific knowledge of its remote location and it seems likely that its betrayal was the work of an informer.

～

Gaynor had kept Christy's signed pledges in a drawer of a sideboard at his home in Mullagh as proof that Christy had conformed. One day, the curate caught his servant boy – a lad named Tom from Knockerra – rummaging in the drawer of his dressing table. It was only later that he discovered that the papers relating to Christy were missing and he formed the opinion that Christy had induced the young lad to steal them for use as evidence in his claim for £1000 compensation for damages.[40]

The claim was heard at Ennis Court on 20 January 1921 by Judge Matthias Bodkin and Christy's formidable legal team included a King's Counsel, a Barrister at Law and a solicitor. Neither Clare County Council nor the Rural District Council were represented at the hearing, so the Kelly claim was not defended. Christy deposed that he and his family were boycotted, his son was kidnapped, his servants failed to turn up for work and his cows went unmilked.

His own health had suffered immeasurably and Dr Hillery stated that on the basis of what Christy had told him he was suffering from neurasthenia and arthritis in the right shoulder as well as diffused loss of sensation in the left hand. Dr Hillery's assessment of his health was supported by Dr Counihan from Ennis, who stated that Christy's problems would only result from the experiences that he had been subjected to. The doctor said that Kelly's treatment would need to continue for six months and would involve costly massage, hydropathic treatment and electric baths.

Christy also claimed compensation for damage to his house, animals, fowl, crops and meadowing. Indeed, when Judge Bodkin had seen the extent of what was being claimed for, he noted that if Christy '… had a hundred hands and eyes he could not have done all the work in respect of which a claim was now made.'

In the end, the judge awarded Christy a total of £450.

Josie claimed £1000 in compensation for his kidnap ordeal, stating that he was marched through the country and across bogs for the most part of a week. In consequence, he was frightened, nervous and had been waking up with nightmares.

Dr Counihan had examined Josie that morning, but had found no obvious ill-effects. Josie was awarded £40.

Mrs Anne Kelly claimed £1000 in personal injuries for the effects that the whole affair, especially Josie's kidnap, had on her. She claimed that her weight had dropped from 15st 2lb to 12st 8lb on account of her ordeal.

Dr Hillery stated that on 27 June Mrs Kelly was suffering from nervousness and acute rheumatism and that her condition had been aggravated by the events of three nights previously. Dr Counihan told the court that her heart 'went tumultuously' when she was excited.

Mrs Kelly was awarded £50.[41]

All three Kellys later appealed against the awards granted to them by Judge Bodkin. Having heard the evidence, the Lord Chief Justice halved Josie's decree to £20, increased Christy's to £475 and affirmed Bodkin's award to Mrs Kelly.[42]

Unlike many other claims, however, the Kelly case was not referred on to the Compensation (Personal Injuries) Committee, as the British Government accepted liability, describing the Kellys as 'British Supporters'.

Following a review of the Bodkin awards, compensation was paid with interest in March and September 1922. Josie's award amounted to £32.8s, his mother received £77.10s.3d and Christy was paid a total of just under £590.[43]

That was not the last that was heard of the 'Christy documents' that were stolen from Gaynor's sideboard, however.

On the night of 31 March 1921, Constable Stanley Moore, a Black and Tan described as '... a harmless poor fellow ... being addicted to drink', was shot dead after he had had a few drinks in Wilson's Pub on the main street of Miltown Malbay.

The following morning two lorry loads of angry police and military arrived at the home of the two Mullagh curates, where they were accused of being involved in the shooting of Constable Moore.

Fr Gaynor and Fr McKenna later made a number of serious allegations against the raiding party. A number of the soldiers were drunk, it was claimed, the tabernacle at Mullagh church had been opened and frightful desecration had been committed.

The military produced the documents that had been stolen from Gaynor's sideboard and used them as an excuse for arresting the two priests. Having been threatened that they would be shot, the pair were brought in separate lorries to Miltown Malbay, where they were brought into the room where Constable Moore was laid out. Later, Fr Gaynor was brought to Ennistymon and shots were fired over Fr McKenna's head after he had been released at Rineen.[44]

The latter, not fancying the long walk home, waved frantically at a passing westbound train in the hope that it would stop for him. The driver, thinking that he wanted a newspaper, threw him one.

Fr Gaynor, when questioned at Ennistymon RIC station, explained how the offending documents had enabled him to mediate in the Kelly affair, bringing it to a successful conclusion. He was released but both priests were later summonsed to appear in court on 9 May. They ignored the summons, but emptied their house of its furniture in the expectation that it would be confiscated.

Gaynor was arrested on 12 May and McKenna the following morning and they were lodged in Limerick Prison.[45] Their court-martial took place at the New Barracks, Limerick on 23 May. They were charged with:

Having, on 1st April, in their house at Mullagh a document containing statements the publication of which would cause disaffection – namely, a paper refusing to recognise the protection of the British Government, and

placing their house under the protection of the Irish Republic;
With having in their possession on 1st April a document purporting to relate to the affairs of an unlawful association – namely, Dáil Éireann.[46]

Gaynor acknowledged having had possession of a document entitled 'Judiciary', which did relate to Dail Éireann affairs, but he denied that the other document was in the house. Fr McKenna made no statement.[47] Sitting in the courtroom was a familiar figure about whom Gaynor later wrote:

> Fr John Francis Maguire (Christy Kelly's brother in law) was seated there by the wall, having been brought in by the Tans from Tulla in their lorry, to gloat over our humiliation. I believe, therefore, that Fr Maguire and Christy Kelly were responsible for our arrest and imprisonment ... I, rather than Fr McKenna, was the object of their spite. Being suspicious by nature and deceitful, they believed that I – not Seán Liddy – had imposed the conditions on Christy Kelly, which obliged him to sign a resignation of his commission as Justice of the Peace.

They were both found guilty and sentenced to six months imprisonment without hard labour.[48] Gaynor wrote later that it was a rather pleasant sojourn. It helped that the governor had acceded to Gaynor's demand that they be allowed to celebrate daily Mass in the prison chapel and of course that they had been granted a political status of sorts. They were released on Saturday 22 October 1921.[49]

Gaynor's antipathy towards Christy didn't dissipate with time, but he was more circumspect in his appraisal of the role of the military, who '... would have let Fr McKenna and me go our way undisturbed, but for the reports against us which were sent to them by traitors and cranks among our own people in west Clare.'[50]

# The Rob Roy Hotel

Out 'mid the bog and the heather
Out where the dreary winds blow
Tired and weary and hunted
Ever dreading some treacherous foe.[1]

Stephen Madigan chose aptly when he gave the nickname 'The Rob Roy Hotel' to one of the hideouts that he used while on the run.

Immortalised in historical fiction by Sir Walter Scott, the outlaw Rob Roy MacGregor was something of a role model for Scott's young revolutionary readers in west Clare. Indeed, there was a little of Rob Roy in each and every west Clare rebel and there was a lot of him in some, whether it was the cattle driver, the kidnapper, the chivalrous outlaw, the raider, the soldier, the prisoner or the all-round folk hero.

Dan Sheedy, a highly-respected Republican activist from Kilmacduane, who held the rank of Brigade Adjutant in mid-1920, probably filled the boots of the chivalrous outlaw.

Following the passing of a Cooraclare Sinn Féin Club resolution on 27 May 1918, only Sinn Féin members were to be elected as Chairmen and Vice-Chairmen of County and District Councils. Sheedy's election as Chairman of Kilrush District Council in the June 1920 elections brought him into conflict with official Government policy and he was targeted for arrest.[2]

Having been on the run on and off for some months, Sheedy's luck ran out on the night of 21–22 October 1920. Earlier, he had presided at a courtmartial at Callinans', a vacant house a couple of miles from Cree.[3]

Brigade Commandant Liddy and his shorter, stockier Quartermaster, Tom Marrinan were sleeping in an attic room in Sheedy's the same night. No sentries were on duty and the pair were awoken by police banging on the

Stephen Madigan (right) with a fellow Republican outside one of their hideouts, which they nicknamed the Rob Roy Hotel.
*(Courtesy Annelen Madigan)*

door at 1.30am. Sheedy delayed answering the door until he had hidden the court-martial papers in a bed.[4]

Marrinan hastily jumped into Liddy's trousers, rushed downstairs, tied a neckerchief around his head and climbed into the bed with an elderly bedridden family member. When the police torches shone into the room he succeeded in passing himself as an old woman with a toothache.

Liddy jumped into Marrinan's trousers, but only made it to the top of the staircase. It was thanks to the discretion of Constable O'Neill, a 'friendly Peeler' who recognised him, that he was able to convince the police that he was a hired farm labourer.[5]

The less fortunate Sheedy was arrested and later interned in Ballykinlar until his release in December 1921.[6]

This was one of a number of close shaves that Liddy and Marrinan had while they were on the run. When he heard of the ill-fitting trouser episode, one local wag christened the pair 'Too Long' and 'Too Loose'.

On another occasion, Liddy and Marrinan had been sleeping in Honan's house in Churchtown for only three nights. They were awoken by a tap on the bedroom window by one of their scouts, who reported having seen motor lights a half an hour earlier. The pair got up and left the house with seconds to spare before the place was surrounded by police and military who had abandoned their vehicles some distance away and continued to the house on foot.[7]

As Brigade Commandant, Liddy had to be careful not to allow any of his correspondence to find its way into enemy hands. He cleverly instructed that letters to him were to bear a special mark and that they were to be addressed to Miss K Murphy of Danganelly. The local postman was made aware of the arrangement so that he would deliver the letters to Liddy. But it was a measure of enemy intelligence that Dublin Castle was also made aware of the procedure.[8]

IRA dugout at Greygrove, Kilmihil.
ABOVE: The tunnel entrance.
RIGHT & BELOW: Views of the interior following renovation by Kilmihil Community Employment Scheme, under the supervision of Martin Keane.
(*Courtesy James McAlpine*)

When safe houses were no longer safe, Volunteers who were on the run were forced to consider alternative forms of accommodation.

In the sandhills of Doughmore, the current site of a prestigious golf links, the word bunker had an entirely different connotation for the Flying Column of the West Clare Brigade.

Tess McNamara, acting OC of the 3rd Battalion, Cumann na mBan – whose brother Michael was tortured and killed by British soldiers in December 1920 – took care of the bunker's on-the-run residents by doing their laundry and preparing and delivering their meals under cover of darkness.[9]

In west Clare, Bill Haugh was undoubtedly the flamboyant folk hero and anecdotal accounts of his escapades while evading capture survive locally to this day.

After the shooting of John Hanlon in Kilrush on 21 August 1920 (see 'Hanley' page 165), Haugh was top of the 'wanted list' and he slept at various times in the homes of sympathisers or in specially-constructed dugouts in isolated parts of the bogs of Shragh and Einagh, Monmore.

One cold night, while he was staying at the home of Seán Chambers of Dromelihy, Haugh woke up to find his two sentries warming themselves by a roaring fire. He drew his revolver and shot the cat, with the warning, "That's what will happen to you if you don't stick to your posts."[10]

The typical dugout was built on the side of a turf bank and would measure 9ft by 6ft, with 6ft headroom. The inner walls were lined with straw and the roof was formed using sally branches topped with rushes. Dugouts were used in rotation and armed sentries were posted nearby at night time.[11]

Apparently, at one of these locations, a large hare used to come in and bed down close to Haugh. Haugh was the hunted one; in those days the tamer hare not so much. Occasionally, when police and military got word about his whereabouts, they would organise a raid and it was during such a raid that they found themselves up to their knees in a boghole when they jumped off the road.

One pained soldier directed his frustration at his superior, "The only ones that can negotiate those bogs are the wild ducks and Shinners."

Thereafter they resorted to firing at suspected hideouts from a distance.

Once, Haugh and Frank Marrinan had a close shave as they sheltered in a rick of turf, lined on the inside with sheet iron and rocks.

When the military opened fire on the rick, Marrinan remarked, "The hailstones are heavy tonight".[12]

When members of the IRA captured the 6th Division British Weekly Intelligence Summary documents, dated 17 May 1921, at Kilteely, County Limerick, they discovered references to the IRA dugouts in Shragh and Moyasta.

John McCarthy, Adjutant of the East Limerick Brigade quickly forwarded extracts to the West Clare Brigade and those on the run were forced to abandon their shelters. Martin Chambers would sleep in the open under cover of a tarpaulin until the Truce in July 1921.[13]

Throughout this period, those who were on the run were universally welcomed into people's homes and Haugh later remarked that, 'There was not a single instance in which food and shelter was refused to the wanted men.'[14]

Sonny Donnelly and Jimmy O'Dea were welcomed at Huxley's of Six Crosses, where a new house was being built. The pair had been cycling nearby when they heard the rumble of a military lorry. They jumped from their bicycles and got busy mixing concrete until the danger had passed.[15]

The rough and hilly land of the 4th Battalion area was frequented by many of those who were on the run. Following the ambush of RIC at Tiernaglohane, outside Cooraclare, on 19 January 1920 that resulted in the drowning of Michael Darcy, Seán Liddy, Michael Campbell, Patrick Burke, John Morrissey and Michael Breen spent three weeks in the safe house of M J McMahon at Launfreigh House, Dromin, near Mullagh.

Following the shooting of Detective John Hanlon in Kilrush on 21 August 1920, Bill Haugh spent much time in the same house over a period of three months.[16]

It was in A Company, Doolough, that Haugh, Martin Chambers, Seán Liddy, Stephen Madigan, Conor Whelan, Matthew Bermingham and Stephen Haugh were billeted after the 22 April 1921 Kilrush raid on police and military garrisons.[17]

The rick of turf was a common hiding place for both rebels and weapons and, following the Lendrum ambush, the Magistrate's car was reputed to have been built into a rick of turf or hay for a time.

In time, the authorities got wise to these practices and their searches involved tossing the ricks, firing into them or even burning them. In the village of Doonbeg, next door to Mickey Matt's forge, lived a labourer named Tommy Chadwick who was known locally as Tommy Shaddick.

Close by the fair green was a low, curved wall. On either side was a rick of turf, one belonging to Igoes and the other belonging to Clarkes. The resourceful Tommy had expertly hollowed out the inside of one of the ricks, while maintaining the integrity of the neatly-clamped exterior. There he would hide whenever there was a raid on the village.[18]

In Cranny, Walter Stephens and Sonny Donnelly spotted six 'Tans' going in to Brown's Pub for a few drinks. For devilment, they stole one of their bicycles from outside the pub and dumped it in a boghole, before returning to hide in the bushes across the road from the pub. When the constables found themselves short of transport for the journey to the barracks, pub proprietor Micho Brown advised:

> Two of ye go to the Six Crosses, two more go to Behan's Cross and the remaining two go to Shessive Cross and by the time ye come back I'll know where the bike is.

Walter later broke all of the windows of Brown's pub, saying 'You'll have something to tell them now!'

Not surprisingly, Stephens ended up on the run and spent six weeks in an ingenious dugout that he had constructed in the middle of a dunghill. Michael Brooks sealed up the door for him with cow dung each night and he only abandoned it when a hive of bees took up residence there.[19]

Cemetery vaults were a favourite haunt for the less squeamish of those who were on the run and the ones in Kilmacduane were in regular demand.

Further north in the parish of Kilmurry, one outlaw rebel was hiding in a vault when his home was raided. When the young man's father was questioned about the whereabouts of his son, he replied, "He's out looking for ye, and 'tis a pity ye don't meet."[20]

Walter Stephens slept in a vault in Churchtown for two nights. When he was asked if he was afraid of the dead, he replied, "I wasn't afraid of the dead at all. It was the living I was afraid of!"[21]

At this time, householders were obliged to record the names of all who were sleeping in the house on a sheet of paper that was pinned to the inside of the main door.

Sentries would be posted on approach roads and they would raise the alarm whenever they saw the lights of approaching police cars or military lorries. Those men whose presence in a house was suspect were often beaten and forced at gunpoint to repair trenched roads.

During a raid at a house in Kilkee the RIC looked for the list behind the door and found a list of all of the local lads with details of the number of press-ups they could do. To the amusement of the householder, they spent considerable time speculating on the significance of the numbers.[22]

Being on the run was not without its hazards and one of the most common of these was scabies.

Known locally as 'Republican Itch', the condition manifested itself in the form of boils on the neck and the bottom. Sufferers could spend up to an hour scratching before getting to sleep. Chemists did a roaring trade in medications such as sulphur ointments and Bill Haugh even found relief by stripping off all his clothes and immersing himself in a pool of bogwater. Bridget Liddy contracted the rash herself after she had treated a number of the afflicted in their dugouts.[23]

Exhausted from lack of sleep, some would return briefly to their homes in search of a night's sleep, but the enemy had other ideas:

> Rebel Flying Columns are suffering heavily from scabies. In order to cure this disease men are returning to their homes and lying up there for a week or two. It is essential that these men be kept on the move by frequent visits to their houses, thus driving them back to the Column.[24]

# Hanley

In the romanticised tales of the Wild West, gunfighters carved a notch on the grip of their pistol for every man they shot. Wild Bill Hickok, the prince of pistoleers, reputedly boasted 40 notches, though he was known to exaggerate.[1]

West Clare had its own gun-toting revolutionary in the person of one William Haugh, a rather harmless-looking former US Marine who would become one of the most ruthless rebels in west Clare and one of the most wanted men in Ireland.

Wild Bill Haugh was no comic book hero, but his exploits during the War of Independence would become the stuff of legend.

Bill Haugh was born into a farming family in Monmore on 9 December 1891.[2] At the early age of 17 he boarded the ocean liner *RMS Baltic* at Queenstown and emigrated to New York in the company of his aunt, Mary McInerney, arriving on Ellis Island on 5 September 1907.[3]

During his early years in New York he worked as a streetcar conductor, a semi-clerical position that required workers to remain standing for long periods without rest on a wage of about 25cents per hour.[4]

On 6 April 1917, the US entered World War 1 with its allies, Britain, France and Russia. Haugh joined the Marine Corps almost immediately and his first training assignment began in Naval Station Norfolk, Virginia, on 4 June 1917. Later, he served on the training ship *USS Louisiana*, but developed kidney trouble, which he blamed on the ship's poor quality drinking water. He was later discharged on pension following an operation to remove his right kidney, which left an open wound that only '... healed [in spite] of neglect ...' while he was on the run.[5]

Haugh's discharge was fortuitous for, had he remained in the Marines, his next posting would have been on the *USS Cyclops*, which disappeared without trace with the loss of more than 300 lives in March 1918 in the area that later claimed spurious notoriety as the 'Bermuda Triangle'.[6]

Despite having secured a job in the New York State Civil Service, Haugh had other things in mind and, on 31 May 1920, he returned to Ireland on the *Baltic*.

Helped by a 23-year-old nurse named Martha McEntee, the daughter of a retired RIC sergeant from Kingscourt in County Cavan, he smuggled through customs two revolvers, 100 rounds of ammunition and a miniature rifle.[7]

While searching Haugh's trunk, a vigilant Customs Officer spotted the rifle and asked, "What's this?"

Haugh reached for one of his revolvers, pointed to it and answered "It's a tripod for this camera I have in my hand. Do you understand?"

There were no further questions.[8]

Haugh set to work immediately as a member of the 3rd Battalion, West Clare Brigade, where he was quickly identified by his colleagues as something of a loose cannon.

Time after time, he argued for radically extreme actions against the enemy, which were only averted following the intervention of his superiors. Indeed, some of his proposals were so drastic that he was even under suspicion as an enemy agent at one point.[9]

One of his first major encounters was with a rather inquisitive Kilrush policeman, Detective Constable John Hanlon, who was the first of two RIC officers who were shot dead in Kilrush during the War of Independence.

Hanlon would be seen regularly at the train station studying the comings and goings and fishing for information.[10] He kept a close watch on known IRA men and regularly cycled out of town visiting known suspects, one of whom was Thomas Howard of Lisladeen.

Howard worked occasionally for a farmer in Tarmon, where he slept in a garret. Once, when Hanlon came looking for him he found that Howard had already left. Not wishing to leave empty-handed, he took with him some of Howard's clothes.

The owner of the farm commented, "Little Lloyd George will thank you for what you have done."[11]

~

In late July, a plan was hatched by Brigade officers to ambush a lorry that carried rations between Kilmore and Kilmihil every Monday.

When locals spotted a number of men checking out the area around Burrane School, they knew that something of a military nature was afoot. Fearing reprisals in the event of an ambush of Crown forces, they began to move their furniture from their homes to places of safety.

Shortly after, local Volunteer John Daly overheard the officer in charge of the Kilmore Garrison telling a Kilrush officer that an attack on the lorry was imminent. Daly sounded the alarm, Liddy called off the ambush and when, on the day of the planned action, military forces converged on Burrane from both Kilrush and Kilmore, they found nothing.[12]

The O'Donnell home in Tullycrine was the central hub of Republican activity in west Clare throughout this period and Hanlon would continue to take a keen interest in the comings and goings.

Towards the end of July 1920, General Headquarters ordered that, where possible, Flying Columns would be formed in each Brigade area. One Volunteer from each company would attend for training at Simon O'Donnell's house in Tullycrine. There, during the first three days of August, Haugh put the men through their paces with the aid of his miniature rifle and a Lee-Enfield rifle.

On Wednesday 4 August, the fourth day of training, O'Donnell's was raided by a combined force of RIC and Royal Scots soldiers, who carried out a thorough search for arms. Forty-three trams of hay were tossed about but, fortuitously, no arrests were made, as the two guns were taken away each night and the men had not yet assembled for training.[13]

Detective Constable John Hanlon was identified as the coordinator of enemy intelligence and the Brigade Council, having temporarily disbanded the Flying Column, decided to execute him.

Bill Shannon, who was in the process of reorganising the Brigade on instructions from Headquarters, had the task of making preparations to have Hanlon shot and part of his plan was to arrange transport to and from the scene of the shooting.

It so happened that Limerick-native John Joe Quilty was holidaying in Kilkee at this time. It was Quilty's car that was used on Good Friday 1916 to transport three men to Cahirciveen in order to seize transmitting equipment for the purposes of communicating with the German arms ship *Aud*. The *Aud* was carrying 20,000 rifles and a million rounds of ammunition, all to be landed at Fenit on the Kerry coast to support the Easter Rising.

Quilty's pride and joy was a c.1915 Briscoe Model B Deluxe Touring car. But it had only one headlamp and when driver Tommy McInerney took a wrong turn outside Killorglin and on to the pier at Ballykissane he and his passengers thought that they were on a road. The car plunged into the River Laune and the three passengers were drowned.

McInerney's telegram to Quilty the following morning said it all: 'Car Gone. Passengers Drowned. Tommy Safe.' His three passengers were the first casualties of the 1916 Rising.

Quilty was arrested three times in the aftermath of the tragedy, but he avoided gaol by sticking to a story that he had rehearsed with McInerney; it was some months before he was allowed to reclaim the Briscoe.[14]

Quilty remained under suspicion, however, and it was only following his most recent arrest and imprisonment in March–April 1920 that he succeeded in convincing the authorities that he was no longer 'a dangerous suspect.'[15]

As evidenced in the cases of Michael Fahy and Paddy Hassett, there were significant restrictions on the use of private motor cars and local car-owners risked being shot at if they ventured beyond their own restricted areas. Petrol was only available by permit, a further curtailment to freedom of movement.

But Quilty had recently been downgraded from 'dangerous suspect' to 'law abiding citizen' and, as a tourist, his car could move freely in the peninsula.

Having secured the use of the Briscoe, Bill Shannon, Tom Marrinan and Jim Talty were driven to Knockerra by John Crowley of O'Curry Street, Kilkee. There, they met the men who had been chosen to assassinate Detective Hanlon: John O'Dea and Martin Melican of Kilmihil and Paddy Clancy of Coolmeen.

John Joe Quilty's Briscoe Touring Car, after the Ballykissane tragedy. The car featured in a planned assassination attempt on Detective Constable John Hanlon in August 1920.
*(Source: Hackett Papers, Archives of the Society of Jesus, Australia)*

Crowley drove the men to Kilrush and parked at the lower end of Moore Street while the men waited near Hanlon's home in Moore Street.[16] Hanlon duly arrived on the scene but a woman pushing a pram came between them and their target and the mission was aborted.[17]

In March 1966, Quilty's son John presented the windscreen frame of the Briscoe to President Éamon de Valera at Áras an Uachtaráin. It was subsequently donated to Kilmainham Gaol Museum.[18]

~

On 10 August Brigade Commandant Seán Liddy, Adjutant Bill Haugh, Frank O'Donnell. William Shannon, Paddy Clancy and Tommy Marrinan decided to assassinate Hanlon themselves at Tullycrine Grove.

While attempting to commandeer a car to transport them to and from Kilrush, they unwittingly approached a fully-occupied police lorry and were lucky to escape with their lives.[19]

On 18 August, Hanlon wrote a memo to Dublin Castle in support of Resident Magistrate Alan Lendrum's repeated requests to be allowed to relocate to Kilrush. Armed Sinn Féiners, the memo stated, were on the lookout for Lendrum at Doonbeg railway station.[20] It is conceivable that Hanlon's statement was intercepted during raids on the mail trains at Craggaknock and Doonbeg the following day, Thursday 19 August (the raiders escaped on bicycles) and that a reference in it to an unnamed local informant made the detective's execution more urgent.[21]

Hanlon, who was now a marked man, would incur the wrath of one 'Motions' Casey after he relentlessly pursued him over some issue in relation to Casey's horse. Casey's patience wore out on Friday 20 August when, in a chillingly portentous retort, he threatened the detective, "You'll be shot tomorrow".[22]

On Saturday 21 August Bill Haugh cycled into Kilrush and waited on Moore Street where, by chance, Paddy Hassett of Cooraclare Company and Constable John Hanlon arrived on the scene simultaneously.[23] Just as Haugh was lining up his target, two women got in the line of fire and for a brief moment Hanlon seemed once again to have thwarted the odds.

But, at 4.30pm, when the detective turned into Rick Walsh's public house, his fate was sealed. Barman Tom Moloney had just served him a drink when Haugh followed him in, engaged his prey in conversation about a permit and asked him to sign some documentation on the pretence that he intended to return to America.[24]

Hanlon asked the proprietor for a pencil before going to the back kitchen with Haugh to conduct their business. Haugh shot him once through the back of the head, the bullet lodging over the right eye before he made good his escape.[25] When Moloney entered the kitchen he found Hanlon sprawled on the floor.[26]

There was some consternation in the streets and Haugh cycled about a mile outside of town, where he left his bicycle with friends before returning to watch through pocket-glasses from a hill overlooking the town.

In the commotion following the shooting, one lady abandoned her shopping expedition and rushed back to her donkey and cart. She lifted her

Bill Haugh.
LEFT: As a young streetcar conductor in New York.
*(Courtesy Sheila Haugh)*
MIDDLE: In the uniform of the US Marines
*(Source: IE MA BMH CD 075/6/7, Bureau of Military History Contemporary Documents, MA)*
RIGHT: Haugh in 1920
*(Courtesy Liam Haugh Jnr)*

cart onto her donkey's straddle but in her haste she forgot to tie the drawing chains to the hames. Having sat up on the cart she cracked the loop of the reins off the donkey's backside, whereupon Neddy took off in a canter and left both herself and her cart behind.[27]

In the aftermath of the shooting, the town was in the grip of fear of reprisals for some time and the homes of prominent Sinn Féiners were searched.

Rick Walsh and his wife were arrested and held overnight before being released on bail.[28] For some nights, police and military fired rifle charges in the air to clear the streets. At masses in the local Catholic Church, Vicar General Dean McInerney, PP and Fr Moloney, CC both condemned the 'heinous crime' while offering the small consolation that the perpetrator was not from the town.[29]

It had been a weekend of bloodshed for the RIC throughout the country. Including Hanlon, five RIC constables, two sergeants and DI Oswald Swanzy were shot dead.

Swanzy, who had been held responsible for the murder of the Lord Mayor of Cork, Tomás MacCurtain, by the Inquest Jury, had shortly afterwards been transferred to Lisburn for his safety. He was tracked down by Michael Collins' intelligence network and was shot dead on the street after Sunday matins.[30] The incident sparked widespread burning of Catholic-owned homes and businesses in Lisburn.[31]

The Inquest into the death of Detective Constable John Hanlon, aged 32, was held by Coroner Thomas Lillis JP at Kilrush National School on Tuesday 24 August. A verdict of wilful murder by a person unknown was recorded by a jury headed by Joe Keating of Market Square. At Kilrush Petty Sessions Court, Captain Lendrum, RM proposed the resolution:

> That this court expresses its profound sympathy with the widow and orphans of Constable Hanlon who was foully murdered at Kilrush on the 21st inst., and expresses its condemnation of these brutal crimes which are staining our

country with blood and her name with dishonour.[32]

John Hanlon was highly regarded by his superiors. The Ennis DI, Horace Frederick Munro noted in court that the detective was on the promotion list. His basic wage was £234 per year with added allowances of £16 towards rent, £3.18s towards footwear, an added £18.5s for service in Munster and £3 for using his own bicycle.

Hannah Hanlon was later awarded £3,900 – one third of the capitalised value of his earnings – for the loss of her husband.[33] She was left with three children, Hannah Frances aged four, Maria Josephine aged two and James Brendan, who was five weeks old at the time. Jimmy died of meningitis at age ten.[34]

Haugh later wrote of having left his name and address in the hands of the RIC at the scene of a 'particularly lurid exploit' (probably the Hanlon shooting), a mistake that would have consequences for his family in Monmore.[35]

He would spend the remainder of the war period on the run.[36] During that period, he was one of Ireland's most wanted men and his photograph, in the uniform of the US Marines, was published in Hue & Cry alongside fellow revolutionaries Michael Collins, Piaras Béaslaí, Cathal Brugha and Micheal Brennan, OC East Clare Brigade.[37]

He is reputed to have carved the letter H three times on the butt of his revolver, a coded testimony to the boast that 'Haugh shot Hanley with Howard's gun.'[38]

# Patrick (Sonny) Burke

On the evening of 21 August 1920, following the assassination of Detective John Hanlon in Kilrush, Brigade Commandant Seán Liddy led a party of ten in two cars to Kilballyowen.

They were on protection duty for William J Studdert, who had been subjected to a campaign of intimidation by locals with a view to taking over some of his land. Among Liddy's party were Brigade Quartermaster Patrick Burke, Paddy Hassett and Frank O'Donnell, brother of Art.

During a protracted campaign of intimidation, cattle had been driven from Studdert's land and on one occasion a bomb had exploded on the window sill of Kilballyowen House, the family home.[1]

The intimidation had intensified since August 1919. Shots were fired into his herdsman's home and at Studdert himself and a chilling message was delivered in the form of a freshly-dug grave. Studdert secured an injunction and he sought and got protection from police and military as well as the West Clare Brigade.

But when the RIC withdrew from Carrigaholt on 19 August 1920, the intimidation began again. On the night of 20 August 1920, seven tons of Studdert's hay were burned, fencing was torn up and burned and 135 trams of hay that were saved in the sunlight were tossed about in the moonlight.[2]

Burke, Hassett and O'Donnell visited Studdert the following day and assured him that they had come to protect his property and that nothing would happen to it that night. On the following day all three, together with an unnamed young woman were travelling in a Ford car driven by Frank Marrinan.[3] They were executing orders in relation to a disputed farm in Ballinagun.[4]

Meanwhile, an RIC Crossley car en route from Miltown Malbay to Kilrush was overheating and had stopped on the roadside at Ballinagun while Sergeant Patrick McLoughlin and a constable walked to a nearby house for water. Presently, Marrinan's Ford happened along in the same direction and was stopped by the police.

Sergeant Ed Sullivan searched Burke and recovered a pouch with belt containing 23 rounds of ammunition. As Burke was being arrested, Sergeant Sullivan spotted an automatic pistol with six rounds in the chamber on the ground and a six-chamber, loaded revolver was also recovered from the scene.

Police reports of what happened next indicate that the arrest and detention of Burke, Hassett and O'Donnell were in line with protocol.

According to a number of other accounts, however, the police were 'demonstrating wildly' in the wake of the shooting dead of Detective Hanlon the previous day.

Marrinan had escaped across the fields when he saw the police car, but the police trashed the car and the remaining three were badly beaten and taken to Kilrush. As they were being loaded onto the Crossley, Mick Honan came upon the scene and fired repeatedly on their captors. This merited further beatings in Kilrush RIC Station as the men were paraded through the room where Constable Hanlon's corpse was laid out.[5]

Over the next two days, the men were beaten repeatedly. Hassett was taken outside alone and beaten on a number of occasions and he was threatened to be shot if he would not give information about the shooting of Constable Hanlon but he steadfastly refused.

It was only following the pleadings of clergy that the prisoners were handed into military custody and transferred to Limerick Gaol. Sinn Féin

Headquarters sanctioned a full defence for Hassett in the event that he was connected to the shooting of Hanlon, but the evidence was not forthcoming and both he and O'Donnell were released.[6]

Burke, however, was not so lucky, despite the best efforts of William Studdert, whose property the three men had guarded through the night. Studdert wrote in mitigation to General Nevil Macready, the Commander-in-Chief of the Irish Forces '... so that justice may be done in this case':

> On Saturday 21st instant three young men whom I afterwards ascertained to be Messrs Burke Hassett and O'Donnell called to my house at Kilballyowen, and made enquiries regarding the destruction of my property the previous night; they told me their names; said they came to protect my property, and assured me that they would see that nothing would happen that night. I didn't see them again until 2 o'clock on Sunday 22nd instant when they came to my home and said they were leaving. I heard afterwards they were arrested near Cooraclare, and that arms and ammunition were found on them. I am perfectly satisfied as to the identity of the three young men.[7]

Studdert's petition fell on deaf ears and Burke was charged with possession of 23 rounds of revolver ammunition. He was tried by court-martial in Limerick at 9.00am on 3 September 1920, where he was sentenced to two years imprisonment with hard labour.[8]

From Limerick, Burke was taken first to Cork Gaol, where, it was noted that he had cut marks under his left eye and his upper teeth were missing. On 18 September 1920 he was transferred by the military to Wormwood Scrubs Prison in London.[9] He would never again save hay in Cooraclare and his fight to save Ireland would continue in British prison cells and hospital beds.

On 24 June 1921, Burke was transferred to Wandsworth Prison, where he and others went on a hunger strike that lasted 24 days. For refusing to take food, he was moved to a small cell, where a water hose was turned on him repeatedly, after which he was left in the clothes he was wearing. What began as a severe cold developed into pleurisy, pneumonia and tuberculosis.

In a greatly weakened state, he was discharged from the prison hospital at the end of October 1921 and readmitted to a London hospital, where he received treatment until December. Burke's physician eventually recommended that his patient's best hope of survival would involve repatriation. On arrival at Ennis Infirmary in December 1921, three quarts and 17 fluid ounces of fluid were drained from his lungs.

Patrick Burke died on 7 March 1922.[10]

Patrick Burke was undoubtedly one of the most trusted and respected Volunteers in west Clare.

After his arrest on 22 August 1920, he had ensured that every penny of £400 in his safe-keeping was handed over to Brigade staff.

At Kilmacduane Cemetery on Easter Sunday 1928, watched by a crowd of between 2000 and 3000, a Celtic Cross, fashioned from native limestone and draped with a tricolour and purple cloth, was unveiled by Brian O'Higgins at the grave of Patrick Burke. Floral wreaths were placed on the grave and two buglers sounded the *Last Post*.[11]

# Ambush Season

It is no exaggeration to state that the West Clare Brigade was ambush-shy during the War of Independence.

Some attributed this to a reluctance on the part of Brigade OC Seán Liddy, acting on instructions from Headquarters, where it was believed that the terrain was unsuited. Following the shooting of Detective John Hanlon, the Flying Column was reactivated and the autumn of 1920 was destined to be 'ambush season'.

The Column's first engagement under Liddy took place at Burrane National School, Knock at 1.00pm on 27 August 1920. The target this time was the lorry that travelled regularly between Kilrush and Kilmore House, where there was a garrison. The ambush was carefully planned and the 20-strong Column was armed with shotguns and rifles.

But there was disappointment at about 12.30pm when the first military to arrive were two unarmed Royal Scots privates on a limber (a two-wheeled cart used for transporting artillery and supplies) that was being drawn by two heavy draft horses. Privates Keith and Nicholls were ordered off the limber and were taken into a field, where they were kept sitting behind a wall for an hour.

Some of the supplies aboard the limber were destroyed and more were stored for a time at the home of Kathleen Bonfield. The limber was burned and the two soldiers were freed unharmed on condition that they go in the direction of Kilrush.

Since each of the horses had the Government mark on its flank and a number burned on their hooves, they were brought to the remote Coore area where they were kept for a time before being sold on – probably at a discount on their combined value of £120 pounds – to generate funds for the Brigade.[1]

On 2 September, John Mulqueen, John Brown and William Moody were arrested and Privates Keith and Nicholls identified Mulqueen and Brown. Moody was released for lack of identification.

Mulqueen and Brown were remanded in custody and tried by district

Horse-drawn Limber similar to the one that was ambushed at Burrane, Knock, on 27 August 1920.
*(Source: Peadar McNamara)*

court-martial in Limerick on 10 September. Despite being identified by the two Privates, they were acquitted following the discovery of eight irregularities in the preparation of the case against them, in addition to lack of evidence that they were armed.[2]

~

Police reports acknowledged that the RIC in Clare was struggling. The number of indictable offences had almost doubled from July to August and County Inspector H F Munro's August Report was uncannily prophetic:

> The situation is becoming more dangerous in this county and may at any moment culminate in more determined attacks on military and police, to cope with which a much larger force of military will be required.[3]

During the month of August a Captain Fitzgerald, an Auxiliary bomb instructor attached to Kildysart RIC station, was attacked, wounded and disarmed by a number of Volunteers from the local B Company. Two of those who were involved, Thomas O'Connor and Patrick Burke (both of Kildysart) were arrested and interned in a subsequent round-up.[4]

On Tuesday 14 September 1920, the Column had planned an ambush of a military Crossley car at Drumdigus, Kilmurry McMahon. The Crossley would normally travel from Kilmihil to Kilrush and it was expected to pass through Drumdigus at about 3.00pm, as it had done for six weeks previously.

At dawn that Tuesday morning, the Flying Column assembled at Paddy Haugh's house under the command of Seán Liddy. There, they were served with tea before they set about preparing for the ambush.

Scouts were positioned on either side of the chosen ambush site for the duration of the preparations in order to warn about any unexpected approach by Crown forces and to manage civilian traffic.[5]

A large trench was cut across the road between Drumdigus Cross and Paddy Haugh's house. It was three feet wide and two and a half feet deep and it was carefully camouflaged with wire mesh, straw and gravel.

The main party, armed with shotguns, revolvers and grenades, took up position in Haugh's vegetable garden on the right hand side of the road in the direction from which the lorry was travelling. Riflemen Willie Shanahan and Paddy Hassett were across the road, accompanied by Joe Kelly who was armed with hand grenades.

Martin Chambers and ex-soldier Pat Haugh, each armed with Lee-Enfield rifles, were positioned on the same side as the main group about 50 yards closer to the crossroads.

By 11.00am the men had been allocated their positions and were in the

Wedding of Seán Liddy, TD, to Anna (Nano) Breen on 27 September 1922.
FRONT ROW, LEFT TO RIGHT: Col Commdt P Brennan, TD, Jennie Breen, Mr and Mrs Liddy, Gen Eoin O'Duffy, Fr Lavin, CC, Ennistymon.
BACK ROW, LEFT TO RIGHT: Inspector Seán Scanlon, 'Babs' Liddy, Superintendent O'Neill, Commdt D Sheedy and Mrs Breen.
*(Source: Freeman's Journal, 5 October 1922)*

process of making them more secure. Pat Haugh was unhappy with his level of cover and he went in search of a furze bush.

At the same time, 23-year-old medical student and Column OC Bill Shannon, who was in charge of scouts, had just finished giving final instructions to the outposts. As he returned with Tom Culligan and Jack Coughlan, the Crossley arrived on the scene ahead of schedule.[6]

When the driver spotted the three men, he stopped on the road, right next to where Chambers was, and the military opened fire and initiated a circular movement.

By every account, Shanahan and Hassett saved the day and saved the lives of the Column members by opening rapid fire, thereby forcing the military to take cover, some of whom crawled under the lorry. Together they kept the military at bay for long enough to enable Liddy and the main body to begin their retreat. Critically, they neutralised the machine-gunner before they themselves retreated.

The soldiers advanced towards Haugh's house, their advance delayed by a few valuable seconds when some of them fell into the trench that had been dug across the road. By the time they reached Haugh's, the main ambush party, some of whom had thrown away their guns, were about 200 yards away and, even though they were still well within range, made good their escape.

The Column regrouped at O'Donnell's of Tullycrine.

Meanwhile, Chambers remained under cover lying on his rifle on the inside of a four foot high boundary fence within yards of the lorry. He had a close shave when a soldier climbed on the fence and knocked over a bush that he had placed there for cover.

He had to lie there for about two hours, while the soldiers blocked the road, filled in the trench and searched the area. Bill Shannon, who had hidden behind a hedge, was captured and arrested, together with local men Michael McCarthy and Martin and Patrick McGrath, who had been working in a nearby field.[7]

McCarthy was released without charge, but Shannon and the two McGraths were tried by district court-martial in Limerick on 6 October 1920.

The McGraths were released due to lack of evidence, but Shannon was found guilty of endangering the safety of members of His Majesty's Forces and he was sentenced to one year's imprisonment with hard labour which he served in England.[8]

# Conflict at Kilmore

Throughout the summer of 1920, in marked contrast with the exponential growth of the West Clare Arbitration Courts, the Petty Sessions Courts of Alan Lendrum RM were in decline. In Kilkee, many of the sittings heard only one or two cases.

On 12 July, Lendrum heard the only case that had been processed in Kilrush in a month and that case was adjourned until the next sitting.[1] By the end of August, police authorities were beginning to acknowledge the extent of the decline:

> ... the ordinary administration work in the county has been suspended. The courts of law are practically neglected by the general public. Disputes are settled by the S Fein [sic] arbitration courts. SF magistrates have been selected generally through the county. In view of police attention these courts are not sitting openly but are adopting the same precautions of secrecy as when first instituted. S Fein [sic] police have been appointed but the police have been able to suppress their activities in the places where our stations exist. All the public bodies have sworn allegiance to Dail Eireann [sic] and intend to ignore the LGB. The Clare Co Council have taken steps to safeguard their funds from being attached to most malicious injury claims. This council has also passed a resolution calling on all DCs and JPs throughout the county to resign their commissions. In the case of their officials this will be enforced

by refusing to pay their salaries. In the case of others matters will be made unhealthy for them in the event of failure to comply.[2]

A number of special court sittings did take place at Ennis Courthouse during the months of July and August. These sittings, presided over by Alan Lendrum, RM, resulted from a labour dispute at Kilmore House, the 'Big House' residence of F W Gore-Hickman in Knock.

The Hickmans owned about 3,500 acres of land in west Clare, of which 3000 acres were let to tenants. Hickman himself was a solicitor, who lived at Hazelwood, near Ennis and he employed a steward, Alex Martin, to manage Kilmore House and another 500 acres having moved his mother and his sisters from the estate due to threats and intimidation.[3]

Two of Hickman's employees, the sons of nearby resident James Cleary and his wife Margaret, had refused to join the Transport Union.[4] This brought both the Clearys and Hickman's steward into conflict with the Republican movement.

At about 11.00pm on 30 June 1920 a number of armed and masked men arrived at the Cleary home. According to the depositions of the Cleary family, the raiders banged on the door and the window and demanded to speak with James Cleary Senior.

Mrs Cleary kept them in dialogue while her husband got dressed and made his escape through a back window. Three of the men then forced their way into the house and searched for Cleary, who, they were told, was visiting with his brother in Kildysart.

Fifteen-year-old James Cleary Junior claimed that John Daly, armed with a revolver, and William O'Dea, who carried a stick, entered his bedroom and searched it for his father using a lighted candle. He said that he recognised both men by the clothes they wore and Daly by his stance.

Margaret Cleary identified John Daly's brother Pat as one of the raiders. He had warned that he and his friends were union men, that he had a seven-chambered revolver in his pocket and that he would blow Alex Martin's brains out. Pat Daly had then ordered another man, whom she believed to be Patrick Lynch, to go around the back of the house.

James Cleary Snr said that he had recognised one of the raiders, who he named as Joe Kelly before he (Cleary) had climbed through a rear window to the safety of the woods.

On 6 July, Sergeant Patrick McLoughlin, RIC Kilrush, visited the homes of the Daly brothers at Burrane and Kelly, Lynch and O'Dea at Knock and arrested them.

All five were duly charged the following day, but Lynch was released on bail and was later discharged when it was determined that there was insufficient evidence to connect him to the raid. The other four were scarcely in custody when the main prosecution witness James Cleary was kidnapped and held captive in the 4th Battalion Coore, Doolough, Mullagh area for eleven weeks, as a result of which the case against the accused was significantly compromised.[5]

Meanwhile, Hickman's steward, Martin, ignored a Sinn Féin Court ruling on the matter and vowed to resist any attempt at enforcement, even to the point of sourcing workers in Dublin.[6]

The Brigade took a serious view of his obstinacy and, at 6.30am on 13 July, up to 30 armed Volunteers under the command of Frank O'Donnell arrived at Kilmore House with a view to relieving him of some of his arms. Martin was out and about early and when he became aware of some activity on the road he went to investigate. Suddenly, he was challenged and ordered to put up his hands. He did as he was told but, as he approached the men, he drew two revolvers from his pockets and opened fire. In the ensuing exchange Killimer Company Adjutant Patrick Hassett, a native of Burrane, was accidentally shot in the shoulder by one of his own men.

Alex Martin headed back towards the house but was shot through his side and seriously injured. Having crawled inside, he discovered that the communication wires had been cut, thus delaying medical attention.

Nevertheless, Martin made a good recovery and succeeded in his subsequent claim for £800 compensation in respect of his injuries.[7] Meanwhile, during the period of his recovery, the RIC and military moved in to Kilmore House and Hickman now found it impossible to get workers. As a result of the boycott, he lost 26 acres of corn, four acres of roots and 70 acres of hay.[8]

The injured Patrick Hassett was moved quickly to the Cree area, but there was some difficulty in finding a driver willing to risk driving him to hospital, as the police and military were aware that a Volunteer had been wounded and were actively trying to find out who it was.

He was attended to by Dr Hillery and nursed by Mary O'Dea (née Reidy) while Lott O'Neill and Tom Neville cycled to Kilkee to ask hackney man and IRA activist Willie Hynes if he would drive the injured man to hospital. Hynes agreed to take him to Limerick, but it was now four days since he had been wounded.

Knowing that the car would be stopped at military checkpoints, it was agreed that Hassett would travel under an assumed name and that he would pretend that he had been kicked by a horse. He made it to Limerick, accompanied by Knockerra men James Driscoll and William Cooper, but he died on or about 18 July 1920 in Limerick's St John's Hospital.

Owing to the levels of secrecy about his identity, no death certificate was issued and he was buried quietly in Mount St Lawrence Cemetery in Limerick. However, in late October or early November 1921, Hassett's body was re-interred with military honours in the family grave at Burrane. Large numbers of volunteers and members of the public attended the funeral.[9]

During the months of July, August and September, John and Pat Daly, William O'Dea and Joe Kelly appeared at six special court sittings at Ennis Courthouse that were presided over by Alan Lendrum RM. The prosecuting DI was none other than Lendrum's wartime friend and comrade, George Harris Noblett, DI, Kilrush.[10]

On the occasion of the defendants' sixth court appearance on Thursday,

12 August 1920, Noblett was driving Lendrum, Sergeant McLoughlin and another constable to Ennis in a 10cwt Model T Ford van. IRA Volunteers had hatched a plan to ambush them by cutting a 18-inch deep trench across the road close to a crossroads near Tullycrine.

As the Ford rounded a corner, Noblett spotted the trench, increased his speed and circumvented it by driving partly up on the ditch. The ambush party opened fire and a number of bullets hit the van, but none of its occupants were injured.

As it happened, it was not possible to transport the prisoners from Limerick Prison to Ennis, due to a motor breakdown, so Noblett drove to Limerick, where the prisoners were further remanded to Limerick Gaol until the date of their trial.[11]

The trial went ahead eventually in the early days of October and, due to the absence of the chief Crown witness, all four prisoners were found not guilty and released.

There was one other notable absence from the courtroom – Alan Lendrum had been ambushed and killed at Caherfeenick, near Doonbeg on 22 September.

# Captain Lendrum

Alan Lendrum's tenure as Resident Magistrate was brief, as were his court sessions. Following his appointment in April 1920, he rented comfortable, if damp, quarters at 4 Albert Place, Kilkee and purchased a Ford two-seater car from John McGrath in the town.

In common with many of his 66 fellow RMs, Lendrum's main difficulty was in sourcing 20 litres of petrol per month to run it. Apart from Kilkee, his regular court sessions were in Kilrush, Miltown Malbay, and Ennistymon and while each town was serviced by the West Clare Railway, the trains were irregular and locals would refuse to hire out a car for official business.[1]

Lendrum was of slight build, he was hard of hearing and he spoke '... with an educated drawl.'[2] He had just come from the ordeal of serving the entire length of the First World War where he was wounded on at least five occasions and was decorated for gallantry. By every anecdotal account, the new RM was personable and well-liked locally, where he was known to offer lifts to random strangers he encountered walking the roads.

But it was his car as well as the nature of his work, rather than his endearing qualities, that brought him to the attention of the IRA in west Clare. Lendrum's car, according to Brigade Adjutant Bill Haugh, '... looked good in the eyes of some Volunteer officers ...' and Brigade Headquarters had given the go ahead to take it from him on condition that he was not to be harmed.[3]

His quarters were twice searched in his absence and his letters to Dublin Castle were probably intercepted during the many raids that were conducted on the mail trains. Among those letters were his monthly reports and it may have been one in particular that prompted unproven suspicions locally that Lendrum was engaged in intelligence work:

Kilkee. Co Clare (Captain Lendrum).

A Increased motor transport is greatly needed for patrol work. It is obvious that a great deal of harm is done by large areas being left with no police or military.

B Considerable annoyance is expressed at the rate levied by Sinn Féin (6d in the £.) from householders for payment of their police.

C Motor cars are increasingly used for illegal purposes.[4]

In fact, Lendrum's June report was fairly typical of RM reports but, whether or not it was intercepted, the magistrate was certainly being monitored and one account of the period claimed that he was suspected of directing the enemy Secret Service in the area.[5]

From 1 August 1920, he had written regularly to the Chief Secretary's Office asking permission to transfer his headquarters to a house that was close to the Coastguard Station in Kilrush, where the Royal Marines were based. Detective Constable John Hanlon had written in support, stating that a 'most reliable' informant had told him that armed Sinn Féiners had been monitoring Lendrum's movements.[6]

It was only on 15 September, following a bureaucratic tic-tacking between the Chief Secretary's office and the RIC, that one official acknowledged the gravity of Lendrum's situation and issued an ominous warning:

This application should be dealt with promptly, or we may have the murder of an RM laid at our door.[7]

By 17 September 1920 Lendrum had finally secured permission for his move

Captain Alan Lendrum, RM, MC and Bar.
*(Courtesy Geoff Simmons)*

to Kilrush.[8] Three days later, he attended at Kilrush Petty Sessions Court for what was probably his last appearance in a courtroom.

In the event, due to the wide popularity and continuing success of the Sinn Féin Courts, not a single case was listed for hearing.[9] His last journey would have brought him to Ennistymon Courthouse on the fateful morning of 22 September.

~

As Lendrum left Kilkee, six-year-old Tomás Meade was leaving his Caherfeenick home to go over to a neighbour's house to tell them that his folks would be putting in hay that day.[10] At the nearby level crossing, Meade met four young men who were putting on masks and asking each other, 'Would I be known?'[11] They were Jim McGrath from Dromelihy and James Neylon, Paddy Boland and James Griffin, all of Caherfeenick.[12]

Presently, neighbour Paddy Burns passed by on his way west to sell pigs to the Hennessys in Doonbeg. He would meet Lendrum's car beyond Behan's Cross but, aware that an ambush awaited Lendrum, thought better of sending the Magistrate by an alternative route when he considered the consequences for himself.[13]

When Lendrum arrived at the railway crossing, the gates were closed.

He was then challenged and he drew an automatic pistol.[14] One of the men fired and the bullet pierced Lendrum's chest close to his heart.[15] He was brought to a nearby field and held there while they tried to move the car, no easy task for men who didn't have first-hand knowledge of the function of the steering wheel, so their initial efforts pushed the car onto the grass margin.

When Willie Shanahan arrived on the scene, he approached Lendrum and the badly-wounded magistrate beckoned him to finish him off. Shanahan later said that he declined, as he had believed that Lendrum's case was hopeless.[16]

The botched ambush had yielded two guns, some ammunition, a Ford car and a badly-wounded government official.

Shanahan drove the car eastwards along quiet country roads to Doolough, where J O'Dwyer, a native of Scarteen in Limerick, took possession of it. O'Dwyer, helped by Patrick O'Dea (Scropul) and Con Donnellan, dismantled the car and disposed of it in Doolough Lake.[17]

Back in Caherfeenick, the two guns and ammunition were a welcome addition to the Brigade's arsenal but, in Lendrum himself, they had both a logistical and an ethical dilemma.

Before long, the place would be crawling with police and military in search of the missing magistrate. What would they do with him, how would they do it and, critically, who would do it?

～

The historical record of the last hours of Alan Lendrum and the aftermath of his death has, for decades, been blurred by those who remained silent and confused by those who didn't.

Danny Garry, born on 1 January 1916 and who later knew many of the central characters of the period, explained the culture of secrecy that existed:

> Whatever you knew about Lendrum you didn't say nothing to no one about it. You had to be very solid, cool and sincere about what you knew and who you would tell it to.[18]

Locally, the ambush would be spoken of in hushed tones, with the exception of pub banter around the time of the anniversary each year.

On one such occasion in the local hostelry, ambush participant Paddy Boland found himself fielding the light-hearted quips of a fellow-drinker.

"Ah, they'll be celebrating in Caherfeenick tonight, ha?"

"Ten men to kill one man, ha?"

Boland kept his counsel until he was leaving, but he turned back at the exit, stretched out an arthritic hand with only the little finger pointing forward and announced for all to hear …

194

"This is the hand that held the gun that shot Lendrum."[19]

Boland's carefully-chosen words only added to the intrigue of the saga, for the hand that held the gun was not necessarily the hand that held the finger that pulled the trigger.

It may never be possible to state definitively which of the four ambush participants fired the first shot that entered Alan Lendrum's body close to the heart. All four men went on the run immediately, they were never identified as suspects and, critically, they were never betrayed.

Of the four ambush participants, only James Neylon left the country in the aftermath of the Lendrum affair. Having made his way secretly to Queenstown, County Cork, he boarded the *Celtic* for New York on 24 November 1920 and arrived at Ellis Island on 3 December. From there, he took a train to Chicago, where he later married Thomas Quealy's sister Mary.

He never spoke to his family about his revolutionary past and he never again set foot in his native Caherfeenick.

Neylon's sister Suzanne, who was born in 1896 and who lived to be over 100 years-old, later recalled that James:

> ... left Ireland because the Black and Tans were after him. He left because I guess they were going to kill him ... he had to be secreted or the Black and Tans would get a hold of him, I believe.[20]

~

What is known for certain is that Lendrum lived for some time after he was first shot and he was first taken to a nearby field, where he remained for several hours. Some said that he blew repeatedly on a whistle, but that he was unheeded, despite the fact that police and military were scouring the countryside both day and night.[21]

Alan Lendrum's final moments would remain clouded in secrecy until one Wednesday night in Kilmurry in the 1970s, when the now-ageing Joe Daly was visited by his son of the same name.

Joe Junior had heard rumours that his father, then aged 24, had been called upon to manage the unfortunate and tragic situation that existed following the Lendrum ambush. The young history teacher and former clerical student broached the question of the old man's preparedness to meet his maker with a view to easing his conscience in respect of his exploits during the War of Independence.

By way of introduction, he cited his father's hero, Dan Breen, from a television interview that he had given in 1967:

I don't make any bones about killing. Anyone that comes into my house or

LEFT: Chicago's Clare Football Team in the 1920s.
*Bottom row:* second from left is James Neylon and far right is his great friend Michael Shannon, from Kilmihil; *Top row:* third from left is John Quealy, Dromelihy.
*(Courtesy Maureen Neylon)*
RIGHT: Joe Daly, Kilmurry Ibrickane
*(Courtesy Daly Family)*

my country and tries to take over by force, I'm going to kill him and I'll use any and every means to do it.[22]

Joe Senior recalled that he had been summoned to the place where the badly injured magistrate had been held captive. There, he offered Lendrum a pencil and paper so that he could write a note to his family. Lendrum declined.

Daly volunteered the services of a pastor, but Lendrum again declined. Having consulted with Brigade officers, and in what was clearly determined to be a necessary act of mercy, Daly then took charge of the execution.[23]

There were reports that Lendrum's body was first buried in the sand close to the nearby home of Larry Healy and on the site of the current Trump International Golf Links. Some said that cattle were driven over the freshly-dug grave in order to conceal the activity. Healy, it was said, had asked for the body to be removed, as he feared reprisals in the event that the location was divulged, so the body was dug up and moved to Lough Donnell, a saltwater lake about a mile to the north.[24]

At Kilrush Barracks, word reached Lendrum's best friend, DI George Noblett, that a police car had been ambushed outside Miltown Malbay and that Lendrum had failed to turn up at Ennistymon Courthouse.

Noblett and a number of RIC policemen retraced the magistrate's steps in two motors. Word spread quickly and in Caherfeenick and all along the route from Kilkee through Doonbeg and Quilty there was panic as houses were searched and their occupants were questioned. Blessed candles were lit in the windows and householders moved their furniture and their families from their homes in fear of reprisals.[25]

Some moved to neighbouring townlands and villages and men took refuge in bogs. Young Tomás Meade and his sister Nora were taken to stay with their O'Leary cousins near Cree, while their father camped out in the middle of Steele's Lake to avoid questioning. Nora later recalled that the man of the house would give her the top of his boiled egg each morning.[26]

~

By coincidence, the Mid Clare Brigade had ambushed a police Crossley car around midday at Dromin Hill, Rineen, between Miltown Malbay and Lahinch. A police sergeant, four RIC constables and their Black and Tan driver were all fatally injured. On the same morning, a warning had been received by post at Ennistymon RIC barracks, from where the Crossley had set out. It read:

Dear Sir,

I am giving you a warning to make your men look out for themselves for the S.F. is going to make a raid on them some day. Let your men look out and the two officers that is going by themselves in the black motor. They will give them a downfall as sure as you are reading this. They would want to look out for themselves: we cannot stop our young innocent sons. Sure the leading man of all of them is John O'Loughlin the man that is going to all the races..

Jim McGrath, Dromelihy, who participated in the Lendrum ambush.
*(Courtesy Jim Tubridy, Kilrush)*

why he has plenty of powder and firearms. We would have an easy mind if you would frighten these murderers. They want more blood ...[27]

At 11.00am, a non-commissioned military officer was alerted to the possibility that a police car might be attacked. He reported immediately to his barracks in Ennistymon and a lorry of troops was sent towards Miltown Malbay to check for likely ambush sites.[28] When word reached Ennis a military party also set out from there.[29]

The near 60-strong ambush party subsequently came under heavy fire, but managed to make it to safety without casualties. Subsequent military reports accused the ambush party of using flat-nosed rifle bullets to disable their targets and of finishing them off with shotguns at close range.[30]

The reprisals that took place in the aftermath of the ambushes at Caherfeenick and Rineen resulted in the sacking of Ennistymon, Lahinch and Miltown Malbay and the violent deaths of six men.

During the night, two lorry-loads of soldiers went on a rampage, burning ricks and winds of hay and cabins all the way from Cree through Doonbeg and Bealaha to Kilkee. When they reached Kilkee they shot up the town and raided the Victoria Hotel and the Concert Hall.[31]

~

Meanwhile, the search for Captain Lendrum, led by his friend George Noblett DI, continued day and night and, within 24 hours of his disappearance, the tracks of his car on the grass verge and the loopholed fence at Caherfeenick betrayed the location of the ambush.

The following day, the *Freeman's Journal* reported the generally-held view that by then he was dead and buried.[32]

As fears grew for his safety, further reprisals were threatened. At Cooraclare National School, the children were at play when twelve year-old Michael Considine was shot in the shoulder by police who were firing indiscriminately from a motor lorry as they searched for Lendrum.

In Kilkee, Mick Blake was arrested, badly beaten and forced to carry a placard warning that he would be killed if Lendrum's body wasn't given up. He was prodded with bayonets as he was paraded through the streets of the town by RIC and Black and Tans. Blake was badly beaten while in custody and he was only released after Lendrum's body was handed over.[33]

Then, on Sunday 26 September 1920, notices were posted around the town warning that if Captain Lendrum had not returned to Kilkee by midday on the following Wednesday the towns and villages of Kilkee, Carrigaholt, Doonbeg, Kilrush, Mullagh, Cooraclare and Kilmihil would be burned to the ground. Many visitors fled the town in panic.[34]

In the meantime, Alan Lendrum's brother James travelled from the family home in Kilskeery, County Tyrone, to help with the search and presumably to identify the body in the event that it were to be found.

Dean McInerney from Kilrush and Canon Glynn from Kilkee urged the IRA to give up the body and pleaded with the police and military for restraint.

On 26 September two civilians reported to DI Noblett that his friend Alan Lendrum had been killed at Caherfeenick on 22 September 1920.

They had been compelled, under threat by Sinn Féin, they said, to inform the authorities that the body would be given up if police and military withheld from reprisals for long enough to facilitate the recovery, but that 'there were difficulties in the way.'[35] Following this, notices were posted in Kilkee to the effect that the threatened reprisals would be postponed for a further 24 hours pending the release of the body.[36]

The 'difficulties in the way' referred to the recovery of Lendrum's body, which is believed to have been concealed in or near Lough Donnell, a nearby coastal lagoon.

In the targeted towns and villages, preparations were made to defend against the threatened reprisals. All members of the 3rd Battalion were ordered to assemble at centres of population to defend against possible attacks. Arms and ammunition were borrowed from the Mid Clare Brigade and were distributed among the different companies.[37]

In Mullagh on 26 September, Fr McKenna mobilised his battalion for their only military operation of the period and strategic plans were developed by Joe Daly, Danny Montgomery and Padla Sexton. In common with many of the other villages, nearly all of Mullagh's inhabitants fled to the safety of the homes of friends and relatives in remote locations and some even slept outdoors.

Jackie Kelly's and Pat Sexton's played host to more than 80 people and there was merriment into the early hours of the morning. Back in the village, however, there was tension.

Daly's men were armed mostly with shotguns, a few single shot rifles and some hand grenades. For some, who had never engaged in armed combat, the prospect of tangling with trained forces was daunting, 'a lot of shakey [sic] fellas were there, praying and hitting their chests.'

Flagstones that had recently been removed from the floor of the church were stood on edge to provide cover for defending Volunteers and publicans buried their whiskey in their gardens. The area's top marksman, Michael Griffin, occupied the best vantage point in the church gallery and the remainder of the men were positioned at strategic locations around the village.

Jim McKeogh and John Corry refused to budge from their homes, the latter believing that the plan to defend Mullagh was an elaborate deception that would enable rowdy elements within the IRA to engage in the looting of empty premises. In the end, the Crown forces never arrived and the Volunteers dispersed at 4.30am.[38]

The logistical operation for the recovery of the body of the third Irish RM to be killed in 18 months proceeded under the shadow of threatened reprisals and involved large numbers of Volunteers.

One who played a prominent part was Mick Killeen, a former RIC constable, Toronto policeman and American soldier. The King's soldiers who had, with arms reversed, marched through the village on either side of his brother's coffin just over a year previously were now threatening to burn the homes and businesses of Killeen's family, his neighbours and his friends.[39]

After the body was taken from Lough Donnell, local sources report that it was taken to a shed next to Davy Walsh's home in Parkduff.

Some accounts state that a coffin was made from rough planks at a workshop situated next to Kilmurry Cemetery by Johnny McCarthy and others say that it was made by Pat Wright. Lendrum's body was placed in the

 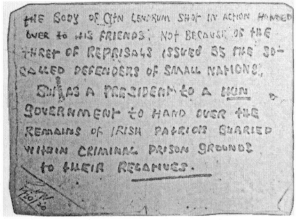

ABOVE LEFT: George Harris Noblett, DI, Kilrush. *(Courtesy Phyllis Winslow)*

ABOVE RIGHT: Copy of note found with the body of Alan Lendrum, RM. The note was initialled and dated by Lendrum's friend George Noblett.
*(Source: Noblett Depositor Papers, T2569, Deputy Keeper of the Records, PRONI)*

Copy of death certificate of Alan Lendrum.
*(Source: https://civilrecords.irishgenealogy.ie)*

coffin and the words 'To Kilkee' written on it.

They brought it to the railway track and moved it to Kilmurry Station on a bogey cart and had intended leaving it at that station, but Joe Daly argued that the Station Master's wife was ill and that the poor man had enough trouble on his hands, so they left it in a cutting between Kilmurry and Craggaknock Stations.[40]

On the morning of 1 October 1920, linesman Stephen O'Halloran made the grim discovery of a roughly-made coffin on the cutting and immediately raised the alarm.

DI Noblett arrived on the scene with five lorries of police and military at 11.00am.[41] There they found the magistrate's coffined body, wrapped in a sheet, together with a note that had been written in blue pencil.[42]

> The body of Cptn Lendrum shot in action handed over to his friends: not because of the thret [sic] of reprisals issued by the so-called defenders of small nations, but as a president [sic] to a hun government to hand over the remains of Irish patriots burried [sic] within criminal prison grounds to their relatives.[43]

After Lendrum's brother James had identified the body, Noblett brought the coffin to Kilkee. There, a procession took place through the streets with Catholic and Protestant clergymen in attendance.

Later, the body was removed to Kilrush Military Barracks where a Military Court of Inquiry investigated the cause of his death.[44]

The findings of this inquiry informed the wording of the magistrate's death certificate, 'Murder by shooting by persons unknown'.

On Saturday night 2 October, the body was taken by motor-lorry from Ennis to the family home at Corkil, Kilskeery, County Tyrone, passing through Ballinamallard at about midnight, where 100 UVF members lined the streets. He was laid to rest the following day in the graveyard at Kilskeery Church.

ABOVE: A 20-strong firing party of Inniskilling Fusiliers, flanked by a guard of the Bedfordshire Regiment, lead the funeral procession of Captain Alan Lendrum, RM at Kilskeery, County Tyrone on 3 October 1920.

BELOW: Pallbearers from the Inniskilling Fusiliers carry the coffin from Lendrum's home in Corkil, Kilskeery.

*(Sources: NAUK, CO 904 168 2. ©NAUK)*

# Telling tales

Alan Lendrum's fate was to become the stuff of myth and legend to such an extent that the task of separating fact from fiction became increasingly difficult with the passing of the decades and of the main players.

Social networking was a common feature of life in the 1920s, both in oral (gossip and rumour) and written (letters and postcards) form. In the absence of social media regulation, harmful and untrue content was easily peddled.

Accounts of the magistrate's death took on a life of their own and, having found their way into the print media, were quickly manipulated and embellished, substituting mythology for fact.

Lendrum's captors allegedly dragged the wounded magistrate to a nearby beach, where they buried him up to his neck and callously left him to drown in the incoming tide. On their return the next morning, they found him still alive and they allegedly dug him up and reburied him closer to the shoreline. Later accounts added the gruesome detail that the victim was deliberately faced towards the advancing tide, so that he might witness his own impending fate.

These lurid new versions soon became entrenched as 'the truth' of what happened and they remained unchallenged for 90 years.[1]

The myth had its genesis in a story that was published in May 1921 under the title, 'The RM' in Blackwood's *Edinburgh Magazine*.

The *Maga*, as it was commonly known, was an effective Unionist propaganda vehicle that enjoyed high circulation figures at home and abroad and whose typical loyalist readership comprised Civil Servants, Constabulary and Military types.

'The RM' was one of a series of stories that had been submitted for publication by Major Aubrey Waithman Long, who may have been a member

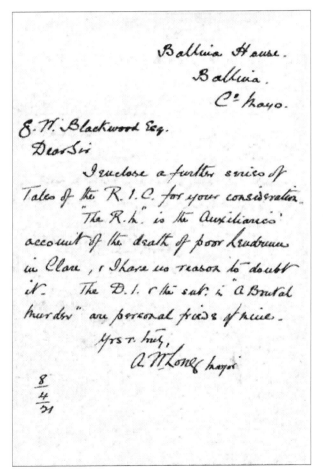

JUST OUT.

POPULAR EDITION.

2/- NET.

# TALES

OF THE

# R.I.C.

*CONTENTS.*

CHAP. I. The Informer—II. On the Run —III. The Landing of Arms—IV. The Red Cross—V. The R.M.—VI. An Outlaw—VII. The Stranger within the Gates —VIII. Mr Briggs' Island—IX. The Reward of Loyalty—X. Poteen—XI. The Mayor's Conscience—XII. A Brutal Murder—XIII. Seal Island—XIV. A Family Affair—XV. The American Nurse —XVI. Father John—XVII. The Bog Cemetery—XVIII. A Jew in Gaelic Clothing — XIX. Mountain Warfare— XX. The Great Round Up—XXI. The Truce.

'Tales of the R.I.C.' leave the reader wondering whether it is possible that the men and women of Ireland can really be living lives in which hazardous adventures, worthy of the pen of Dumas, are decked with the trappings of present-day warfare. Yet they bear truth's indefinable stamp.

WILLIAM BLACKWOOD & SONS,
EDINBURGH AND LONDON

LEFT: Birth of a myth. Letter that accompanied Major A W long's story, The RM, which he submitted for publication in Blackwood's Magazine on 8 April 1921. *(Source: NLS MC, Blackwood Papers, MS.30193).*

RIGHT: Advertisement for *Tales of the R.I.C.*, which included the story 'The R.M.'. *(Source: Blackwood's Magazine, October 1922)*

of the Auxiliary Division, RIC. In the story, a Resident Magistrate named Mayne is buried to his neck on a beach by rebels and left to drown in the incoming tide. In a letter to *Maga's* editor, Long wrote:

> The RM is the Auxiliaries' account of the death of poor Lendrum in Clare. I have no reason to doubt it.[2]

Blackwood's editors were clearly pleased with the boost in circulation figures that followed the publication of Long's stories and they expressed the hope that Long's 'Tales' would prompt decisive action from the British government:

> I am delighted to hear that 'Maga' is being widely read in Dublin and one can only hope that the inevitable indignation that must arise from the publication of facts concerning the condition of affairs there will compel our procrastinating government to take some effective action soon.[3]

The May edition of *Maga* had sold out in Easons by early June and Major Long reported that there was a copy of Blackwood's magazine in every house he visited in the capital.[4] 'The RM' had earned for Long a fee of £32.10s.

Later the same year, the story was reissued by Blackwood's in *Tales of the RIC*, an anonymous book of short stories. The *Fortnightly*, Volume 110, advertised 'Read Tales of the RIC and you will there find THE FACTS and no longer be bored'. The 'Facts' in question made for gruesome reading: 'And the next flood tide put an end to a torture the like of which Lenin and Trotsky could hardly exceed for sheer malignant devilry'.

Because it presented a macabre vignette of the callous cruelty of the IRA, this fiction was retold as fact by successive commentators of varying backgrounds.

In 1951 in *The Last Of The Irish RMs.*, Sir Christopher Lynch Robinson referred to a magistrate being 'buried alive in the sands' in Galway.

In his 1959 best-seller, *The Black and Tans*, Richard Bennett repeated the story, listing the fictional *Tales of the RIC* as his source in his bibliography.

Rex Taylor's 1961 version in *Assassination: The Death of Sir Henry Wilson and the Tragedy of Ireland*, baldly stated that Lendrum was buried alive on the beach: 'In all the history of Irish sadistic violence, there is nothing to equal this atrocity committed against a gallant and decent man'.

The myth was recycled through the years in several publications, including *Life World Library: Ireland* by Joe McCarthy in 1964, *A History of Ireland* by Peter and Fiona Somerset Fry in 1991 and *The Irish Constabularies 1822–1922* by Donal J. O'Sullivan in 1999.

In 1966 Tim Pat Coogan gave the myth the full treatment in his *Ireland since the Rising*, including the reburial facing the tide. A fictional interlude was provided by best-selling novelist, Eilis Dillon who, in 1967, reintroduced the story in *The Interloper*:

> I was staying in a house in County Clare … The men I was with were rejoicing – that's the only word I can use – in the lingering death inflicted on a resident magistrate, buried in the sand and left to drown in the rising tide on a desolate shore.

A character in J G Farrell's highly-regarded 1970 novel, *Troubles*, is singled out for a similar fate.

≈

The content and timing of these accounts of the 'barbarity' had a collateral effect in the North.

Generations of the magistrate's relatives and friends may have gone to their graves believing that the horrific drowning had actually happened. As recently as 1989, a niece of Lendrum's was in receipt of a letter from a former Northern Ireland judge and Unionist politician that contained the most absurdly fictitious account of his final moments. The letter repeated the version that the writer had heard from Major J D Mc Callum, who succeeded Lendrum as Resident Magistrate in Clare. It stated that Lendrum:

... was captured by the IRA and taken to the sands off Lisdoonvarna, where the sands were very far out. He was buried except for his head in the sands while he was still alive and the tide gradually came in and he was slowly drowned. Apparently according to Major McCallum he was secured in the sands with rope and stakes driven into the beach. This is as it was related to me by the man who succeeded him.[5]

In 2000, in his *Police Casualties in Ireland 1919–1922*, Richard Abbott referred to resultant 'serious disturbances and lawlessness that spanned both the political and religious divides' in the north of Ireland.

In 1972 Arthur Hezlet had fleshed out this oblique comment in his *The "B" Specials: A History of the Ulster Special Constabulary*: 'In Ulster itself tension was further increased by the murder of Captain Lendrum, a resident magistrate ... from Trillick [*sic*: Kilskeery] in Co. Tyrone.'

Hezlet detailed the burial and reburial, followed by the dead body being brutally discarded on a manure heap. He opined:

I make no apology for recalling this atrocity ... for unless some such cases are mentioned it is difficult to understand the pressures and tensions of the time and the hatreds that exist in Ireland to this day.

This work was published in one of the darkest years of the Troubles, during which close on 500 people lost their lives.

In 1989 Kevin Myers, writing with characteristic gusto in the *Irish Times*, rehashed the standard 'burial on the beach' story, although he honourably retracted it later, blaming Basil Clarke and his propaganda machine for the misinformation.

In west Clare, people shrugged off reports of an atrocity: 'Sure, everybody knows that didn't happen'.

Nevertheless, there was a sense of helplessness in the absence of definitive proof to the contrary and the extended families of the men involved had to live with the shadow of this cruel atrocity hanging over their lives.

It was not just outsiders who repeated the story.

Fr. Patrick Gaynor ministered locally and was a member of the Supreme Executive of Sinn Féin. In his memoirs *The Gaynors Of Tyone*, written between 1945 and 1949 and published in 2003, Eamonn Gaynor wrote: 'After a subsequent autopsy the police claimed that he had been buried while still alive: that death was due to drowning.'

In 2003 in his *A History Of County Clare*, Seán Spellissy gave a similar account.

In 1987 Brian Dinan repeated the 'burial, reburial and drowning' account in *Clare And Its People: A Concise History*.

In a more recent treatment of the period in 2009, *Blood On The Banner* Pádraig Óg Ó Ruairc stated that Willie Shanahan, 'thinking Lendrum was already dead, took him to a lake, tied a weight to him and threw him into the water, where the unconscious captain died of drowning'. Ó Ruairc later acknowledged the error and corrected it.

≈

On 2 and 3 October 1920 in Kilrush, a Military Court of Inquiry in lieu of an Inquest was held into the death of Captain Lendrum.

It found that death resulted from 'Murder by shooting by persons unknown'. However, the exact nature of the Captain's injuries is uncertain due to the lack of visibility of the Inquiry Report and the only clues are to be found in news reports. The first of these is in the form of a letter written by Lendrum's mother to the Editor of the *Impartial Reporter* on 6 October 1920, when she wrote:

'He was shot in the face by a shot gun, and a bullet wound in the back between the shoulders ...'[6]

It is likely that her information came from Dublin Castle, where Basil Clarke and his cohorts in the propaganda department had been closely monitoring the unfolding sequence of events subsequent to the discovery of the body. Clarke wrote:

> It looks as tho' Lendrum RM had been buried & dug up to disclose his fate & avert the reprisal. Can you ascertain if this is so? It could help in the show-up.

The response to Clarke's query was that the body had not been dug up, but that it appeared to have been taken from the sea, a theory that was supported by DI Noblett, who later stated that the hair showed traces of having been in the sea. There were two bullet holes on the body, he added, one close to the heart and the second to the head.[7]

The suggestion that the body had been in the sea is explained by the fact that it had been put in Lough Donnell, a coastal lagoon. This, together with the 'difficulties in the way' that had delayed the recovery, would also prompt speculation about how and why the body ended up there.

And all of these factors coupled with the inference in Lendrum's mother's letter that there was damage to the face, could have fuelled the onset of rumours among the Auxiliaries that Lendrum had been the victim of a cruel and barbaric atrocity.

It is difficult to ascertain the extent to which shocking tales of a drowning atrocity influenced the efforts of police and military to track down those who were involved in his killing. But it may be stated with certainty that they were relentless in seeking revenge and ruthless in exacting it.

# Mac and Shanahan

The hunt for those associated with Captain Lendrum's death spread far and wide and continued for months.

Martin Moroney, who worked in Mahoney's shop in Kilrush, together with his brother and Sinn Féin District Court member Jack O'Dwyer (none of whom had any involvement in the affair) emerged as early suspects for the Lendrum ambush. Moroney, it was thought, had an interest in a taking over a house that Lendrum had hoped to rent from the Methodists in Kilrush, either because he wanted it for himself or because he sought to prevent Lendrum from getting it.[1]

In January 1921, Walter O'Brien, a native of Mullinahone in County Tipperary, who had a motor and bicycle business at Callan in Kilkenny, was arrested on a charge of being implicated in the Magistrate's death. Suspicions were aroused when he had attempted to sell a car in Dublin for which he had no permit.[2]

Though Willie Shanahan had no involvement in the death of Lendrum, his participation in the disposal of the car became known to the authorities.

His home at Ocean View, Doughmore and the homes of his friends were subjected to repeated night-time raids by Crown forces. On one occasion, the raiders were violent towards his parents and threatened to destroy the family home.

"We're here to butcher Willie Shanahan," the military officer-in-charge announced, "... we'll shoot him if he doesn't tell us who shot Lendrum."

"And I'll shoot him if he does," replied Shanahan's father.

The soldiers then arrested one of Willie's brothers and threatened to butcher him. It was only after the intervention of an RIC sergeant, who had previously been stationed in Mullagh, that this brother was released.[3]

Raids were conducted throughout west Clare with greater intensity and the homes of known Republican activists were targeted in the months following the events of 22 September 1920.

A number of Auxiliaries were drafted into Kilkee and at about 2.00am on 11 October 1920, Crown forces shot up the town. The roof of Talty's Newsagents on O'Connell Street was riddled with bullets and all of the front windows were broken. Marrinan's of Albert Road was singled out for similar treatment. The raiders then turned their attention to the Station where a fitter and a steamraiser were preparing a train for the next morning's outward journey, forcing the pair to flee.[4]

Meanwhile, Shanahan, together with his great friend Michael McNamara from Mountrivers, near Doonbeg, were to spend the next three months on the run, sleeping in safe houses and in the sandhills of Doughmore.

Both were members of the recently-formed West Clare Brigade Flying Column and their ongoing activities included the raiding of mail trains, raiding for arms, trenching of roads and cutting of enemy lines of communication. McNamara proudly carried the revolver that had belonged to Thomas Ashe.[5]

Both McNamara and Shanahan had nationalist pedigrees.

McNamara's grandfather, Patrick McNamara, had been the leader of the pre-famine Terry Alt organisation in west Clare that was at its most active during the period 1828–1831. Named after a rather unobjectionable Corofin-based loyalist, the agrarian Terry Alt movement sought to relieve the plight of the poorer peasant classes.

The Terry Alts did this by organising nocturnal raids for arms as well as intimidating landlords and wealthy farmers and their herdsmen. Many hundreds of men, women and children would assemble in broad daylight and march in formation, accompanied by bands of musicians to targeted pasture lands, which they would dig up with forks and shovels.

In 1831, Patrick McNamara had been leading a group of men to Querrin, near Kilkee, in a raid for arms. Following a tip off, however, they were surprised by a large party of loyalist planters and all but himself were arrested. McNamara was wounded in the leg, the hip and the back, but survived the ordeal. [6]

Friends in need.
Willie Shanahan (left) and Michael McNamara, who were tortured and killed by British soldiers on 22 December 1920 after they refused all information about the ambush and killing of Captain Alan Lendrum RM.
*(Source: Clare Champion, 4 January 1964)*

Willie Shanahan's grandfather of the same name, a prominent Fenian, had provided a safe house for leaders of the Fenian Rising in west Clare in 1867 and had been instrumental in arranging for their safe passage out of the country.[7] And his uncle, John S Carroll, had been a trustee of the fund for the erection of a monument in Kilrush to perpetuate the memory of the Manchester Martyrs.[8]

Shanahan had been appointed Brigade Chief of Republican Police. He had a narrow escape on the day that Tom Curtin was fatally wounded at the Cloonagarnaun Sinn Féin Court sitting on 6 December 1920, when vigilant scouts signalled the approach of military lorries, enabling him to escape through the fields with Court papers.

∾

Since mid-November, both Shanahan and McNamara had been staying in the safe house of Mr and Mrs Denis Reidy at Newtown, a remote spot less than a mile from Doonbeg.

On the night of 16 December 1920, the pair were joined for a drink in Igoe's Pub Doonbeg by Pat McNamara, Mick Thomas (McGrath) and Michael Killeen of Clifden House. The five were last to leave.

Michael Mac and Mick Thomas left first, followed by Shanahan, Pat Mac and Michael Killeen, who stopped to relieve themselves at a crossroads close by Killeen's home. There, Killeen noted that Shanahan and McNamara had been a month at Reidys' and warned of the danger of staying for so long in the same house.

Shanahan agreed, adding "I was going to ask you could we go down with you for a couple of weeks?"

Killeen suggested that they do so immediately, but Shanahan needed to give the Reidys a few pounds, so the move was postponed until the following night.[9]

It so happened that news had reached Granda McGrath's house that a family member had died in the United States and Mac and Shanahan called there on their way to Reidys' to sympathise. There they met Bill Haugh.

"Ye are badly wanted," observed Haugh.

"Wherever we get a warm bed we'll sleep in it," they responded.

Sometime after 2.00am on 17 December 1920, a party of military, and police, acting on a tip-off and with clear knowledge of the location, burst in the door of Reidys' and arrested Mac and Shanahan. The pair were identified by Constable John Mullee, originally from near Naas, County Kildare, who later worked as an insurance agent in the Manchester area.[10]

Among the raiders was one 20 year-old Royal Scots soldier named Brenton Haliburton Ashmore who would go on to have a distinguished army career, serving in Shanghai and Singapore.

In September 1982, Conrad Wood recorded an interview with him for the Imperial War Museum in which Ashmore spoke of his time in County Clare in 1920–21. He had, he said, been stationed at Ennis and Ennistymon, where he used to go out hunting 'Sin Féiners' [sic] who were on the run:

Actually, I caught one of them one night. Don't know what happened to him in the end … Well I went out one, eh, one evening with my patrol and eh into the into the Ennistymon into the village eh where we were stationed and em of course we always had a an RIC fellow with us, a Royal Irish Constabulary policeman, and em we went to this house which belonged to a family called Shanahan and em w we got a tip off that Willie, that's one of the family who'd been on the run he was there and so we went in with I went in with the policeman and em he was I went up to his bedroom and he was in bed and em ehhh actually he ran out of the (word muffled by a chortle) eh em ehhhhaou we took him into custody and em and em marched him back to the barracks and em he told me he said he was thankful that at last he'd been caught. He'd been on the run for I don't know how long three years only. He seemed quite pleased (chuckles) … He weh he was quite pleased that he'd been caught and he wee wouldn't be have to be on the run anymore (chuckles) …[11]

Sixty-two years after his short posting in Clare, Shanahan's name came effortlessly to Ashmore's mind (there was no mention of McNamara). What Ashmore did not disclose was that Denis Reidy had been given a bad beating for having harboured the fugitives. Nor did he describe how the two prisoners were beaten with rifle butts outside the Reidy house, or how the Royal Scots treated their two prisoners over the next five days.[12]

～

Mac and Shanahan were taken to Kilrush Military Barracks, where Shanahan was identified by Privates Keith and Nicholls as one of the party that had ambushed a limber at Burrane on 27 August 1920. They were accused of involvement in the Lendrum ambush and the taking of his car and they were tortured for information about this and other IRA activities.

On 22 December, soldiers of the 2nd Battalion, Royal Scots, took them from Kilrush by military lorry to Ennis via Kildysart and Ballynacally. During the journey they were stabbed and kicked and when the pair resisted their hands and feet were tied. McNamara was singled out for particular torture in the hope that Shanahan would tell what he knew. Throughout his ordeal, McNamara is believed to have repeatedly proclaimed his loyalty to the Republic.

At Ashline, he was thrown on the road, jumped upon and prodded with bayonets, before being tied to the lorry and dragged behind it. Finally, he was told that he was free to go and he was shot in the back after he had stumbled a few steps.[13]

At Ennis, McNamara's body was brought to the County Infirmary, where the Royal Scots first indicated that he had been shot while attempting to escape and this was reported in the *Irish Times*.[14] They quickly changed their story, however, possibly in light of growing concern at the number of men who were being shot ostensibly while attempting to escape.

By midday the following day, 23 December 1920, the Ennis DI had reported to Basil Clarke in Dublin Castle that McNamara had been:

Last photo of Willie Shanahan outside his home at Ocean View, Doughmore.
*(Courtesy Martha Shanahan)*

... accidently [sic] shot dead by Discharge [sic] of soldiers [sic] rifle when being conveyed under escort from Kilrush to Ennis 22nd inst.[15]

Meanwhile, Shanahan was lodged in the custody of one Company Sergeant Major William Strath, C Company, 2nd Battalion, Royal Scots – a one-time bus conductor who was in charge of Battalion police at Ennis Gaol and whose brutal methods at least matched and probably exceeded those of Provost Sergeant David Findlay.

When Strath and his cohorts had finished with him, Shanahan's body, bound hand and foot, was dumped near the mortuary of the County Infirmary in Ennis.[16]

Last rites were administered to both victims by Fr John Considine, who had ministered in Kilmurry parish between 1910 and 1920 and who was now based in Ennis. His family recounted that what he saw had a profound effect on his health.[17] The injuries to Shanahan's body were described as:

... mangled and covered with bayonet wounds. The back of his head was blown away and the distorted appearance of his countenance betrayed terrible agony.[18]

Others stated that almost every bone in Shanahan's body was broken and that most of his finger nails and toenails had been pulled out.[19] McNamara had suffered three severe bayonet thrusts and he had been shot. His sister Tess, who cycled the round trip of 18 miles daily to visit him in Kilrush Military Barracks, noted that he had been '... tortured and beaten beyond recognition.' She retained his clothes as proof that he had been bayoneted through the heart and shot in the back.[20]

Back in Ennis Gaol, the Royal Scots set in process the charade that was to inform the official record of the last hours of Shanahan and McNamara. At the Military Court of Inquiry into the death of Michael McNamara, Private T Brotherston stated that:

> I was sitting at the forward end of the car at the near side & there was a lot of
> kit bags & boxes & I was rather cramped. Going over a big bump in the road
> I fell forward & my rifle accidentally went off –
> The two prisoners were sitting on a form in the middle of the car facing the
> off side. The bullet struck the prisoner in the back.

The medical examination of the body was done by Captain H A Haskell, RAMC, the results of which were reported in a single sentence 'He was dead – evidently from shock & haemorrhage the result of a gunshot wound of the chest.' The Court of Inquiry found that McNamara had been shot accidentally and that he died of '… a gunshot wound in the chest entering from the back.'[21]

The official record of Shanahan's death is contained in the report of a Court of Inquiry in lieu of Inquest that was held at Ordnance House, Ennis on 23 December 1920.

Company Sergeant Major Strath and one of his battalion policemen named Henderson identified the body as that of a prisoner named Shanahan who was brought in to the gaol and given over to Strath's 'safe custody' at about midday on 22 December 1920. Strath stated that he was escorting Shanahan to the latrine at about 7.45pm when the prisoner attacked him:

> I escorted him along the passage keeping about three yards behind him. I
> passed through a gate in the passage with him and ordered him to halt while
> I closed the gate. Whilst in the act of closing the gate, the accused [sic] struck
> me with his clenched fist in the right eye and immediately tried to escape down
> the stairs. I closed with him again on the stairs and struggled with him. During
> the struggle I managed to get out my revolver and shot him in self defence.

When Captain Haskell, RAMC arrived at about midnight Shanahan's body was in a cell and *rigor mortis* had set in. There is no evidence that any medical examination was conducted on the body.

The medic's report was brief, 'He was then dead as a result of a bullet wound in the head.' The inquiry found that Strath had shot Willie Shanahan '… in self defence and while in the execution of his duty.'[22]

Strath's version of events might have seemed plausible were it not for St Flannan's College Professor Éamon Waldron's account of his brutal treatment by Strath in Ennis Gaol.

Waldron had been walking between St Flannan's College and Ennis at 11.50pm on Christmas Day, four days after Shanahan and McNamara had been killed. A number of Black and Tans in the charge of DI Byrne stopped him. Byrne shone a torch in his face and said 'This is our man'.

As Waldron was marched to Ennis Gaol he was repeatedly kicked and struck with revolver butts, all the while being first knocked to the ground and then ordered to get up. When he entered the gaol, he was handed over to the 'safe custody' of Company Sergeant Major William Strath. Waldron later wrote:

The Sergeant Major jumped off his bed as soon as I arrived, and without asking me any questions struck me a punch in the eye, which tumbled me over a barrack room form. I was told to get up; I did so and my clothes we [sic: were] stripped forcibly from me. The Sergt. Major made another attempt to strike me in the face. I put up my hands to defend myself. He levelled a revolver at me telling me to take down my hands or to "take this". I was then beaten with portion of a webb belt which contained buckles, and was told to run along the corridor. I did so and was ordered into a cell where I remained all night without food or bed clothes of any kind.

In the morning I demanded my clothing but was refused, in the presence of the Chaplain (Rev. Fr. Meade, C.C., Ennis) to allow my clothes to be returned without his (the Sergt Major's) permission. Later that day however I got my clothing back.

I remained in Ennis Jail for eight weeks and was then sent to Limerick Barracks. As a result of the treatment I received on the night of my arrest I was under medical treatment for the greater part of the time. The Military authorities at Limerick sent for a specialist from Corkand [sic] he in consultation with Dr. Fogarty of Limerick ordered my release for medical treatment. I was released on Parole from Limerick Barracks on March 3rd. A fortnight afterwards I came to Dublin and have since been undergoing dieretic treatment at the convalescent home Linden, Blackrock.

During my detention in Ennis Jail a number of cases of ill treatment of prisoners far worse than my own came unde [sic] my notice.[23]

The Scots were clearly frustrated that the information they wanted about the Lendrum ambush was not forthcoming, despite their efforts to force it from Mac and Shanahan.

On the day after the two had been killed, eleven lorryloads of military poured into Doonbeg village. All of the men, married and single, were taken and lined up outside Mrs McGrath's house, where they were saved from worse treatment by the intervention of an officer.

"We had a sorrowful Christmas Day here," wrote a Doonbeg mother in a letter to her son in the United States, "Willie Shanahan and Michael McNamara were taken by the Black and Tans and shot dead."[24]

The brutal killing of Mac and Shanahan merited few column inches in the newspapers of the day, but their refusal, in the face of frightful torture to divulge the names of those involved in the Lendrum affair, earned them a special place in the hearts of many and in the memory of one – Brenton Haliburton Ashmore.

In 1984, they were honoured locally, when Doonbeg's GAA Club named their new football grounds Shanahan McNamara Memorial Park.

Some time later, Shanahan's sister May, a teacher, was returning to England following a visit to her parents at Doughmore. She found herself sharing a train carriage with some soldiers of the 2nd Battalion, Royal Scots, who were reminiscing about the time they spent in Ennis.

Suddenly, the conversation came around to the killing of Willie Shanahan and how one of them had gotten his good leather boots.

"That was my brother," May interrupted, "which of you shot him?"

There was no response, the soldiers being shocked into silence.[25]

On the recommendation of the Compensation (personal Injuries) Committee, a grant of £300 was paid to the McNamara family in respect of the loss of Michael McNamara. His sister Tess was awarded £250 of this and £50 went to his brother Arthur. An additional gratuity of £60 was awarded to Tess under the Army Pensions Act, 1923.[26]

Shanahan's parents were awarded £200 under the Criminal Injuries Act 1919 and 1920.[27]

# Trench warfare

In mid-1920, British forces were stationed at a number of key locations in the West Clare Brigade area.

In Quilty and Kilrush, there were a number of Coastguard Marines, who were not regarded as particularly hostile. Kilkee had an RIC Barracks and a detachment of Coastguards. Both Kilrush and Kilmihil had RIC stations and military barracks that were manned by soldiers. There was also a military detachment at Kilmore House and an RIC station at Kildysart.

When Crown forces ventured out they did so with caution, since roads were regularly made impassable by rebels, using a variety of means, the most common of which was trenching.

This involved the cutting of a trench across a road, work usually carried out under cover of darkness using picks, shovels and spades. The trench was then camouflaged using a fine netting that was covered with straw and gravel in such a way as to make it indistinguishable from the road.[1]

Trees were also felled across roads and obstacles such as old farm machinery was strategically placed near bends, allowing for little reaction time on the part of the driver.

When a police or military vehicle drove into a trench, it could take some time to get it out.

On 25 April 1921, a quick-thinking driver saved one party of Royal Scots soldiers on their way from Ennis to Kilrush. By the time he spotted the trench, which was 8ft long and 6ft deep, it was too late to stop, so he accelerated in an attempt to jump it. Five of the occupants were injured, some of them being thrown from the car.

When he awarded compensation to all five at Kilrush Quarter Sessions, Judge Bodkin noted that the soldiers were lucky to have sustained their injuries in 'this war'. Had they gotten a blow on the nose in 'the other war' there would be no compensation.[2]

Invariably, locals were rounded up and forced to fill in the trenches at gunpoint, but the IRA would reopen them that night. Once, when soldiers encountered a trenched road that had been dug by Joe Daly in Kilmurry, they ordered Mullagh curate and OC of the 4th Battalion, Fr Michael McKenna, to fill it in. McKenna refused, but he was held in a two-hour downpour while the soldiers filled it in.[3]

The cutting of trenches could cause considerable inconvenience to local farmers as well as to military and police. Farmers were obliged to use circuitous routes through fields or via boreens to draw home cartloads of turf from the bog or hay from the meadow. But even when alternative routes were unavailable the filling of trenches was strictly forbidden.[4]

Two Knockerra farmers filled in a trench (an offence that warranted a court appearance) so that they could draw farmyard manure using horses and carts. They were duly accompanied to a Sinn Féin court in Darragh where the judge was none other than Matthew Bermingham, in whose family quarry the men had worked. To the embarrassment of their escort, the pair shook hands and struck up a friendly conversation with Bermingham, who let them off lightly.[5]

≁

Cooraclare man Patrick Falsey was not so lucky.

During the first week of February 1921, a number of local Volunteers had trenched the road at various locations near the home of the Falsey family of Cooraclare. Michael Falsey's farm was in two parts, the family home and grassland being separate from the part which was comprised of tillage.

On 11 February, his 20-year-old son, Patrick, was working in the tillage garden to prepare it for sowing and was soon going to need to cart manure to it from the home section, but one of the trenches prevented this. That evening, when neighbouring farmers John Marrinan and Matt Honan found themselves in the same predicament, they asked Patrick to help them to fill in part of the trench.

The men had been filling it in for about an hour when word reached some local Volunteers who were staying in a nearby safe house. Angry that their trenching work was being undone, they fired seven or eight shots, presumably as a warning. The filling party ran for cover but when Michael Falsey turned

| C | Locality. | Date of Incident. | C.R. Number. | Date. | Div. Number. | Bde. Number. | Unit Number. |
|---|---|---|---|---|---|---|---|
| | CLARE | | 2/41158 | 9.3.21 | Signal message no: 7826 dated 9.3.21 | | |

| Civilians Involved. | PRECIS OF REPORT. |
|---|---|
| 1 | Road cutting in Clare, Killaloe and in |
| 2 | several areas. Consequent danger of police |
| 3 | being cut off. Compelled to requisition |
| 4 | bicycles as means of transport; motor |
| 5 | transport at present useless. |
| 6 | |
| 7 | |
| 8 | |
| 9 | |
| 10 | |
| 11 | |
| 12 | |

| Casualties. | K. | W. | M. | Total |
|---|---|---|---|---|
| Officers ... | | | | |
| O.R.s ... | | | | |
| Police ... | | | | |
| Civilians ... | | | | |
| Men | | | | |
| Women | | | | |

For particulars of Court of Inquiry see Reverse.

Army Incident Report, 9 March 1921.
Having driven the RIC to the safety of larger towns, the IRA's widespread trenching of roads greatly limited vehicular movement throughout the county.
*(Source: NAUK, WO 35, ©NAUK)*

to see if his son was following him, he was nowhere to be seen. When he retraced his steps he found Patrick lying the road with a bullet wound on his left side.

Patrick was anointed by Fr Hehir before he was stretchered on a door to his home, where he died at 3.00am.[6]

A military Court of Inquiry found that Patrick Falsey died from shock and haemorrhage from a bullet wound in the chest that was inflicted by a person unknown and that that person was guilty of wilful murder.[7]

His father Michael later claimed £3000 in compensation for the loss of his son.[8] He was awarded just over £700 on 4 April 1921, which was finally approved and paid in September 1924.[9]

The shooting of Patrick Falsey was widely condemned throughout west Clare. Brigade OC Seán Liddy ordered that a Court of Inquiry be held to investigate the circumstances of the tragic event and Martin Chambers was given the task of presiding over it.

The court, which was opened in Cooraclare, had just begun taking evidence from two IRA officers when scouts announced that Crown forces were on their way. Chambers dismissed the court and it never re-convened.[10]

~

In September 1921, a racehorse owner named T H O'Gorman was driven through the windscreen of his car when it drove into a trench at Johnston's Hill, Quilty.

The car was written off and O'Gorman and his passenger were reported to have lost large quantities of blood. Subsequently, the Volunteers filled in the trench.[11]

The early months of 1921 saw a veritable epidemic of road-cutting that served to contain police and military and safeguard those who were on the run.

According to one account, the enemy resorted to indiscriminate shooting when they failed to round up men to fill in trenches. They began to carry wooden planks, which they would use to bridge the trenches, only to find that the width of the trenches was doubled or even trebled.[12]

By mid-April, with the towns of Kilkee, Kilrush and Miltown Malbay practically isolated by a combination of trench-cutting and the destruction of bridges, police and military patience ran out.[13]

On 23 April 1921, the day after the Kilrush raid that ended the life of Sergeant John McFadden, they surrounded the town and rounded up all of the men in Bank Square before marching them under guard to fill the many trenches that had been dug that week.

Although this exercise was repeated in Quilty, Mullagh and Kilmurry, many of the trenches were reopened that same night.[14]

# Secret Murder

By early 1921, martial law had been extended to Clare. A further proclamation was issued by General Macready, General Commander of the British Forces in Ireland.

Under this proclamation, offences such as possession of arms and ammunition, possession of military uniforms and harbouring of rebels would be punishable by sentences ranging from penal servitude to death.[1]

The composition of police stations in west Clare had undergone dramatic change since the previous year. Following the closure during 1919 of barracks at Doonbeg, Mullagh, Cooraclare, Quilty and Labasheeda, 1920 had seen further losses at Carrigaholt, Kilmore, Knock and Kilmihil.

By January 1921, the number of RIC stations in the West Clare Brigade area had been reduced to four – Kilrush, Kilkee, Kildysart and Miltown Malbay.

Also, during 1920, the number of regular police constables in the area had dropped from 69 to 32 and the deficit had been addressed by the introduction of 37 Black and Tans (see Appendices 1 and 2). These forces were later augmented by a number of Auxiliaries, who were drafted in to Kilkee following the Lendrum killing.[2]

But, despite the high rate of attrition in the Constabulary, a number of hardy annuals remained and among them was Kilkee-based 'Fite Jinnet',

Constable Michael Monaghan, who was rewarded for his loyalty with promotion to the rank of sergeant.[3]

Monaghan's new role brought new challenges, one of which was the management of an undisciplined cohort of Tans. Once, during a raid on the home of Michael McNamara of Tullaroe (possibly during the search for his Mountrivers-based namesake), some Black and Tans shot the family's dog and burst in the door. They smashed a picture of the Sacred Heart before dragging McNamara and neighbour Jack Lardner from the house.

The 'Fite Jinnet' was reputed to have interceded with the Tans to save them from being shot, pleading that both men had young children.[4] He himself, together with Constables Thomas Kelly and John O'Keefe, had allegedly been targeted for assassination by the IRA after they had arrested Michael Roche from Doonaha on 12 April 1921. Roche was subsequently interned in Spike Island Prison.[5]

On 7 April 1921 the *Irish Times* and *Cork Examiner* carried a report from Dublin Castle on the killing of Tom Shannon, a respected west Clare farmer. These reports stated that Shannon, who had served as a magistrate in the popular Sinn Féin Courts, had attempted to distance himself from Sinn Féin when he found himself in disagreement with court methods.

Furthermore, Dublin Castle claimed that he had refused to pay local Sinn Féin rates – the inference being that the killing had been carried out by fellow Republicans.[6] The report was an exercise in propaganda that remained unchallenged for almost 100 years.

Forty-year-old Tom Shannon farmed a substantial holding at Moyasta where he lived on the side of the public road with his wife Bridget. On Sunday night 13 March 1921, after he had cleaned some mangolds in the kitchen, he took a lighted lantern and went outside to the cabin to tend to his cows.

Bridget was feeling unwell, so she undressed and went to bed. At about 9.30pm she heard the dog barking and the footsteps of what she believed to be two men passing through the stone stile in the low parapet wall that ran parallel to the road. She did not answer the subsequent knocking on the front door but it started again when Tom returned to the house. His repeated calls for his visitors to identify themselves were met with demands that he open the door.

The voice from outside asked, "Are you Mr. Shannon?"

He answered, "Yes", and was again ordered to open the door.

Finally, holding the lantern in one hand, he undid the bolt with the other.

With the words, "You'll open the door now", his assailant aimed a revolver at his neck and fired.

The bullet entered just above the left collar bone and exited at the level of the seventh vertebrae on the right of Shannon's spine.

Bridget found her husband lying on the floor at the door of the kitchen, against a bucket, into which his cap had fallen. She asked who had done this and her husband said that he didn't know. When she undid the band of his shirt she saw that he was bleeding profusely from the neck so she said an Act of Contrition, which Tom repeated.

Bridget ran for help to neighbour John Tubridy's house and he was joined by John Smith and John Keane. By this time, Tom was unconscious and he died some minutes later. It was a long night in the Shannon home and the neighbours, afraid to venture outside to call a priest, spent the night consoling Bridget.[7]

At 11.30am the next day an armed party of RIC and officers of the 2nd Battalion Royal Scots arrived at the house for the purpose of holding a Court of Inquiry in lieu of Inquest.

Under the Restoration of Order in Ireland Act, inquests had been replaced by Military Courts of Inquiry since August 1920. Previously, inquests had regularly returned verdicts of murder against Crown forces so the new system allowed for more control of the findings. Needless to say, there was great public mistrust of these courts and victims' relatives often refused to cooperate with them.

In some cases, where such courts might find it difficult to avoid incriminating British forces, the authorities simply didn't hold Military Inquiries at all, such as in the cases of those who were killed in the reprisals for the Rineen Ambush on 22 September 1920.[8] In other cases, the inquiry reports were simply deprived of detailed medical evidence, as in the cases of Willie Shanahan and Michael McNamara the previous December.[9]

In the case of Tom Shannon, the Inquiry was postponed for a week due to Bridget Shannon's illness. Significantly, at the re-convened Inquiry on Monday 21 March, one critical piece of evidence – that Tom's killers spoke with a strange accent – was not included in Bridget's signed statement. It may have been this omission by the court that prompted an approach to the *Clare Champion*, which published the correct version of events on 26 March 1921. This account brought to public knowledge the fact that the killers' accents were not local and it left the reader in no doubt that Tom, up to the time of his death, had been a proud and respected member of the Arbitration Courts.[10]

Predictably, the Court of Inquiry reported findings of murder by person or persons unknown. This cleared the way for Dublin Castle to peddle the story that Shannon had been killed by fellow Republicans and this version of events was subsequently repeated in a number of publications.[11]

While it is not possible at this time to determine who was responsible for the shooting of Tom Shannon, there is little doubt that he was shot by British forces.

On 25 May 1921, Bridget Shannon lodged a claim before Judge Bodkin at Ennis Quarter Sessions for £5000 in respect of the loss of her husband.[12] Bodkin informed the County Court that he had been prohibited by the military authorities from hearing cases where there were allegations that Crown forces had committed criminal damage.[13]

Any such allegations in this case, therefore, would at least delay (and possibly rule out) a compensation award in Bridget's favour. Cleverly, Counsel for Mrs Shannon declared that the applicant made no allegation against anybody, thereby clearing the way for the case to proceed. Throughout her evidence, Bridget Shannon was careful not to apportion blame, even though she had no doubt that Crown forces were responsible for her husband's death. She was awarded the sum of £3000 with £19.16s.3d in costs. The British Ministry of Finance honoured the decree, having agreed to accept full liability.[14]

Not for the first time Bodkin availed of the opportunity to point the finger at British forces when he stated that there was no evidence that Shannon had any quarrel with Sinn Féin and that there was only one conclusion any rational man could come to.[15]

～

Bill Haugh, Adjutant and OC ASU West Clare Brigade, believed that the deed was done by Black and Tans from Kilkee.[16] But the attribution of the Shannon assassination to the Black and Tans warrants caution, since the notorious hybrids were wrongly blamed for some of the most high profile killings of the period in west Clare. Many of these killings were in fact the hot-blooded and rather brutal work of Royal Scots soldiers, whose *modus operandi* differed from that of the Shannon killing.[17]

However, there can be little doubt that for one year beginning in June 1920 there existed in the RIC a policy of 'secret murder' that was sanctioned at the highest level of government. Evidence of this policy is found in a report by Brigadier-General Cecil Prescott-Decie, RIC Divisional Commissioner, to John Taylor, Assistant Under-Secretary at Dublin Castle which described a besieged police force where morale was so low that his men were '… very near throwing up the sponge'. Prescott-Decie continued:

I have been told the new policy and plan and I am satisfied, though I doubt its ultimate success in the main particular – the stamping out of terrorism by secret murder. I still am of the opinion that instant retaliation is the only course for this, and until it is stamped for good and all, the same situation is only likely to recur.

The 'secret murder' referred to by Prescott-Decie would be directed at prominent and well-respected people in the community as well as front line Republican activists.[18] Often, the victims were elected representatives and it was believed that targeting them would '... shock the general public into submission ...'[19]

Two such killings took place in Limerick on the night of 6–7 March 1921 – just a week before the shooting of Tom Shannon – when Mayor Seoirse Clancy and former mayor Michael O'Callaghan were assassinated in their homes in what would become known as the Curfew Murders. The circumstances of the shooting of Tom Shannon were remarkably similar to the shooting of the mayors.

In each of the three cases, the assassins struck at night and announced their presence by loud knocking on the front door, after which they ascertained the identity of their victims. The killers spoke with distinctive accents and all three victims were shot in the hallway of their homes. When Clancy refused to go outside with the raiders the man who shot him said, "Then take this". Shannon's reluctance to open the door was met with "You'll open the door now" just before he was shot.

All victims were highly respected members of the community, having been elected to positions of honour. Finally and in typical fashion, Dublin Castle inferred that all three were shot as a consequence of local disputes.

It is likely that Clancy and O'Callaghan were shot and killed by a gang of Auxiliary cadets, led by one George Montague Nathan, who were billeted at the nearby Cruises Hotel.[20] And, while it may not be inferred that the same gang were responsible for Shannon's death, the similarities in the circumstances of the outrages lend some considerable weight to the theory that Shannon, like Clancy and O'Callaghan one week before, was a victim of RIC-sponsored 'secret murder' as described by Prescott-Decie and that members of either the Auxiliary Division or the Black and Tans were responsible.

Locally, it was believed by some that the Shannon shooting was in retaliation for the killing of Kilkee-based Alan Lendrum, Resident Magistrate in the British court system, following an ambush at Caherfeenick on 22 September 1920.[21] By coincidence, Shannon had appeared before Lendrum at Kilkee Petty Sessions Court on 3 September 1920 on a charge of having an unlighted vehicle on the public road during the hours of darkness.[22]

Lendrum's court sittings had been quite poorly attended due to the popularity and success of the recently-formed Sinn Féin Arbitration Courts. There was, and is, general acknowledgement that there was no intention to kill Lendrum who, like Shannon, had been well-liked in the area.

Perspectives on the arbitrary nature of the Shannon killing (he was not even known to his assassins) were illuminated by a number of October 1947 newspaper reports of the death of P J Shanahan, the father of Willie Shanahan and a former west Clare Sinn Féin magistrate. These reports stated that early in 1921 the names of five local Sinn Féin magistrates were put up for lottery to be shot by British forces and Tom Shannon's name was drawn.[23]

Because the victims of the Limerick assassinations had held high office, the Curfew Murders dominated the headlines for some time, while reports of Shannon's killing commanded few column inches.

Dublin Castle propaganda about the killings was robustly refuted in the cases of Clancy and O'Callaghan but not in the case of Shannon. And, while the Limerick mayors are remembered in their native city and in the history books, the Moyasta magistrate has been largely forgotten in his native west Clare. The only monument to his memory, a simple granite slab, was erected over his grave in November 1953 by members of the 5th Battalion, West Clare Brigade IRA Memorial Committee which, in furtherance of national unity, honoured pre-Treaty, pro-Treaty and anti-Treaty comrades in simple graveside ceremonies.[24]

Tom Shannon was buried in Old Shanakyle Cemetery, Kilrush on Wednesday 16 March 1921.

# The siege of Kilrush

An attack on Kilrush that was carried out by a joint force of East and West Clare Volunteers on 22–23 April 1921 had been jointly planned by Seán Liddy, OC West Clare Brigade and Michael Brennan, OC East Clare Brigade.

The essential local knowledge, including details of patrol routes, military movements and timetables, was provided by Joseph McNamara, Intelligence Officer for Kilrush, Stephen Madigan, 1st Lieutenant Kilrush Company and Michael McMahon, Battalion Adjutant.[1]

Liddy had become somewhat disenchanted with the West Clare Brigade's failure to deliver any spectacular hit on Crown forces and he was anxious to emulate the achievements of similar brigade units throughout the country.[2]

The Brigade had experienced difficulty in procuring quality arms and ammunition and support from Headquarters had been somewhat limited because it was believed that adverse terrain would compromise any significant engagement with enemy forces. In particular, morale in the Flying Column was low and some of its members were being openly critical of leadership in the Brigade.[3]

Attacks on police and on police barracks had forced the RIC into the safety of the towns. There, the enemy remained largely unthreatened and were less and less inclined to venture out into the hostile countryside. When they did they travelled in convoy and the greatest threats were trenched roads and felled trees.[4]

On one famous occasion, a detachment of Royal Scots soldiers rounded a corner at speed in a charabanc, only to crash into and kill a cow that had been left grazing the long acre. Having informed the owner of the cow, the driver nursed his damaged vehicle back to Kilrush, where he struggled to explain the situation to an unsympathetic officer. In his distinctive Scottish accent, the driver began:

"You see sir, the cow was wonderin' on the road and ..."

"She was wonderin' alright", the officer interrupted, "she was wonderin' who allowed an idiot like you to drive a charabanc!"

～

The primary purpose of the Kilrush raid was to attack and disarm the nightly police patrol which was particularly brutal in its treatment of men who broke curfew.[5] The success of such engagements was determined more by the number of guns and ammunition that were appropriated than by the number of casualties that were inflicted.[6]

The movements of this patrol, numbering between twelve and 16, had been monitored and mapped nightly for a month by Joseph McNamara, Michael McMahon and Stephen Madigan.

It would depart the barracks at about 9.00pm, from where it would travel via Back Road to Henry Street and through Vandeleur Street.

Turning right on to The Glen, it would proceed along High Street before turning right again on to Burton Street and on straight to Market Square where it remained for some 15 minutes.

Next, it travelled down and back Moore Street, stopping for some time at Market Square before returning to the barracks at 11.00pm. The District Inspector would check periodically on the whereabouts of the patrol.[7]

Every night for the previous fortnight or three weeks, the patrol had stood around the Protestant Church chatting and smoking, having stacked their rifles in the adjacent square. They had been secretly monitored by Willie Donnelly from the upstairs window of his nearby home.[8] Stephen Madigan had meticulously recorded the routes that were travelled and the times that were taken at each of the routes' stages and all of the data were collated at a Brigade meeting. The plan was to attack the patrol on Moore Street.[9]

Brennan later claimed that a feint attack was planned on the RIC barracks on Toler Street. The police would surely send up Verey-light signals with a view to provoking a response from the various barracks.[10] Any attack on the RIC barracks or on the nightly patrol would undoubtedly draw out police and military in response and any emerging forces would be sitting ducks for strategically positioned and well-armed Volunteers.

In west Clare, the greatest concentration of police and military was in Kilrush. Here, there was a detachment of about 50 Royal Marines who were stationed at Cappa, somewhere in the region of 150 soldiers of the 2nd

The O'Donnell family of Tullycrine.
REAR FROM LEFT: Jim, Simon, Nora, Frank, Mary, Jack, Art.
FRONT FROM LEFT: Susan, Con, Dick, Mary (mother), Tom, Simon (father), Lizzie, Alice, Willie. Missing is Kathleen.
*(Courtesy Paul Markham)*

Battalion Royal Scots who lodged in the old Workhouse (on the Cooraclare Road on the northern edge of town) and about 50 police in the RIC barracks on Toler Street. All of the barracks were well fortified with sandbags, barbed wire and steel shutters.[11]

~

Brennan's Column, numbering about 25 men, assembled at Rineanna on the night of 21 April and crossed the river Fergus in two boats. They disembarked at Crovahan, near Kildysart, where they were met by guides from the West Clare Brigade.

They headed first for Kildysart, where they proposed to entice some police and Black and Tans onto the street. A couple of Volunteers, feigning drunkenness, paraded up and down the street outside the RIC barracks shouting rebel slogans and singing seditious ballads; they even threw stones and broke windows, but there was no response from inside.[12]

From there, the Column marched through the night, arriving at the home of Simon O'Donnell in Tullycrine at about 4.00am. There, Mrs O'Donnell had prepared a fine meal for them, after which they were billeted in local houses at Tullycrine and Knockerra. There they rested and planned the raid until about 5.00pm, when they set out for Kilrush.[13]

The united columns, armed with over 30 rifles as well as shotguns and revolvers, marched in pairs. Scouts had been positioned along the route and locals gathered by the roadside to witness the spectacle.[14] When they were about a mile from Kilrush, instructions were given and posts were allocated. Scouts from Kilrush Company led each squad to its position.

The Toler Street RIC barracks would be covered from the convent field; Toler Street itself from Bonnie Doon on Frances Street, the road to the Workhouse from Kelly's field on the Kilkee Road, Market Square from Patterson's Mills, the Marine Station from a suitable point at Cappa and Workhouse Road from the Cut Hill area.[15]

One Micho O'Brien had cut notches on the blade of his scythe, which he used to cut communication wires between Toler Street and the Workhouse.[16] Communication with Ennis would be disabled by the cutting of telegraph wires and most approach roads were trenched and bridges were made impassible by the Ballykett men.[17]

During the day, Intelligence Officer Mikie Reidy gave regular updates to Cumann na mBan member Susie Bermingham about the situation in the town and her brother Matthew made three visits to Tullycrine to update his comrades.[18]

On Friday night, 22 April, District Inspector Captain Walter May, Auxiliary Division, RIC, absented himself without leave from his post in Toler Street Barracks and got drunk in a local hotel. Sergeant Foley took charge of the curfew patrol.

On leaving the barracks and, unaware that two local scouts were monitoring their movements, he led his men in pairs north along Toler Street, right on to Back Road and onto the Ennis Road before swinging right again onto

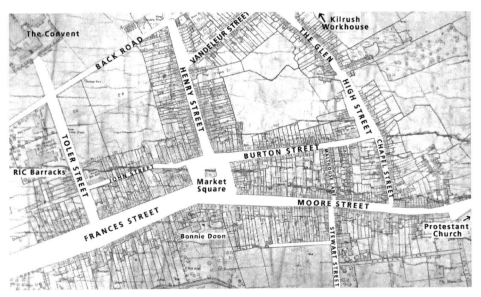

Kilrush Street map showing some of the main locations of events of 22 April 1921.
*(Adapted from Valuation Office Map of Kilrush 1895-1925 © Valuation Office)*

Vandeleur Street. Turning left at Henry Street, they continued on to Market Square, where they rested awhile. Then the sergeant, either taking advantage of May's indisposition, or sensing some impending danger, allowed his patrol to return to barracks via Frances Street without completing its route.[19]

Sergeant McFadden and Constable Fallon, armed with revolvers and in full uniform, left the barracks again at 10.15pm and went drinking first to Madigans and later to the pub of Denis Sheehan on Vandeleur Street.[20]

Constable Hopkins, a Black and Tan, had gone for a walk with a girl and by 11.15pm was having a drink in Crotty's pub at the Market Square end of Henry Street.

Meanwhile, Brennan had sent a party of about twelve men, led by Brigade Quartermaster Tom Marrinan, Brigade IO Paddy Clancy and Michael McMahon to secure the causeway to the Coastguard Station in Cappa in order to prevent marine reinforcements from entering the town.[21] They were joined by Jack McCormack and a man named Lynch from Monmore as well as two east Clare men.[22] They had come from the south of the town through the Vandeleur Wood.[23]

The ambush of the police patrol was to take place in Moore Street and Brennan and Bermingham had carefully selected and positioned three men on each of Ball Alley Lane, Malthouse Lane and Stewart Street and Jim Hannon had charge of six men in a nearby lane.[24]

Seán Liddy brought eight men to the rear of the Workhouse, while Bill Haugh and his men covered its front gate, which opened on to a long narrow lane with high walls on either side, at the end of which was Workhouse Cross, a T-junction whose horizontal boundary was a fence that offered perfect cover to Haugh's party.[25]

Haugh had made it clear that, in the event that soldiers emerged from the Workhouse, no firing would commence until they were within 20 yards and nobody was to fire before Haugh.

The strategy had two purposes. Foremost in Haugh's mind was a desire that no harm would come to a Royal Scots officer who, when Haugh's father's life was threatened during a raid at his house in Monmore, had ordered his men to 'unhand the old man'. Second, Haugh wanted to maximise the potential to secure arms and ammunition.[26]

Haugh's party included Martin Chambers and Miko Moroney (Monmore Co), Mike O'Dea (Tulla), Tom Martyn (OC 3rd Battalion), Jack Lynch, Stephen Haugh and John Haugh, as well as local guides Martie Mulqueen, Micho Tubridy and Bill Keating.

Pat Mulqueen and Mikie Bermingham were stationed at the back of the Workhouse. They were armed only with shovel handles, as the number of guns that were supplied by the Cooraclare contingent was fewer than anticipated.[27]

~

While McFadden and Fallon were relaxing in Sheehan's, Brennan and a party of four or five men made their way to Toler Street to implement stage one of their plan – an attack on the RIC barracks.

Their local guide was poorly informed, however, and he misdirected them to the Convent on Back Road at its junction with Toler Street.

As the men took up firing positions near the Convent gate at about 10.45pm, Private Ernest Sack, a Royal Scots soldier of English extraction, was making his way, unarmed, along Back Road on his way to the barracks. When Brennan's men challenged him from inside the boundary wall, Private Sack made a run for it, but they caught up with him at the corner and brought him into the field, where he was detained for about 20 minutes by a man he described as being six-foot-six in height. He was questioned at gunpoint about the RIC patrols and was told that they would blow his brains out if he didn't divulge what he knew, but he refused.

Just then, an armed military officer in civilian clothes was intercepted as he walked along outside the wall. He immediately opened fire and escaped via O'Dea's field. Amid the confusion, Sack again made a run for it under fire from his captors. He escaped, but not before he was struck by a revolver bullet in the shoulder and shotgun pellets in the back.[28]

Brennan's local guide's navigation skills were called into question when he directed Brennan to the Kilrush Convent, a large imposing building on Convent Road opposite the north end of Toler Street, and declared that it was the RIC Barracks.

A dubious Brennan asked again and his guide responded emphatically.

"There it is, straight forninst you."

A volley of shots was fired at the building, but the response from within, if any, was prayerful.

Brennan waited and watched, but there was no retaliation from the nuns. Following Brennan's repeated calls for clarity, the guide eventually realised his mistake ...

"God almighty, that's the Convent".[29]

Brennan's party went back down Toler Street, firing into the RIC barracks as they passed, and headed for Market Square.

When McFadden and Fallon heard the gunshots they immediately left Sheehan's and moved along Vandeleur Street, turned left onto Henry Street where they heard more shooting and proceeded in the direction of Market Square.[30] Had the pair turned right onto Henry Street, then left onto Back Road, it is likely that they would have reached the barracks without incident.

Constable Hopkins, who was still drinking in Crotty's, also heard gunfire and rushed out into the street where he met an unarmed Royal Marine named Clifton. The two crossed to the east side of Henry Street, where they met with McFadden and Fallon.

Having discussed the gunfire, they decided to return to the barracks.[31]

At the same time, Brennan and his men had made their way along Frances Street and when they reached the western side of the square they were saluted by the McFadden group standing in the shade of Ryan & Son's shop on the far side.

Brennan crossed alone to Market House, which was in the centre of the square and, holding his rifle across his left forearm, moved cautiously around it to get a better view of the group. Again, someone called to him in an Irish accent and Brennan crossed the street in their direction.

He initially mistook McFadden's outstretched hand as a gesture of friendship and only realised the danger when the sergeant moved from the shadow and the bright moonlight revealed the sergeant's stripes and the revolver in his hand.[32]

Brennan swung his rifle around and fired, shattering the joint of McFadden's right arm before racing for the cover of Market House. From there, he kept firing and ordered his men to do likewise, covering the western side of Market House.

Fallon and Hopkins returned fire and when he had emptied his revolver Fallon ran northward along Henry Street with Private Clifton and returned to the barracks via Convent Road. Hopkins and McFadden, pursued briefly by Tom Bentley and Joe Clancy, ran northward along the eastern side of Henry

LEFT: Sergeant John McFadden, RIC.
*(Courtesy The Royal Irish Constabulary Forum)*
MIDDLE: Seán Liddy, OC, West Clare Brigade.
*(Source: Lynch Family)*
RIGHT: Michael Brennan, OC, East Clare Brigade.
*(Source: IE MA BMH CD 075/6/7, Bureau of Military History Contemporary Documents, MA)*

Street, swung right onto a lane by Brew's and sheltered in a cabin, where they remained for about 20 minutes while Hopkins tended to McFadden's wound.

When they felt that it was safe they came back out to Henry Street and turned right, heading northward with the intention of returning to the barracks via Convent Road.

If McFadden's earlier choice of route to his barracks was unfortunate, this subsequent choice was disastrous. For Brennan, Tom McGrath, Joe Clancy and Matt Bermingham had already made their way up Henry Street on their way to the Workhouse.[33] As McFadden and Hopkins approached the Back Road junction, they found their route blocked by Brennan's men who ordered them to halt.

Thinking that they were military from the nearby Workhouse, McFadden approached the cordon and called out, "It's alright. We are police".

Brennan opened fire and McFadden fell. Calling on Tom McGrath and Joe Clancy to retrieve McFadden's gun, Brennan pursued Hopkins along Vandeleur Street towards The Glen, where the constable narrowly escaped by hiding under a cart until the coast was clear. Before Brennan and his men had a chance to regroup, firing broke out, probably at Workhouse Cross.[34]

There, Haugh and his men had been waiting for two hours when the military officer who had a narrow escape on Back Road returned to the Workhouse with news of what had happened. Presently, a detachment of soldiers marched through the front gate but, despite the clarity and strictness of Haugh's instructions, one trigger-happy volunteer opened fire almost immediately.[35]

The soldiers were able to retreat to the safety of the compound and only one of their number, Sergeant Clapperton, was injured.[36]

Haugh was livid at the wasting of such a golden opportunity to inflict casualties and to sequester guns and ammunition. Later that night he even went so far as to formally request Brennan's permission to shoot the offending Volunteer, whose inexperience was what saved him in the end.[37]

~

The marines at Cappa were regarded locally as less aggressive and less threatening than the police and military.

On their way to Cappa from Vandeleur's Wood, Micho McMahon and Jack McCormack spotted a uniformed and unarmed marine out walking with the daughter of a former British soldier.

"Hands up!" they called.

"All roight Paddy," came the response and he duly obliged.

The prisoners were marched with the group before a second marine and his belle were forced to join them further on. The girls were detained in the house of Paddy Moloney until the attackers withdrew and the marines were held in the corner of a field for the duration of the hostilities.

McMahon and his men covered the Coastguard Station from a hill that overlooked the building, where they waited until the firing began in the town. Then, as expected, the marines emerged through the gate, but had to make a hasty retreat when Jack McCormack opened fire on them.

For the remainder of the night, the attackers were sprayed with bullets from a machine gun that was positioned in a lofty turret. Every burst of fire from the coastguard building was returned, accompanied by the wild cheers of McMahon and his comrades, who kept the garrison at bay until the signal to withdraw was given.

The men then made their way to Bermingham's and the two marines were finally released unharmed at Ballykett Fair Green when their captors were well clear of the town.[38]

The pair were well treated and were fed misleading information about where the volunteers were coming from, where they were going and what mode of transport they were using.[39] At dawn, Susie Bermingham opened her door to six hungry men, who feasted from a keave of milk and a cake of bread which McMahon later described as one of the best meals he had ever eaten.[40]

~

Constable John Horan was one of a police patrol that was sent to the military barracks. As they returned at about 2.30am, Horan found the body of

Sergeant McFadden slumped on the road. He had been shot once in the arm, once in the throat, twice in the chest and once in the abdomen.[41]

It was not the 31-year-old sergeant's first brush with death since he was posted in Feakle on 17 May 1919. There, when still a constable, he was wounded and narrowly escaped when a police patrol was ambushed and two of his fellow constables were fatally injured on 7 October 1920.[42]

McFadden was later reported to have led Black and Tans to the homes of suspect Volunteers in an orgy of burning and had already begun to make a name for himself in Kilrush.[43]

On 8 October Brennan's mother Mary's home was burned and she lodged a claim for £7,000. During this incident, it was reported that police had presided over the burning alive of the Brennans' pig, which greatly infuriated the family and McFadden was linked anecdotally with the deed.[44]

When police later visited the Brennan home Brennan's sister threatened them with the same fate as Captain Lendrum RM, who was ambushed and killed in west Clare in September. The police report unashamedly described the burning as accidental.[45]

Three weeks after the Feakle ambush Constable McFadden was awarded the Constabulary Medal for gallantry and he was promoted to the rank of sergeant.

~

The Column withdrew in the early hours of 23 April and assembled at Jimmy Canny's of Derha, about a mile and a half outside the town in the Cooraclare direction, where Cumann na mBan member Cissie Canny fed them with milk and bread.[46]

Brennan and his men had been left stranded when their guide disappeared following the killing of McFadden, so they were unable to make their way to join Haugh and his party at the nearby Workhouse.[47] Having spent an hour wandering aimlessly within and without the town, they eventually met up with the rest of the Column, which travelled to Cree via Cooraclare, where food and billets had been organised.[48] In Cooraclare, Brennan bought one drink for each man before they continued onward to Cree.[49]

There, they rested in a number of houses that had been prepared for them on the east of the village. Then, following Sunday Mass, there was a memorable session of music, song and dance before it was time to move on. All approach roads to Cree had been trenched, preventing vehicular access to the area and the whole of C Company guarded the houses where the men were billeted through the night and for the following two days.[50]

Cappa resembled a 'bombed village' in the aftermath of the attack on the Marine outpost. The houses were riddled with bullets and residents had left their homes and fled across the fields. Elsewhere in the town there was panic and people got out of bed and sat by the fire through the night.

At 6.00pm the following evening, the remains of Sergeant McFadden were brought the short distance from the RIC Barracks to St Senan's Catholic Church, where the Rosary was recited and the killing of McFadden was condemned at all Sunday masses. Police ordered the suspension of all business and many of the town's residents fled to the safety of friends' and relatives' homes in fear of reprisals.[51]

Sergeant McFadden's failure to identify Brennan as a foe may have sealed his fate since Brennan's military style outfit rendered him practically indistinguishable from the Auxiliaries.[52] At 11.30am on Monday 26 April the slain sergeant's funeral left St Senan's Church for Kilrush Railway Station. There, the *Last Post* was sounded as the train moved off from the station.[53]

The burial was initially planned for Carrigart in northern Donegal, where he grew up. However, this was not possible as the approach roads had been trenched and the railway was closed. Interment was in Derry City Cemetery.[54]

As McFadden's funeral took place, Captain May, who had been posted to Kilrush as a Permanent Cadet on 10 November 1920 was being dismissed from the police force '… in consequence of his misconduct on the occasion of the recent attack on the police post of which he was in charge in the Martial Law area.'[55]

By this time, Haugh and Liddy were two of the most wanted men in west Clare. Haugh's parents' home in Monmore was regularly raided and his family terrorised.[56]

The killing of Sergeant McFadden, however, would provoke a stronger reaction. Ever since General Strickland had authorised, under martial law, the burning of several Midleton houses by way of reprisal for the occupants' failure to warn of an impending ambush, official reprisals in the form of burnings had become commonplace.[57]

On 26 April at 4.00pm, as Sergeant McFadden was being laid to rest, several lorry-loads of police and military pulled up outside Haugh's home, where they found only women and children. They immediately set about loading useful items onto their lorries, after which they sprinkled the house with petrol and placed a mine near the fireplace before exploding it. The house and outbuildings were completely destroyed.

The explosion sent a stone splinter flying through the air, knocking out one of the raiding soldiers. Haugh maintained that the soldier later died, but the claim is unsupported.

Earlier, Brigade Commandant Liddy's home was similarly destroyed.[58] Strickland's 6th Division later acknowledged responsibility for the reprisals.[59]

The occasion was not without its lighter moments.

Some neighbours had gathered in solidarity with the Haughs and were praying the rosary. Among them was Murty Keane, a local wit.

At the height of the blaze, a woman remarked to Keane, "It's a sad day for Monmore. That was always a warm house."

"That's true", said Murty, "but 'twas never as hot as it is now."[60]

There is a saying in west Clare 'If you want a pig to go esht (east), turn him wesht and if you want him to go wesht turn him esht'. In Haugh's haggart that day was a sow that was suckling her litter of 14 banbhs. Porky was not accustomed to taking direction from anybody, least of all soldiers, and when one of them attempted to steer her clear, she ran straight for him, forcing him onto the safety of a wall.

"A Sinn Féin pig!" he cried, "A Sinn Féin pig!"

Seeing her large family, he wondered, 'So 'ow many toimes woz she married then, eh?'[61]

The destruction of the Haugh home came at a time when Denis Haugh had entered an arrangement to purchase his holding of just over 40 acres at Monmore under the Land Purchase Acts for £301. Pending completion of the sale, Haugh was obliged to pay interest on the purchase price to the Land Commission at a rate of 3.5 percent, which fell due twice yearly in instalments of £5.5s.4d. Not surprisingly, he fell into arrears while he awaited compensation for his loss. In a letter to the Land Commission, he wrote:

> There was nothing saved but the clothes we were wearing, we would not be allowed to remove even our Sunday clothes or milk separator or dairy utensils, therefore I was obliged to dispose of my milch cows, and am since then with my wife and children living on the generosity of kind neighbours.[62]

Bill Haugh's family home in Monmore after it was bombed and burned by British military on 26 April 1921.
*(Courtesy Kathleen Haugh).*

The following night, a vain attempt was made to set Market House alight, but it was destroyed by fire in the early hours of Friday 29 April. An official army memo blamed Sinn Féiners, though there was little doubt that crown forces were responsible. At the time Kilrush Urban Council had been in the process of buying the building from the Vandeleur family.[63]

On 14 June 1921 the military also made attempts to destroy the Manchester Martyrs monument. Their efforts to demolish the railing succeeded only in bending it, but they managed to pull down the Maid of Erin statue from the top, breaking one of the arms.

Jack Moody and Thomas Culligan bundled the damaged statue into a wheelbarrow and transported it for safe keeping to the *seamlas* near Stewart Street. Following the troubles Judge Bodkin awarded the sum of £200 compensation to the monument's Trustees and the Maid was reinstated.[64]

~

An unusual compensation claim was lodged at Judge Matthias Bodkin's Kilrush Petty Sessions Court in January 1922.

Mary Anne Sheedy, a dressmaker and milliner of Feakle, sought £5,000 compensation for the loss of RIC Sergeant John McFadden, who was shot dead in Kilrush on the night of 22–23 April 1921.

Sheedy claimed that she had first met McFadden in June 1919, one month after he had been posted in the Clare village. By November, the friendship had blossomed and she deposed that Sergeant McFadden had given her an engagement ring in July 1920, together with a promise of marriage.

In November 1920, two men had visited her at her home to warn her against keeping company with an RIC officer and threatened to shoot them both if they married. McFadden was transferred to Kilrush in February 1921 and Ms Sheedy claimed to have received a letter from him the following month (which she had destroyed) declaring his intention to marry her. She told the court that on 13 September 1921, almost five months after McFadden's death, she gave birth to his child.[65]

Mary Anne Sheedy's account of the relationship was indeed plausible and she had given birth to a baby girl on that date at Bauroe, Feakle, whom she named Maureen Joan Sheedy.[66]

A number of McFadden's letters to Mary Anne were read out in court, but there was no evidence of his intent to marry her and Bodkin, with some reluctance, found himself obliged to dismiss the case.[67]

On 22 April 1922 a poignant notice was published in the In Memoriam section of the *Irish Independent* marking the first anniversary of Sergeant McFadden's death. It read:

In cherished memory of Sergt. John McFadden, R.I.C., shot at Kilrush, April 23 1921. On his soul, Sweet Jesus have mercy. Dear John, forgotten by some in this world you may be, but never forgotten a moment by me. Inserted by M.A.S.[68]

Similar notices were published on subsequent anniversaries, with wording such as 'In sad and ever-loving memory ... Fondly remembered by M.A.'[69]

Following medical assessment, Private Ernest Sack – the Royal Scots soldier questioned by Brennan's during the April attack on Kilrush – was deemed to be medically unfit and he was discharged from the army. At the Kilrush Quarter Sessions on 7 October 1921, he claimed compensation of £2,000.[70] He was later awarded £600 for his injuries.

Sergeant Clapperton, injured at the Workhouse, was awarded £1,000.[71]

∾

The April attack on Kilrush was something of an embarrassment to the forces that were garrisoned there, considering that a small column of men had held them virtually under siege for so long without meaningful response.

General Strickland reported that the attackers comprised 40 IRA men who were drafted in from Cork and Kerry, supported by the Cooraclare Battalion and the West Clare Flying Column. The Kilrush Volunteers, he claimed, had been compelled at bayonet point to act as guides.[72]

The Brigade men were no strangers to exaggeration either, having claimed that as many as eight of the enemy had been killed.[73] They also claimed that Strickland had embellished the report on the Kilrush raid by exaggerating the number of attackers to 400.[74]

As the Kilrush nuns gave prayerful thanks for their deliverance, Brennan's men took their leave of their west Clare comrades and began their march homeward singing the popular songs of the day.

Martin Chambers, dressed in a lounge suit and wearing a British military helmet, was overheard to lament the end of the relationship:

"Ye may well sing, but we have to creep into our holes and stay in them until ye come back again."[75]

Brennan would later lament the fact that the effort only yielded a sergeant's revolver and a few rounds of .45 ammunition.[76] Nonetheless, there was general agreement that the collaborative engagement had given a significant boost to morale in the West Clare Brigade.

As a direct result of the killing of Sergeant McFadden, from 6 May 1921 stricter military restrictions were enforced in the town and within a radius of two miles. The Military Governor for Clare under Martial Law declared a curfew between the hours of 10.00pm and 3.00am and fairs and markets were banned within a five mile radius of the town.[77]

The editors of the *Clare Champion* and the *Saturday Record* were given strict instructions by the military authorities about the insertion of advertisements and reports on behalf of third parties. Such advertisements and reports would have to be traceable to those who submitted them for publication and noncompliant editors would face summary military courts. Furthermore, editors were prohibited from reporting the movements of troops, civilian prisoners or internees before, during or after such movements took place.[78]

# Operation Frustration

In early January 1921, Martial Law was extended to Clare. From that time, any unauthorised person caught in possession of arms or explosives or wearing a uniform would be liable on conviction to the death penalty.

Men on the run came under pressure from a ruling that the death penalty could be applied in cases where safe harbour was given to armed insurgents.[1]

On Fair Day in Kilrush on 17 January, soldiers were sticking to the letter of the law when they spotted an elderly man from out of town wearing a pair of old army breeches. To the amusement of all, save himself, he was forced to remove the offending garment on the spot and had to go home in his drawers.[2]

The wanted man was still welcomed in the homes of west Clare, but householders became decidedly more nervous in his company. On arrival, he was quickly seated at the table while a family member kept watch outside. Food was produced without delay, but as soon as it was eaten the guest was sprinkled with holy water and was given a 'here's your hat and what's your hurry?' type of send-off.[3]

Once, while visiting a safe house in Monmore, Bill Haugh left his revolver on the kitchen table and placed his flat cap on top of it. When his rather jumpy hostess went to move the cap, the gun fell off the table and discharged a bullet that passed under her oxter.[4]

The dreaded Tans had a significant presence in west Clare at this time and by

January 1921, there were six in Kilrush, eight in Kilkee, six in Kildysart and 20 in Miltown Malbay.[5]

Patrick Reilly was one of a number of Kilkee-based Tans who '… had made themselves obnoxious during this period.' Reilly was singled out for assassination and a Brigade man was chosen do the deed. But the Kilkee men, indignant at any implication that they were less than fitted for the task, asked for time to plan the attack and the guns to expedite it. The Brigade supplied them with four rifles, but OC Seán Liddy abandoned the idea three weeks later, when the job hadn't been done.[6]

The brutal treatment of Mac and Shanahan signalled the determination of the military to establish control over west Clare by fair means or foul and a captured report from Brigade Commandant Liddy to Headquarters, dated 30 December 1920, indicated a diminution in grass-roots support for the armed struggle:

> The civil population, especially the farmers, in a great many districts, have become, in fact I may put it, hostile to the Volunteers. I find of late in a great many companies that the Volunteers themselves are rather inclined to fall in with the views of the old people to remain quiet. For instance, in one particular place where an ambush had been planned, the Volunteers in the vicinity refused to take any part whatever in it …[7]

Many local activists, however, told of operations that were carried out with limited resources and of others that were aborted due to lack of support from Brigade Headquarters.

In February 1921, Jim Talty and Matt Blake lay in wait on Lower O'Curry Street, Kilkee, for an RIC and Tan patrol. Scouts Jack McSweeney and Mick Blake were strategically positioned nearby on Circular Road to signal the patrol's approach. It was on the fifth night that Blake reported that two of the enemy were on their way.

The pair entered a pub on Lower O'Curry Street and when, 20 minutes later, a lone Tan came out onto the street, the men prepared to shoot … but a passing woman got in the line of fire, causing a delay of some vital seconds. Talty and Matt Blake, armed with double-barrelled shotguns, fired as soon as it was safe to do so, wounding the Tan in the arm. The Tan returned fire, but the men made it to the outskirts of the town before reinforcements arrived (see plan below).[8]

∼

Following the killing of Captain Lendrum, the increased presence of Auxiliaries and Black and Tans had brought terror to the streets of the main towns.

In Miltown Malbay on a dark November night despatch-rider Pat

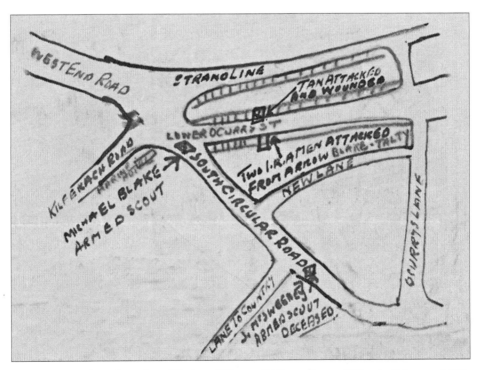

Map showing plan of attack on Black and Tans at O'Curry Street, Kilkee in February 1921.
*(Source: MA MSPC A24, Maps of West Clare Brigade, MSPC)*

O'Connor had just delivered a message from Ignatius O'Neill to a house in the town when he was surrounded by six 'Black and Tans'.

Having turned his pockets inside out, they ordered the young lad to run. O'Connor refused, believing that he would become another 'shot while attempting to escape' statistic like the ones he was reading about in the newspapers every day. He was beaten and kicked instead before taking a blow to the head that cut through the leather band of his flat cap.

In Kilkee, the homes of Republicans and their sympathisers were subjected to raids of increasing intensity. In a possible bid to emulate the siege of Kilrush, a joint daylight attack on Kilkee RIC station was agreed and planned for 26 June 1921 by Commandant Jim Talty of the 5th Battalion and Brigade staff. Over 100 men were involved in scouting operations and trenches were cut on approach roads to the town.

The Brigade Flying Column would supply men with rifles and Talty's men would provide cover with shotguns and revolvers. On the appointed night, Talty and some of his most trusted men waited all night at the rendezvous point, but there was no show by the Column. A Brigade despatch later explained that the operation would have involved too much risk for the Column, as it would have been easy for the Kilrush military to surround the area.

The decision led to a quarrel that must surely have led to a split were it not for the intervention of the Truce.

Though they were frustrated at the lack of Brigade support and the paucity of resources, Talty and his men were determined to use the resources they had to launch an offensive on Kilkee. On the chosen night they entered the town in three groups. Two of these groups sniped continuously at the RIC barracks, while the main party laid siege to a private house on O'Connell Street, where Black and Tans were entertained on a nightly basis.

Afterwards, the Volunteers smashed the windows of houses in the town that had dealings with RIC. The RIC and Tans responded in tit-for-tat fashion, by breaking all of the remaining windows the following morning.[9]

Talty, McSweeney and Matt Blake were greatly sought after at this time and the authorities spared no effort in trying to find them. When a cousin of Talty's died in Querrin, the wake was raided by two lorry-loads of military and Tans in the expectation that the three men would be in attendance:

> The enemy surrounded the house and rushed in. All those present were ordered to put their hands up and all were searched, asking each one if the wanted men were present.

> They entered the corpse room, searched under the bed, lifted the clothes off the corpse and the corpse itself and searched under the mattress. Next several of those present, including J. Talty's father, were taken out in the street and threatened them [*sic*: with] death if they did not divulge the whereabouts of the wanted men.[10]

~

When compared with counties like Cork and Kerry, west Clare was undoubtedly quieter during the War of Independence. Relatively few serious attempts were made to attack Crown forces, something that was the cause of widespread frustration to many Volunteers who had prepared diligently and engaged in significant levels of fund-raising in support of the armed struggle.

The Fifth Battalion area, incorporating companies at Carrigaholt, Kilbaha, Kilkee and Kilferagh and under the direction of OC Jim Talty, reported that all of its members were well-trained and ready for combat, but that they simply did not have the weaponry.

> A supply of arms and ammunition was now the only thing needed. The Battalion was badly in need of such supplies. At this time an arms levy collection was put into operation in conjunction with other Battalions of the Brigade and large sums of money that were collected and forwarded to G.H.Q. to get in return a supply of Rifles, Revolvers, Ammunition etc. never were supplied thus handicapping the officers and men of the 5th Battalion

who were ready if armed properly to launch attacks against the enemy.[11]

In fact, not only were the men of the west deprived of the luxury of additional guns, but they were apt to lose the ones they had.

At a time when the Battalion was 'pitifully short of weapons', David Conroy had managed to purchase a German automatic pistol and 50 rounds of ammunition from a returning soldier. Conroy's great mistake was to show off his prized acquisition to Micheal Brennan, who was visiting the area. Brennan took a shine to the firearm and declared that he had identified a greater need for it. It was the last that Conroy would see of it.[12]

In the 3rd Battalion area, there were many instances of ambushes that were prepared for police and military that failed to materialise either when the intended target didn't travel or when Brigade Headquarters called them off.

On or about 18 June 1918, after Brigade Headquarters had issued a directive that RIC patrols were to be attacked in west Clare, Martin Chambers had planned an ambush on four RIC men from Doonbeg Barracks. His ambush party were armed with shotguns and conscription pikes.

At the eleventh hour (both literally and metaphorically), T V Honan of Ennis and Christy McCarthy, OC of the 4th Battalion, visited Conor Whelan's house in Shragh with orders to abort the attack.[13]

On 15 August 1920 Martin Chambers and Bill Haugh had planned to ambush a lorry carrying twelve soldiers at McGrath's Cross, Moyasta. They gathered a party of 40 men, armed with nine Lee-Enfield rifles, five revolvers and double-barrelled shotguns.

Having attended Mass that morning in Monmore Church, they were finalising their plan of action when Jack Hassett arrived with a despatch from Brigade OC Seán Liddy. Liddy was not in favour of going ahead with the ambush and he would hold Chambers personally responsible if it did.

Later, Liddy explained that '... there was not enough rifles to cover off the retreat.' Chambers called off the ambush, but he was greatly frustrated, believing that the planned the operation had every chance of success.[14]

In mid-November 1920 four men, travelling in a car, asked Monmore IRA man Tom Lynch for directions to Kilkee. Lynch, believing them to be Black and Tans, tipped off his company captain, Martin Chambers, who quickly rounded up seven men, including Bill Haugh, with a view to interrupting the Tans' return journey at Monmore.

It was well after dark when the sound of a motor car was heard approaching from the Doonbeg direction. As soon as it came into view Haugh fired and the others followed suit. When they heard a woman's screams they knew that they had made a big mistake.

Kilkee hackney-man Willie Hynes was driving a dairy instructress named Gallagher who worked in a creamery. The pair had a fortunate escape, though the car was peppered with gunshot and the petrol tank was holed.[15]

Towards the end of 1920 Haugh's home in Monmore was regularly raided by Kilrush troops. On a number of nights in December, Martin Chambers and about 20 men armed with shotguns lay in wait for them at Higgins's Hill, about a mile and a half outside the town.[16]

After Moyasta Bridge was blown up on 2 July 1921, motor travel between Kilrush and Kilkee was only possible via the nearby shoreline at low tide.

On one occasion, ten RIC members from Kilkee barracks travelled by train to Ennis to give evidence at a Quarter Sessions Malicious Injuries hearing. Realising that the police would be prime targets for a few pot shots on the return journey, Martin Chambers organised his men for a sniping operation.

When the train came along, however, there was no sign of the police. As Chambers and his party were disbanding, they spotted nine military lorries, accompanied by an armoured car, escorting their targets westward via the shore.[17]

Members of the 5th Battalion claimed that they could have played a far more active role if support had been forthcoming from the Brigade. And their frustration was shared by members of the 4th Battalion, under the leadership of Battalion Commandant Christy McCarthy from Cloonlaheen.

Both Battalions had repeatedly sought sanction for large-scale engagements and the resources to expedite them. But the repeated response from Headquarters was that these areas were unsuited to such operations.[18]

In exasperation, McCarthy took the decision to relocate to the East Clare Brigade area.[19] On 15 June 1921, he was one of a party of eight members of an East Clare Brigade active service unit who set out to raid a mail train at Meelick, between Longpavement and Cratloe stations.

When a scout relayed the message that there were military on the train, the OC of the 2nd Battalion, John McCormack, decided to abort the mission. Instead, he decided to cut some telephone lines and sent a cover party of six riflemen to a nearby hill. McCarthy was to take charge of the cover party, but he and Michael Gleeson opted instead to cover the men who were cutting the wires. However, as the train passed, McCormack fired a shot at a soldier who was looking out the window and the main outposts interpreted this as the signal to disperse.

Meanwhile, when the train reached Cratloe station, Lieutenant Alexander Gordon, the Royal Scots officer in charge of the military on the train detrained the passengers. He then ordered the driver to reverse the train to Meelick, shutting down the steam as it neared the spot where the men were cutting the wires.

By the time the men realised that the train was coming, it was almost upon them. McCarthy and Gleeson were hotly pursued. McCarthy was wounded in an early exchange and Gleeson, who was by then in a position of comparative safety, returned to help him. Gleeson was shot down and McCarthy was pursued by Gordon, who gained on him after nearly a mile before finishing him off. McCarthy's body was identified on the following day by Fr John Considine, who had served as a curate in Mullagh parish. [20]

At about 10.00pm on 26 May 1921, two Kildysart-based Black and Tan constables, Edgar Budd and Robert Irvine, were cycling to Kildysart from Ennis, where they had spent a day's leave.

Kildysart men John Kelly, Seán McNamara and Michael McMahon from the local B Company, West Clare Brigade, were lying in wait at Cooga, about two miles on the Ennis side of Kildysart[21].

Captain Martin Chambers, Monmore Company, in army uniform.
*(Courtesy Berna Kirwan)*

Budd's ear was blown off when he was shot in the temple and he died instantly. Irvine was slightly injured, but managed to flee across the fields. He was hotly pursued by one of the ambush party and only escaped as a result of a malfunctioning IRA shotgun cartridge. While all accounts agreed that the two men were in mufti, there were conflicting reports about whether Budd and Irvine were armed[22].

On 2 June, by way of reprisal, the homes of Mary McNamara of Ardnagla, Ballynacally and Mrs Cusack of Paradise Hill were burned. Furniture and hay were burned at John Clancy's of Glencunnane and damage was done to the property of John Cusack of Ballynacally.[23]

In the weeks running up to the Truce, there were few military engagements of any significance on either side. The British military conducted one final sweep of the bogs around Monmore in June 1921 in an effort to round up wanted men like Bill Haugh, who had evaded them for so long.

As many as 300 arrived by train and set about combing the bogs in search of dugouts.

The same Bill Haugh was attending a meeting miles away in Scropul.[24]

# 'Traitors and Cranks'

Fr Pat Gaynor famously wrote that west Clare was reeking with spies.

His parish priest, Fr Glynn, had been informed by a Miltown Malbay RIC sergeant that the sergeant had '… a pile of reports a foot high' that had been sent in by Gaynor's own parishioners. The curate had even come into possession of a police telegram in cipher that had been intercepted en route from Ennis to Ennistymon which read 'Information received Sinn Féin court being held in Mullagh Tuesday time unknown.'

On the due date, Crown forces had raided every house in the Mullagh area but nothing was found.[1]

Gaynor even attributed the constant attention he received from the military to '… the reports against us which were sent to them by traitors and cranks among our own people in west Clare.'[2]

In Kilkee during the summer of 1920, John Joe Keane's Arcade was boycotted after he was suspected of breaking windows in the town, telling stories to the police and even sleeping in the RIC barracks. Indignant at these charges and concerned that business at his family's drapery and flour and meal store would suffer during the coming holiday season, Keane wrote to the Editor of the *Saturday Record*:

I deny that I ever did those acts, that I ever knew they were to be done, or that

I know who did them. I am ready and willing to face my maker now as I write this letter, or at any future time ...[3]

Keane sang a very different song before the Irish Grants Committee in February 1927, when he openly acknowledged his family's friendship and support for the British Police Forces all through the period of the troubles. This, he claimed, coupled with the fact that his sister was married to an RIC policeman, resulted in harassment and boycott that had cost him £4,958. Keane claimed that the family's premises were frequently fired into and that he and his father were tried on a charge of supporting the RIC by a Republican Military Court on 16 and 20 September 1921.

Between the months of May and December 1921, twelve of the Keane's cows had to be milked onto the ground when the townspeople refused to buy milk from them. Interestingly, Keane included one Rev Charlie Culligan CC among his referees.[4]

Patrick Keane, of 49 Albert Road in Kilkee, was a self-declared loyalist who was 'on terms of the most intimate friendship' with the local RIC. In May 1921 his shop windows had been broken, his house had been fired into and his two daughters had to be housed in Limerick and Cork for the summer as they were afraid to sleep in the family home. He claimed too that visitors had boycotted his wife's boarding house during the summer season. His long-held position as school attendance officer had been taken over by Sinn Féin.

He also maintained that he had been a newspaper correspondent for some Dublin, Cork, Limerick and Clare newspapers, but that he couldn't forward reports of local happenings for fear of being shot.[5]

On 27 September 1920, two masked men held up a postman between Miltown Malbay and Dunsallagh and demanded to see the 'Coor [sic: Coore] letters.'

Having gone through the bag, the men took one letter that was addressed to Miss MB Walsh in the city of London. Miss Walsh was believed to be a daughter of Michael Walsh of Caherogan and the motive was '... to seize letters addressed to London where local Sinn Féiners believe there is a secret agency of information for Government.'[6]

British forces didn't have to go to London for information, however, as Christy McCarthy was to find out.

Following his period of incarceration in Belfast Gaol, McCarthy continued from where he left off in the Republican movement and was forced to go on the run. British forces thought that they were about to seize McCarthy after they arranged for a man from Miltown Malbay to approach him after Mass in Mullagh and to identify him by placing a hand on his shoulder.

But locals got word of this plan. As they left the church a number of them crowded around the informer and ushered him around the side of the church and down through the graveyard.[7]

When two Brigade officers stopped off at George Comerford's pub in Doonbeg to ask for directions, they confided in him that they were on their way to deal with a suspected informer named Tony who lived between Doonbeg and Doonmore and was alleged to have been passing written messages to the RIC in Kilrush. Realising that his visitors had the wrong man, Comerford offered to accompany them to the home of the accused.

On arrival at the man's home, George took the initiative.

"Tony," he began, "these men are from the West Clare Brigade and they are investigating reports that you have been giving information by letter to the peelers in Kilrush."

Tony's response brought the affair to a speedy conclusion.

"Now George, you and I know very well that this can't be true, since I can neither read nor write."[8]

Kilrush man Mikie Reidy was the trustworthy Intelligence Officer in the town. Being the only Volunteer who drank, he could visit any pub without raising suspicion, so the local Volunteers ensured that he would have drink money whenever they needed information.

The Kilrush Volunteers took a dim view of Charlie Dunleavy, an ex-British soldier, buying potatoes for the Marines in Cappa and some had suspected him of spying. Mikie was given the task of finding Dunleavy and he was arrested at John Street, near Looney's, one night and was brought first to Bonnie Doon. After he had shown some reluctance to go any farther Jerry Crowley fired some shots in the air by means of persuasion.

Dunleavy was brought to Glenmore, where he was detained pending trial. There, his hostess (the mother of a Volunteer) discovered that Dunleavy was quite an accomplished cook. He was eventually released after being given some stern warnings.

~

The finger of suspicion was pointed at many throughout the first half of 1921. Subsequent to the brutal killing of Mac and Shanahan on 22 December 1920 it was clear that very specific information had been received from one or, more likely, a number of sources. Following the shooting of Alan Lendrum, police and military began to raid the home of Willie Shanahan after they had received information that he had been involved. The nature and the detail of that information was later revealed by ex-RIC Sergeant Laurence Nolan, who had been stationed at Doonbeg and Miltown Malbay during the period of the troubles:

> … an unsigned letter was written to Captain Woods at Milltown-Malbay [sic] denouncing Willie Shanahan and Michael Macnamara [sic] and another local man who was known locally as 'Sheldrake' Kelly as the murderers of Captain Lendrum. That letter was given to Head-Constable Hunt by Captain Woods, and Head-Constable Hunt showed it to me and asked my opinion on it. Both he and I were perfectly satisfied that it was the work of some girl and a badly educated girl at that. It was a very badly written letter but it was done well enough to convey all that it was intended to convey by way of information for the British forces. Captain Woods who was a personal friend of Captain Lendrum was furious at the contents of the letter. Soon after Willie Shanahan and Michael

Macnamara [*sic*] were arrested, but 'Sheldrake' Kelly was not found.[9]

In fact, John 'Sheldrake' Kelly had a lucky escape when Crown forces came to his farm at Cloonagarnaun to arrest him. He hid in a drain after a female visitor to his home spotted police or military lorries on the road. Kelly's suitors stuck pikes and bayonets into his hay and knocked his rick of turf in their search for him.[10]

When Crown forces raided an Arbitration Court sitting in Colunagarnaun on 6 December 1920, they were on the trail of wanted men and Shanahan and McNamara were at the top of their list. From the manner of the approach of the military lorries, it was clear that they knew exactly where they were going, despite the remoteness and inaccessibility of the location. Shanahan barely escaped with the court papers, but the raid cost local farmer Tom Curtin his life.

Fr Gaynor believed that Christy Kelly was responsible for the betrayal and, by implication, the death of Tom Curtin.[11] Gaynor later wrote:

> I should say, without qualms of conscience, that of those who knew in advance where the court would sit, Christy Kelly was by far the most likely person to have sent information to the police; if he did so, he has the murder of Mr Curtin on his mean and miserable soul.[12]

But Brigade headquarters had identified another suspect, about whom Bill Haugh wrote:

> Towards the end of this month (December 1920), the first enemy intelligence agent was executed. To him was traced the betrayal of the second Burrane effort, also that of the Sinn Féin Court at Clohanes [*sic*] in September [*sic*].[13]

Haugh was referring to 52-year-old Joe Greene from Toonavoher, near Knock. Greene, originally from Kilmacduane and, having spent some time in the US, married and settled in Toonavoher where he ran a farm. When

Greene and his wife fell out, the IRA became involved and they put him out of the house before appointing two Volunteers to run the farm. Greene was incensed and he took to spying on the IRA as well as burning hay belonging to the Mahonys, the Mescalls and the Duggans.[14]

At 8.30pm on Monday 3 January 1921, Greene, accompanied by his friend Paddy Synan from Churchtown, was sitting in his home by the fire reading a newspaper. A shot was fired through the window, striking him in the chest and killing him instantly. Synan, fearing for his life, tried to hide up the chimney, but was pulled down by two men whom he didn't know and told to get outside.[15]

There, he was held at gunpoint, before being sent back inside with a warning to remain there until the following morning. He left at 3.00am and informed Greene's brother John, who in turn alerted the police.[16] Kilrush Auxiliary DI Captain Walter May arrived at the house at 3.00pm the following day and found Greene stretched on his back on the floor. He had three large wounds and a number of smaller ones on the chest.[17]

Bill Haugh's Bureau of Military History Witness Statement is the only one that refers to the fact that two spies were eliminated in the West Clare Brigade area. Pádraig Ó Ruairc's detailed and well-researched register of suspected spies lists only Patrick Darcy for the west Clare area, while favouring the notion that Greene's assassination was the consequence of an agrarian dispute.[18] And newspaper reports of the shooting indicated that there was no political motive and that Greene was shot in connection with a land dispute.[19]

Indeed, Greene's assassination was the last of a series of actions relating to a land dispute that was triggered when he fell out with his wife. It had none of the hallmarks of an execution; there was no formal court-martial or questioning and the customary spy note was lacking.

Haugh's explanation for the unofficial nature of the execution was that the target was closely related to a number of Volunteer officers.[20]

The assertion that Greene was informing was given some extra weight by

Margaret Daly, (sister of Patrick Darcy who was himself to be shot as an informer in June 1921) in a letter she wrote to the Military Service Pensions Board in May 1947. Mrs Daly described a military raid on her mother's house during which she believed ammunition was planted in her brother's room. She wrote:

> I can place this raid as having taken place in the month of December (1920), because on the same day the military were accompanied by a local civilian named Joseph Greene who was shot as a spy a little time afterwards.[21]

Further support for the spy theory came from Haugh's 1924 application to the Pensions Board for a Certificate of Military Service, where his handwritten memo lists 'sniping spies' among his contributions to the struggle for independence in west Clare.[22]

The Court of Inquiry in lieu of Inquest into the death of Joe Greene was held at Kilrush on 14 January 1921. Since the body had been removed to Cooraclare for burial, there was no medical examination. Coincidentally, or perhaps not, Lieutenant Tuffield, who shot Tom Curtin at Cloonagarnaun on 6 December, was one of the members of the court. There was no medical evidence other than the opinion of Captain May that death would have been instantaneous due to the nature of the wounds. The court found that Greene died of shock and haemorrhage due to a gunshot wound in the chest.[23] The report concluded:

> The deceased was a farmer and a bad lot. The local Sinn Féiners had turned him out of his farm; left his wife there to look after the farm and put two Sinn Féinmen in to help her carry on. At a later date the deceased returned to his farm, beat the two men and kicked them out and then threw all his wife's clothes out, burnt them and then threw her out. The murder followed as a sequence to above.[24]

When all efforts failed to remove the stain of Joe Greene's blood from the flagstone where he fell, it was eventually turned upside down.[25]

# Patrick Darcy

Margaret Darcy's life was punctuated with moments of tragic personal loss that saw her burying her husband and no less than three of her seven children by 1921.

Her husband Michael died in 1906, her eldest daughter died in a convent at age 20 in 1914 and 22-year-old Michael drowned in January 1920 following an attack on RIC personnel. Mrs Darcy farmed 13 acres of land, on which she kept five milch cows.[1]

The Darcys had good pedigree in the Republican movement. Michael's mother would later be in receipt of a posthumous award of a Service Medal and another son John was an active member of Mid Clare IRA. But it was the allegation that her son Patrick had given information to the authorities about Willie Shanahan and Michael McNamara and his subsequent execution that would give rise to controversy that endures to the present day.

Born in Cooraclare on 19 October 1895, Patrick Darcy had qualified as a national teacher (NT) at St Patrick's Training College, Dublin, in 1916. Having served a probationary period, he was awarded his Teaching Diploma and gained further qualifications in the teaching of Irish from O'Curry College in Carrigaholt.[2]

During the War of Independence he taught as an assistant teacher at

Patrick Darcy, from Cooraclare, who taught at Doonbeg National School.
*(Courtesy Paul Daly)*

Doonbeg National School with Principal Pádraig Ashe, a cousin of Thomas Ashe. Darcy joined the Volunteers on their formation in Cooraclare about 1917 and played some part in the disarming of two policemen in April 1918, though the extent of his role in this incident is unclear.[3]

Battalion Commandant Dan Sheedy was one of the first to raise concerns about the young teacher. According to Sheedy, Darcy was being used by the Brigade for intelligence work, but Sheedy had been unhappy about this. During the boycott of Murphy's in Danganelly, Dan Sheedy had received reports that the young schoolteacher had been breaking the ban.[4] Darcy had been frequenting a pub in Vandeleur Street, Kilrush that Denis Sheehan was renting from Francis Ryan.[5]

Sheehan's was a favourite haunt of Crown forces, where they could be confident of an after-hours drink. Sheedy noted 'and Darcy himself was that kind of a type, that he would be inclined to boast or talk about what he knew when he had a sup taken ...'

Sheedy made his concerns known to Liddy and he recalled one incident in particular that made him wary of Darcy when Cumann na mBan held a dance in the Mullagh area in order to generate funds. The dance, which took place prior to Sheedy's arrest and imprisonment on 22 October 1920, was attended by Sheedy, together with John O'Donnell, Liddy, local Captain Paddy O'Dea (Scropul) and Patrick Darcy.

Before the men left that night, Sheedy and O'Dea made plans to meet again the following Sunday at 4.00pm to deal with some outstanding Battalion matters. Luckily, Sheedy couldn't keep the appointment, as the venue was raided by British forces at 4.00pm.

Sheedy confronted Darcy, who admitted to disclosing the arrangement in a letter to a female friend. Sheedy later advised Liddy not to bring Darcy along anymore, as he felt that Darcy was '... too loose to be going in our company.'[6]

Indeed, Darcy was as likely to be seen drinking and singing with Black and Tans as with local Volunteers. He drank with Constable Michael Hurley, who had at one time been based in Doonbeg, though they were seen only as 'social comrades'.

Darcy was described as ' ... a bit wild in the matter of taking drink with any person with whom he came in contact and he was fond of reckless living and amusements'.[7] Another noted that he was '... an odd kind of individual ... not very stable ... a fidgety and erratic individual' and 'light-headed' and his brother-in-law, John Daly, acknowledged that he was a 'harum scarum' who was 'addicted to drink'.[8]

As time went on, Brigade officers became increasingly wary of Darcy and were reluctant to share knowledge of a sensitive nature with him.[9]

Battalion Transport Officer Michael Russell's Bureau of Military History Witness Statement was the only one that gave a comprehensive account of the Patrick Darcy affair. Russell wrote:

> A number of wanted I.R.A. men who were "on the run" stayed most of their time around the Cooraclare and Doonbeg areas where Darcy resided and taught. It became obvious from police raids that information regarding the whereabouts of these wanted men was being given to the police authorities. Any man at the time who was known to be keeping company of R.I.C. or any member of the British Garrison naturally came under suspicion, and Darcy, who was the only one from this side of the country who was ever seen in this type of company, came to be regarded by the local I.R.A. as a dangerous man and a potential spy.[10]

During an IRA operation at Kilteely, County Limerick in May 1921, the 6th Division British Weekly Intelligence Summary documents, dated 17 May 1921, were captured by members of the IRA. These documents, which had been compiled by General Strickland, contained information about key IRA personnel and their activities in each of the Munster counties. John McCarthy, Adjutant of the East Limerick Brigade quickly circulated extracts of the report to the relevant Brigade officers throughout the province and to General Headquarters.[11]

A number of these extracts related to the West Clare Brigade personnel and their movements:

West Clare Brigade. Has been in the Doonbeg-Cooraclare-Kilmihil area and intended attacking the RIC Barracks at Kilkee on the 6th inst. It is now believed to have moved up (north) towards Quilty. Its only activity has been the cutting of roads in the southern part of the County [sic].

The following information re the attack on the Kilrush Barracks on 22nd ult. Has [sic] been obtained and corroborated:-

The attackers comprised about 40 men of a Flying Column from Kerry or County Cork and the Cooraclare Bn and West Clare Flying Column.

The Kilrush members of the IRA were used as guides, very unwillingly and apparently on point of the bayonet. Simon Breen's house at Kilmacduane, Cooraclare was used as the meeting place for the attack.

John Liddy, Michael Honan (misspelled as Hinan in the original document) and Michael Killoughrey [sic] have been living in a dug-out in the townland of Clonreddan, which was discovered on the 8th instant. This was large enough to hold 6 men and apparently a tent had been erected, as a number of tent pegs had been found.

Liddy's party were rationed from Cooraclare and obtained money and despatches through a woman who cycles from Ennis to Clonreddan once a week. Willie Haugh is reported to have taken over command of this Brigade. One of the rebels who was killed (during the attack on Kilrush on 22 April 1921) is reliably reported to have been buried at Doonbeg on the 24th ult.

Willie Haugh and 20 others had been living in a dug-out in a bog in Moyasta – Shragh district.

The Madigans of Banmore, Moyasta and Miss Irene Kennedy of Lisdeen were reported to be harbouring rebels.

Information has been received that the Marine Dispatchment at Seafield Quilty is to be attacked and that a lodge which is situated about 100 yards (away) is to be used by the rebels to fire from.[12]

It was no great surprise that the Weekly Summary comprised propaganda and factual inaccuracy. Indeed, there were elements of complete fabrication in respect of the attack on Kilrush. However, the officers of the West Clare Brigade were concerned that some of the information in the hands of the British appeared to have come from a source or sources with intimate knowledge of their movements.

The locations of safe houses where Seán Liddy and Tom Marrinan were sleeping were disclosed three times in the space of two months and Liddy later remarked that:

... it was by a miracle, by a sheer miracle that we are alive today to tell the tale. No; they were getting the information red hot for a long period before we took steps to stop it.[13]

Bill Haugh confirmed that Patrick Darcy had been under suspicion for a considerable period. His suspicions were heightened when he received a report from a lad named Maguire from Derryard that the teacher had been asking his students if their parents had mentioned where Haugh was sleeping at a time when Haugh had been hiding out in the same place for four months.[14]

The matter was taken seriously, since some pupils from Doonbeg School used to deliver food to the dugouts. Liddy later recalled a Black and Tan raid on Doonbeg School, where IRA documents were being held for safekeeping. The fact that the Tans knew exactly what they were looking for convinced Liddy that Darcy had given the information.[15]

Then, immediately following the killing of McNamara and Shanahan,

Darcy was reported to have gone to Ennis to claim the bodies. Before he left, he called to the home of Martin Chambers, where it was noted that he was '... very worried and sorry about the shootings, actually hysterical about the incident'. But it was his bizarre query about where Bill Haugh and Martin Chambers were hiding out that worried Chambers's sister.[16]

There was widespread revulsion in west Clare at the manner of the killing of Michael McNamara and Willie Shanahan. Kilrush Police and military were shunned, even by those who were not in sympathy with the Republican movement. Yet Patrick Darcy continued to socialise with them.

~

On Friday 17 June 1921, Head-Constable James Treacy received word that a man had been shot dead in Doonbeg. He arrived at the scene at about 3.00pm and found the body of Patrick Darcy lying on his back on the street outside the door of Daniel Hayes's public house. Hayes had stumbled on the gruesome scene at 7.00am. A white cloth was tied around his eyes and a note was pinned to his body that read 'Sooner or later we get them. Spy. Tried convicted and executed by IRA'.

Treacy took possession of two documents that he found on Darcy's clothing – his will and a farewell letter to his mother. His purse contained two keys and £3.1s.7d. Treacy's enquiries established that the likely time of the shooting was 12.30am. The body was taken by motor to Kilrush Mortuary.[17] At 7.45pm, the officer commanding the Royal Scots in Ennis sent a telegram to Dublin with news of the execution:

Patrick Darcy school Teacher [sic] Cooraclare murdered last night by I.R.A. spy notice pinned to coat but man never gave us any information ...[18]

A military Court of Inquiry in lieu of Inquest was held on 27 June 1920 to investigate the circumstances of the death of Patrick Darcy. A post-mortem, carried out by Dr Richard Counihan revealed that three bullets had entered

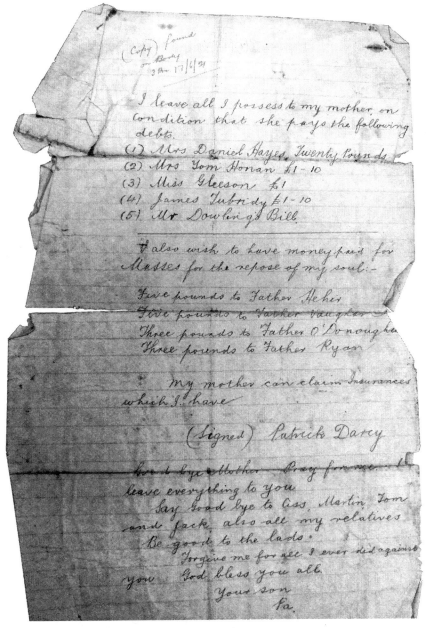

RIC copy of the last letter and will of Patrick Darcy.
*(Courtesy Paul O'Looney)*

the body via the temple, the chest and the abdomen and the fourth had struck the shoulder bone.

The inquiry concluded that Patrick Darcy had died from shock and haemorrhage resulting from wounds inflicted by persons unknown and that those persons were guilty of wilful murder.[19]

After the Inquiry, Margaret Darcy collected her son's body from Kilrush and brought it to Cooraclare by horse and cart. Accompanied by two youngsters, she walked beside the cart on his final journey home.[20]

Patrick's burial in the family plot at Kilmacduane Cemetery was a lonely spectacle:

> Without any tricolour and without any comrades or friends except a few near relatives we laid him with his brother, the one covered with glory and the other with shame.[21]

Some time later, an RIC sergeant visited Darcy's mother and handed her a single handwritten page, which he said was a copy of the two documents that were found on her son's body. It read:

> I leave all I possess to my mother on condition that she pays the following debts.
> Mrs Daniel Hayes Twenty Pounds
> Mrs Tom Honan £1.10
> Miss Gleeson £1
> James Tubridy £1.10
> Mr Dowling's Bill
>
> I also wish to have money paid for Masses for the repose of my soul:-
> Five pounds to Father Hehir
> Five pounds to Father Vaughan
> Three pounds to Father O'Donoughue [sic]
> Three pounds to Father Ryan

My mother can claim Insurances which I have
    (Signed) Patrick Darcy

Good bye Mother. Pray for me. I leave everything to you
Say Good bye to Ciss, Martin, Tom and Jack, also all my relatives.
Be good to the lads.
Forgive me for all I ever did against you. God bless you all.

    Your son
    Pa[22]

To this day, there has been no explanation for the RIC decision not to deliver to Margaret Darcy the two original documents that were written by her son on the night he was shot.

In the absence of his will, Patrick's mother swore an oath one month after he had been executed that he had died intestate.[23] At the 1947 sworn inquiry, Commandant Tom Marrinan, who was in the execution party, stated that he was almost certain that Darcy had protested his innocence in his final letter to his mother, and that the police must have deleted it. But the Pensions Board Referee doubted this; if the police were deleting a protestation of innocence, they would hardly include the phrase 'Be good to the lads' – which he understood to be a clear reference to those who were responsible for his execution.[24]

The Mr Dowling whose bill was to be discharged from his estate was a moneylender, whose offices were in Moore Street, Kilrush.[25]

∽

An inquiry into the Patrick Darcy affair was conducted by General Eoin O'Duffy at Ennis Courthouse towards the end of July 1921, when he visited Clare for the purpose of reorganising the 1st Western Division. However, there has been no visibility of O'Duffy's report, if indeed there was one. All that remains are conflicting accounts of comments attributed to O'Duffy at the time.

On the one hand, Liddy recalled that, as he was leaving after the inquiry, O'Duffy asked him 'Have you many men in town with you?' Liddy replied in the affirmative and O'Duffy cautioned 'You had better be careful.'[26]

Commandant Tom Marrinan had claimed that O'Duffy had informed him of his belief that Darcy's sentence was justified.[27] Darcy's brother John maintained that O'Duffy had informed him in the presence of Commandant Frank Barrett that the only justification for any action against Patrick Darcy related to his association with enemy forces. O'Duffy, he claimed, had promised to publish his report.[28]

Commandant Joe Barrett claimed that O'Duffy had told him that Darcy's case was similar to that of Limerick Volunteer Captain James Dalton and that it would be treated in the same manner.[29] Dalton, a father of eleven, had been seen entering the home of an RIC policeman at 1.00am and he hadn't left for some hours, which led to suspicions that he was giving information. After an attempt was made to assassinate him, Dalton had demanded to have his case heard by a Sinn Féin Court. This had happened on 8 May 1920 and he had been vindicated, but he was shot dead before the written verdict had been promulgated. The Dáil Éireann verdict was made public at the inquest into the circumstances of Dalton's death:

> The main point was not disputed that the plaintiff (Mr Dalton) had entered certain premises at 1am and remained there till morning, the fact which had brought suspicion upon him. Having heard the evidence, I was of opinion that the plaintiff had been guilty of a grave indiscretion and error of judgment in acting as he had done, and that his conduct very naturally gave rise to such suspicions. As against this I was clearly of opinion that there had been no guilty or dishonest motive on his part, and that the suspicions in this respect were unfounded.[30]

Joe Barrett recalled that O'Duffy, on the morning after the latter's investigation of the Darcy affair, had told him that the findings of the Dalton case would be published and that compensation would be paid to Dalton's family.[31] Indeed, Dáil Éireann's cabinet approved an ex-gratia payment of £500 to Dalton's widow on 24 July 1920. The Compensation Personal Injuries Committee awarded her a further £700 on 29 September 1924.[32]

Margaret Darcy's application for compensation of £5000 in respect of the loss of her son was heard by County Court Judge Bodkin KC at Kilrush Quarter Sessions on 6 October 1921.

There, she stated that Patrick had worked as an assistant teacher at Doonbeg NS. He had earned a salary of £217 per annum and that sum was supplemented by annual income of £40 from teaching Irish. He was tutoring his sister Margaret, who hoped to become the second teacher in the family.

Judge Bodkin awarded Mrs Darcy £600, of which £100 was to be paid to her daughter Margaret.[33] The amount of the award was in keeping with the conventions of the day. But in marked contrast with the Dalton case, the British government accepted full liability and on 3 October 1924 they paid Margaret Darcy the sum of £724.6s.7d, inclusive of interest and costs. The British side also accepted full liability in respect of Martin Counihan and John Reilly, both of whom were shot by the IRA as alleged spies.[34] In his comprehensive treatment of the Darcy affair, Pádraig Óg Ó Ruairc writes:

Of the forty-three compensation cases for County Clare listed in the commissions [sic] register, 'British Liability' was admitted in just three cases: Martin Counihan, John Reilly and Patrick Darcy, all three of whom had been shot by the IRA as suspected spies. Counihan and Reilly's cases were described as 'Agreed to accept as a British Liability,' with Darcy having the distinction of being the only one described as a 'Full British Liability'... The British acceptance of liability in these cases, though not conclusive proof, gives a strong indication that those killed were involved in espionage.'[35]

In February 1933, Patrick Darcy's sister, Margaret, married John Daly, from

Burrane, formerly an active Volunteer. Willie Shanahan's brother Patrick was best man at the wedding. With Patrick Shanahan's support, the Dalys would go on to make every effort to have Patrick Darcy exonerated.

～

In 1945, Colonel Dan Bryan was instructed by An Taoiseach, Éamon de Valera, to investigate two matters of relevance to the Patrick Darcy affair:

> If a number of specifically named officers still serving in the Army knew of any reasons which had arisen since Darcy was shot which might alter the original decision in the case.
>
> and
>
> If it were possible to trace any official notes or records of the enquiry which General O'Duffy held in connection with this incident at some time after the Truce in 1921.

Colonel Bryan's enquiries, which he had even extended beyond the scope of his brief, realised no new knowledge in respect of point number one. With regard to the O'Duffy inquiry, there was no trace of a report and little optimism that one would be discovered.[36]

Bryan referred to the conflicting accounts of Marrinan and Barrett about O'Duffy's findings. He also referred to the only official record of the activities of the West Clare Brigade in the Military Archives. This record referred only in vague terms to the execution of Patrick Darcy, but it was clear that '… his execution in the account is regarded as completely justified.'[37]

In December 1946, Margaret Daly applied to the Department of Defence for the posthumous award of a Service Medal with Bar in respect of services rendered by her late brother, Patrick Darcy.

The complexities of the case necessitated some sort of inquiry and the advice of an army expert, Colonel George P Hodnett, BL, was sought. Hodnett was reluctant to recommend a tribunal of inquiry:

The evidence now put forward in favour of the executed man is largely hearsay, as to what people now dead (and who, therefore cannot be examined or cross-examined) are alleged to have sa [*sic*] or omitted to say … My opinion is that this case should be left to be reviewed by persons who, like the minister and yourself, have intimate knowledge of the conditions of the time, and who re [*sic*] free to judge it by the standards of the time as set by the necessities of guerrilla warfare.[38]

The hearsay evidence included statements that were said to have been made by unnamed people or people who had since died.[39]

Kilkee IRA men relaxing in Pound Street.
Tom (Nap) Marrinan is on the left and Tom Prendergast (the Little Corporal) on the right.
*(Courtesy Mary Driver)*

The Minister referred the matter to the office of the Pensions Board Referee. Subsequently, an extensive investigation in the form of a Sworn Inquiry was undertaken under the chairmanship of Tadhg Forbes and an advisory committee comprising Séamus Robinson, a Mr McCoy and Hugh Brady.

Between 20 May and 8 July 1947 sworn evidence was taken by interview from those who were most closely associated with Darcy's execution as well as others whose testimony was of interest, namely Margaret Daly (sister of Patrick Darcy), John Daly (her husband), John Darcy (brother of Patrick Darcy), Patrick Shanahan TD (brother of Willie Shanahan), Commandant Joseph Barrett and James Spellissy (formerly Mid Clare Brigade), Major Conor Whelan, Commandant Thomas Martyn, Commandant Tom Marrinan, Commandant Liam Haugh, Martin Chambers, Michael Melican, Stephen Hanrahan, Dan Sheedy and Michael Russell (all formerly of the West Clare Brigade).

The purpose of the inquiry was to establish whether Patrick Darcy had given active service that would entitle him to the posthumous award of a Service Medal with Bar. The question of whether or not he was a spy would only be addressed in the event that active service was first proven.[40]

Before the majority of the witnesses had been interviewed, the Referee advised Margaret Daly that '… it might be in her best interest to withdraw the application'.[41] On the second day of the inquiry, Forbes informed the Dalys that their application for a Service Medal with Bar had actually defeated its own purpose:

You have launched this application on two qualifications to which I have drawn your attention – first, the statement that he (Patrick Darcy) was excused from Volunteer work by reason of his occupation, and the second was that up to the 19th Jan. (1920) he was actively and closely associated with officers in the Bde. (Brigade) area and that after that differences arose between him and the Commandant but that he was still friendly and helpful to other volunteers.

The Referee explained that, to qualify for a Service Medal, it would be necessary to establish that a Volunteer had continuous service. To qualify for a Service Medal with Bar, service of such quality as would qualify a living applicant for a pension would need to be proven. It would not be enough to show that Darcy associated with other Volunteers, since 'A lot of people who don't go to school meet the scholars.' On the strength of the application before him, the Referee concluded 'You have not a hope of getting it, I can say that straight away, unless with a wealth of additional evidence.'[42]

Through the months of June and July 1947, after the Referee had ruled out any possibility of making a posthumous award of a Service Medal with Bar to Patrick Darcy, the sworn inquiry would concentrate much of its efforts on evidence related to the circumstances leading up to his execution.

The effort was indeed worthwhile from the perspective of the historian, because evidence was gathered from a number of key players who did not provide witness statements to the Bureau of Military History.[43]

In the course of the inquiry, evidence was gathered from Russell and Bill Haugh, both of whom had intimate knowledge of the arrest and execution. But there was key testimony also from Brigade Commandant Seán Liddy, Dan Sheedy, Michael Melican, Conor Whelan, Thomas Martyn, Tom Marrinan, John Daly and Stephen Hanrahan, some of whom had played a critical role in the arrest and interrogation of Denis Sheehan and none of whom would later give statements to the Bureau.

The record, which makes for compelling reading, brings new insights into the affair, notwithstanding the fact that 26 years had passed and memory for detail had faded. The file is populated with a number of irreconcilably conflicting accounts, subjective and uncorroborated hearsay allegations and statements that were attributed to people who had by this time passed on. There are, in fact, contradictions in the sworn evidence of some individual interviewees.

There were statements from John Daly and Joe Barrett that the late Francis

W Gore-Hickman, a proud loyalist and legal advisor to the British Military Southern Command during the War of Independence, had told them that Darcy was not a spy.[44] Daly's sworn affidavit referred to conversations that he had with Hickman:

> He informed me on countless occasions that he had access to every item of information that the British authorities received from their agents and spies and from every source whatsoever ... He assured me that he knew the names of every agent, spy or person who supplied information of every description... He immediately assured me that he could testify on oath if necessary that the name of Patrick Darcy was never at any time on the list of agents or spies in the British Intelligence Department.[45]

A statement by Martin McCarthy claimed that, on the day after Darcy was executed, Seán Liddy had told McCarthy '... it is alright if we did not make a mistake and shoot the wrong man.'[46]

Ex-RIC sergeant Laurence Nolan, who had been based in west Clare, had furnished a signed statement through the Dalys. Referring to Darcy, he stated:

> He had never to my knowledge given any information to the British Forces or to the R.I.C. at Doonbeg, Milltown Malbay or any other place...I would go so far as to say that had he given any information I would have been informed or consulted about the accuracy of such information.[47]

Ex-Sergeant E M Sullivan, who had been involved in some of the significant events of the period in west Clare, including the arrest of Patrick Burke, wrote to the Dalys 'I never knew of the late Patrick Darcy to be an informer, not to the slightest degree.'[48]

One of the most sensational allegations concerned Massie McInerney of Mountrivers, close by Doonbeg railway station, whose sister was married to Kilrush publican Denis Sheehan. John Daly claimed that letters written by

Massie to an RIC man had been intercepted in one of the many raids on the mail train. According to Daly, she had sworn that she would swing for Shanahan and McNamara after these letters had been published.[49]

New insights were gained into the critical role that was played by Denis Sheehan in the determination of alleged guilt on the part of Patrick Darcy.

In June 1921 Sheehan had been identified as a suspect for the giving of information that led to the arrest of McNamara and Shanahan on 17 December 1920. The inquiry heard that Martin Chambers had received orders from the Brigade Commandant to assassinate Sheehan. Each Sunday, the Sheehans would make the journey to Mountrivers by pony and cart to visit Minnie's family. They would typically travel the most direct route via Monmore and Shragh. Chambers claimed that he had been less than happy with his assignment:

> I got the order from the Brigade O.C. to shoot Sheehan as being a spy. I am on my oath now and that is the truth. I questioned the authority of taking a human life because his wife would be in the car and she would be a mix-up on the job.

Chambers believed that he was chosen for the job because his company area in Monmore was on the route that the Sheehans would travel. He chose Tim Neenan, Jack Honan of Dangan, Danny and Michael Campbell (pronounced locally as 'Camel'), first cousins of Patrick Darcy, as well as Jack O'Dea, who was Captain of A Company in Cooraclare. There were two other Volunteers named Simon Moroney and John Lynch.

The ambush party lay in wait from 10.00am until 6.30pm or 7.00pm on 13 June 1921 and, when there was still no sign of the Sheehans, they returned their guns to their dump in a field. Suddenly, a Volunteer reported that the Sheehans' pony and trap were approaching and Chambers and O'Dea ran to retrieve their weapons. Sheehan stopped to shelter under a bush from a rain shower, but he had moved on by the time Chambers and O'Dea returned.[50]

Liddy, however, maintained that he had not given the order to shoot Sheehan and claimed that those who said that he had were 'romancing.' Conor Whelan was also quite adamant that Chambers had been ordered to arrest Sheehan, not to shoot him.[51] Nonetheless, the Referee and his advisory committee deemed it to be a proven fact that Chambers had been tasked with shooting Sheehan.

Interestingly, the report of Colonel Dan Bryan's 1945 inquiry had suggested a very different picture of Sheehan, who:

> ... is alleged to be a relative of Seán Moylan, who is alleged to have given someone described as Seán Hogan given [sic] Sheehan's family record in Cork as good, and that Sheehan or his family had given a lot of arms to a Cork Brigade. This was before the Truce.

Moylan, who would later serve as a government Minister, had been OC of two North Cork Brigades prior to the Truce.[52]

Bryan's report contained a reference to a statement by Martin Chambers that he and Willie Shanahan had actually '... personally collected at Sheehan's house (when Tans were in it) revolvers that had been bought through Sheehan.' And Bryan's notes referred to '... rumours about other "peculiar" dealings in arms in which Sheehan would seem to have been concerned'.[53]

When Sheehan visited Greygrove, near Kilmihil, at around midday on 14 June 1921 he was arrested and held in a cabin that was owned by Peter McMahon, who had played an important part in the attack on police at Kilmihil on 18 April 1920. McMahon had a specially constructed IRA dugout in a remote location on his farm, where prisoners could be brought for interrogation, but it was considered too dangerous on this occasion, as it was suspected that British forces had some knowledge of it.

The written record of the proceedings of the sworn inquiry of May–July 1947 contains testimony from three Brigade members who were present for some or all of the interrogation of Denis Sheehan at Greygrove on 14–15 June 1921. They were Brigade Commandant Seán Liddy, Lieutenant Michael Melican, C Company, 2nd Battalion and Vice Commandant Stephen Hanrahan, 2nd Battalion.

Stephen Hanrahan, who lived about three miles from Greygrove recalled that he had received a despatch to attend at McMahon's cabin, though he acknowledged that he had not been present for the entire period of the interrogation:

> When I entered the shed, Sheehan was standing in the middle of the floor, blind-folded with a white handkerchief. Commdt. Liddy was standing about apace [*sic*] or so in front with a Mauser rifle pointed at his heart, and he was interrogating him in a very sharp, snappy voice, and the fellow was trembling like a leaf ... He was asking Sheehan questions of what people were visiting his premises ... Sheehan replied to all the questions but did not incriminate himself in any way nor any of the people whom he was asked about ... He denied all those questions, but I remember him to say at one time that he himself was innocent but he could not be responsible for his wife ... or he didn't know whether she gave information to the Tans or not. I remember that distinctly for him to say that.[54]

Hanrahan had earlier given a statement to the effect that Sheehan had not incriminated Darcy during his interrogation, but acknowledged that he had not been present for the whole period of Sheehan's questioning.[55]

Michael Melican stated that Liddy and Tom Marrinan had called to his home at Greygrove after they had got word that Sheehan had been arrested. Melican brought Liddy to the cabin where Sheehan was being held. There, the prisoner was questioned at length by Liddy, as various officers and Volunteers came and went – among them Stephen Hanrahan and Peter McMahon. The dramatic scene where Sheehan was questioned was described by Melican:

> Liddy put on goggles; (Tom) Marrinan also had goggles, and started to

question him … We went out to the end of the cabin. They were not satisfied with the evidence given and used a threat that he was going to be shot and to write a word to his wife, and then left him. And Liddy was at the end of the cabin with the Volunteers and myself, and someone told Liddy he was wanted again and he went back. I did not. And, after an absence of 5 or 10 minutes he came back and said "Darcy was the man".

In one of the most charged sequences of the inquiry, Melican was taken through the copy of a statement that he had made in August 1946 and which had been submitted to the inquiry:

Q. Did you make that statement?
*A. Not the exact words. I signed that statement.*
Q. But you say the words are not the exact words you used?
*A. No.*
Q. Take the first sentence, "I remember the Courtmartial of Jackie [*sic*: Denis] Sheehan at Glanmore in June 1921."
*A. It was Greygrove.*
Q. "I was a member of the Court."
*A. I was present.*
Q. Were you a member of the Court?
*A. It depends on what you call it. I was there.*
Q. Is that what you thought you were?
*A. I never for a moment thought it was a court.*
Q. You didn't?
*A. No.*
Q. "Before the court assembled, Seán Liddy, Brigadier, told me under no circumstances would Sheehan be reprieved."
*A. I used the words I used to you, "under no circumstances was he to be let go soft."*
Q. And "I understood that Sheehan was to be shot regardless of any evidence he gave." Did you understand that?
*A. I did not understand that he was to be shot at that time.*

Q. Did you say last August you thought so?

*A. I signed the statement.*

Q. In the belief that it was true?

*A. I signed the statement in the belief that it was true.*[56]

Tom Martyn, who succeeded Dan Sheedy as OC of the 3rd Battalion following Sheedy's arrest, gave evidence on oath that he had been a close friend of Darcy's first cousins, Danny and Michael Campbell. Both, he claimed, were of the opinion that 'nothing unjust was done' to Patrick Darcy.[57]

The testimony of Liddy at the sworn inquiry of 1947 would be the only recorded first-hand account of what Sheehan had said that incriminated Patrick Darcy that night in McMahon's shed at Greygrove:

> ... and there was a little fellow who drove the Tans and it was he got the information from D'arcy – there was some nickname on him, I can't tell you now, he was killed after the Truce in Ennis, absolutely kicked to pieces on the road ... By the lads in Ennis, the I.R.A. fellows. That was the gentleman that got it from D'arcy, we know that ... this fellow boasted that he got the dope off D'arcy and that is why he was afterwards killed in Ennis ... Sheehan told us that he knew that D'arcy had given away Shanahan and McNamara, where they were sleeping, and that this Tan driver told Sheehan himself and he boasted that it was he got the information from him.[58]

The 'Tan driver' referred to by Liddy was almost certainly Provost Sergeant David Findlay, a non-commissioned officer of the 2nd Battalion, Royal Scots. According to Seán Liddy, Darcy had befriended Findlay. The diminutive Findlay would appear to have sealed Darcy's fate with what Haugh described as 'an incontinent slip' to Sheehan that set in train the investigation that led ultimately to the identification of Darcy as a spy and his subsequent execution.[59]

A native of Scotland, Findlay, who was known locally as '... a bad egg, a very bad type', was notorious for the severe beatings and kickings that he and his gang gave to IRA prisoners in Ennis Gaol. One of his victims was John Joe 'Tosser' Neylon, who '... was covered with cuts and bruises; he was bleeding from the scalp and his fingers were damaged when, with his hands, he tried to ward off kicks.'[60]

James Spellissy, a Mid Clare Battalion IO who worked on the West Clare Railway, would take advantage of Findlay's fondness for drink to elicit information:

... one Saturday evening in Ennis, after British troops had left, there was a Provost Sergeant there; he was coming up the street; David Fenley [sic] was his name; and he was intoxicated; and I saw an opportunity of getting some information from him; so I brought him into Kelly's publichouse [sic] in Ennis; and I gave him a few bottles of stout or whiskey or whatever he drank at the time; and I said "Have you any information about Willie Shanahan and McNamara?" – who had been previously murdered; so he told me he had, that the British troops were touring around West Clare looking for I.R.A. men, and about eleven o'clock at night time, coming into the town of Kilrush, they saw a man in the street, outside Sheehan's publichouse [sic] in Kilrush; so he hailed them; and they got off; and he told them to go back one mile on the road and they would see a white house; and they got the two lads in it, McNamara and Shanahan; so that is how they were captured; but at the time – I forget now the date of that particular incident – but at the time it was thought that Darcy was the man ...[61]

Around 10 January 1922, Tom McDonagh, Transport Officer with the Mid Clare Brigade, was in the Queens Hotel Ennis when Findlay, in civilian clothes, spotted him. Wagging his finger at his target, Findlay crowed 'I know you; you are so-and-so and you are one of the Shinners.'

Findlay had signed his death warrant. That night, as he left the Queens, he was waylaid and beaten so badly by local IRA men that he died of congestion of the lungs and syncope at the Gaol on 18 January 1921.[62] Claims that

Findlay had been the soldier who shot Willie Shanahan at Ennis Gaol on 22 December 1920 were later found to be incorrect.[63]

Hanrahan also recalled that Tom Marrinan was present at Sheehan's interrogation, though he acknowledged vagueness due to the passage of time. But Marrinan denied that he had been present and there was some dispute about whether Conor Whelan had been present.

$\approx$

In July 1947, following a request from solicitors for the Dalys, the War Office in London responded with a statement that Patrick Darcy '... is unknown to this department and has never acted as an agent, or in any other capacity

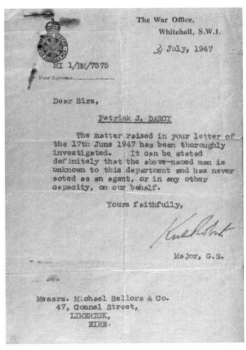

Letter to Solicitors for Daly family from the War Office, London, 31 July 1947.
*(Courtesy Paul O'Looney)*

on our behalf'.[64] John Daly forwarded this information to the Referee's Office and to the Department of Defence with the comment '... it speaks for itself'.[65]

The decision of the Committee was communicated on 31 July 1947:

We recommend that no medal should issue in this case.

Our recommendation is based solely on the grounds that no satisfactory evidence has been forthcoming to prove either that patrick [sic] D'arcy was a member of the forces at any time later than 1920 or that he rendered continuous service to the forces during any of the months in 1921 preceding his death in June of that year.[66]

Referee Tadhg Forbes and Advisory Committee members Robinson and Brady were unanimous in all of their conclusions and it was their considered opinion that the following facts were proven:

1. That the late Patrick D'arcy joined the Volunteers on their formation in Cooraclare about 1917, and that, about March, 1919, he took part, with Seán Liddy, Paddy Lynch and Tom Miskelly [sic], in the capture of two rifles from two RIC constables ...[67]

2. That his services were used by officers of theBrigade [sic] for the purpose of intelligence at various dates prior to the arrest of D.P. Sheedy in October, 1920 ... and that no satisfactory evidence was forthcoming of connection with the Forces subsequent to that date.

3. That Patrick D'arcy frequented a public house in Kilrush, owned by an ex R.I.C. man, named Denis Sheehan, during the year 1920, that the fact was well known to the officers of the Brigade, that at no time was any disapproval expressed to him ...

4. That on the Sunday prior to D'arcy's death on June 17th 1921, Company Captain Martin Chambers was ordered by Brigade OC Seán Liddy to shoot Denis Sheehan, and that an abortive attempt was made by Chambers to comply with this order ...

5. That on or about 14<sup>th</sup> June, 1921, Denis Sheehan was arrested, by orders of the Brigade OC, and interrogated at the point of a gun, that Sheehan was threatened with death, and that, in these circumstances, he is alleged to have said something which incriminated D'arcy – what exactly he said we have been unable to establish – that Sheehan was released, and that orders were given by the Brigade OC, Seán Liddy, for the arrest of Patrick D'arcy ...

6. That a search was made forthwith for Patrick D'arcy at his home and school.

7. That Patrick D'arcy was then absent in Ennis for innocent reasons ...

8. That on his return home on the night of Friday, 16<sup>th</sup> June, 1921, Patrick D'arcy was arrested by a party of Volunteers, including Liam Haugh and Michael Russell ...

9. That on the orders of the Brigade OC, Seán Liddy, Patrick D'arcy was shot that night by Liam Haugh and Thomas Marrinan ...

10. That Patrick D'arcy was shot without trial ...[68]

The Report of the sworn inquiry was disappointing for the Dalys, who were to make one final effort to extract some modicum of mitigation for Patrick Darcy.

On 28 August 1947, John Daly, in a letter to An Taoiseach, Éamon de Valera, acknowledged that a very thorough investigation of the circumstances of Patrick Darcy's execution had taken place. He agreed that continuity of service had not been established, but expressed disappointment that the report contained no measure of exoneration. He and Mrs Daly would settle for a statement from the Minister to the effect that the circumstances of Patrick Darcy's death would not preclude the awarding of a Service Medal if continuity of service had been established.[69]

The response from the Minister for Defence was unequivocal:

... the matter raised in Mr Daly's letter has been carefully and sympathetically considered but the Minister regrets that he is unable to issue a communication to Mrs Daly on the lines suggested in the penultimate paragraph of Mr Daly's letter.[70]

A short time later, John Daly submitted his resignation from the Chair of Fianna Fáil's West Clare Comhairle Dáil Ceanntair to An Taoiseach, Éamon de Valera. The report of the Referee and Advisory Committee, he stated '… leaves the family still under a cloud and gives rise for suspicion by all concerned that the deceased was not exhonerated [sic] at the investigation.' He would be retiring from public life.[71]

A 1955 *Sunday Press* article by Ernie O'Malley ignited the controversy once again. O'Malley, without naming Patrick Darcy, referred to the execution of a British spy in west Clare who, he wrote, 'gave away' Mac and Shanahan. The column provoked a stinging response from Margaret Daly, who wrote:

In his article headed "British Reprisals" Mr. Ernie O'Malley has placed on record a story which is obviously based on hearsay, utterly devoid of personal knowledge or historical fact.

When he refers to the man who "gave away" Commdt. Shanahan and Capt. McNamara and whose "labelled body was found on a roadside," he is referring to one of four brothers who were all active members of the I.R.A. and served it faithfully to the very end, the D'arcy brothers of Cooraclare.

Michael D'arcy (R.I.P.) died in action with his company early in the struggle and I hold the Service Medal which was posthumously awarded to him. Jack D'arcy (R.I.P.) served in a Flying Column and was later captured and under sentence of death. He escaped, to die at an early age as a result of the wounds and hardships of active service. Martin D'arcy emigrated after the wars were over.

Patrick D'arcy (R.I.P.) took part in one of the first engagements of the struggle for Independence when a party of police were disarmed. He had many other activities as a volunteer too numerous to mention here, but, nevertheless, he met his death as described by Mr. Ernie O'Malley as great a martyr for Ireland as his dead brothers.

As the only surviving sister of the D'arcy brothers, I am happy in the knowledge that the late Tadg [sic] Forbes in his official capacity as Chairman or "Referee" of the I.R.A. Pensions Board held a searching investigation into all the factors connected with the activities and death of Patrick D'arcy.

It is sufficient for me that such an efficient and unbiased Officer [*sic*] (God rest his noble soul) as Tadg [*sic*] Forbes publicly stated in the Courthouse at Ennis in June, 1954, to a large gathering of Old I.R.A. Officers, "that his investigations of the D'arcy case convinced him beyond doubt that the man was innocent."[72]

Willie Shanahan's brother, Patrick, wrote in support:

I have read with no little surprise the final paragraph of Mr. O'Malley's account of the shooting of a man who was alleged to have given information on my brother (the late Commdt. W. Shanahan) and Capt. M. McNamara in December 1920.

My whole family and myself are conversant with the happenings of that period, and I assure you that we would not agree with the version quoted by Mr. O'Malley.

We never believed that the man who was shot was guilty of spying, and we have never been supplied with any evidence to connect him with it, although it was asked for.[73]

O'Malley's apology was printed underneath. He explained that his information was based on the account of Vice Commandant of the West Clare Brigade, Bill Haugh, who did not actually name Darcy.

∾

After Denis Sheehan had implicated Patrick Darcy during his interrogation at Greygrove, Michael Melican suggested to Liddy that Darcy be brought face to face with Sheehan. Sheehan could have been brought to Peter McMahon's underground dugout, which was used extensively by the Brigade for the holding of prisoners.

However, this was considered too dangerous, as the Tans had been snooping around and there were fears that they had some knowledge of its location. Also, it was known that Sheehan used to visit a house in the locality and searches would begin when he failed to return to his home. Sheehan was released and, according to Melican, Liddy and others went back to Melican's house, where it was decided to arrest Patrick Darcy.[74]

In his evidence at his brother's Court of Inquiry in Lieu of Inquest, Martin Darcy recalled the events leading up to the arrest of his brother:

About midnight on 15th inst. Four or 5 masked men came to our house in Cooraclare. They entered the house. They had dirty white clothes over their faces & Brown belts with revolver holsters. Their clothing appeared to be torn and shabby. They asked if we kept Players cigarettes & when told no would not believe us & searched the house superficially. They then asked all about my brothers. I told them I had 3 alive, one aged 17, Thomas at home – one John who lives with his aunt Mrs Morris [sic: Maurice] Quinlivan Jail St. Ennis & one Patrick aged 27 schoolmaster at Doonbeg who lives at home. The latter had gone to Ennis by train on 14th inst to see his aunt, but I did not tell them this.[75]

The masked men were Michael Russell, Tom Marrinan, Michael Fitzmartin, Michael Cunningham, John Golden and Michael Briody. Russell later added that when they returned to Cree empty-handed Liddy, believing that Darcy had fled, sent them back to get a photograph of Darcy. When Darcy's sister Margaret questioned their motives, Russell responded 'he (Patrick) is the man that spied on Shanahan and Macnamara [sic] and took the blood money.'

As soon as Liddy got the photo he dictated a despatch to the OC of Ennis Company and Michael Fitzmartin was sent at about 6.30am to deliver it by bicycle. The despatch requested the Ennis OC to '… get in touch with a secret service agent who had gone to Ennis from west Clare and should be found dead or alive …'

When Fitzmartin delivered the despatch, the Ennis Company OC was able to inform him that Patrick Darcy had been in Ennis to see his brother

Jack and that he would be on the evening train to Doonbeg.[76]

By this time, it would appear that Darcy had become aware that he was a wanted man, as James Spellissy later reported that he had met Darcy in Ennis and that Darcy had told him 'That the Volunteers had come for him the previous night, and that he was more or less on the run'. Spellissy was of the understanding that Darcy was in some trouble with the Volunteers in west Clare.[77]

Though Liddy had no recollection of sending despatches with anybody other than Fitzmartin, Michael Melican asserted that he had also carried despatches for the OC of the East Clare Brigade and the OC of the Mid Clare Brigade. Fitzmartin, he said, had accompanied him to McNamara's pub in the town. There he met William Crowley, who informed him that Darcy was at Maurice Quinlivan's (Darcy's aunt's pub). Melican continued:

> While we were talking, Crowley and myself, the Bartender [sic], who was a sister of Crowley, says, "You must carry out a letter to Jack D'arcy when going out in the evening," and I pinched or kicked him, and she gave him the letter, and Crowley and I opened the letter out in the back.

The Referee asked what was in the letter. Melican replied:

> I am on my oath and I cannot give you the exact words. It was brief, more like a telegram than anything else. It was "came over to meet you today; wanted to see you badly. Come back to where you were immediately. You would be safer there than where you are at present. I am leaving at 3.30 or 3.45 train. Goodbye. Pa.

Melican and Fitzmartin then knew that Patrick Darcy would be returning to west Clare, so they cycled west themselves. Melican went to his home, which was nearest, while Fitzmartin continued on to update Liddy on the situation.[78]

It was later argued that Patrick Darcy's mother had sent him to Ennis after word had reached her that his brother Jack had been wounded in an ambush at Darragh. The ambush by the Mid Clare Brigade on an Auxiliary bicycle patrol had actually taken place one week previously, at Darragh Cross on 9 June 1921. While there were no casualties on the Republican side, a rumour had been put out by the Auxiliaries that two men had been killed and this was reported in the *Saturday Record* of 18 June, after Darcy's execution.[79]

When Darcy reached Ennis Railway Station, he enquired for the whereabouts of Major Kershaw, the British IO for County Clare, and he was on his way to meet Kershaw when he met Sylvester Barrett. When Darcy told Barrett that he was on his way to claim his brother's body Barrett informed him that his brother was safe and well and the pair went drinking in a number of public houses for the day.[80]

On the evening of 16 June, Patrick Darcy travelled west on the train but, before he reached his home, Russell and his men arrived there in search of him. When Liddy got word that Darcy would be on the train, he went to the dugout where Russell and others were sleeping and roused them. They were to go straight to Doonbeg Station to take custody of Darcy from local IRA police, who had been ordered to arrest him on arrival.

When they arrived there, however, Darcy had not been arrested, as the local Volunteers believed that there were a number of British troops on the train.

Bill Haugh arrived on the scene and sent four men in pairs along different roads to Cooraclare with a view to apprehending Darcy. Russell and Johnsie Cunningham along the Doonbeg route and James Fitzmartin and John Golding took the Cree road. Russell and Cunningham arrived first.[81] Martin Darcy was at the house when they called:

At about 17.30 hours the same number of masked men came again to our house and asked where Patrick was. I told them that he had not come back & that I did not know where he was. They said that Patrick had taken blood money and given information about Shanahan & Macnamara [*sic*] – two men (now dead) who had been on the run. They then left the house.[82]

Seán Liddy would subsequently clarify that there was no evidence that Darcy had been in receipt of money.

Darcy's sister Margaret later claimed that her brother had, in fact, been at school that day, 16 June and that it was only when he came home that his mother informed him that he was wanted. Patrick had claimed that he had done nothing wrong, but at the behest of his mother he had gone to speak with parish priest, Canon Hehir.[83] Martin Darcy continued:

Half an hour after at about 18.00 hours Patrick returned & entered the house. I told him that masked men were after him & said that they said that he had given information against Shanahan & Macnamara [*sic*]. He said it was a lie and decided to go and ask advice from Fr Hehir the parish priest. He left the house to do this. I was standing in the doorway of my house & saw Patrick coming back from the priest. I saw the masked men go up to him & stop him. I went up to them to see what was happening & Patrick told me he was going away with them for a few minutes & asked me to fetch his bicycle. I

Michael Russell, Transport Officer, 3rd Battalion, West Clare Brigade.
(*Courtesy Michael Russell Jnr*)

went back to the house & gave him the bicycle & saw him go away with the masked men, also on bicycles, in the direction of Creagh [sic]. I have no idea who the masked men were.[84]

Russell told Darcy that Bill Haugh, who was waiting a short distance away, wished to have a word with him, to which Darcy replied 'What would Bill Haugh or anyone else want with me?'

When they reached Haugh, Darcy's mother approached and asked what were they going to do with her son. Haugh replied that he would be responsible for him. 'You take my bike Micky,' he called to Russell and, addressing Darcy, he called 'You come with me. I want to have a few words with you.' Darcy's last words to his mother were 'If anything happens to me you can curse them all your life because I am innocent.'

Haugh took his prisoner across the fields to Cree, while Russell and Cunningham cycled.[85]

There is little agreement about where Darcy was brought next and even less consensus about who was present at his court-martial and whether or not there was a trial.

Some said that the location was Dan Sheedy's house, Michael Russell thought that it was O'Donnell's of Cree and Bill Haugh recalled that the prisoner was held at Kelly's of Cree. Haugh also said that Darcy was held there until dark, so it is reasonable to infer that people were coming and going and that their awareness of who was present and their impressions of what was going on was determined by the timing and duration of their visits.[86]

At some point during his detention, Darcy was given a pen and two sheets of paper. He wrote his will on one and a letter to his mother on the other. Haugh then wrote the customary spy note.

According to Russell, when Darcy came out after his court-martial, he asked John Cunningham to plead with Liddy on his behalf. Russell and Cunningham suggested to Liddy that Darcy and Sheehan be brought face to face, and even offered to go to Kilrush to arrest Sheehan, but Liddy declined.

When they put the same proposal to Haugh, he replied 'Have you a bike, a whistle, a gun and stuff. You are to be No. 1 scout on the way to Doonbeg.' Russell, together with fellow scouts Tom Martyn and Tommy Marrinan, were to clear the road as far as McNamara's of Mountrivers.[87] There, Bill Haugh informed McNamara's sister, Tess, that the spy who had betrayed her brother had been captured and was about to be executed. He could not, he said, tell her what evidence there was against the prisoner, as he was simply carrying out orders.[88] Darcy was about to be shot when Paddy Healy, a local company policeman intervened, arguing that the McNamaras had already lost one son at the hands of the British and that their home would be burned in reprisal if Darcy were to be shot there.

Patrick Darcy was taken to Daniel Hayes's public house, where he was stood on the street outside the main door. A white cloth was tied across his eyes and there he spoke his last words 'I forgive ye, boys. Ye are shooting me in the wrong,' before he was shot by Haugh and Marrinan and the spy note was pinned to his clothes.[89]

⤳

The execution of Patrick Darcy has been, for almost a century, the most controversial episode of the War of Independence in west Clare. The charge against Darcy was that he had betrayed the whereabouts of Michael McNamara and Willie Shanahan at a time when they were on the run and lodging at the home of Denis Reidy and his wife at Newtown, near Doonbeg.

Three investigations were held at the behest of Darcy's family.

The first of these was conducted in Ennis a short time after the Truce by General Eoin O'Duffy. O'Duffy's findings were never published and there are conflicting anecdotal accounts of what he said after his investigation.

Colonel Dan Bryan held a second investigation into the affair in 1945 with a view (a) to finding O'Duffy's report and (b) to establish whether any serving army officers who had been involved in the Darcy affair had any reason to believe that the decision to shoot him was misinformed. There was no sign of the O'Duffy Report and none of the army officers had seen any reason to revise their position on Darcy's execution.

The third and final investigation took place between the months of May and August 1947. This extensive sworn inquiry took place following an application by Darcy's sister for the posthumous award of a Service Medal with Bar. The medal was not awarded, but the transcripts, which are now available for scrutiny, provide valuable insights into the affair. The passage of time had clearly taken its toll on the memory of those who were interviewed and there were many conflicting testimonies. Nonetheless, File No. MA MSPC, MD/6954, when it is triangulated with other archive material, facilitates a comprehensive reconstruction of the last days and months of Patrick Darcy.

The last days and months of Michael McNamara and Willie Shanahan were spent on the run. During that period, they were betrayed at least three times. The first of these was by handwritten letter that was delivered to Captain Woods in Miltown Malbay. This letter named McNamara, Shanahan and John 'Sheldrake' Kelly as the men who killed Alan Lendrum at Caherfeenick on 22 September 1920.

The second betrayal concerned the date and location of the Sinn Féin Court sitting at Cloonagarnaun on 6 December 1920. The police and military raid on that court resulted in the death of Tom Curtin. Mullagh curate, Fr Pat Gaynor, blamed local magistrate Christy Kelly for giving away the location of the court, but it is likely that Joe Greene was shot dead in the belief that he had done so.

Patrick Darcy was blamed for the third betrayal and he paid the ultimate price when it was decided that he had revealed the whereabouts of Mac and Shanahan on 16–17 December 1920.

This book makes no pronouncement about the guilt or innocence of Patrick Darcy, nor does it seek to speculate about the rights or wrongs of his execution. It simply provides a comprehensive factual account of what happened.

# Cogadh na mBan

It is only in recent years that the role of women in the War of Independence has been given the scholarly treatment that it undoubtedly deserved.

With a membership of about 10,000, Cumann na mBan (the Women's League), had, as its primary purpose, the support of the IRA's guerrilla campaign. Recent releases by the Bureau of Military History of women activists' post-war applications for Pensions and Service Medals enable historians to begin to record the contribution of these women to the Republican cause.

It is noteworthy that the applications of some of the most active members were initially turned down and applicants were obliged to seek corroborating testimony from former senior Brigade officers and in some cases they were obliged to give sworn evidence in support of their applications.

Then there was Rita Fahy, sister of Michael, who had died aged 19 in March 1920. Rita served as Captain of Kilkee Branch, before becoming President of West Clare Brigade, which position she held in July 1922.[1]

She is believed to have been a founding member of Cumann na mBan in west Clare. She is also remembered as the woman who went between Free State soldiers and de Valera when an attempt was made to shoot him in Ennis during the Civil War. She got shrapnel in her back for her trouble, but she refused to apply for a pension.

Her brother-in-law, Brodie Lillis, had repeatedly reminded her that she had earned her pension and that she only needed to apply for it.

'I didn't do it for the money,'[2] she said.

The most active Cumann na mBan members engaged in a wide variety of activities, including organisation of fundraising dances, provision of first aid, door-to-door collection of funds in support of prisoners, preparation and mailing of food parcels for prisoners, delivery of despatches, storage and delivery of guns and ammunition, and provision of lodgings for men on the run.

Tess McNamara was probably the quintessential Cumann na mBan activist. From Mountrivers, near Doonbeg, she was a sister of Michael McNamara, who had suffered a cruel torture and death at the hands of British soldiers in December 1920.

At organisational level, Tess filled the roles of Acting OC, Adjutant and Secretary of the 3rd Battalion District Council, West Clare Brigade and she presented her members for review by Éamon de Valera when he visited Doonbeg in September 1921.

On the ground, she played a supportive role in almost everything that was happening locally. Once, when she and Minnie O'Grady were en route to alert Volunteers to an impending raid, they were stopped by Tans at 2.00am. They were, they declared, on their way to find a priest to attend to a dying man.

McNamara was regularly on hand to sort through and to intercept letters during the frequent mail train raids that took place at Doonbeg and Craggaknock stations. She attended to the needs of the participants in the Lendrum ambush at Caherfeenick on 22 September 1920 and attended to the wounded and the dying pending the arrival of a doctor following the raid on the Arbitration Court sitting at Cloonagarnaun on 6 December 1920.

When the West Clare Brigade Flying Column hid out in the Doughmore sandhills, she supplied them with bedding, washed their clothes and delivered food to them under cover of darkness as well as oiling guns and managing a nearby arms dump. Then, when the strain of it all took its toll on her health, she was sent by GHQ to The Hostel in Baldoyle, Dublin for a period of five weeks recuperation. McNamara's home was raided after the Lendrum ambush and hay and cabins were burned. She wrote later that at this time she was '… tortured beyond speaking of by Military & Tans while they were performing their revenge.'[3]

First prize for bravery must have gone to Kathleen Bonfield, a member of the Republican Mahoney family, who stood in the line of fire of some Tans who had drawn their revolvers to shoot at Jim Talty in Kilkee during the Truce. Talty credited her with saving his life.

This intrepid woman entered Kilkee RIC station on the pretext of visiting a prisoner and was caught escaping with a bandolier of ammunition. Her home was a safe house for men on the run, who were fed and boarded for periods of up to five days and consequently the house was subjected to

Cumann na mBan stalwart Rita Fahy (later Duggan), at Cliff Road, near Dunlicky Castle, Kilkee.
*(Courtesy Mary Driver)*

frequent police and military raids. Bonfield also fed a large contingent of men on the eve of the April 1921 attack on Kilrush forces. Conor Whelan, ex Brigade Vice Commandant, later wrote:

> On a number of occasions she kept and stored arms and ammunition and on one particular occasion she succeeded in safeguarding a dump of ammunition which was located at her home, while British forces were actually searching it.[4]

Sisters Ellen and Mary McMahon of Dromin, Mullagh, who lived next door to each other, provided for most of the main players who were on the run during the War of Independence.

Following the Tiernaglohane ambush on RIC, which resulted in the drowning of Michael Darcy, members of the ambush party, including Patrick Burke and Michael Campbell, took refuge in their homes. Following the shooting of Detective John Hanlon in Kilrush on 21 August 1920, Bill Haugh would spend over three months with them. Ellen would carry dispatches to and from him and even did sentry duty.

Once, Haugh made his way to safety in advance of a raid, but left some personal papers behind. She saved the day by hiding the documents before they were discovered. Again, following the siege of Kilrush on 22 April 1921, her home was the hideout of Seán Liddy, Bill Haugh, Stephen Madigan, Tom Marrinan and Conor Whelan.

But the McMahon homes also doubled as 'detention centres' for female prisoners who had disobeyed some Sinn Féin court order or who had transgressed in some other way.

Bridie Burke of Leadmore, Kilrush worked in the office of a military officer in Cork, so when she arrived home on holidays Seán Liddy, Conor Whelan and others arrested her and deposited her in the care of Mary and Ellen McMahon. The Brigade officers had hoped to get some information from her and PJ Murphy intercepted 'an important letter' that she had written to a military captain in Cork.[5]

TOP: Kilkee girls posing in military dress.
*(Courtesy Mary Driver)*

LEFT: Una Fahy, the 15-year-old sister of Michael Fahy, takes aim as her colleague stands to attention.
*(Courtesy Mary Driver)*

Ellen was even reported to have stored the motor car of Alan Lendrum RM after he was ambushed and shot at Caherfeenick on 22 September 1920.[6]

When referring to the care he received from Mary McMahon, Bill Haugh later wrote:

> Mary McMahon was the most useful and active member of the Cumann na mBan organisation in west Clare during the Anglo Irish war … If I may speak from personal experiences – hers was the first house in which I was received when worst wanted & suffering from an open wound in the right side which required attention for a considerable time, & received same at her hands.[7]

Haugh was referring to the wound that resulted from the removal of a kidney during his time in training with the US Marines. This wound had never properly healed, causing him some difficulty while he was on the run.

~

In late 1919, Mick Honan and Michael Breen hid out in the home of Mary O'Dea (née Reidy, Ballinagun) at Tullabrack. During Honan's incarceration in Dundalk Gaol, she had mailed parcels of food to him.[8]

Bridget Liddy, sister of the Brigade OC, who lived in Danganelly, served first as President of the Cooraclare branch of Cumann na mBan from 1917 until the end of 1918. The following year she was elected to the position of Brigade OC, which rank she held until the Truce in July 1921.

Following the boycott of the Murphy family of Danganelly in 1918, the nearby Liddy home was subjected to repeated military raids and Bridget was singled out for particular attention:

> I was three weeks without lying in the bed; just lying in front of the window to save myself; not even take my clothes off. The brunt of the rifle morning, noon and night, and as for a bed, you could not get a bed, because it was torn asunder when they came in, and as for abuse!

IRA dugout at Greygrove, Kilmihil.
*(Courtesy James McAlpine)*

Early in 1920, Bridget had succeeded in delivering to the Brigade a trunk full of gelignite, detonators and hand grenades by train from Dublin on behalf of William Shannon.

Following the siege of Kilrush on 22–23 April 1921, the Liddy home was bombed and burned in an organised military reprisal. Bridget was taken hostage that day in case any attack would be launched on the military during the operation. Before they left, the military warned her that any family who would give her shelter would suffer the same fate.

Those who were on the run at this time slept in dugouts in remote locations in Clonreddan and in Greygrove, where one still exists today in land owned by Raymond and Martina Coughlan. Once, during a large-scale round-up, the military had surrounded a large area, within which a number of Volunteers were sleeping in a dugout. When Bridget Liddy became aware of the operation, she hastened across country to alert the men, who had to break through the military cordon to escape. Her description of crawling through a tunnel to alert the men most likely refers to the Greygrove dugout.

Bridget herself spent the night in a drain, not daring to move until the military had left.[9]

～

Romance blossomed on a regular basis between members of Cumann na mBan and their Volunteer counterparts. In fact, Volunteers on the run in west Clare had a better chance of being struck by Cupid's arrow than by a Lee-Enfield rifle bullet.

Except for Mick Honan, of course, in whose case the rifle bullet came first. Honan had participated in a particularly dangerous and protracted ambush on RIC at Cahercanivan on 22 September 1919, during which he was shot in the chest. Bridget Liddy cycled up to four times daily for a fortnight to dress Honan's wound. It was the beginning of a relationship that would last for the rest of their lives, for they married in June 1924.[10]

Lendrum ambush participant James Neylon and Danny Campbell, who took part in many engagements, including the Drumdigus ambush, married Thomas Quealy's sisters, Mary and Jane, in Chicago.

Seán Liddy married Nano Breen, sister of Mickey 'Saddler' Breen. Martin Chambers married Margaret McNamara, the sister of Michael McNamara who was killed with Willie Shanahan on 22 December 1920 and Jack McNamara of Kilmihil married Cumann na mBan activist Mai Clancy. The same Mai Clancy, together with Susan Ryan had to keep cool heads when they were stopped by Tans at Shaughnessy's Cross as they cycled from Kilrush to Kilmihil. They had bullets strapped to their waists inside their clothes.[11]

Help and support for the Republican cause sometimes came from the most unlikely sources, and so did romance.

While on the run, John McCarthy Adjutant of the East Limerick Brigade

Romance in the dugout. Mick Honan (Leitrim) and Cumann na mBan activist Bridget Liddy, (Danganelly) on their wedding day, 24 June 1924.
*(Courtesy Michael Honan Jnr)*

and member of the Flying Column, had occasion to visit Kilrush on personal business. There, his accommodation was looked after by one of the local Volunteer officers. On a visit to Williams's Hotel on Frances Street, he was surprised to discover that Catherine McCreery, the daughter of a retired RIC man who lived in Kilfinane, was working there.

His initial fears that the young lady would disclose his presence were quickly dispelled when she informed him that the local RIC had intended to arrest him for questioning. McCreery arranged for McCarthy's safe passage to Limerick on a departing cargo steamer, guided him to the boat and even provided him with food for his all-night journey. In September 1923 she would marry West Clare Brigade officer Conor Whelan.[12]

Bill Haugh, one of Ireland's most wanted men and whose photograph had been published in *Hue and Cry*, once found himself on the platform of a train station facing an oncoming RIC patrol. He grabbed a nearby young lady and engaged her in an extended passionate embrace until the danger had passed.[13]

On another occasion, he succeeded in getting arms and ammunition through customs with the help of Martha McEntee, a 23-year-old nurse who was the daughter of an RIC constable from Kingscourt in County Cavan.[14]

~

Women were strongly discouraged from walking out with police or military personnel, a practice that was far more common in the towns than in rural areas. Fr Pat Gaynor believed that girls were motivated by '... a desire for attention and admiration from any source ...'

Apart from the inherent lack of patriotism and the potential for betrayal of their secrets, the Volunteers were less than impressed that they themselves were not first in the queue. Offending girls could expect to have their hair cropped, and on rare occasions their bare heads were tarred. Gaynor disapproved of this punishment, believing that it ought to be inflicted only on women who were proven spies:

With most girls vanity – not lust – is the ruling passion, they desire primarily to exercise their power of fascination and to win affection and attention.

It may be inferred that the pastor's insights into what motivated those he described as the 'gentle sex' were informed by his experience of the confessional.

A number of Quilty girls were in the habit of chatting with members of a detachment of Royal Marines that occupied the Coastguard Station outside the village. The matter was brought before the Battalion Council, where Battalion Commandant Fr Michael McKenna was asked to sanction the clipping of their hair by the Quilty Volunteers. Gaynor, who held no rank in the Battalion, was less than happy with the outcome:

The local swains in the volunteers, whether through jealousy or outraged principles, brought this trivial occurrence before the Battalion Council and very unwisely, Fr McKenna – though usually tender-hearted – allowed the Council to impose sentence of 'hair-clipping' on the Quilty girls. He took for granted, I am sure, that the sentence would be carried out in open day and would be a mere formality: he did not avert that the Quilty volunteers, with their 'moonlighting' instincts, would drag the girls from their homes after dark and might subject them to worse insult than hair-clipping. Miss McInerney, a very refined young lady, complained to me that she had been insulted, being under the impression that I had imposed the unjust penalty... Fr McKenna, on hearing that I was blamed for the hair-clipping, went to see Miss McInerney and took responsibility and gave all possible consolation.[15]

At a dance in Quilty, a number of unmasked young men entered the building and cropped the hair of four girls who had ignored warnings against keeping company with soldiers. When a fifth target pleaded that she was about to emigrate to America she was brought outside and marched through the village blindfolded[16].

Two young Miltown Malbay women ignored repeated warnings about keeping company with soldiers to their cost. On Saturday night 10 April 1920 their hair was cut by a group of men, after which they hid the damage by wearing wigs.[17]

Elsewhere, in Kildysart, a domestic servant who had been friendly with police was accosted by three armed men on her way from her home to the home of her employer. She was thrown to the ground and all of her hair except for a small amount at the front of her head was cut off.[18]

Young Annie O'Shea from Lack West, Kilmihil, would suffer a similar fate when it was discovered that she was visiting Denis Sheehan's pub on Vandeleur Street in Kilrush, a popular haunt of military, police and Black and Tans. She had also been seen in the company of groups of four and five policemen in the town.

O'Shea later claimed that on 7 December 1920 she was visited in her home by as many as twelve men who were armed with knives, sticks, scissors and a revolver. There, she was forced to the middle of the kitchen floor, where the man with the scissors proceeded to cut her hair.

A compensation award in the County Court of £60 was later increased on appeal to £100. Annie O'Shea had denied the accusations that had been levelled against her and even claimed partial deafness as a result of her ordeal. It was stated that a marriage which was on the cards had fallen through following the hair-cropping incident.[19]

The British side agreed to pay half of the sum awarded.[20]

~

Gender-based violence was not the sole prerogative of Republicans, however, and a number of instances were directly attributable to police and military.

In October 1920, Babe Hogan, secretary of Cumann na mBan in Miltown Malbay district, heard knocking on her front door at 1.00am. Sensing that members of the British forces had come to cut her hair, she ran through the back door and on to the garden wall before she was surrounded by uniformed men. She was brought inside, where one of the men identified her and another aimed a revolver at her. Hogan put up a brave fight and although her attackers succeeded in cutting some of her hair, she unmasked one of them and made her escape through the back door and into a neighbour's garden, where she spent the remainder of the night.[21]

In Kilmihil, Delia Browne was subjected to harassment in her own home by RIC over a prolonged period of time. The terrorising of the 24-year-old dressmaker had begun prior to April 1920 when two drunken constables named McGowan and Creavin entered her house late one night and refused to leave for two hours. She had reported the matter to DI Barrett but one of the men had written that they were drunk and that they didn't know what they were doing. The pair had since left the area.

The harassment continued, however and another two drunken policemen entered her home in December 1920 and started to sing and refused to leave. Once again she reported the matter to DI Barrett, but was later visited by a policeman who threatened to kill her and burn her house down for having reported his friends.

On the night of 25 January 1921, Delia was in her house with a young local girl named Minnie Carey, when she was awakened by the sound of a lorry outside. When she answered a knock at the door, eight or ten masked men entered and ordered her to light a lamp. One of the men then cut her hair with a scissors, while another pointed a revolver at her. One of the men demanded money from Minnie Carey, who went upstairs to get a light and she was followed by one of the men who remarked that she '... would not need much light to shoot a policeman.' Having cut Delia's hair quite bare, the men then threatened to burn the house down if they didn't get money.

Throughout the War of Independence, householders were obliged to display on the inside of the front door the names of those who were sleeping in the house. After the men had left, the list was found on the floor. Written on it with pencil were the words, 'Anti Sinn Fein [*sic*] Gang; Beware, your doom is sealed.' Delia Browne had no doubt that it was police who had been harassing her. They had, after all, threatened to cut her hair on three previous occasions.

As a consequence of this harassment, she lost her business and had to go and live with her father. In awarding compensation of £400, Judge Bodkin remarked that it would be '... an utterly preposterous travesty of justice to have the ratepayers called on to pay this compensation.'

In cases where there were allegations against forces of the Crown, Bodkin had always given ample notice so that they could be represented at compensation hearings, but invariably they failed to attend. The matter was raised in the House of Commons in May 1921 by Mr Thomas Griffiths, who asked the Chief Secretary about the Delia Browne award.

In response, Mr Denis Henry refused to accept the validity of such awards, since those against whom the allegations had been made were not present in court to answer them.[22]

# The Blackened Tans

History and folklore have rightly blamed the Black and Tans for much of the terror that attended the operations of British forces in the War of Independence.

Stories of indiscriminate firing, shooting of animals, burning, looting, floggings, torture and murder invariably conjure up images of drink-fuelled hybrids terrorising civilian populations. Tan terror made world headlines, causing widespread revulsion at home and abroad and brought international pressure to bear on the British government.

Yet, for all their notoriety, the reputation of these two-tone police recruits is less than warranted in west Clare. There, many of the most violent misdeeds that have been attributed to the RIC and Black and Tans were the work of regular soldiers of the 2nd Battalion, The Royal Scots, the regiment that was known as Pontius Pilate's Bodyguards.

The Black and Tans were temporary constables who were recruited in late 1919 and 1920 in response to the inability of a dwindling police force to contain a crisis of lawlessness that existed in Ireland at the time.

Many had served in the Great War and had not yet taken up full time employment. A shortage of proper uniforms meant that they were often issued with a mix of army (khaki) and police (dark green-black) outfits.

And it was their dress, together with the manner of their deportment, which earned them a moniker that had been coined for a pack of foxhounds.[1]

1920 was the year of the unofficial reprisal when Crown forces, frustrated at the guerrilla tactics of the IRA and the difficulty of securing convictions, took the law into their own hands. Rebel attacks on police and military were answered by lightning raids on nearby towns with widespread burning and looting and the killing of civilians. Then, in the first half of 1921, official reprisals became more common.

Some of the most severe reprisals occurred in September 1920. In Balbriggan, in the north of County Dublin, the shooting dead of HC Burke, who had stopped off for a drink in a local hostelry on 20 September was to have devastating consequences. When Black and Tans and Auxiliaries in Gormanstown Camp got word of the attack on Burke they descended on the town and went on a drunken orgy of destruction, killing James Lawless and John Gibbons and burning numerous homes and buildings. After an *ad hoc* firing squad had shot the two men, a drunken Tan moved in to finish the job, stabbing Gibbons three times, watched by an elderly man from a nearby window:

> [Gibbons] moaned each time, the last moan being very weak. The man who stabbed him fell over him, and the bayonet grazed along the concrete wall with a tearing sound. When he got up he stabbed the body again. He passed the body of the man with the bandaged head and lifted the head with his bayonet.[2]

The Tan was in fact slicing the muscles on the back of Lawless's neck with his bayonet, inflicting a deep laceration.[3]

≈

Word spread quickly that the sack of Balbriggan, which left two men dead, 50 families homeless and 400 jobless, was the work of Black and Tans from Gormanstown, about four miles away.[4]

The atrocity made world headlines and gave centre stage to this motley cohort of RIC temporary cadets who would go down in history as the villains of the Anglo-Irish War.

More severe reprisals occurred in County Clare on the night of 22–23 September after the Lendrum ambush at Caherfeenick and another at Rineen, between Miltown Malbay and Lahinch, where six policemen were shot dead.

In a random shooting immediately following the Rineen ambush, farmer John Keane was fatally wounded by Royal Scots soldiers. As in the cases of the other five victims of the Rineen reprisals, the army did not hold the obligatory Court of Inquiry.

Later, a best-selling book on the period reported that Keane had been shot by RIC and Black and Tans.[5]

A spree of retribution by Crown forces resulted in the deaths of six men, the sacking of Ennistymon, Lahinch and Miltown Malbay and extensive burning of property along the route of Lendrum's last journey between Kilkee and Cree.

Fresh from the horror of Balbriggan, the first newspaper reports attributed these reprisals to Black and Tans.[6] Amid calls for an independent inquiry, the English Parliamentary Labour Party conducted its own investigation and the subsequent report depicted a people-friendly military that was resentful of any suggestion of complicity with Tans and Auxiliaries in the reprisals.

One British Army officer who was serving in Ireland at the time wrote to Field Marshall Sir Henry Wilson to complain about the importation of '... crowds of indisciplined men who are just terrorizing the country.'[7]

The sacking of these three west-Clare towns would come to be almost universally misrepresented as the hot-blooded vengeance of police and Black and Tans.[8]

∽

There were early indications, however, that the reality was very different. The local *Manchester Guardian* correspondent, having sent an initial report on the ambush at Rineen, was promptly arrested by British forces and held prisoner for two days, being thus prevented from reporting on the reprisals.[9] Another correspondent, having made detailed enquiries in the Clare towns, wrote:

> I have spent a couple of days carefully sifting the accounts of the happenings in Ennistymon and Lahinch furnished by eye witnesses. If the authorities are able to confute it they should do so at once, but the statement is made here, not by one witness, but by many – some of them holding responsible positions, – that in the sacking of Ennistymon the men were led by commissioned officers ... To take Ennistymon, the worst case, first. Within a very short time of the soldiers' arrival – eye-witnesses insist they were soldiers with officers from a garrison near by [*sic*] – two men named Connole and Linnane had been done to death, several shops and the wooden Town Hall set ablaze, and nearly the whole of the terrorstricken [*sic*] population put to flight.[10]

Tom Connole, a trade union official who had played no part in the Rineen ambush, was sitting in his home reading the newspaper at about 10.00pm on the evening of the ambush when he heard loud knocking on his door. When he opened it he saw about 25 soldiers outside. Having identified himself, he was taken outside for questioning.

His wife, Helena, pleaded with the soldiers, saying that her husband had no involvement in politics; everybody knew him – even the local police, but they simply stared blankly at her. Then one of the soldiers who was in the house said that it was time to burn it. Helena took a child under each arm and showed them to the officer in charge:

> "For God's sake," I said, "have mercy; my husband is an innocent man." He told me to clear away or he would make it worse for me. I then knelt on the road. He caught and dragged me to my feet and called the soldiers to clear me away ... the soldiers drove me at the point of the bayonet up the road. When about 15 yards I heard two shots and the next thing I saw was the house in flames.

Connole was then shot, after which his body was thrown into the hallway of his burning home.

The following morning, a simple cross, fashioned from stones, marked the bloody spot where he was shot; his cap and a piece of his skull were nearby.

Joe Flaherty gave evidence of having seen Connole's charred body inside the front door of his home. Flaherty had been held up by military personnel the previous night when they arrived in the town from the Workhouse. They were all soldiers, he stated.[11]

A short time later, P J Linnane was shot dead as he attempted to quench fires that were started by the soldiers.

Limerick-based Jesuit Fr Willie Hackett took this photograph of the bombed-out 22 Main Street in Ennistymon around noon on 23 September 1920, the day after the town was sacked. Fr Hackett had brought some visiting Quakers there to show them examples of British atrocities in Ireland. He described his guests as 'Mr Barlow, chief Quaker of the world, the Quaker Pope, Mr Clarke, chief Quaker of England and Miss Ellis.' His caption read: 'This photograph Ennistymon Black and Tannism, midday after it happened exemplifies the widespread attribution of the Rineen reprisals to Black and Tans.' *(Photograph Fr Willie Hackett; courtesy Archives of the Society of Jesus, Australia, Hackett Papers)*

In nearby Lahinch, visitor Joe Sammon was staying in Walsh's boarding house when the soldiers broke in at 2.00am. Hearing the noise from downstairs, both Sammon and a female guest jumped from the window onto the back yard. The soldiers caught him and took him to the kitchen. He was found dead the following morning with a bullet through his head.[12]

Pake Lehane, who had earlier participated in the Rineen ambush, had heard that some of his men had gone to Lahinch that night. He went into the town with the intention of organising a car to get them away.

It so happened that Major Meldon, a visiting Resident Magistrate, was staying at the Aberdeen Arms Hotel in the town and his car was in the garage attached to the Old Golf Links. At about midnight, some men (probably including Lehane) came to the hotel to commandeer Meldon's car, but the RM refused to have anything to do with them. When the car didn't materialise, Lehane went to Thomas and Bridget Flanagan's pub.

At about 2.00am the military burst in. Lehane was reported to have been shot and burned with the house and his charred body was found the next day.[13]

Fr Willie Hackett, a Limerick-based Jesuit priest, had been showing some English Quakers examples of British brutality in Ireland when a friend suggested that they visit Clare, where there were reports of terrible reprisals.

Having hired a car, Hackett brought his visitors to Ennistymon, Lahinch and Miltown Malbay. On Friday 24 September they arrived in Lahinch '… to a scene of indescribable misery,' where they were shown the body of Pake Lehane:

> The pretty little village of Lahinch had been gutted on Wednesday night (we were there on Friday). Water taps were still running, houses still smouldering, and the people were in terror. No one knew what was going to happen next. Everyone seemed dazed at the magnitude of the disaster. A large body of troops had poured into the town and without giving the people time to dress or even leave the houses had proceeded to sprinkle the houses with petrol

ABOVE: The home of Michael Howard in Main Street, Lahinch (today's Claremont Bar and Nightclub), containing 20 apartments, which he leased from Michael Linnane of Ennistymon, was burned during the reprisals that followed the Rineen ambush on 22 September 1920. Linnane was later awarded £6000 in compensation.

BELOW: Main Street's Vaughan Hotel (today's Atlantic Hotel) also suffered the same fate and the Vaughan family subsequently received £6351 in compensation.

*Photographs by Fr Willie Hackett (courtesy Archives of the Society of Jesus, Australia, Hackett Papers)*

and to throw in incendiary bombs ...They proceeded with such expedition—they had to carry destruction over a large area that night—that Mrs. Hanley of Limerick had to jump from the second storey to escape being burned to death. She broke her two legs. Her husband made the same leap but escaped with a shaking.

In another house hardby [*sic*: nearby] one of the inhabitants was actually burned to death. They showed us his body on the Friday. It was simply a trunk. Arms were burned away and legs were gone. The people had taken the remains out of the house where the tragedy had happened and had wrapped it in linen very neatly but then in their panic they had placed it in an outhouse—a kind of pigsty ... I took many photoes [*sic*] in Lahinch but I could not bring myself to photo the terrible corpse.

Hackett's hired car was borrowed to collect a coffin from Ennistymon for Lehane's body.[14]

～

In a letter to the *Freeman's Journal* on 11 October, Connole's brother Joe emphasised that it was soldiers who had brutally killed his brother in Ennistymon on that fateful night:

These were no drunken soldiers who broke loose from barracks, but disciplined men who knew what they were about and, acting under the orders of their officer, did it only too effectually. Connole, with the other victim, young Linnane, was buried without even the pretence of a military inquiry.[15]

Later, Judge Matthias Bodkin, citing the sworn testimony of litigants in the County Court, highlighted the involvement of military personnel.

The publicity surrounding Bodkin's intervention and Connole's letter may have influenced Chief Secretary Sir Hamar Greenwood's acknowledgement of limited military culpability. But the definitive proof of army participation comes from a Royal Scots' memo in the National Archives at Kew. Referring to the Ennistymon reprisals, the document clearly states that:

> ... the houses of well known Sinn Feiners were selected for destruction and burned by organised parties under officers.[16]

The Royal Scots' memo gives the lie to Greenwood's assertion that the Rineen reprisals were carried out 'in hot blood'.

By way of justification, The Chief Secretary had claimed that expanding bullets (commonly known as dum dum bullets) had been used in the ambush by rebel forces, provoking outrage among the victims' colleagues and driving them to reprise.[17]

The Royal Scots memo that proves that the Ennistymon reprisals were planned and conducted by soldiers under officers.
(*Source: NAUK, WO 35 89, Army incident Report Ennistymon, 22 September 1920, ©NAUK*)

The fatal shooting of civilian Thomas Curtin at an Arbitration Court sitting in Craggaknock on 6 December 1920 was widely ascribed to Black and Tans.[18]

In fact, the subsequent Military Court of Inquiry reported that the raid was carried out by a mixed force of police and soldiers of the 2nd Battalion, Royal Scots. Curtin was shot by Lieutenant A W Tuffield, 2nd Battalion, Royal Scots – the officer in charge – as he fled the scene.[19]

Local curate Fr Patrick Gaynor wrote that another man was shot on that occasion while standing facing the soldiers with his hands in the air. Gaynor, a member of the supreme executive of Sinn Féin, and fellow Mullagh curate Fr McKenna (a former army chaplain and Commandant of the local battalion of Volunteers) had their own troubles with the soldiers.

In his memoirs, Gaynor recalls numerous raids on the curates' house in Mullagh. During one raid a military officer threatened to break McKenna's face while his fellow soldiers drank the priests' whiskey. Both priests were subsequently arrested and gaoled on trumped-up charges. At their trial by Field General Court-martial in May 1921, McKenna detailed a catalogue of petty tyrannies, including 'frightful desecration of the tabernacle' by the military in the local church.[20]

In a rare occurrence, a Royal Scots private named Munroe and James Huddleston, a County Leitrim-born Black and Tan and ex-Marine, were charged with attempted rape of Kate Kelly at Knock, near Kilrush, on 25 September 1920, at the height of the west Clare reprisals.

The pair had visited the house earlier on the pretence of searching for arms. The soldier was convicted of common assault offences and had his sentence of six months hard labour commuted to detention by the military authorities. There was no mercy for the Tan who was convicted as charged and sentenced to one year's hard labour.[21]

The torture and shooting on 22 December 1920 of Doonbeg IRA men ,Willie Shanahan and Michael McNamara, while in military custody is represented in song and story as the dirty work of Black and Tans. Even in the immediate aftermath of their deaths, a letter from a Doonbeg woman to her son in the United States represented the killings as a Black and Tans outrage.[22]

The subsequent Courts of Inquiry in lieu of Inquest were no more than a pretence, being devoid of medical evidence. Nevertheless they revealed that both men had been shot by named soldiers of the 2nd Battalion Royal Scots.

~

Ten violent deaths during the War of Independence in the western half of County Clare have been widely attributed in varying degrees to the Black

This cartoon, published in the London newspaper, *The Catholic Herald*, was confiscated in October 1920 from elderly Glengarriff hotelier Mrs Violet Annan Bryce. The wife of a former MP, she had been arrested while on her way to address a meeting in Wales on the subject of reprisals in Ireland.
*(Source: NAUK, WO 35 214, ©NAUK)*

and Tans, the RIC or a combination of the two.

John Keane, Tom Connole, Tom Curtin, Willie Shanahan and Michael McNamara were killed by Royal Scots soldiers and Joe Sammon was last seen in the custody of soldiers shortly before he was shot.

P J Linnane was shot during the sack of Ennistymon which is now known to have been an organised military reprisal and Pake Lehane was shot and burned in a similar military operation in Lahinch.

Because of the widespread tendency to rush to judgment on RIC and Black and Tans, there is no certainty of police or Tan culpability in the deaths of Tom Shannon and Dan Lehane. In Shannon's case, the only account to assign culpability came from Bill Haugh, who blamed Black and Tans from Kilkee.[23] But Haugh was incorrect in stating that Tom Curtin was a victim of the Tans.

And in the case of the shooting of Dan Lehane at his home in Cragg, his wife's evidence referred to 'men dressed in uniform.'[24] Other later accounts stated that Black and Tans were responsible.[25]

Furthermore, the reprisals that left six men dead, three Clare towns in ruins and hundreds of people dispossessed were executed with significant engagement by soldiers of the 2nd Battalion, Royal Scots.

In fact, Royal Scots soldiers were responsible for many if not most of the outrages that have traditionally been attributed to the police and the Black and Tans in the western half of the county. Yet Pontius Pilate's Bodyguards, like Pilate, walked away with clean hands while the ballad sheets and the history books heaped scorn on their constabulary cousins.

It is unlikely that the Black and Tans sat at home reading the newspaper while Royal Scots soldiers terrorised the west Clare population on the night of 22–23 September 1920. But it is clear from the sworn testimony of the victims that these reprisals were systematically conducted by soldiers under the command of officers and that any role played by the Tans was secondary.[26]

How, therefore, did it happen that the Black and Tans became the villains of the War of Independence in west Clare?

The sack of Balbriggan on 20 September 1920, followed by a similar one in Trim, County Meath, on 27 September, had been quickly, correctly and universally reported as Black and Tan atrocities.

Sandwiched between the two, the Ennistymon, Lahinch and Miltown Malbay outrages bore all of the hallmarks of and came to be identified as RIC and Black and Tan reprisals, with secondary attribution in a few accounts to the military.

These incidents caused widespread revulsion, demonising the Black and Tans both at home and abroad. In Clare, it was a convenient narrative for everybody, except the Black and Tans who were transitory and without structure or voice.

Clare Republicans now had universally acknowledged figures of hate upon whom these and other future atrocities could and would be pinned. In a

Richard Bennett's best-seller *The Black and Tans* (1959) grossly sensationalised the Lendrum affair and attributed the Rineen reprisals solely to police and Tans. The 2010 reprint of this book continued to perpetuate the myths:

'Reprisals also provoked some members of the I.R.A. to acts of insensate savagery. On the day the Black and Tans ran wild in Ennistymon, Lahinch and Miltown Malbay, for example, a party of Volunteers a few miles away buried a Resident Magistrate up to his neck in sand, just below high water mark, as they imagined. He had been kidnapped and condemned to death as a traitor, but the appointed executioner had wounded him in the head without killing him. The Volunteers returned the next day to find the victim still alive. They dug him out and buried him again farther down the beach, where he could watch the next tide advance, to put him slowly out of his long agony."

war that was seen as '... a battle between Ireland and England, us and them, good and evil,'[27] an ephemeral cohort of hybrids who were committing daily atrocities nationally were perfect scapegoats.

～

In west Clare, the Royal Scots, were in control of the all-important Military Courts of Inquiry in lieu of Inquest, whose *raison d'etre* was to report on the circumstances of each death.

No such inquiries were held in the cases of the six men who died violent deaths as a result of the Rineen reprisals, which meant that there was no official record of culpability which, in turn, did nothing to dispel the enduring myth that the RIC and Black and Tans were largely to blame.

Then, as time went on, the people of west Clare came to accept the Black and Tan moniker as a descriptor for all British forces. This was in sharp contrast with Dublin where the distinction between 'gentlemen' military personnel and 'riff raff' Black and Tans was more clear-cut and people were more inclined to differentiate.[28]

And, of course, the Tan moniker was populist and guaranteed to sell books as evidenced by the success of Richard Bennett's *The Black and Tans*, published in 1959, which ascribed the Rineen reprisals to police and Tans ... and went on to break all sales records in Ireland by being the first paperback to sell more than 100,000 copies.[29]

The extensive oral history research of historian Tomás Mac Conmara has noted this also, though he stresses that people did know the difference:

Two considerations are important. Firstly, while the categorisations can be technically inaccurate, I have found that the collective description 'Tans' does not indicate an inability to distinguish. Instead, it is often a recognition of the divided nature of the war, which saw the British on one side and the IRA on the other. For many, the Black and Tans, RIC, Auxiliaries and even British army could acceptably be labelled as 'Tans' ... In the same way, their counterparts in the republican movement were referred to as 'Sinn Féiners' and 'IRA', despite the technical distinction.[30]

It is indeed true that the widespread practice of collective description served to reflect the popular Republican conception of the 'us and them' and the 'good and evil' referred to by David Leeson.[31]

But historians are duty bound to go beyond a convenient, collective description and, when they fail to do so, the historical record is compromised.

The 'historical' record in the textbooks of generations of Irish schoolchildren taught that the burning of Ennistymon was the work of Black and Tans.[32]

By wrongly attributing the deaths of as many as eight men to Black and Tans, the 'historical' record enabled Pontius Pilate's Bodyguards – the soldiers of the 2nd Battalion, Royal Scots – to wash their hands of their responsibility.

It clearly mattered to Joe Connole to set the record straight by insisting that regular soldiers were responsible for the death of his brother Tom.

Should it matter any less to the descendants of Ennistymon-based RIC and Black and Tans, whose names are now readily accessible on internet archives, that they were blamed for shooting Tom Connole before throwing him into his burning home?

# Reclaiming the Streets

Traditionally, the streets of Kilrush have borne the names of members of the Landlord Vandeleur family. And every time a new street was developed a new Vandeleur name was chosen for it.

Gender equity was the accepted practice at the Kilrush Big House long before the term came into popular use, as evidenced when the town's main street was given to Lady Frances Vandeleur as a wedding present and named Frances Street in her honour.

The people of west Clare had something of a 'We-love-them, we-love-them-not' relationship with the Vandeleur family. On the one hand, they were responsible for planning and building much of the modern town that is Kilrush. But on the other, this family and their agents would preside over some of the most heartless dispossessions that were seen in Ireland during the famine years and beyond.

And the advent of photojournalism ensured that the world was informed about what came to be known as the Vandeleur Evictions. The world was duly horrified.

In June 1930, in one of its 'we-love-them, but-we-love-our-own-even-more' phases, Kilrush Urban Council adopted a resolution that a number of the town's main streets be renamed in memory of west Clare Republican activists who died or were killed during the republican struggle and the Civil War or in consequence of their service in these wars.[1]

While much has already been written about the casualties of the War of Independence, less is known about those who were active during that war but who died or were killed during or after the Civil War.

One of these was Dan Crawford, from Shanaway in Mullagh, who achieved the rank of section Commander in Coore Company.

Following the Truce in July 1921, Crawford participated in the IRA occupation of Kilrush and Knock. Having taken the anti-Treaty side in the Civil War, he became a member of the West Clare Active Service Unit in 1922. While on the run, he spent many nights on Mount Callan, which was thought to have had a detrimental effect on his health. He was arrested by troops from Miltown Malbay at a friend's house and was lodged in Limerick Prison.

John O'Gorman (left), Lisdeen and Cloonagarnaun and Patrick O'Dea, Carrowmore, who were active during the War of Independence and killed during the Civil War.
(*Source: Author's Colloection*)

There. he experienced chronic stomach trouble, which was probably exacerbated by a subsequent hunger strike. Crawford died on 16 June 1924, some time after the prison doctor had ordered his release. Grace Street, Kilrush was renamed in his memory.[2]

Thomas and Michael Keane were remembered in the renaming of Burton Street and Crofton Street.

Kiltrellig-born Thomas Keane's tragic death happened in a field at Cross village on Sunday 5 March 1916. His Volunteer unit had assembled for miniature rifle practice and the 17-year-old was accidentally shot in the head while examining the workings of the gun.[3]

Michael Keane had deserted from the Irish Guards to join the Republican struggle in his native Shragh. He became a member of the Flying Column and participated in a number of their engagements. Keane took the anti-Treaty side in the Civil War, but contracted pneumonia on active service and died on 4 November 1922. He was buried in Doonbeg's Republican Plot.[4]

Back Road was renamed O'Dea's Road in memory of 18-year-old Patrick O'Dea from Carrowmore North in the parish of Doonbeg.

An accomplished long-distance swimmer, O'Dea had been active in the IRA since 1920. On 15 July 1922 he was shot in the chest during an engagement with Free State soldiers at Monvana, outside Kilrush and died the following day. He was buried with honours in the Doonbeg Republican Plot.[5]

O'Dea's friend and neighbour, John O'Gorman, had Pound Street renamed in his honour.

O'Gorman had taken an active part in the War of Independence and had been badly wounded by an exploding bomb in an attack on Free State soldiers in Kildysart Barracks on 7 August 1922. He died in Ennis Hospital on 14 August and was buried with full military honours in the Republican Plot in Doonbeg.

Jack McSweeney of Kilkee, who was similarly injured in the same attack, also died. McSweeney had been an active member of the 5th Battalion during the Republican struggle. Hector Street was renamed McSweeney Street.[6]

Patrick Keating from Rahona died in Kilrush Hospital on 29 August 1922 following a failed ambush on Free State soldiers on 25 August. Keating, aged 30, had also been active during the War of Independence. He was buried in Kilballyowen with Military Honours. Chapel Street, Kilrush, was renamed Keating Street.[7]

Finally, Market Square was renamed Martyrs Square.

Officially, however, the changing of a street's name requires the holding of a plebiscite of the street's residents in order to determine their wishes. When no such plebiscite was held, the town's business people were free to advertise their addresses in accordance with their political leanings. So it was not uncommon to see two advertisements for businesses on the same street, one of which bore the surname of a patriot and the other the Christian name of a Vandeleur.

In the end, most of the previously 'renamed' streets reverted to their original status in 1981 and bilingual signs were erected accordingly.[8]

LEFT: Christy McCarthy, Clounlaheen.
*(Source: McCarthy Family)*
RIGHT: Peadar Clancy.
*(Source: http://source.southdublinlibraries.ie/handle/10599/9958)*

| Original Name | New Name |
| --- | --- |
| Vandeleur Street | Breen Street<br>(*John Breen, Kilmihil, 18 April 1920*) |
| Frances Street | Shanahan Street<br>(*Willie Shanahan, Doughmore, Doonbeg, 22 December 1920*) |
| Henry Street | McNamara Street<br>(*Michael McNamara, Mountrivers, Doonbeg, 22 December 1920*) |
| The Glen | Burke Street<br>(*Patrick Burke, Carhue, Cooraclare, 7 March 1922* |
| Moore Street (part of) | Clancy Street<br>(*Peadar Clancy, Cranny, 21 November 1920*) |
| Grace Street | Crawford Street<br>(*Dan Crawford, Shanaway, Mullagh, 16 June 1924*) |
| John Street | Darcy Street<br>(*Michael Darcy, Cooraclare, 19 January 1920*) |
| Stewart Street | Hassett Street<br>(*Paddy Hassett, Burrane, circa 20 July 1920*) |
| Burton Street | Keane Street<br>(*Michael Keane, Shragh, 4 November 1922*) |
| Crofton Street | Keane's Road<br>(*Thomas Keane, Kiltrellig, Kilbaha, 5 March 1916*) |
| Chapel Street | Keating Street<br>(*Patrick Keating, Rahona, 29 August 1922*) |
| Hector Street | McSweeney Street<br>(*Jack McSweeney, Kilkee, August 1922*) |
| Moore Street (part of) | McCarthy Street<br>(*Christy McCarthy, Clounlaheen, Mullagh, 15 June 1921*) |
| Market Square | Martyrs Square<br>(*Manchester Martyrs, 22 November 1867*) |
| Back Road | O'Dea's Road (part)<br>(*Patrick O'Dea, Carrownore, Doonbeg, 16 July 1922*) |
| Pound Street | O'Gorman Street<br>(*John O'Gorman, Lisdeen and Cloonagarnaun, 14 August 1922*) |
| | Russell's Lane<br>(*Thomas Russell, Ballyferriter, County Kerry, 24 March 1918*) |
| | Fahy's Road<br>(*Michael Fahy, Kilkee, 19 March 1920*) |

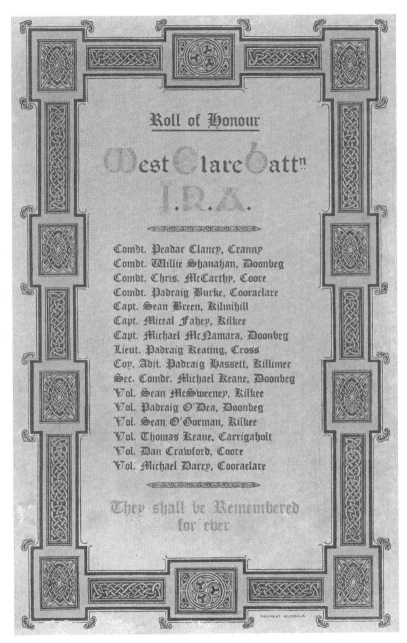

A unique Roll of Honour memorial scroll for members of the West Clare Brigade.
*(Courtesy James Stephens)*

# Calm before the storm

In the months following the Truce, IRA men could carry arms openly and there were tense moments when they met old armed foes on the streets. Michael Brennan recalled one standoff between his men and a large group of Auxiliaries near Lisdoonvarna, when weapons were drawn.[1]

By the end of July, the only reported breaches of the truce were being attributed to British Forces, though a drunken Ennis mob drew a stinging rebuke from County Council Chairman, Michael Brennan:

> It is not very creditable to Ennis to say that numbers of its residents were drunk on the streets and could be heard until a late hour shouting about dying for Ireland. They know it is quite safe to shout now. How many of them shouted in a similar strain a week ago? Not one! I have been told that if 100 men were selected from those that carried on in that scandalous fashion on Monday night, not even one of them could be classed as a good Irishman ... They will shout about fighting police and soldiers now when they know the police and soldiers are not allowed to fight ... Get a good brick and hit on the head anybody who is trying to cause disturbance especially the people who kept behind the door and under the bed while the war was on.[2]

In Kilrush on 18 July, there were complaints that people had been jostled about by soldiers using rifle butts. An RIC District Inspector had called to a hotel in the town on Saturday 25 July asking if the murderer _____ was there. He was referring to an officer of the IRA.

In Kilkee, police were openly carrying arms and clearing the streets of young men.[3]

          ~

The Truce period saw the return of passable roads after the trenches had been repaired. But for months afterwards donkeys, ponies, jennets and horses tended to zig-zag as they always had done when they came to the locations of historical road cuttings.[4]

There was a general feeling that the Truce would not last and training camps were held throughout the Brigade area. The 2nd Battalion was the favoured location and camps were held at Kilmihil, Drumdigus, Tullycrine, Knock, Knockerra and Kilrush.

Barracks were occupied at Kilkee, Kilkee and Kilrush Coastguard Stations, Kilrush RIC, Kilmihil and Kilmore House and these were held until the outbreak of the Civil War, when they were destroyed.[5]

British intelligence summaries struggled for news in Truce times and found themselves descending to the level of gossip. In Kilkee, those whom Michael Fahy had trained so well in the art of signalling, practised their skills by sending messages to each other across Kilkee Bay. The opposition, in turn, got to practise their deciphering skills and one of the messages that was relayed to Dublin Castle read:

Who is in charge of the home waters now?
The Volunteers under the command of de Valera, the present king of Ireland.[6]

One of the most imaginative and sensational of these intelligence reports, which reached Dublin Castle from Limerick in October 1921, concerned Seán Liddy, who had been elected MP for East Clare in May 1921.

Michael Brennan, it was claimed, had presided at an IRA court-martial in the Ancient Order of Hibernians building in Kilrush on 21 October 1921, at which Liddy had been charged with misappropriating £26,000 of County Council money. Liddy had been suspended, the report maintained, and had been replaced by Simon McInerney of Kilferagh.[7]

Brennan's own account of the period was unequivocal. The rates that were set by the County Council were collected by the three Brigades since many of the existing rate collectors were older men who were fearful for their safety. Every pound, he emphasised, was accounted for.[8]

The reprisals that followed the Lendrum ambush on 22 September 1920 were to cause considerable difficulties for affected farmers.

In Bealaha, hay and property were burned at the homes of Patrick Downes (120 tons), Daniel Greene (70 tons), Patrick Mahony (40 tons), Susan Clohessy (18 tons) and John Haugh (35 tons).

In Doonmore, Bridget McKee lost a sidecar, a dairy cabin and dairy equipment; John Power lost 60 tons of hay and out-offices were burned and Mary Sexton lost 35 tons. George Comerford and John Downes, both of Doonbeg lost 33 tons and 23 tons respectively and 12 tons of ryegrass and 47 tons of hay were burned at John McMahon's of Glascloon.

In Caherfeenick, there were burnings at Sinon Behan's (16 tons), Thomas Griffin (36 tons) and Sinon Keane (24 tons). Nearby, in Mountrivers, Thomas O'Grady had 95 tons burned as well as a hayshed, and Mary O'Sullivan lost 22 tons. Further west in Lislanihan, 32 tons of hay was destroyed at Mary O'Mara's and 45 tons at John Corry's.

Many faced fodder shortages while they awaited compensation for the hay that was burned. The impending crisis was averted when, under the auspices of the Farmers' Union, unaffected farmers throughout west Clare contributed hay to those who had suffered losses. Those who didn't have hay to spare, or where distance was an impediment to the sharing of resources, contributed money on the assumption that it would be paid back out of future compensation awards.

Since it was not feasible to transport hay due to the distance involved,

Éamon de Valera in Ennis.
*(Courtesy Mary Driver)*

the farmers of Carrigaholt collected £67.5s.6d, which was given to Timmy Chambers, Treasurer of the Doonbeg Hay Committee, for distribution. The Doonbeg Farmers' Association, finding that the fodder needs of the sufferers had already been met, allocated £27.10s to a man whose outhouses had been burned. When that man received compensation he returned the money with interest – a total of £30 – to the Doonbeg Committee. The remaining £40 had been given to the sister of Michael McNamara, who had found herself in some hardship following the killing of her brother by British soldiers on 22 December 1920.

A dispute arose when a number of the Carrigaholt contributors sought the return of the money they had donated to the Doonbeg Relief Fund and the matter ended up in Kilrush District Court in May 1926.

The action, which was of a friendly nature, was taken in order '… to get the ruling of the court on the disposition of such funds as had been recouped to Mr Chambers.' The judge, noting that Chambers had '… behaved with perfect propriety in the matter,' ruled that there was no legal contract and that the £30 should be paid into the court. Both sides' costs would be paid out of it and the court would decide later on how to dispose of the remainder.[9]

~

When de Valera came to Tullycrine during the Truce huge crowds assembled in O'Donnell's field where The Chief addressed them. The occasion was celebrated in song:

> And very soon we'll see him dressed
> In a coat so very fine
> Inspecting troops once more down there
> On the hills of Tullycrine.[10]

In 1936 (possibly on Easter Sunday) there was a big commemoration in Killernan graveyard and Mary McSwiney, widow of Terence, attended it.

A detective who did not share her political views was on duty. Approaching

Mrs McSwiney, he asked out of the corner of his mouth, "Are you still sleeping with de Valera?"

Ned Welsh, a Cree publican who did share her ideologies, overheard and thumped the detective, who promptly drew his revolver. Welsh solemnly warned him, "If you pull that trigger you'll never leave Killernan alive."[11]

There was a carnival atmosphere in Mullagh on 26 October when the parish's two gaoled curates, Fr Gaynor and Fr McKenna were released from Limerick Prison. The pair were accompanied to their home by Mullagh Band and hundreds of IRA men marching in formation and wearing the Republican colours.

That night, bonfires were lit in celebration.[12]

Bonfires blazed once again on 8 December in Quilty, Mullagh, Dunogan, Shanaway, Mountscott and Coore and windows were aglow with lamps and candles.

News that had reached the area of the signing of the Anglo-Irish Treaty on 6 December 1921 was met with jubilation in west Clare.

At Miltown Malbay railway station a Black and Tan, having read the terms of the settlement, threw his newspaper over his head and exclaimed, "All is up now."[13]

It was the calm before the storm ...

# Afterword

In the West Clare Brigade area over 1,500 IRA Volunteers and over 500 Cumann na mBan members were active during the War of Independence.

The area was policed at any one time by around 90 RIC and Black and Tans and an undetermined number of soldiers.

During the period, one Resident Magistrate, three policemen, one Black and Tan, two suspected spies and one civilian who was filling in a road trench were shot dead by the Republican side.

Two IRA men died as a result of accidental shootings while on active service and one died as a consequence of ill-treatment while in British prisons.

One drowned and one was shot dead during separate attacks on RIC.

A Sinn Féin judge was shot dead in his home, possibly by Auxiliaries or Black and Tans and two civilians were fatally wounded by British army officers.

Two IRA men were tortured and killed by British soldiers.

When compared with counties like Cork and Kerry, west Clare's military contribution to the War of Independence might be viewed as marginal. Indeed, while many ambushes were planned in the area, most failed to materialise and those that did had limited success.

Yet, it may be argued that west Clare's greatest contribution to national freedom was its dismantling of the British justice system. For it was in west Clare that the first Arbitration Courts were set up and it was the model that evolved in west Clare that was later adopted successfully throughout the country.

And it was in west Clare that the eyes and ears of the British Government, the RIC, were made practically redundant when they were driven from their barracks to the larger towns, where they were isolated by the widespread trenching of roads and the threat of attack.

Mullagh curate, Fr Pat Gaynor, a member of the Ard Chomhairle of Sinn Féin, noted that the battle for Irish freedom was not won by armed conflict:

> ... there was a stark resolve to hold fast and to run the civic affairs of the country, despite the handicap of British terrorism, in loyal support of Dáil Éireann. It was that stark resolve, and the people's patient endurance – not the few ambushes here and there – which made Britain's position untenable outside Ulster and which, to the extent we know, won the war of freedom.[1]

This 'stark resolve' was evident in abundance in west Clare among IRA Volunteers, Cumann na mBan members, members of the clergy and civilian men and women who remained loyal in the face of terror.

# Chronology of significant events
## January 1917 – July 1921

**January 1917 …**
Independent Brigade established in Clare, consisting of eight battalions.

**Late 1917 and early 1918 …**
Escalation of agrarian strife in Clare.

**Late 1918…**
Clare divided into three Brigade areas – West Clare, Mid Clare and East Clare.

**26 February 1918 …**
County Clare declared a Special Military area in response to what was described as widespread lawlessness.

24 March 1918 …
British soldiers stab up to six attendees at a packed Sinn Féin meeting in Carrigaholt; 21-year-old Kerry-born teacher, Thomas Russell, is gravely injured.

27 March 1918 …
Thomas Russell dies of his wounds at Kilrush Hospital.

12 April 1918 …
Lance Corporal Joseph Dowling arrives at Doolin, having disembarked from a German submarine, sparking suspicions of a Sinn Féin conspiracy with Germany, which became known as the German Plot.

21 April 1918 …
Conscription Pledge is signed at every parish church. Patrick Burke makes daring escape when police and military attempt to arrest him.

16–17 May …
Seventy-three Sinn Féin leaders, including Éamon Waldron and Brian O'Higgins, arrested and deported to England.

8 August 1918 ...
Cooraclare RIC Barracks is one of the first to be shut down.

14 December 1918 ...
Sinn Féin wins seventy-three out of one hundred and five seats in the General Election. Brian O'Higgins, who was in Birmingham Gaol, and Éamon de Valera elected unopposed in Clare.

**21 January 1919 ...**
Two RIC policemen shot dead at Soloheadbeg, County Tipperary, by Irish Volunteers.

21 January 1919 ...
Dáil Éireann meets for the first time in Dublin's Mansion House.

11 April 1919 ...
Dáil Éireann declares a boycott of RIC.

13 April 1919 ...
Failed attack on an RIC sergeant and two constables at Knockerra; five Volunteers and a youth arrested.

29 June 1919 ...
Farmer Pat Studdert shot and fatally wounded by British soldier.

20 August 1919 ...
Irish Volunteers renamed Irish Republican Army (IRA).

22 September 1919 ...
Ambush of RIC at Cahercanivan, Kilmihil; Mick Honan wounded.

1 November 1919 ...
First West Clare District Arbitration Court or Circuit Court formally set up.

*circa* 8 December 1919 ...
Michael Fahy accidentally wounded in Kilkee.

**19 January 1920 ...**
Michael Darcy drowned following ambush of RIC at Tiernaglohane, Cooraclare.

19 March 1920 ...
Michael Fahy dies in Limerick Hospital.

18 April 1920 ...
John Breen and Sergeant Patrick Carroll shot dead during a planned attack on RIC.

*circa* 18 July 1920 ...
Patrick Hassett dies in Limerick Hospital after being accidentally wounded during attack on Kilmore House on 13 July.

21 August 1920 ...
Detective John Hanlon shot dead by Bill Haugh in Kilrush.

27 August 1920 ...
  Burrane ambush.

14 September 1920 ...
  Drumdigus ambush.

20 September 1920 ...
  Sack of Balbriggan.

22 September 1920 ...
  Resident Magistrate Alan Lendrum ambushed and shot at Caherfeenick, near Doonbeg. Widespread burning of hay and outhouses in reprisal.

22 September 1920 ...
  Rineen Ambush. Five RIC and one Black and Tan are shot dead by a large force from Mid Clare Brigade at Dromin Hill, between Miltown Malbay and Lahinch. Reprisals result in the sacking of Ennistymon, Lahinch and Miltown Malbay and the deaths of six men, only one of whom had been involved in the ambush.

1 October 1920 ...
  Body of Captain Lendrum found on railway line between Kilmurry and Craggaknock stations.

25 October 1920 ...
  Lord Mayor of Cork, Terence McSwiney, dies on hunger strike.

1 November 1920 ...
  Kevin Barry executed at Mountjoy Gaol.

21 November 1920 ...
  Bloody Sunday. Peadar Clancy killed in Dublin.

6 December 1920 ...
  Police and Military raid Republican Court sitting at Cloonagarnaun. Civilian Tom Curtin fatally wounded.

11 December 1920 ...
  Cork City burned.

17 December 1920 ...
  Willie Shanahan and Michael McNamara captured at Newtown, Doonbeg.

22 December 1920 ...
  Willie Shanahan and Michael McNamara killed by British soldiers.

23 December 1920 ...
  Government of Ireland Bill partitions Ireland.

**3 January 1921 ...**
  Joe Greene shot at his home in Toonavoher, as he was believed to have given information to British Forces.

January 1921 ...
  Martial Law extended to Co Clare.

11 February 1921 ...
  Patrick Falsey shot and fatally wounded while filling a trench at Cooraclare.

February 1921 ...
  Attack on Black and Tan in Kilkee.

6/7 March 1921 ...
  Limerick Mayor Seoirse Clancy and former Mayor Michael O'Callaghan assassinated in their homes.

13 March 1921 ...
  Sinn Féin magistrate Tom Shannon shot dead at his home in Moyasta. Dublin Castle attempts to blame local IRA members.

22-23 April 1921 ...
  Siege of Kilrush by a joint force of East Clare and West Clare IRA.

May 1921 ...
  First publication of the myth that Captain Alan Lendrum was the victim of an atrocity.

23 May 1921 ...
  Mullagh curates Fr Pat Gaynor and Fr Michael McKenna gaoled for six months.

26 May 1921 ...
  Constable Edgar Budd, a Black and Tan, shot dead in an ambush at Cooga, near Kildysart.

15 June 1921 ...
  Christy McCarthy shot dead at Meelick.

17 June 1921 ...
  Doonbeg schoolteacher Patrick Darcy executed in Doonbeg village.

9 July 1921 ...
  Truce is called.

11 July 1921 ...
  Truce begins at midday.

6 December 1921 ...
  Anglo-Irish Treaty signed.

# Appendix 1

## Officers of West Clare Brigade, 11 July 1921

| | 1st Battalion |
|---|---|
| OC | James O'Dea |
| Vice OC | Michael Falahee |
| Adjutant | James Corbett |
| Quartermaster | Mitchell Shannon |
| | Sinon Haugh (Coolmeen) had been Quartermaster at the time of his arrest and imprisonment on 20 November 1920 |

| A Company: Coolmeen | | Strength: 115 |
|---|---|---|
| Captain | Michael Kennedy (Coolmeen) | |
| 1st Lieutenant | Michael Sexton (Derrylough) | |
| 2nd Lieutenant | Tom McMahon (Aylroe Shanahea) | |
| | Denis Shannon (Coolmeen) had been 2nd Lieutenant at the time of his arrest and imprisonment in November 1920 | |

| B Company: Kildysart | | Strength: 104 |
|---|---|---|
| Captain | Patrick McMahon (Kildysart) | |
| 1st Lieutenant | Jack Grace (Kildysart) | |
| 2nd Lieutenant | Tim McMahon (Kildysart) | |

| **C Company: Cranny** | | Strength: 99 |
|---|---|---|
| Captain | M A Donnelly (Cranny) | |
| 1st Lieutenant | Martin Corry (Clondrina) | |
| 2nd Lieutenant | John Brann ( Cranny) | |

| **D Company: Labasheeda** | | Strength: 128 |
|---|---|---|
| Captain | Michael Breen (Kerry) | |
| 1st Lieutenant | Matt P Kelly (Kilkerrin, Labasheeda) | |
| 2nd Lieutenant | Daniel O'Neill (USA) | |

### 2nd Battalion

| OC | Seán Flanagan (Tullagower, Tullycrine) |
|---|---|
| Vice OC | Stephen Hanrahan (Wood Road, Kilrush) |
| Adjutant | Percy Cooper (Donaile, Killimer) |
| Quartermaster | P J Shannon (Drumdigus) |
| | Seamus Lorigan (Lack West, Kilmihil) had been Adjutant at the time of his arrest and imprisonment on 10 April 1920 and on 1 November 1920 |
| | P McInerney (Kilmihil) had been Quartermaster at the time of his arrest and imprisonment on 3 July 1921 |

| **A Company: Knockerra** | | Strength: 78 |
|---|---|---|
| Captain | Michael Brown (USA) | |
| 1st Lieutenant | Tim Clune (Coolminga, Killimer) | |
| 2nd Lieutenant | Michael Ryan Knockerra | |

| **B Company: Kilmurry McMahon** | | Strength: 123 |
|---|---|---|
| Captain | John Coghlan | |
| 1st Lieutenant | Frank O'Donnell (Tullycrine) | |
| 2nd Lieutenant | Michael Hassett (Crossmore, Kilmurry McMahon) | |

| **C Company: Kilmihil** | | Strength: 118 |
|---|---|---|
| Captain | Michael Killoury (Clonakilla, Kilmihil) | |
| 1st Lieutenant | Patrick Normoyle (Cahercanivan) | |
| 2nd Lieutenant | Michael Melican (Kiltumper) | |

**D Company: Kilmihil**                                            Strength: 98

| Captain | Michael Honan (Leitrim) |
|---|---|
| 1st Lieutenant | Martin Melican (Glenmore, Kilmihil) |
| 2nd Lieutenant | Peadar McMahon (Boulinameala, Kilmihil) |

**E Company: Killimer**                                            Strength: 82

| Captain | James Driscoll (Burrane) |
|---|---|
| 1st Lieutenant | Lott O'Neill (Burrane) |
| 2nd Lieutenant | John Cleary (Kilmurry McMahon) |

**F Company: Kilrush**                                            Strength: 91

| Captain | Jerry Crowley (Ballynote) |
|---|---|
| 1st Lieutenant | Matt Bermingham (Ballykett) |
| 2nd Lieutenant | Thomas Crowley (Ballynote) |

3rd Battalion

| OC | Thomas Martyn |
|---|---|
| Vice OC | Vacant |
| Adjutant | M McGrath (Dromelihy, Cree) |
| Quartermaster | Patrick Hassett |
|  | Daniel Sheedy (Bridge House, Clarecastle) had been OC at the time of his arrest and imprisonment on 21/22 October 1920 |

**A Company: Cooraclare**                                            Strength: 126

| Captain | Jack O'Dea (Tullabrack) |
|---|---|
| 1st Lieutenant | Tim Neenan (Mullagh) |
| 2nd Lieutenant | Pat Clohessy (Moneen, Kilbaha) |

**B Company: Monmore**                                            Strength: 89

| Captain | Martin Chambers (Monmore) |
|---|---|
| 1st Lieutenant | Patrick McGuire (Monmore) |
| 2nd Lieutenant | Pat Sheehan (Monmore) |

| C Company: Cree | Strength: 91 |
| --- | --- |
| Captain | Michael Fitzmartin (Cree) |
| 1st Lieutenant | T Walsh (Clohanes) |
| 2nd Lieutenant | W Crowley (Leitrim) |

| D Company: Doonbeg | Strength: 109 |
| --- | --- |
| Captain | Tom McMahon (Doonbeg) |
| 1st Lieutenant | Michael Doyle (Doonbeg) |
| 2nd Lieutenant | Senan McGrath (Caherfeenick) |

| E Company: Bealaha | Strength: 78 |
| --- | --- |
| Captain | Patrick Downes (Bealaha) |
| 1st Lieutenant | Charles Clancy (Bealaha) |
| 2nd Lieutenant | Patrick Haugh (Bealaha) |

| F Company: Clohanmore | Strength: 63 |
| --- | --- |
| Captain | John Mullins (Clohanmore) |
| 1st Lieutenant | Timothy Meaney (Clohanmore) |
| 2nd Lieutenant | David Walsh (Cloonagarnaun) |

| 4th Battalion | |
| --- | --- |
| OC | Patrick Kelly (Ennis) |
| Vice OC | Patrick Clancy (USA) |
| Adjutant | John Griffin (Australia) |
| Quartermaster | James Kelly (Clohauninchy, Kilmurry) |

| A Company: Doolough | Strength: 44 |
| --- | --- |
| Captain | Con Donnelan (Mullagh) |
| 1st Lieutenant | John McGuane ( Doolough, Mullagh) |
| 2nd Lieutenant | Michael Donnelan (Carhungry Mullagh) |

| B Company: Coore | Strength: 105 |
| --- | --- |
| Captain | Thomas Killeen (Coore, Miltown Malbay) |
| 1st Lieutenant | Pat Gleeson (Coore, Miltown Malbay) |
| 2nd Lieutenant | M Killeen (Killernan, Miltown Malbay) |

### C Company: Mullagh

Strength: 82

| | |
|---|---|
| Captain | P Moloney (Mullagh) |
| 1st Lieutenant | P Sexton (Mullagh) |
| 2nd Lieutenant | J Darcy (Mullagh) |

### D Company: Kilmurry Ibrickane

Strength: 119

| | |
|---|---|
| Captain | David Walshe (USA) |
| 1st Lieutenant | Pat Clancy (USA) |
| 2nd Lieutenant | N Broady (Crigane, Kilmurray) |

### E Company: Quilty

Strength: 61

| | |
|---|---|
| Captain | Patrick Boyle (Seafield, Quilty) |
| 1st Lieutenant | Michael Ryan (USA) |
| 2nd Lieutenant | John Fennell (Seafield, Quilty) |

### 5th Battalion

| | |
|---|---|
| OC | James Talty (O'Connell Street, Kilkee) |
| Vice OC | Matt Blake (USA) |
| Adjutant | John Keane (Querrin) |
| Quartermaster | Patrick McGrath (USA) |
| | Michael Roche (Doonaha, Kilkee) had been Adjutant at the time of his arrest and imprisonment on 2 April 1921 |

### A Company: Carrigaholt

Strength: 71

| | |
|---|---|
| Captain | Tim Haier (USA) |
| 1st Lieutenant | P Keating (Kilcrona, Carrigaholt) |
| 2nd Lieutenant | D O'Gorman Kilcrona, Carrigaholt) |

### B Company: Kilkee

Strength: 66

| | |
|---|---|
| Captain | J McSweeney (Kilkee) |
| 1st Lieutenant | P Sullivan (Corbally) |
| 2nd Lieutenant | D O'Gorman ( Corbally) |

### C Company: Kilferagh     Strength: 37

*(This company was disbanded and its members transferred to B Company during the truce)*

| | |
|---|---|
| Captain | M Costello (Limerick Junction) |
| 1st Lieutenant | T McInerney (Fouagh) |
| 2nd Lieutenant | Michael McInerney (Kilferagh, Kilkee) |

### D Company: Doonaha     Strength: 67

| | |
|---|---|
| Captain | J O'Brien (Querrin) |
| 1st Lieutenant | M Scanlan (Rahaneska) |
| 2nd Lieutenant | J Houlihan (Tullaroe) |

### E Company: Moveen     Strength: 54

| | |
|---|---|
| Captain | M Crotty (Moveen) |
| 1st Lieutenant | P McMahon (Moveen) |
| 2nd Lieutenant | P Deloughrey (Moveen) |

### F Company: Cross     Strength: 50

| | |
|---|---|
| Captain | J Corbett (Newtown) |
| 1st Lieutenant | J Brennan (Cross) |
| 2nd Lieutenant | T Murray (Cross) |

### G Company: Lisdeen     Strength: 62

| | |
|---|---|
| Captain | J Blackhall (Kilkee) |
| 1st Lieutenant | P Prendergast (Moyasta) |
| 2nd Lieutenant | P Carey (Kilkee) |

*Adapted from: MA MSPC RO 222-226, 1st Western Division, West Clare Brigade*

# Appendix 2

## Officers of Cumann na mBan West Clare Brigade
## 11 July 1921

| | 1st Battalion | |
|---|---|---|
| OC | Bridget Liddy | |
| Secretary | Mrs McMahon | |
| Treasurer | Alice Counihan | |

| | Cranny Branch | Strength: 16 |
|---|---|---|
| Captain | Mrs Eily Gallery (Rockmount, Ennis) | |
| Adjutant or Secretary | Miss Jane Corbett (USA) | |
| Treasurer | Miss Margaret Shannon (USA) | |

| | Kildysart Branch | Strength: 20 |
|---|---|---|
| Captain | Nurse M Kelly (Kildysart) | |
| Adjutant or Secretary | Mrs Jenny McMahon (Kildysart) | |
| Treasurer | Mrs Siney Haugh (Coolmeen) | |

| | Coolmeen Branch | Strength: 12 |
|---|---|---|
| Captain | Miss Winifred Farrell (Coolmeen) | |
| Adjutant or Secretary | Miss Bridget Lynch | |
| Treasurer | Mrs Tom Connolly (Kildysart) | |

### Labasheeda Branch — Strength: 16

| Captain | Miss J Kelly (Labasheeda) |
| --- | --- |
| Adjutant or Secretary | Miss M Falahee (Labasheeda) |
| Treasurer | Miss McNamara (Labasheeda) |

### A Company Branch — Strength: 14

| Captain | Mrs James Clancy |
| --- | --- |
| Treasurer | Miss E Gallery |

## 2nd Battalion

| OC | Susan Shannon (Cranny) |
| --- | --- |
| Secretary | Lizzie O'Donnell (Tullycrine) |
| Treasurer | Mrs Bonfield (Knockerra, Killimer) |

### Kilmurry McMahon Branch — Strength: 30

| Captain | Mrs Meehan (Kildysart) |
| --- | --- |
| Adjutant or Secretary | Lizzie O'Donnell (Tullycrine) |
| Treasurer | Mrs Liddane (nee Coghlan) |

### Knockerra Branch — Strength: 26

| Captain | Mrs B Crowley (Tullagower, Killimer) |
| --- | --- |
| Adjutant or Secretary | Mrs Power (Killimer) |
| Treasurer | Mrs Bonfield (Tullagower, Killimer) |

### Killimer Branch — Strength: 28

| Captain | Mrs P O'Connell (Tullycrine) |
| --- | --- |
| Adjutant or Secretary | Miss Cooper (Killimer) |
| Treasurer | Miss O'Neill (Burrane) |

### Kilrush Branch — Strength: 32

| Captain | Miss Queally (Frances St, Kilrush) |
| --- | --- |
| Adjutant or Secretary | Mrs N O'Dwyer (Market Square, Kilrush) |
| Treasurer | Miss C Considine (Frances St, Kilrush) |

| Kilmihil Branch | | Strength: 30 |
|---|---|---|
| Captain | Mrs McMahon (Breen St, Kilrush) | |
| Adjutant or Secretary | Mrs J Flanagan (Tullagower, Killimer) | |
| Treasurer | Mrs M O'Mahony (Australia) | |

## 3rd Battalion

| President | Miss Jennie Breen (Churchtown, Cooraclare) |
|---|---|
| Acting President | Miss Tess McNamara (Mountrivers) |
| Adjutant or Secretary | Miss Tess McNamara (Mountrivers) |
| Treasurer | Miss Maggie McNamara (Mountrivers) |

| Cooraclare Branch | | Strength: 30 |
|---|---|---|
| Captain | Miss Aggie O'Dea | |
| Adjutant or Secretary | Miss Kathleen Sheedy | |
| Treasurer | Miss Nora Reidy | |

| Doonbeg Branch | | Strength: 28 |
|---|---|---|
| Captain | Miss Minnie O'Grady (Mountrivers) | |
| Adjutant or Secretary | Miss Tess McNamara (Mountrivers) | |
| Treasurer | Miss Maggie McNamara (Mountrivers) | |

| Bealaha Branch | | Strength: 15 |
|---|---|---|
| Captain | Mary Ellen Downes | |
| Adjutant or Secretary | Eily Downes | |
| Treasurer | May Power | |

| Monmore Branch | | Strength: 20 |
|---|---|---|
| Captain | Miss B Haugh | |
| Adjutant or Secretary | Miss Nora Downes | |
| Treasurer | Miss Nora Haugh | |

| Cree Branch | | Strength: 31 |
|---|---|---|
| Captain | Miss Mary Kate Martyn | |
| Adjutant or Secretary | Miss Angela Ryan | |
| Treasurer | Miss Delia McInerney | |

### 4th Battalion

| | |
|---|---|
| President | Miss Bridget Liddy (Brigade OC) |
| Adjutant or Secretary | Miss Mary McMahon (OC 4th Battalion) |
| Treasurer | Vacant |

### South Coore Branch      Strength: 26

| | |
|---|---|
| Captain | Miss Mary McMahon (Dromin, Mullagh) |
| Adjutant or Secretary | Kathleen Donnellan |
| Treasurer | Miss M A Montgomery |

### North Coore Branch      Strength: 20

| | |
|---|---|
| Captain | Miss Mary McGuane |
| Adjutant or Secretary | Vacant |
| Treasurer | Vacant |

### 5th Battalion

| | |
|---|---|
| President | Miss Bridget Liddy (Brigade OC) |
| Adjutant or Secretary | Miss Tess McNamara (Mountrivers) |
| Treasurer | Miss Annie McGrath |

### Kilkee Branch      Strength: 30

| | |
|---|---|
| Captain | Miss Rita Fahy (Kilkee) |
| Adjutant or Secretary | Annie McGrath (Kilferagh) |
| Treasurer | Annie Talty (Kilkee) |

### Doonaha Branch      Strength: 16

| | |
|---|---|
| Captain | Josephine Roche (Doonaha) |
| Adjutant or Secretary | Gretta Haugh (Doonaha) |
| Treasurer | Mago Queally (Doonaha) |

### Carrigaholt Branch      Strength: 32

| | |
|---|---|
| Captain | Maire Behan (Carrigaholt) |
| Adjutant or Secretary | Mary Ellen Keane (Carrigaholt) |
| Treasurer | Margaret Ginnane (Carrigaholt) |

| **Blackweir Branch** | | Strength: 12 |
|---|---|---|
| Captain | May Corry (Blackweir, Lisdeen) | |
| Adjutant or Secretary | Miss Lynch (Blackweir, Lisdeen) | |
| Treasurer | Miss Clancy (Blackweir, Lisdeen) | |

*Source: MA MSPC CMB 70, West Clare Brigade.*

# Appendix 3

## Nominal Return of RIC men serving in the West Clare Brigade area on 1 January 1920

*Note*: In the cases of Head Constables and Sergeants, the second date represents the date of appointment to the present rank.

| Number | Rank | Name | Religion | Date of Appointment | Marital Status | Station |
|--------|------|------|----------|---------------------|----------------|---------|
| 56509 | Sgt | Martin McGrath | RC | 2.7.94 / 1.9.12 | M | Miltown Malbay |
| 60202 | Sgt | James Hunt | RC | 16.5.01 / 1.7.14 | M | Miltown Malbay |
| 61758 | Con | James Walsh | RC | 26.3.06 | S | Miltown Malbay |
| 66416 | Con | James McDonald | RC | 15.2.12 | S | Miltown Malbay |
| 60996 | Con | Patrick McShera | RC | 6.9.02 | M | Miltown Malbay |
| 67388 | Con | James Mahoney | RC | 1.7.13 | S | Miltown Malbay |
| 58695 | Con | Michael Ronan | RC | 16.1.99 | M | Miltown Malbay |
| 63243 | Con | James Donovan | RC | 16.10.07 | M | Miltown Malbay |
| 60763 | Con | Terence Cooney | RC | 2.6.02 | M | Miltown Malbay |
| 66217 | Con | Patrick Breen | RC | 1.11.11 | S | Miltown Malbay |
| 58464 | Sgt | Michael O'Shea | RC | 1.10.98 / 1.2.19 | S | Kilrush |
| 64365 | Sgt | Martin Gleeson | RC | 21.9.08 / 8.12.19 | M | Kilrush |
| 56866 | Sgt | Timothy Sheehan | RC | 2.1.95 / 1.6.10 | M | Kilrush |
| 59495 | Sgt | Patrick McLoughlin | RC | 8.5.00 / 1.2.12 | M | Kilrush |
| 58743 | Sgt | Patrick J Carroll | RC | 1.2.99 / 1.3.18 | S | Kilrush |

| Number | Rank | Name | Religion | Date of Appointment | Marital Status | Station |
|--------|------|------|----------|---------------------|----------------|---------|
| 57153 | Sgt | Timothy O'Dwyer | RC | 16.9.95 / 1.9.12 | M | Kilrush |
| 56866 | Sgt | Timothy Sheehan | RC | 2.1.95 / 1.6.10 | M | Kilrush |
| 62074 | HCon | James Sweeney | RC | 3.9.06 / 1.1.18 | S | Kilrush |
| 61169 | HCon | William Reilly | RC | 1.6.02 / 2.1.03 | M | Kilrush |
| 62715 | Con | Michael Salter | RC | 26.6.07 | M | Kilrush |
| 67731 | Con | Michael O'Malley | RC | 2.3.14 | S | Kilrush |
| 68703 | Con | John O'Neill | RC | 5.9.16 | S | Kilrush |
| 52601 | Con | James O'Shea | RC | 8.8.87 | M | Kilrush |
| 64481 | Con | Patrick Palmer | RC | 26.11.08 | S | Kilrush |
| 52206 | Con | James McDermott | RC | 15.10.86 | M | Kilrush |
| 65685 | Con | Patrick Mullany | RC | 3.1.11 | S | Kilrush |
| 67646 | Con | Patrick Murphy | RC | 2.1.14 | S | Kilrush |
| 69455 | Con | John Horan | RC | 4.6.18 | S | Kilrush |
| 69682 | Con | Henry J Hughes | RC | 1.4.19 | S | Kilrush |
| 66446 | Con | John Fitzgerald | RC | 15.2.12 | S | Kilrush |
| 64249 | Con | John Hanlon | RC | 20.7.08 | M | Kilrush |
| 57708 | Con | Timothy Donovan | RC | 1.5.96 | M | Kilrush |
| 66910 | Con | John Browne | RC | 1.11.12 | S | Kilrush |
| 69580 | Con | Hugh Monaghan | RC | 5.11.18 | S | Kilrush |
| 61008 | Sgt | Edmond Sullivan | RC | 2.1.03 / 1.9.19 | S | Kilmihil |
| 57690 | Sgt | Thomas Gilman | RC | 1.5.96 / 1.5.14 | S | Kilmihil |
| 68709 | Con | Michael Sloyan | RC | 19.9.16 | M | Kilmihil |
| 66647 | Con | Jeremiah O'Callaghan | RC | 18.6.12 | S | Kilmihil |
| 58263 | Con | Michael Power | RC | 1.7.98 | S | Kilmihil |
| 68612 | Con | Daniel Reidy | RC | 6.4.15 | S | Kilmihil |
| 68100 | Con | Patrick Martyn | RC | 22.9.14 | S | Kilmihil |
| 69563 | Con | Patk J McGowan | RC | 5.11.18 | S | Kilmihil |
| 65358 | Con | Martin Creavin | RC | 15.6.10 | M | Kilmihil |
| 69261 | Con | W J Armstrong | RC | 4.12.17 | S | Kilmihil |
| 61255 | Con | William Costigan | RC | 16.2.13 | M | Kilmihil |

| Number | Rank | Name | Religion | Date of Appointment | Marital Status | Station |
|--------|------|------|----------|---------------------|----------------|---------|
| 59615 | Sgt | Richard Sullivan | RC | 1.6.00 1.8.19 | S | Carrigaholt |
| 55885 | Con | Robert Walwood | P | 16.6.93 1.11.19 | S | Carrigaholt |
| 67340 | Con | Daniel Collins | RC | 2.6.13 | S | Carrigaholt |
| 57275 | Con | Daniel Shea | RC | 8.11.95 | M | Carrigaholt |
| 62735 | Con | Lawrence Nolan | RC | 1.7.07 | S | Carrigaholt |
| 60799 | Con | Jeremiah Murphy | RC | 16.6.02 | S | Carrigaholt |
| 67262 | Con | Michael Hurley | RC | 1.5.13 | S | Carrigaholt |
| 67754 | Con | Patrick Hopkins | RC | 16.3.14 | S | Carrigaholt |
| 69336 | Con | Denis Driscoll | RC | 4.2.18 | S | Carrigaholt |
| 67000 | Con | James Coyle | RC | 16.12.12 | S | Carrigaholt |
| 60236 | Sgt | Michael Corduff | RC | 1.6.01 / 1.11.10 | M | Kilkee |
| 57004 | Sgt | Edward M Sullivan | RC | 1.7.95 / 1.4.13 | M | Kilkee |
| 65114 | Con | John O'Keeffe | RC | 20.12.09 | M | Kilkee |
| 60794 | Con | Daniel Nelson | RC | 2.3.03 | S | Kilkee |
| 68824 | Con | Martin Mannion | RC | 1.11.16 | S | Kilkee |
| 61106 | Con | Michael Monaghan | RC | 17.11.02 | M | Kilkee |
| 68529 | Con | John Mullee | RC | 1.3.15 | S | Kilkee |
| 68607 | Con | Simon Kelly | RC | 6.4.15 | S | Kilkee |
| 66931 | Con | Martin Boland | RC | 18.11.12 | S | Kilkee |
| 64547 | Con | James Conway | RC | 5.1.09 | M | Kilkee |
| 57599 | Sgt | William Wood | P | 16.3.96 / 1.8.19 | S | Kilmore |
| 54632 | Sgt | Thomas Kearney | RC | 15.11.90 / 1.7.12 | M | Kilmore |
| 68579 | Con | John Nagle | RC | 1.4.15 | S | Kilmore |
| 67544 | Con | Jas F Mannion | RC | 2.1.17 | S | Kilmore |
| 67115 | Con | John T Keeffe | RC | 17.2.13 | S | Kilmore |
| 63858 | Con | James Doyle | RC | 16.9.08 | S | Kilmore |
| 69089 | Con | Patrick J Brennan | RC | 17.4.17 | S | Kilmore |
| 69759 | Con | Humphrey Courtney | RC | 3.6.19 | S | Kilmore |

| Number | Rank | Name | Religion | Date of Appointment | Marital Status | Station |
|---|---|---|---|---|---|---|
| 55800 | Sgt | Daniel Boyle | RC | 27.3.93 / 1.1.13 | M | Knock |
| 54435 | Sgt | John Daly | RC | 1.7.90 / 1.6.12 | M | Knock |
| 63984 | Con | James Mannion | RC | 1.7.08 | S | Knock |
| 57028 | Con | Nicholas Morgan | RC | 15.7.95 | S | Knock |
| 69525 | Con | Robert J Woods | P | 3.9.18 | S | Knock |
| 68999 | Con | Patrick Nagle | RC | 1.2.17 | S | Knock |
| 59809 | Con | Maurice Foley | RC | 17.9.00 | S | Knock |
| 67848 | Con | Frederick Gannon | RC | 3.10.16 | S | Knock |
| 61534 | Con | William Hayes | RC | 1.12.05 | M | Knock |
| 56637 | Con | Thomas Daly | RC | 1.9.94 | M | Knock |
| 61176 | Sgt | John Moynihan | RC | 2.1.03 / 1.7.15 | M | Kildysart |
| 55941 | Sgt | Patrick Mullany | RC | 1.7.93 / 1.1.14 | M | Kildysart |
| 68972 | Con | Peter Hevican | RC | 17.1.17 | S | Kildysart |
| 55684 | Con | Michael Kiernan | RC | 10.12.92 | M | Kildysart |
| 60308 | Con | Patrick Gleeson | RC | 1.8.01 | M | Kildysart |
| 69553 | Con | Michael Cannavan | RC | 1.10.18 | S | Kildysart |
| 65722 | Con | Daniel Burke | RC | 1.2.11 | S | Kildysart |
| 65242 | (Res) Con | Jeremiah Daly | RC | 1.4.10 | S | Kildysart |
| 69310 | Con | Michael Conway | RC | 2.1.18 | S | Kildysart |
| 69179 | Con | Patrick Coolican | RC | 3.7.17 | S | Kildysart |

*Adapted from NAUK, HO 184, Royal Irish Constabulary Service Records 1816–1922, Nominal Returns arranged by counties, County of Clare.*

# Appendix 4

## Nominal Return of RIC men serving in the West Clare Brigade area on 1 January 1921

*Note 1.* In the cases of Head Constables and Sergeants, the second date represents the date of appointment to the present rank.

*Note 2.* Constables whose registration numbers begin with 7 are probably Black and Tans.

| Number | Rank | Name | Religion | Date of Appointment | Marital Status | Station | Black & Tan |
|--------|------|------|----------|---------------------|----------------|---------|-------------|
| 76711 | Con | J R Savage | P | 15.12.20 | M | Miltown Malbay | T |
| 67512 | Con | Patrick Sheehan | RC | 15.9.13 | S | Miltown Malbay | |
| 72200 | Con | Herbert Tattle | P | 3.8.20 | S | Miltown Malbay | T |
| 58695 | Con | Michael Ronan | RC | 16.1.99 | M | Miltown Malbay | |
| 76701 | Con | William Ross | P | 15.12.20 | M | Miltown Malbay | T |
| 70950 | Con | Patrick O'Toole | RC | 29.3.20 | S | Miltown Malbay | T |
| 62735 | Con | Lawrence Nolan | RC | 1.7.07 | M | Miltown Malbay | |
| 68806 | Con | Daniel Nyhan | RC | 17.10.16 | S | Miltown Malbay | |
| 67388 | Con | James Mahony | RC | 1.7.13 | S | Miltown Malbay | |
| 72217 | Con | Stanley L Moore | P | 3.8.20 | S | Miltown Malbay | T |
| 76689 | Con | A Kincaid | P | 15.10.20 | S | Miltown Malbay | T |
| 65965 | Con | P J Kennedy | RC | 21.6.11 | S | Miltown Malbay | |
| 76860 | Con | J Hayes | P | 17.12.20 | M | Miltown Malbay | T |
| 72225 | Con | Charles G Gibson | P | 3.8.20 | S | Miltown Malbay | T |

| Number | Rank | Name | Religion | Date of Appointment | Marital Status | Station | Black & Tan |
|--------|------|------|----------|---------------------|----------------|---------|-------------|
| 71483 | Con | Peter Doorigan | RC | 28.5.20 | S | Miltown Malbay | T |
| 72219 | Con | John J Drewitt | P | 3.8.20 | M | Miltown Malbay | T |
| 63243 | Con | James Donovan | RC | 17.10.07 | M | Miltown Malbay | |
| 70951 | Con | Robert Flight | P | 29.3.20 | S | Miltown Malbay | T |
| 76705 | Con | T Flurrie | P | 15.12.20 | S | Miltown Malbay | T |
| 72083 | Con | Wilfred Cox | P | 27.7.20 | M | Miltown Malbay | T |
| 72193 | Con | H R Cason | P | 3.8.20 | S | Miltown Malbay | T |
| 72197 | Con | V R Cason | P | 3.8.20 | S | Miltown Malbay | T |
| 73972 | Con | John S Collins | P | 8.10.20 | S | Miltown Malbay | T |
| 74114 | Con | H Butterworth | P | 12.10.20 | S | Miltown Malbay | T |
| 73633 | Con | J A Parker | RC | 1.10.20 | S | Miltown Malbay | T |
| 57282 | HC | James Treacy | RC | 15.11.95 / 19.6.20 | S | Kilrush | |
| 59809 | Sgt | Maurice Foley | RC | 17.9.00 / 1.8.20 | S | Kilrush | |
| 63827 | Sgt | Patrick Molloy | RC | 18.5.08 / 23.2.20 | S | Kilrush | |
| 57153 | Sgt | Timothy O'Dwyer | RC | 16.9.95 / 1.9.13 | M | Kilrush | |
| 70944 | Con | Connell Boyle | RC | 29.3.20 | S | Kilrush | T |
| 72208 | Con | F A Carruthers | P | 3.8.20 | S | Kilrush | T |
| 69607 | Con | Patrick Costelloe | RC | 2.1.19 | S | Kilrush | |
| 69971 | Con | F J Fallon | RC | 2.12.19 | S | Kilrush | |
| 66446 | Con | John Fitzgerald | RC | 15.2.12 | S | Kilrush | |
| 68361 | Con | Michael Harrington | RC | 1.12.14 | S | Kilrush | |
| 67754 | Con | Patrick Hopkins | RC | 16.3.14 | S | Kilrush | |
| 69455 | Con | John Horan | RC | 4.6.18 | S | Kilrush | |
| 73762 | Con | David Houston | P | 4.10.20 | S | Kilrush | T |
| 69682 | Con | H J Hughes | RC | 1.4.19 | S | Kilrush | |
| 67389 | Con | John Kelleher | RC | 1.7.13 | S | Kilrush | |
| 72747 | Con | C E E Maslin | P | 3.9.20 | S | Kilrush | T |
| 67646 | Con | Patrick Murphy | RC | 2.1.14 | S | Kilrush | |
| 70920 | Con | Thomas E McEniry | RC | 23.9.20 | S | Kilrush | T |
| 52206 | Con | James McDermott | RC | 15.10.86 | M | Kilrush | |
| 67646 | Con | John O'Neill | RC | 5.9.16 | S | Kilrush | |

| Number | Rank | Name | Religion | Date of Appointment | Marital Status | Station | Black & Tan |
|---|---|---|---|---|---|---|---|
| 71812 | Con | William Reeves | P | 6.7.20 | S | Kilrush | T |
| 62715 | Con | Michael Salter | RC | 26.6.07 | M | Kilrush | |
| 57708 | Con | Timothy Donovan | RC | 1.5.96 | M | Kilrush | |
| | | | | | | | |
| 64547 | Sgt | James Conway | RC | 5.1.09–1.11.20 | M | Kilkee | |
| 61106 | Sgt | Michael Monaghan | RC | 17.11.02–1.11.20 | M | Kilkee | |
| 57004 | Sgt | E M Sullivan | RC | 1.7.95–1.4.13 | M | Kilkee | |
| 72205 | Con | Wm G Burr | P | 3.8.20 | S | Kilkee | T |
| 72202 | Con | John E Higgins | P | 3.8.20 | M | Kilkee | T |
| 67103 | Con | Thomas Kelly | RC | 17.3.13 | S | Kilkee | |
| 68529 | Con | John Mullee | RC | 1.3.15 | S | Kilkee | |
| 65114 | Con | John O'Keeffe | RC | 20.12.09 | S | Kilkee | |
| 72198 | Con | Sydney G Parker | RC | 3.8.20 | M | Kilkee | T |
| 72148 | Con | John W Parrish | P | 30.7.20 | M | Kilkee | T |
| 71065 | Con | Patrick Reilly | RC | 16.4.20 | S | Kilkee | T |
| 70967 | Con | Edward Roberts | P | 30.3.20 | M | Kilkee | T |
| 57275 | Con | Daniel Shea | RC | 8.11.95 | M | Kilkee | |
| 72220 | Con | S H Sydenham | P | 3.8.20 | S | Kilkee | T |
| 72110 | Con | Harrold [sic] G Winsor | P | 3.8.20 | S | Kilkee | T |
| | | | | | | | |
| 57690 | Sgt | Thomas Gilman | RC | 1.5.96 / 1.5.14 | S | Kildysart | |
| 55941 | Sgt | Patrick Mullany | RC | 1.7.09 / 31.1.14 | M | Kildysart | |
| 65722 | Con | Daniel Burke | RC | 1.2.11 | S | Kildysart | |
| 69553 | Con | Michael Canavan | RC | 1.10.18 | S | Kildysart | |
| 56637 | Con | Thomas Daly | RC | 1.9.94 | M | Kildysart | |
| 64477 | Con | John Farrelly | RC | 26.11.08 | S | Kildysart | |
| 69719 | Con | Michael Flynn | RC | 1.5.19 | S | Kildysart | |
| 55684 | Con | Michael Kiernan | RC | 10.12.92 | M | Kildysart | |
| 76760 | Con | F G Meadows | P | 17.12.20 | M | Kildysart | T |
| 69380 | Con | Hugh Monaghan | RC | 5.11.18 | S | Kildysart | |
| 63654 | Con | James Reilly | RC | 27.1.08 | S | Kildysart | |
| 71156 | Con | Edward Higgins | RC | 22.4.20 | S | Kildysart | T |

# APPENDIX 4

| Number | Rank | Name | Religion | Date of Appointment | Marital Status | Station | Black & Tan |
|--------|------|------|----------|---------------------|----------------|---------|-------------|
| 76755 | Con | A Hewson | P | 17.12.20 | S | Kildysart | T |
| 72604 | Con | F W Sargisson | P | 24.8.20 | M | Kildysart | T |
| 69525 | Con | R J Woods | P | 3.9.18 | S | Kildysart | |
| 69972 | Con | Peterin [sic: Peter] Heverin | RC | 17.1.17 | S | Kildysart | |
| 71816 | Con | Robert Banham | RC | 6.7.20 | M | Kildysart | T |
| 72348 | Con | Edgar Budd | RC | 6.7.20 | S | Kildysart | T |
| 76712 | Con | J McIntosh | P | 15.12.20 | S | Kildysart | T |

*Adapted from NAUK, HO 184, Royal Irish Constabulary Service Records 1816–1922, Nominal Returns arranged by counties, County of Clare.*

# Archive abbreviations

| | |
|---|---|
| BMH | Bureau of Military History |
| CO | Colonial Office |
| CSORP | Chief Secretary's Office Registered Papers |
| HO | Home Office |
| IWM | International War Museum |
| MA | Military Archives |
| MSP | Military Service Pensions |
| MSPC | Military Service Pensions Collection |
| NAI | National Archives of Ireland |
| NAUK | National Archives of the United Kingdom |
| NLS MS | National Library of Scotland, Manuscript Collections. |
| PRONI | Public Record Office Northern Ireland |
| REF | Referee |
| UCDA | University College Dublin Archives |
| WO | War Office |
| WS | Witness Statement |

# Endnotes

## Drilling for Ireland

1 Mathún Mac Fheorais interview with Pat Bermingham (Mathún Mac Fheorais Collection, Local Studies Centre, Ennis).

2 Mathún Mac Fheorais interview with Micho McMahon (Mathún Mac Fheorais Collection, Local Studies Centre, Ennis).
Stephen Madigan, untitled and unpublished memoir in author's possession; courtesy Annelen Madigan.

3 BMH WS 1316 (John Flanagan), p. 2.
BMH WS 1322 (Art O'Donnell), p. 9.

4 BMH WS 883 (John M McCarthy), p. 15.

5 Frank Gallagher, *The Four Glorious Years, 1918–1921*, 2nd edition (Dublin 2005), pp. 70–71.

6 David Fitzpatrick, *Politics and Irish Life 1913–1921: Provincial Experience of War and Revolution* (Cork 1977), p. 5.

7 Author's interview with Murt McInerney, 11 April 2019.

8 Farmers who were experiencing a shortage of grass were wont to allow a fettered animal to graze the lush grass that grows on the side of the road. This illegal practice was commonly referred to as 'grazing the long acre.'

9 Author's interview with Pádraig De Barra, 30 September 2009.

10 BMH WS 1322 (Art O'Donnell), p. 23.

11 BMH WS 1252 (Éamon Fennell), p. 3.

12 BMH WS 1324 (Joseph Barrett), p. 12.

13 BMH WS 1322 (Art O'Donnell), p. 23.

14 BMH WS 1252 (Éamon Fennell), p. 8.

15  Matthew Bermingham Jnr. Statement given to Mathún Mac Fheorais. (Mathún Mac Fheorais Collection, Local Studies Centre, Ennis).

16  'Sinn Fein's bark and bite', *Manchester Guardian*, 5 November 1917, p. 8.

17  Mathún Mac Fheorais interview with Brian Mac Lua, Ennis, 14 March 1970 (Mathún Mac Fheorais Collection, Local Studies Centre, Ennis).

18  NAUK, CO 904 151, Letter from Assistant Registrar General for Ireland to Charles E Glynn, 11 April 1919. Glynn had published a pamphlet containing a list of men from the town who had enlisted in the British Army during the Great War.

19  Mathún Mac Fheorais interview with Brian Mac Lua, Ennis, 14 March 1970 (Mathún Mac Fheorais Collection, Local Studies Centre, Ennis).

20  'Republican Flags Displayed at Kilrush and Captured by the Police', *Limerick Leader*, 7 May 1917, p. 7.

21  NAUK, Ireland, Petty Sessions Court Registers. Clare, Ireland, 10 August 1917, Mary Hayes (www.findmypast.co.uk, accessed 07 February 2019).

22  'Republican Flags on Licensed Premises. Prosecutions at Kilkee', *Limerick Leader*, 6 August 1917, p. 3.
    'Kilrush Quarter Sessions', *Cork Examiner*, 18 October 1917, p. 2.

23  David Fitzpatrick, *Politics and Irish Life 1913–1921: Provincial Experience of War and Revolution* (Cork, 1977), p. 8.

24  Birth certificate of John Hanlon, marriage certificate of John Hanlon and Hanna Nyhan, retrieved from https://civilrecords.irishgenealogy.ie.

25  NAUK, HO/184/33, RIC General Register Entry.

26  NAUK, Easter Rising & Ireland Under Martial Law 1916–1921, WO 35 97, Drilling at Knockerra, Co Clare, 5 August 1917 (www.findmypast.co.uk, accessed 29 January 2019).

27  NAUK, Ireland, Petty Sessions Court Registers, Clare, Ireland, 15 October 1917, Richard Behan (www.findmypast.co.uk, accessed 19 February 2019).

28  BMH WS 1251 (Martin Chambers), pp. 1–2.

29  MA MSPC A24, 5th Battalion, West Clare Brigade, pp. 8–9.

30  Tim Pat Coogan, *De Valera, Long Fellow, Long Shadow* (London 1993), p. 92.

31  'Coming Elections East Clare', *Evening Herald*, 20 June 1917, p. 1.

32  BMH WS 1322 (Art O'Donnell), p. 26.

33  'Sinn Féiners Courtmartial in Cork', *Cork Examiner*, 30 August 1917, p. 3.

34  'Results of Cork Courtmartials', *Cork Examiner*, 5 September 1917, p. 3.
    NAUK, WO 35 96 13. Civilians tried by Courtmartial (www.findmypast.co.uk, accessed 24 March 2019).

35  BMH WS 1322 (Art O'Donnell), p. 27.

36  BMH WS 1322 (Art O'Donnell), p. 30.

37  'Two Doonbeg Patriots', *Clare Champion*, 4 January 1964.

38 Maurice (Moss) Twomey, *The West Clare Brigade Papers, IE 2135* (1930), p. 45, Pádraig Burke, University of Limerick Special Collections.

39 NAUK, Ireland, Petty Sessions Court Registers, Clare, Ireland, Special Court, 13 August 1917 (www.findmypast.co.uk, accessed 24 March 2019).
'Sinn Féin Arrests and Fines', *Irish Independent*, 16 August 1917, p. 2.
'Petty Sessions', *Cork Examiner*, 18 August 1917, p. 2.

40 'Courtmartial in Cork', *Cork Examiner*, 8 September 1917, p. 8.
'Courtmartial in Cork', *Freeman's Journal*, 8 September 1917, p. 6.

41 'Four Men Get a Year for Illegal Drilling', *Freeman's Journal*, 17 September 1917, p. 4.

42 'Protest Meetings', *Irish Independent*, 24 September 1917, p. 9.
'Protest Meeting in Athboy', *Meath Chronicle*, 22 September 1917, p. 3.

43 Constance Gore-Booth, *Prison Letters of Countess Markievicz* (London, 1986) p. 295. Countess Markievicz here refers to meeting 'Liddy and Browne'. The latter appears to be Thomas Browne of Toonavoher and Ennis. However, Liddy was arrested on 25 August, tried by District Court-martial in Cork on 7 September and his sentence was promulgated on 12 September. Thomas Browne was arrested on 14 September and tried on 2 October. It is possible that the two men were at Limerick Station on 14 September 1917 when Liddy was being transferred to Mountjoy Prison and Browne was being brought to Cork Men's Prison to await his trial.

44 'Dramatic Scene at Inquest', *Evening Herald*, 11 October 1917, p. 1.

45 BMH WS 1322 (Art O'Donnell), p. 29.

46 BMH WS 1322 (Art O'Donnell), p. 30.

47 Tim Pat Coogan, *De Valera, Long Fellow, Long Shadow* (London 1993), p. 100.

48 Mathún Mac Fheorais interview with Frankie Ronan, Kilrush, September 1975 (Mathún Mac Fheorais Collection, Local Studies Centre, Ennis).

49 Mathún Mac Fheorais interviews with Micho Tubridy and Pat Bermingham (Mathún Mac Fheorais Collection, Local Studies Centre, Ennis).

50 Mathún Mac Fheorais interview with Pat Bermingham (Mathún Mac Fheorais Collection, Local Studies Centre, Ennis).

51 Mathún Mac Fheorais interview with Micho 'Carriga' McMahon, Kilrush, 14 July 1970 (Mathún Mac Fheorais Collection, Local Studies Centre, Ennis).

52 NAUK, WO 35 132, Courts-martial Case Registers No. 89, Joseph Breen (www.findmypast.co.uk, accessed 23 March 2019).
'Civilians Courtmartialled', *Cork Examiner*, 3 October 1917, p. 2.

53 NAUK, Irish Prison Registers 1790–1924, Mountjoy Prison General Register Male 1914–1918, Joseph Breen (www.findmypast.co.uk, accessed 24 March 2019).
NAUK, Irish Prison Registers 1790–1924, Prison Dundalk General Register Male 1917–1931, Joseph Breen (www.findmypast.co.uk, accessed 24 March 2019).

54 NAUK, Irish Prison Registers 1790–1924, Prison Dundalk General Register Male 1917–1931, John Liddy (www.findmypast.co.uk, accessed 24 March 2019).
BMH WS 1322 (Art O'Donnell), p. 32.

## Hunger for Land

1  David Fitzpatrick, *Politics and Irish Life 1913-1921: provincial experience of war and revolution*, (Cork 1977), p. 58.

2  Daniel McCarthy, *Ireland's Banner County. Clare from the fall of Parnell to the Great War, 1890–1918*, p. 15.

3  Erskine Childers, *The Constructive Work of Dáil Éireann, No 2* (Dublin 1921), p. 7.

4  Frank Gallagher, *The Four Glorious Years, 1918–1921*, 2nd ed, (Dublin 2005), p. 71.

5  'Scenes in Ennis Court', *Cork Examiner*, 9 February 1918, p. 5.

6  'Cattle Drives in Clare', *Cork Examiner*, 30 January 1918, p. 4.

7  'Sinn Féin Position', *Freeman's Journal*, 5 March 1918, p. 5.

8  'Sinn Féin Position', *Freeman's Journal*, 5 March 1918, p. 5.

9  *Strabane Chronicle*, 16 March 1918, p. 3.

10  BMH WS 1068 (Michael Brennan), p. 30.

11  'Volunteer Orders. Papers from Headquarters found by Police', *Freeman's Journal*, 26 March 1918, p. 5.

12  BMH WS 1253 (Joe Daly), p. 6.

13  MA MSPC 653221 (Patrick Burke).
'School Teacher's House Fired Into', *Irish Times*, 6 September 1919, p. 7.

14  BMH WS 1322 (Art O'Donnell), p. 25.

15  *Lámh láidir* is an Irish language term that means 'physical force'.

16  'Kilballyowen Cattle Drive', *Clare Champion*, 11 October 1919.

17  'Clare Cattle Drive', *Freeman's Journal*, 9 October 1919, p. 6.

18  'House Fired Into At Kilballyowen', *Saturday Record*, 25 October 1919.


## Bayonet charge in Carrigaholt

1  BMH WS 1252 (Éamon Fennell), p. 8.

2  BMH WS 1252 (Éamon Fennell), p. 10.

3  'The Village Hall Tragedy', *Freeman's Journal*, 5 April 1918, p. 3.

4  Author's interview with Pakie Keane, nephew of Michael Keane, 3 September 2019.

5  BMH WS 1252 (Éamon Fennell), p. 9.
'Kerryman's Death', *Killarney Echo*, 13 April 1918, p. 4.

6  'The Russell Inquest', *The Liberator*, 11 April 1918, p. 3.

7  MA MSPC A24. 5th Battalion, West Clare Brigade, Record of Carrigaholt Company from 1914 to 1923, p. 3.

8  'Carrigaholt Tragedy', *Saturday Record*, 6 April 1918.

9  'Thrust or Mischance. Doctors Disagree on Nature of Carrigaholt Victim's Wound', *Freeman's Journal*, 8 April 1918, p. 6.

10 'Kerryman's Death', *Killarney Echo*, 13 April 1918, p. 4.

11 'The Russell Inquest', *The Liberator*, 11 April 1918, p. 3.

12 'Kerryman's Death', *Killarney Echo*, 13 April 1918, p. 4.
'The Russell Inquest', *The Liberator*, 11 April 1918, p. 3.

13 'Carrigaholt Tragedy', *Saturday Record*. 13 April 1918.

14 'Kerryman's Death' *Killarney Echo*, 13 April 1918, p. 4.

15 Certified copy of death certificate for Thomas Russell, 27 March 1918, No. 377;
retrieved from https://civilrecords.irishgenealogy.ie.

16 Mathún Mac Fheorais interview with Marty Mulqueen (Mathún Mac Fheorais
Collection, Local Studies Centre, Ennis).

17 Mathún Mac Fheorais interviews with Micho Tubridy and Pat Bermingham (Mathún
Mac Fheorais Collection, Local Studies Centre, Ennis).

18 'Correspondence', *Manchester Guardian*, 26 April 1918, p. 8.

19 'Reported Conflict with the Military', *Irish Times*, 30 March 1918, p. 2.

20 'Military Law in Clare', *Irish Times*, 6 April 1918, p. 2.

21 House of Commons. (1918), *9 April Debate* (vol 104, col 1450); retrieved from
https://api.parliament.uk/historic-hansard/commons/1918/apr/09/westmeath-
independent-seizure-1

22 *Irish Independent*, 30 September 1918, p. 2.
'"Champion's" Re-appearance', *Clare National Journal*.

23 'Carrigaholt Tragedy', *Saturday Record*, 6 April 1918.

24 'Sinn Féiners' Version', *Irish Independent*, 10 April 1918, p. 2.
'Kerryman's Death', *Killarney Echo*, 13 April 1918, p. 4.

25 Trinity College Dublin Digital Collections, Letter from Bishop M Fogarty to
Ennis Sinn Féin Club, 5 April 1918; retrieved from http://digitalcollections.tcd.ie/
content/526/pdf/526.pdf.

## Gaoled for Ireland

1 'Kilrush Tragedy', *Cork Examiner* 6, April 1918, p. 7.

2 NAUK, Ireland, Petty Sessions Court Registers, Clare, Ireland, 29 March 1918,
Michael Keane (www.findmypast.co.uk, accessed 07 February 2019).
'Unrest in Ireland. Drilling and Cattle Drives', *Irish Independent*, 30 March 1918, p. 3.

3 Maurice (Moss) Twomey (1930), The West Clare Brigade Papers, IE 2135, p. 45
(Christy McCarthy), University of Limerick Special Collections.

4 NAUK, Ireland, Petty Sessions Court Registers, Clare, Ireland, 29 March 1918,
Christopher McCarthy (www.findmypast.co.uk, accessed 7 February 2019).

5 'Unrest in Ireland. Drilling and Cattle Drives', *Irish Independent*, 30 March 1918, p. 3.

6   NAUK, Ireland, Petty Sessions Court Registers. Clare, Ireland. 5 July 1918, Michael Greene (www.findmypast.co.uk, accessed 19, February2019).

7   'Unlawful Assembly: Proceedings at Crimes Court', *Saturday Record*, 3 August 1918.

8   NAUK, Ireland, Petty Sessions Court Registers, Clare, Ireland, 26, 27 July 1918, Thomas McGrath (www.findmypast.co.uk, accessed 19 February 2019).

9   NAUK,Ireland, Petty Sessions Court Registers. Clare, Ireland, 11 October 1918, Patrick O'Shea and Martin Collins (www.findmypast.co.uk, accessed 15 March 2019).

10  '"Unlawful Assembly". Interesting Appeal at Quarter Sessions', *Clare Champion*, 25 January 1919.
    '"Unjust and Vindictive". Judge's Censure on Sentence', *Irish Independent*. 24 January 1919, p. 2.

11  'Unlawful Assembly at Kilkee', *Saturday Record*, 3 August 1918.

12  NAUK, WO 141 93 195. *Record of the Rebellion in Ireland*, Vol IV, Part 2, Chapter 1; General Remarks on the Rebellion in the 6th Divisional Area (www.findmypast.co.uk, accessed 21 February 2019).

13  'Unlawful Assembly in West Clare', *Saturday Record*, 1 June 1918.

14  MA MSPC A24, Records of Activities of Battalion 1, West Clare Brigade, IRA, 1917–1923, p. 2.

15  MA MSPC, PB/1D285 (Patrick Burke). Letter from Sgt William Breen in support of Patrick Burke Senior's claim for an allowance or gratuity under section 12 of the Army Pensions Act, 1932.
    'Exciting Chase in Cooraclare. Arrest and Escape of a Volunteer', *Saturday Record*, 27 April 1918.
    Maurice (Moss) Twomey (1930), The West Clare Brigade Papers, IE 2135, p. 45 (Pádraig Burke), University of Limerick Special Collections.
    Irish Prison Registers 1790–1924, Cork County Gaol General Register 1915–1924. (Patrick Burke) (www.findmypast.co.uk, accessed 18 February 2019).

16  Maurice (Moss) Twomey (1930), The West Clare Brigade Papers, IE 2135, p. 45 (Michael Fahy), University of Limerick Special Collections.
    MA MSPC DP 7097 (Michael Fahey). Michael Colivet suggests that Fahy went to sea one year later, in September 1917, but the dates given by Mrs Nora Fahy in MA MSPC 2RB4157 are favoured here.

17  MA MSPC A24, 5th Battalion, West Clare Brigade, pp. 7–10.

18  'Illegal Drilling at Kilkee. Boyscouts Courtmartialled', *Saturday Record*, 8 June 1918.

19  'Another Boy Scout Arrested. A Bayonet Charge', *Saturday Record*, 8 June 1918.

20  Email correspondence from Michael Marrinan to Cindy Wood, 6 July 2019.

21  NAUK, MA MSPC A24, Record of 5th Battalion, West Clare Brigade, p. 10 (www.findmypast.co.uk, accessed 18 March 2019).

22  NAUK, MA MSPC A24, Record of 5th Battalion, West Clare Brigade, p. 10 (www.findmypast.co.uk, accessed 18 March 2019).

23 WO 35 101 15, *An tÓglach*, Vol 1 No 6, Official Organ of the Irish Volunteers (www.findmypast.co.uk, accessed 18 March 2019). Daniel Brosnahan is mistakenly named here as David Brosnan.

24 MA MSPC A24, Record of 5th Battalion, West Clare Brigade, p. 10.
NAUK, WO 35 101 15, *An tÓglach*, Vol 1 No 6, Official Organ of the Irish Volunteers (www.findmypast.co.uk, accessed 18 March 2019). James Talty is mistakenly named here as James Tully.

25 MA MSPC A24, Record of 5th Battalion, West Clare Brigade, p. 10.

26 'Collapsible Boat Man. Court Martial Story', *Irish Independent*, 9 July 1918, p. 3.

27 NAUK, HO 141 72, Private Joseph Dowling, Trial By General Court-martial (www.findmypast.co.uk, accessed 2 March 2019).

28 Pauric Travers, 'The Conscription Crisis and the General Election of 1918' in John Crowley, Dónal Ó Drisceoil and Mike Murphy, Eds., *Atlas of the Irish Revolution* (Cork 2017), p. 326.

29 BMH WS 1322 (Art O'Donnell), p. 22. For a comprehensive account of Éamon Waldron's role in the revolutionary period see Mick O'Connor, 'Arrest in Ennistymon', *Clare Association Yearbook* (2017).

30 'English Prison Regime', *Irish Independent*, 21 September 1918, p. 3.

31 'Released Deportee. Birmingham Jail Conditions', *Irish Independent*, 20 January 1919, p. 3.

32 NAUK, HO 144 1496, Postal Censorship Reports on the Correspondence of the Irish Internees, Brian O'Higgins (www.findmypast.co.uk, accessed 21 February 2019).

33 NAUK, HO 144 1496, Postal Censorship Reports on the Correspondence of the Irish Internees – censored extract of letter from Mrs O'Higgins to Brian O'Higgins, 9 December 1918 (www.findmypast.co.uk, accessed 21 February 2019),

34 NAUK, HO 144 1496, Postal Censorship Reports on the Correspondence of the Irish Internees – censored extract of letter from Mrs O'Higgins to Brian O'Higgins, 10 November 1918; censored extract of letter from Brian O'Higgins to Mrs O'Higgins, 17 November 1918 (www.findmypast.co.uk, accessed 21 February 2019).

35 NAUK, HO 144 1496, Postal Censorship Reports on the Correspondence of the Irish Internees – censored extract of letter from Peter O'Hourihane to Rev T O'Molloy, 29 December 1918 (www.findmypast.co.uk, accessed 21 February 2019).

36 'Hedge School' debate on 'The 1918 General Election – political earthquake or 'same old, same old?', *History Ireland*, 17 December 2018, Brian Walker; (www.historyireland.com, accessed 7 March 2019).

37 NAUK, HO 144 1496, Postal Censorship Reports on the Correspondence of the Irish Internees, Brian O'Higgins (www.findmypast.co.uk, accessed 21 February 2019).

38 NAUK, HO 144 1496, Postal Censorship Reports on the Correspondence of the Irish Internees, Brian O'Higgins (www.findmypast.co.uk, accessed 21 February 2019).

39 BMH WS 883 (John M McCarthy), p. 54.

40 'Release of Mr Brian O'Higgins MP', *Saturday Record*, 15 March 1919.

## The conscription crisis

1   'The New Conscription Cry', *Cork Examiner*, 22 September 1917, p. 4.

2   BMH WS 1251 (Martin Chambers), p. 2.

3   Morgie O'Connell in Jackie Elger and Patricia Sheehan (Eds), *Three men From Clare*. (Corofin 2018).

4   BMH WS 1316 (John Flanagan), p. 5.

5   BMH WS 1253 (Joe Daly), pp. 2–3.

6   Mathún Mac Fheorais interview with Marty Mulqueen (Mathún Mac Fheorais Collection, Local Studies Centre, Ennis).

7   'A Dance Raid at Knockerra', *Saturday Record*, 15 November 1919.

8   MA MSPC A24, 2nd Battalion, West Clare Brigade, IRA, 1917–1923, p. 1.

9   'Attack on Dwelling House', *Nenagh News*, 16 February 1918, p. 3.
    NAUK, Ireland, Petty Sessions Court Registers, Clare, Ireland, Special Court, 12 February 1918, John McNamara (www.findmypast.co.uk, accessed 17 February 2019).
    NAUK, WO 35 100 18, Civilians tried by courts-martial, William Moody (www.findmypast.co.uk, accessed 17 February 2019).

10  Mathún Mac Fheorais interview with Marty Mulqueen (Mathún Mac Fheorais Collection, Local Studies Centre, Ennis).
    NAUK, WO 35 100 18, Civilians tried by courts-martial, William Moody (www.findmypast.co.uk, accessed 17 February 2019).

11  'Raids for Arms in Clare', *Irish Times*, 13 February 1918, p. 5.
    NAUK, WO 35 100 18 Civilians tried by courts-martial, William Moody (www.findmypast.co.uk, accessed 17 February 2019).

12  'Raids for Arms in Clare', *Irish Times*, 13 February 1918, p. 5.

13  Mathún Mac Fheorais interview with Pat Bermingham (Mathún Mac Fheorais Collection, Local Studies Centre, Ennis).
    BMH WS 474 (Liam Haugh), pp. 5–6.

14  House of Commons (1918), 9 April Debate (Vol 104, Col 1451); retrieved from https://api.parliament.uk/historic-hansard/commons/1918/apr/09/westmeath-independent-seizure-1#S5CV0104P0_19180409_HOC_431.

15  'Military Precautions in Clare', *Manchester Guardian*, 2 March 1918, p. 7.
    'Proclamations in Clare; State of Clare: Martial Law', *Saturday Record*, 2 March 1918.

16  MA MSPC A24, Records of Activities of Battalion 1, West Clare Brigade, IRA, 1917–1923, p. 3.

17  MA MSPC A24, Record of 3rd Battalion, West Clare Brigade, 1918–1923/4, p. 1.
    MA MSPC, MD/6954, Sworn evidence given before the Referee and Advisory Committee by Chief Superintendent Seán Liddy in the case of Patrick Joseph Darcy (deceased) on 20 May 1947. The Report of this Committee gives the date of the attack as March 1919, but the record of the 3rd Battalion, West Clare Brigade states that it took place in April 1918. Liddy's account of this event differs in the detail from the

official record of the 3rd Battalion. Liddy describes the attack as a spur of the moment decision that was taken while he, Patrick Darcy, Paddy Lynch and another were out walking. The interview transcriber was somewhat confused by Liddy's pronunciation of the name of one of the participants in this attack, which is written as 'Tom Miskelly?' [*sic*]. The author infers that Liddy was referring here to one of three men – Thomas Quealy, Thomas Mescall or Thomas Kelly – all of whom were members of Cooraclare Company but none of whom is named on the official list of participants in this attack. The version in the official (1937) Battalion record is favoured here, as Thomas Quealy was Secretary of the Committee that compiled it.

18 'A New Clare Prohibition', *Irish Independent*, 19 April 1918, p. 2.

19 Cooralclare/Cree Historical Society, *Cooraclare & Cree, Parish of Kilmacduane: history & folklore*, p. 446.

20 RTÉ/Boston College. *Century Ireland*: Robin Adams, *Funding the new Republic: the External Dáil Loan*; retrieved from www.rte.ie/centuryireland/index.php/articles/funding-the-new-republic-the-external-dail-loan.

21 RTÉ/Boston College. *Century Ireland*: Dr William Murphy, *How Ireland was lost in the 1918 Conscription Crisis*; retrieved from www.rte.ie/centuryireland/index.php/articles/how-ireland-was-lost-in-the-1918-conscription-crisis.

22 'Conscription. Irish Leaders meet', *The Kerryman*, 20 April 1918, p. 3,

23 BMH WS 809 (David Conroy), p. 2.

24 'The Anti-Conscription Pledge', *Saturday Record*, 27 April 1918.

25 Mathún Mac Fheorais interviews with Micho Tubridy and Pat Bermingham (Mathún Mac Fheorais Collection, Local Studies Centre, Ennis).

26 Mathún Mac Fheorais interview with Matt Bermingham (Mathún Mac Fheorais Collection, Local Studies Centre, Ennis). Marty McNamara was a member of the Clare Senior football team that contested the 1917 All-Ireland Final against Wexford.

27 Mathún Mac Fheorais interview with Pat Bermingham Junior (Mathún Mac Fheorais Collection, Local Studies Centre, Ennis).

28 RTÉ/Boston College, *Century Ireland*: Dr William Murphy, *How Ireland was lost in the 1918 Conscription Crisis*; retrieved from www.rte.ie/centuryireland/index.php/articles/how-ireland-was-lost-in-the-1918-conscription-crisis.

## Michael Fahy

1 'Alleged Illegal Drilling', *Clare Champion*, 4 January 1919,

2 NAUK, WO 35 102, Easter Rising & Ireland Under Martial Law 1916–1921, Michael Corduff (www.findmypast.co.uk, accessed 08 February 2019).

3 'Cork Sensation. Sequence to Recent Shooting. McNeillis Escapes', *Cork Examiner*, 12 November 1918, p. 4.

4 NAUK, WO 35 102, Easter Rising & Ireland Under Martial Law 1916–1921, Michael Corduff (www.findmypast.co.uk, accessed 08 February 2019).

Maurice (Moss) Twomey (1930), The West Clare Brigade Papers, IE 2135, p. 45, (Michael Fahy), University of Limerick Special Collections.

5   BMH WS 809 (David Conroy), pp. 6–7.

6   Maurice (Moss) Twomey (1930), The West Clare Brigade Papers, IE 2135, p. 45, (Michael Fahy), University of Limerick Special Collections.

7   MA MSPC 2RB4157 (Michael Fahy), Maurice (Moss) Twomey (1930), The West Clare Brigade Papers, IE 2135, p. 45, (Michael Fahy), University of Limerick Special Collections.

8   MA MSPC A24, Record of 5th Battalion, West Clare Brigade, p. 12.

9   MA MSPC 2RB4157 (Michael Fahy), Signed statement of Jim Talty, OC 5th Battalion, West Clare Brigade, 25 October 1939.

10  MA MSPC 2RB4157 (Michael Fahy), Letter from Michael Colivet to Military Service Pensions Board, Griffith Barracks, 3 May 1938.

11  MA MSPC DP 7097 (Michael Fahy), Signed statement of Dr J Roberts, Barrington's Hospital, Limerick, 14 July 1939.
    Maurice (Moss) Twomey (1930), The West Clare Brigade Papers, IE 2135, p. 45, (Michael Fahy), University of Limerick Special Collections.

12  MA MSPC A24, Record of 5th Battalion, West Clare Brigade, p. 13.

13  'Death of Mr. Michael Fahy, Kilkee', Saturday Record, 27 March 1920.

## Hear, hear, Paddy

1   NAUK, WO 35 102 39, Keane, Thomas & 3 others. Waylaiding [sic] a police constable while returning from Kilrush to his station at Carrigaholt (www.findmypast.co.uk, accessed 21 February 2019).
    'Attack On Constable. Cork Courtmartial', Cork Examiner, 14 February 1919, p. 3.
    'Policeman Attacked', Clare Champion, 11 January 1919.

2   'Cork Prison Scenes', Cork Examiner, 13 February 1919, p. 4.

3   'Attack On Constable. Cork Courtmartial', Cork Examiner, 14 February 1919, p. 3.

4   NAUK, HO 144 1496, Postal Censorship Reports on the Correspondence of the Irish Internees – censored extract of letter from Mrs M A Keane, Carrigaholt to Brian O'Higgins, 17 January 1919, (www.findmypast.co.uk, accessed 21 February 2019).

5   Irish Independent, 6 February 1919, p. 2.

6   'Warder and Patient. Cork Guardians' Protest', Cork Examiner, 26 February 1919, p. 3.
    'Cork Prisoner Victim', Cork Examiner, 21 February 1919, p. 4.

7   'Pithy Provincial news. Munster', Irish Independent, 28 March 1919, p. 4.

8   'Cork Prisoners', Cork Examiner, 8 March 1919, p. 5.

9   Irish Prison Registers 1790–1924. Cork County Gaol General Register 1915–1924. Book No. 1/8/38 (www.findmypast.co.uk, accessed 11 March 2019).

10 NAUK, WO 35 102 39, Keane, Thomas & 3 others. Waylaiding [*sic*] a police constable while returning from Kilrush to his station at Carrigaholt (www.findmypast. co.uk, accessed 21 February 2019).

11 'Policeman's Claim', *Nenagh News*, 12 April 1919, p. 4.

12 BMH WS 1252 (Éamon Fennell), p. 10.
'Carrigaholt Man Gets Four Months', *Saturday Record*, 3 May 1919.

13 'Illegal Drilling in West Clare', *Saturday Record*, 22 February 1919,

14 NAUK, Petty Sessions Court Registers. Clare, Ireland, 21 February 1919, Patrick Clancy (www.findmypast.co.uk, accessed 13 March 2019).
'Níl Beann Agam Oraibh. Crimes Act Court At Ennis', *Clare Champion*, 1 March 1919, p. 1.

15 'Prisoner's Homecoming. Enthusiastic Reception', *Clare Champion*, 15 March 1919.

## The shooting of Pat Studdert

1 'Shocking Affair at Kilkee. Fisherman Shot by a Soldier', *Saturday Record*. 5 July 1919. Maurice (Moss) Twomey (1930), The West Clare Brigade Papers, IE 2135, (Pádraig Studdert), University of Limerick Special Collections.

## Saving hay and saving Ireland

1 BMH WS 1316 (John Flanagan), p. 8.

2 BMH WS 1322 (Art O'Donnell), p. 4.

3 BMH WS 1316 (John Flanagan), p. 9.

4 'Co Clare Incident: Courtmartial in Cork', *Cork Examiner*, 9 May 1919, p, 2.

5 'Attack on Clare Police', *Irish Times*, 9 May 1919, p. 6.

6 NAUK, WO 35 45792, General Courts-martial Papers, Trial of Art O'Donnell, Thomas Howard, Michael Mahony, John Grogan, Joseph Sexton.

7 'The Attack on Clare Police', *Irish Times*, 24 May 1919, p. 4.

8 NAUK, WO 35 45792, General Courts-martial Papers, Trial of Art O'Donnell, Thomas Howard, Michael Mahony, John Grogan, Joseph Sexton.

9 NAUK, HO 184 102, Constabulary Force Fund, Thursday 13 May 1919, p. 6.
The Royal Irish Constabulary Forum; https://irishconstabulary.com/viewtopic.php?f=4 4&t=1577&p=5375&hilit=John+Hanlon#p5375, accessed 26 December 2017.

10 NAI, Irish Prison Registers 1790–1924. Cork County Gaol General Register 1915–1924. Book No. 1/8/38 (www.findmypast.co.uk, accessed 11 March 2019).

11 Irish Prison Registers 1790–1924. Mountjoy Prison General Register Male 1918–1923. Book No. 1/43/12 (www.findmypast.co.uk, accessed 11 March 2019).

12 Author's interviews with Michael Howard 30 October 2009 and 20 August 2011.

13 David Fitzpatrick, *Politics and Irish Life 1913–1921: Provincial Experience of War and Revolution* (Cork, 1977), p. 138.

14 *The Police Gazette* or *Hue and Cry*, Dublin, 12 March 1920.

15 Author's interview with Jim Tubridy, 3 July 2019.

16 MA MSPC A24, Record of 3rd Battalion, West Clare Brigade, 1918–1923/4, p. 1.
Author's interview with Martin Quealy, son of Thomas Quealy, 30 October 2011.

17 Cooralclare/Cree Historical Society, *Cooraclare & Cree, Parish of Kilmacduane: history & folklore* (Clare 2002), p. 446.
'Minor Outrages in Clare', *Manchester Guardian*, 28 October 1919, p. 8.

18 BMH WS 1322 (Art O'Donnell), p. 46–48.

19 BMH WS 1322 (Art O'Donnell), p. 48.

20 BMH WS 1322 (Art O'Donnell), pp. 50–51.

21 NAUK, CO 762, Irish Grants Committee, application of Annie Callinan, 10 December 1928.

22 'Obituary Notices. Mr Michael Killeen, Doonbeg', *Clare Champion*, 23 January 1937.

23 Murt McInerney Collection, Letter from Michael Killeen to his sister Mary. 6 August 1919.

24 'Shots from the Hedges. Police Return Fire in Clare', *Manchester Guardian*, 24 September 1919, p. 7.
'More Clare Shooting', *Saturday Record*, 27 September 1919. The date of this ambush is incorrectly reported in a number of accounts.

25 MA MSPC A24, West Clare Brigade, 1 Western Division, 2nd Battalion, West Clare Brigade, p. 1.

26 BMH WS 474 (Liam Haugh), p. 6.

27 'More Clare Shooting', *Saturday Record*, 27 September 1919.

28 'Clare Raiders recoil. Masked Raiders Thrashed', *Irish Independent*, 22 October 1919, p. 9.

29 BMH WS 474 (Liam Haugh), p. 6.

30 'Special Court at Kilkee', *Saturday Record*, 15 November 1919.

31 BMH WS 1226 (Michael Russell), p. 2.

32 Michael Fitzmartin, Handwritten summary of his role in the War of Independence, which formed part of his Pension Application (in author's possession); courtesy of his brother, Senan Fitzmartin.
'Courtmartial Sentences', *Cork Examiner*, 17 December 1919, p. 7.

33 'Barracks Besieged', *Freeman's Journal*, 14 November 1919, p. 3.

34 'Barracks Besieged', *Freeman's Journal*, 14 November 1919, p. 3.

35 'Barracks Besieged', *Freeman's Journal*, 14 November 1919, p. 3.
'Attacks on Police Huts. Burning of Cooraclare Barracks', *Saturday Record*, 31 January 1920.

36 'Attacks on Police Huts. Burning of Cooraclare Barracks', *Saturday Record*, 31 January 1920.

37 MA MSPC A24, Record of 3rd Battalion, West Clare Brigade, 1918–1923/4, p. 2. Cooralclare/Cree Historical Society, *Cooraclare & Cree, Parish of Kilmacduane: history & folklore* (Clare 2002), p. 448.

38 'Courtmartial Sentences', *Cork Examiner*, 17 December 1919, p. 7.

## The drowning of Michael Darcy

1 NAUK, WO 35 109, Corry, Patrick, Harrington, Dan, Attempt to murder police at Cooraclare, Co. Clare. Evidence of Constable William Costigan, Limerick Gaol, 28 January 1920.

2 'The Cooraclare Attack', *Belfast Newsletter*, 21 January 1920. p. 5.

3 Cooralclare/Cree Historical Society, *Cooraclare & Cree, Parish of Kilmacduane: history & folklore* (Clare 2002), pp 448–449.

4 Most accounts of the ambush describe Michael Darcy as a scout. However, Seán Liddy gave sworn evidence 25 years later to the Pensions Board, where he stated that he thought that Darcy was 12–14-years-old, 'just a child', but that he might have been a bit older as he was 'a little fellow who didn't grow up'. Liddy stated that he had told Darcy to '… clear away as quickly as you can and get away to a safe distance', after Darcy had followed the ambush party.

5 BMH WS 474 (Liam Haugh), p. 4.

6 NAUK, WO 35 109, Corry, Patrick, Harrington, Dan, Attempt to murder police at Cooraclare, Co. Clare. Evidence of Constable James Irwin, Limerick Gaol, 28 January 1920.

7 NAUK, WO 35 109, Corry, Patrick, Harrington, Dan, Attempt to murder police at Cooraclare, Co. Clare. Evidence of Constable James Irwin, Limerick Gaol, 28 January 1920.

8 BMH WS 474 (Liam Haugh), p. 4.

9 NAUK, WO 35 109, Corry, Patrick, Harrington, Dan, Attempt to murder police at Cooraclare, Co. Clare. Evidence of Constable James Irwin, Limerick Gaol, 28 January 1920.

10 NAUK, WO 35 109, Corry, Patrick, Harrington, Dan, Attempt to murder police at Cooraclare, Co. Clare. Evidence of Constable William Driscoll, Limerick Gaol, 28 January 1920.

11 NAUK, WO 35 109, Corry, Patrick, Harrington, Dan, Attempt to murder police at Cooraclare, Co. Clare. Evidence of Sergeant John Daly, District Inspector's Office, Kilrush, 20 January 1920.

12 'RIC Attacked at Cooraclare', *The Banner* Claremen and Women's Patriotic, Benevolent and Social Association of New York (New York 1963), p. 169.

NAUK, WO 35 109, Corry, Patrick, Harrington, Dan, Attempt to murder police at Cooraclare, Co. Clare. Evidence of Constable James Irwin, Limerick Gaol, 28 January 1920.

13 'RIC Attacked at Cooraclare', *The Banner* Claremen and Women's Patriotic, Benevolent and Social Association of New York (New York 1963), p. 169.

14 'The Sensation at Cooraclare', *The Liberator* (Tralee), 29 January 1920, p. 3.

15 'The Sensation at Cooraclare', *The Liberator* (Tralee), 29 January 1920, p. 3.

16 'One Man Killed', *Freeman's Journal,* 21 January 1920, p. 1.

17 NAUK, WO 35 109, Corry, Patrick, Harrington, Dan, Attempt to murder police at Cooraclare, Co. Clare. Letter from Captain William C Gover on behalf of Major General, commanding 6th Division, Cork, to General Headquarters Ireland, 29 January 1920.

18 NAUK, Petty Sessions Court Registers, Clare, Ireland, 11 February 1920, Patrick Corry (www.findmypast.co.uk, accessed 08 February 2019),

19 'Drowned, Not Shot. The Jury and the Police', *Saturday Record*, 31 January 1920.

20 BMH WS 1322 (Art O'Donnell), p. 50.

21 MA MSPC, MD/6954, Sworn evidence given before the Referee and Advisory Committee by Margaret Daly in the case of Patrick Joseph Darcy (deceased) on 21 May 1947.

22 MA MSPC, MD/6954, Sworn evidence given before the Referee and Advisory Committee by Margaret Daly in the case of Patrick Joseph Darcy (deceased), 20 May 1947.

23 'West Clare Celebrations', *Clare Champion*, 14 April 1928.

24 MA MSPC, DP 64 (Michael D'arcy).

25 MA MSPC, A24, Records of Activities of Battalion 1, West Clare Brigade, IRA, 1917–1923, p. 3.
'A Rifle Missing', *Freeman's Journal*, 4 March 1920, p. 4.
NAUK, WO 35 139 Report of CI Co Clare on Joseph O'Connor, Handwritten memo by H J Moore (www.findmypast.co.uk, accessed 18 February 2019).

## Republican Courts

1 BMH WS 1253 (Joe Daly), p. 6.

2 'A Political Dog', *Cork Examiner* 22 May 1918, p. 6.

3 'Sinn Féin Courts: The new order in Ireland', *Manchester Guardian*, 6 July 1920, p. 6.
Mary Kotsonouris, *Retreat from Revolution: The Dáil Courts, 1920–1924* (Dublin 1994).
Conor Maguire, 'The Republican Courts', *Capuchin Annual, 1968*, pp 378–388.

4 Mary Kotsonouris, *Retreat from Revolution: The Dáil Courts, 1920–1924*, (Dublin 1994) p. 20.

5 BMH WS 1253 (Joe Daly), pp. 6, 11.

6  BMH WS 1322 (Art O'Donnell), p. 49.
   BMH WS 1251 (Martin Chambers), p. 11.

7  Canon Peter Ryan, PP, *History of Kilmurry Ibrickane* (Clare 1969), p. 48.

8  BMH WS 1253 (Joe Daly), pp. 3–4.

9  'A Patriot Priest', *Clare Champion*, 15 June 1935.

10 MA MSPC A24, 5th Battalion, West Clare Brigade, Record of Carrigaholt Company from 1914 to 1923, p. 4.

11 'Formation of Arbitration Courts. Representative Meeting in West Clare', *Clare Champion*, 24 July 1920.

12 BMH WS 1770 (Kevin O'Sheil) pp. 891–892. O'Sheil also credits the Brennan brothers, whom he describes as '… the local IRA Commandants.' In fact, the Brennans were active in east Clare and the local west Clare commandants of the period were Art O'Donnell and Seán Liddy.

13 Matthew Bermingham Jnr. Statement given to Mathún Mac Fheorais. (Mathún Mac Fheorais Collection, Local Studies Centre, Ennis). Matthew Bermingham's statement is unclear about whether this was a Parish Court or a Circuit Court sitting, though he does refer later to the holding of a Circuit Court sitting at this venue.

14 Seosamh Mac Mathúna, *Kilfarboy, A History of a West Clare Parish*, (Dublin 1976), p. 89.

15 Maurice (Moss) Twomey, *The West Clare Brigade Papers, IE 2135* (1930), p. 45, Captain Seán Breen. University of Limerick Special Collections.

16 MA MSPC A24, Records of Activities of Battalion 1, West Clare Brigade, IRA, 1917–1923, p. 6.

17 BMH WS 809 (David Conroy), pp. 3–4.

18 Seosamh Mac Mathúna, *Kilfarboy, A History of a West Clare Parish* (Dublin 1976), p. 89.

19 CO 904 197 88, Dublin Castle Special Branch Files Eneclann, Trinity College, Dublin.

20 Frank Gallagher, *The Four Glorious Years, 1918-1921*, 2nd ed. p. 74. (Dublin 2005).

21 Stephen Madigan, untitled and unpublished memoir in author's possession.

22 Author's interview with Liam Haugh, son of Bill Haugh, 27 October 2010.

23 Mathún Mac Fheorais interviews with Micho Tubridy and Pat Bermingham (Mathún Mac Fheorais Collection, Local Studies Centre, Ennis).
   BMH WS 1253 (Joe Daly), p. 7.
   MA MSPC, PB/1D285 (Patrick Burke), Letter from Michael Killeen, Clare County Registrar, in support of Patrick Burke Senior's claim for an allowance or gratuity under section 12 of the Army Pensions Act, 1932.
   Maurice (Moss) Twomey (1930), The West Clare Brigade Papers, IE 2135, p. 45. (Pádraig Burke), University of Limerick Special Collections.
   BMH WS 1322 (Art O'Donnell), p. 49.

24 BMH WS 1252 (Éamon Fennell), p. 11.

25 Mathún Mac Fheorais interview with Micho Tubridy (Mathún Mac Fheorais Collection, Local Studies Centre, Ennis).

26 Seosamh Mac Mathúna, *Kilfarboy, A History of a West Clare Parish* (Dublin 1976), p. 89.

27 BMH WS 1252 (Éamon Fennell), p. 11.

28 Éamonn Gaynor, *Memoirs of a Tipperary Family: The Gaynors of Tyone 1887–2000* (Dublin 2003), p. 121.

29 'Land Hunger in Clare', *Manchester Guardian,* 2 March 1918, p. 7.

30 BMH WS 1322 (Art O'Donnell), p. 49.

31 'Arbitration Court, West Clare District', *Clare Champion*, 17 July 1920, p. 1.

32 'Arbitration Court, West Clare District', *Clare Champion*, 17 July 1920, p. 1.

33 'Kilrush Petty Sessions. Light Business', *Clare Champion*, 24 July 1920.

34 'Volunteers' Work in Clare', *Freeman's Journal*, 1 July 1920, p. 3. This report refers to J P Christy Kelly's refusal to attend a Sinn Féin Court on a charge of trespass and states incorrectly that he had been kidnapped. It was his son, Josie, who had been kidnapped.

35 'Miltown Malbay Petty sessions', *Saturday Record*, 22 March 1919.

36 'Sinn Féin's Land Courts. An insurance against Violence. The Attitude of the Bar', *Manchester Guardian*, 9 July 1920, p. 9.

37 Frank Gallagher, *The Four Glorious Years, 1918–1921*, 2nd ed. (Dublin 2005), p. 79.

38 'Kilrush Quarter Sessions. Malicious Injury Claims', *Saturday Record*, 24 January 1920. NAUK, CO 905 15. Ireland, Criminal Injuries to Private Persons. County Clare. BMH WS 1322 (Art O'Donnell), p. 48.
'Another House Attacked near Doonbeg', *Saturday Record*, 25 October 1919. (The evidence that was given by the Whelans at Kilrush Quarter Sessions does not claim that the Whelan home had been attacked or fired into; the *Cork Examiner*, 10 November, p. 5, incorrectly reported that Mrs Whelan had been beaten during an attack on her house.)

39 Éamonn Gaynor, *Memoirs of a Tipperary Family: The Gaynors of Tyone 1887–2000* (Dublin 2003), p. 121.

40 Email correspondence from Paddy Waldro, 4 February 2011.

41 Éamonn Gaynor, *Memoirs of a Tipperary Family: The Gaynors of Tyone 1887–2000* (Dublin 2003), p. 121.

42 'Arbitration Court, West Clare District, McNamara v O'Dwyer.', *Clare Champion*, 17 July 1920, p. 1.

43 Author's interview with Patsy O'Connor (current owner of pub), 26 October 2018.

44 Author's interview with Frank Considine, 20 January 2011.

45 Author's interview with Peadar McNamara, 24 August, 2010.

46 Seosamh Mac Mathúna, *Kilfarboy, A History of a West Clare Parish* (Dublin 1976), p. 89. Mathún Mac Fheorais interview with Pat Bermingham (Mathún Mac Fheorais Collection, Local Studies Centre, Ennis).

47 Mathún Mac Fheorais interviews with Micho Tubridy and Pat Bermingham (Mathún Mac Fheorais Collection, Local Studies Centre, Ennis).

48 Matthew Bermingham Jnr statement given to Mathún Mac Fheorais. (Mathún Mac Fheorais Collection, Local Studies Centre, Ennis).

49 'Extraordinary Story from County Clare', *Irish Times*, 18 October 1920, p. 4.

50 Seosamh Mac Mathúna, *Kilfarboy, A History of a West Clare Parish* (Dublin 1976), p. 89.

51 Hathi Digital Trust, *Newsletter of the Friends of Irish Freedom*, National Bureau of Information, Washington DC. Vol. 2, 1920–21, p. 8.
'Good Story From Clare; Marooned men decline rescue by RIC', *Limerick Leader*, 11 June 1920, p. 4.

52 'Sinn Féin Courts: The New Order in Ireland', *Manchester Guardian*, 6 July 1920, p. 6.

53 MA MSPC A24, Record of 4th Battalion, West Clare Brigade, 1918–1923/4, p. 6.

54 'Parliament and Sinn Féin Courts', *Irish Independent*, 18 June 1920, p. 5.

55 Éamonn Gaynor, *Memoirs of a Tipperary Family: The Gaynors of Tyone 1887–2000* (Dublin 2003), pp. 121–126.
Frank Gallagher, *The Four Glorious Years, 1918–1921*, 2nd ed. (Dublin 2005), p. 72.

56 'Sinn Féin Courts: An Insurance against Violence', *Manchester Guardian*, 9 July 1920, p. 9.

57 Mary Kotsonouris, *Retreat from Revolution: The Dáil Courts, 1920–1924*, (Dublin 1994), p. 35.

58 Éamonn Gaynor, *Memoirs of a Tipperary Family: The Gaynors of Tyone 1887–2000* (Dublin 2003), p. 122.

59 Éamonn Gaynor, *Memoirs of a Tipperary Family: The Gaynors of Tyone 1887–2000* (Dublin 2003), pp. 123–124.
David Fitzpatrick, *Politics and Irish Life 1913–1921: Provincial Experience of War and Revolution* (Cork 1977), p. 150.

60 Éamonn Gaynor, *Memoirs of a Tipperary Family: The Gaynors of Tyone 1887–2000* (Dublin 2003), pp. 123–126.

61 'Formation of Arbitration Courts. Representative Meeting in West Clare', *Clare Champion*, 24 July 1920.

62 Éamonn Gaynor, *Memoirs of a Tipperary Family: The Gaynors of Tyone 1887–2000* (Dublin 2003), p. 133.

63 Matthew Bermingham Jnr, statement given to Mathún Mac Fheorais, p. 4. (Mathún Mac Fheorais Collection, Local Studies Centre, Ennis).

64 BMH WS 0993 (Mr. Justice Cahir Davitt), pp. 33–34.

65 David Fitzpatrick, *Politics and Irish Life 1913–1921: Provincial Experience of War and Revolution* (Cork 1977), p. 149.

66 BMH WS 1252 (Éamon Fennell), p. 11.

67 BMH WS 1252 (Éamon Fennell), p. 11.

68 Frank Gallagher, *The Four Glorious Years, 1918–1921*, 2nd ed. (Dublin 2005), p. 71

69 Frank Gallagher, *The Four Glorious Years, 1918–1921*, 2nd ed. (Dublin 2005), pp. 73–74.

70 Mary Kotsonouris, *Retreat from Revolution: The Dáil Courts, 1920–1924* (Dublin 1994), p. 36.

71 BMH WS 1253 (Joe Daly), pp. 9–10.

72 Frank Gallagher, *The Four Glorious Years, 1918–1921*, 2nd ed. (Dublin 2005), p. 81.

73 *London Daily News*, 5 July 1920. Editorial cited in Frank Gallagher, *The Four Glorious Years, 1918–1921*, 2nd ed. (Dublin 2005), p. 79.

## Kilmihil's bloody Sunday

1 NAI CSORP CO 904 194/45, Statement of Head-Constable Hoare, 60187.

2 'Seán Breen Memorial', *Saturday Record*, 23 April 1927, p. 1.

3 NAUK, Ireland, Petty Sessions Court Registers, Clare, Ireland, 23 March 1918, John Breen, Michael Killoughery and Michael Honan (www.findmypast.co.uk, accessed 18 February 2019).

4 NAUK, Ireland, Petty Sessions Court Registers, Clare, Ireland, 22 March 1918, Peter Daffy and Michael Kelly (www.findmypast.co.uk, accessed 08 February 2019).

5 BMH WS0821 (Frank Henderson), p. 33.
'Seán Breen Memorial', *Saturday Record*, 23 April 1927, p. 1.

6 Éamonn Gaynor, *Memoirs of a Tipperary Family: The Gaynors of Tyone 1887–2000* (Dublin 2003), p. 174.

7 NAI CSORP CO 904 194/45, Statement of Head-Constable Hoare 60187. When questioned at the inquest, HC Hoare stated that it had been the practice for some time for constables attending Divine Service to carry bombs.

8 NAI CSORP CO 904 194/45, Statement of Head-Constable Hoare 60187.

9 *Constabulary Gazette*, 15 May 1920. The precise positioning of the five members of the attacking party and the details of their respective roles during the attack may be deduced from the statements of Constable Martyn, Head-Constable Hoare and the account of Fr. Pat Gaynor.

10 *Irish Independent*, 19 April 1920, p. 5.

11 Éamonn Gaynor, *Memoirs of a Tipperary Family: The Gaynors of Tyone 1887–2000* (Dublin 2003), p. 174.

12 Éamonn Gaynor, *Memoirs of a Tipperary Family: The Gaynors of Tyone 1887–2000* (Dublin 2003), p. 174.

13 Éamonn Gaynor, *Memoirs of a Tipperary Family: The Gaynors of Tyone 1887–2000* (Dublin 2003), p. 175.

14 NAI CSORP CO 904 194/45, Statement of Constable Patrick Martyn 61800, 18 April 1920.

15 NAI CSORP CO 904 194/45, Statement of Constable William Hayes 61534, 18 April 1920.

16 NAI CSORP CO 904 194/45, Statement of Constable Patrick Martyn 61800, 18 April 1920.

17 *The Police Gazette* or *Hue and Cry* (Dublin), 2 August 1921.

18 *Freeman's Journal*, 13 May 1920, p. 5.

19 BMH WS 1316 (John Flanagan), p. 12.

20 *Weekly Irish Times*, 24 April 1920, p. 3.

21 *Freeman's Journal*, 14 May 1920, p. 3.

22 Éamonn Gaynor, *Memoirs of a Tipperary Family: The Gaynors of Tyone 1887–2000* (Dublin 2003), pp 176–177.

23 *Nenagh Guardian*, 15 May 1920, p. 3.

24 *Freeman's Journal*, 13 May 1920, p. 5.

25 *Freeman's Journal*, 13 May 1920, p. 5.

26 BMH WS 1316 (John Flanagan), p. 12.

27 NAUK, CO 904 194/45, RIC Report of Outrage, 18 April 1920.

28 Éamonn Gaynor, *Memoirs of a Tipperary Family: The Gaynors of Tyone 1887–2000* (Dublin 2003), p. 175.

29 NAI CSORP CO 904 197/88, Report by Sgt Edmond Sullivan 61008 of sermon preached by Rev Charles Culligan, CC Kilmihil on 6 January 1920.

30 Éamonn Gaynor, *Memoirs of a Tipperary Family: The Gaynors of Tyone 1887–2000* (Dublin 2003), pp. 175–176.

31 BMH.WS474 (Liam Haugh), p. 7.

32 *Nenagh Guardian*, 10 April 1920, p. 4.

33 *Nenagh Guardian*, 15 May 1920, p. 3.

34 *Irish Independent*, 9 April 1921, p. 7. Delia Browne was later awarded £400 compensation by County Court Judge Matthias Bodkin.

35 NAI CSORP CO 904 194/45, pp. 6–7, Murder Sergt P J Carroll RIC & attempted murder Const Daniel Collins RIC County of Clare Kilmihill, 27 May 1920.

36 'Kilmihill Shooting. Sequel at Quarter Sessions. Compensation Awarded', *Clare Champion*, 25 September 1920.

37 'Seán Breen Memorial', *Saturday Record*, 23 April 1927, p. 1.

38 James T. McGuane, *Kilrush from Olden Times* (Indreabhán 1984).

## New arrivals

1 '2nd Battalion Notes', *Highland Light Infantry Chronicle, 1920–1921*, Vol. XX, No. 2, April 1920, p. 36.

2 '2nd Battalion Notes', *Highland Light Infantry Chronicle, 1920–1921*, Vol. XX, No. 3, p. 63.

3 NAUK, WO 35 139 569–571, E K Strickland, 9 March 1920 (www.findmypast.co.uk, accessed 18 February 2019).

4 'Popular Nenagh Priest', *Freeman's Journal*, 4 February 1920, p. 4.

5 *The Dublin Gazette*, April 1920, p. 1.

6 NAUK, Ireland, Petty Sessions Court Registers, Clare, Ireland. 6 April 1920. Petty Sessions Clerk Thomas Jonas Blackall adjourned the four cases that were to be tried (www.findmypast.co.uk, accessed 30 March 2019).

7 NAUK, HO 184. Royal Irish Constabulary Records 1816–1922, George Harris Noblett (www.findmypast.co.uk, accessed 06 February 2019).

8 NAUK, Ireland, Petty Sessions Court Registers, Clare, Ireland, 16 April 1920 (www.findmypast.co.uk, accessed 30 March 2019).


## Fall from grace

1 BMH WS 1322 (Art O'Donnell), pp. 50–51.

2 BMH WS 1322 (Art O'Donnell), pp. 50–51.

3 BMH WS 1316 (John Flanagan), pp. 12–13.

4 BMH WS 883 (John M McCarthy), Appendix F 2.


## The Belfast boycott

1 'Boycott of Belfast Goods', *Ulster Herald*, 21 February 1920, p. 2.

2 Dooley, T, 'From the Belfast Boycott to the Boundary Commission: Fears and Hopes in County Monaghan, 1920–26', *Clogher Record*, 15 (1) 1994, pp 90–106.

3 Seosamh Mac Mathúna, *Kilfarboy, A History of a West Clare Parish* (Dublin 1976), p. 89.

4 Éamonn Gaynor, *Memoirs of a Tipperary Family: The Gaynors of Tyone 1887–2000* (Dublin 2003), p. 132.

5 'Belfast Trade Boycott', *Clare Champion*, 26 February 1921.

6 BMH WS 1685 (Michael McMahon, p. 5.

7 Mathún Mac Fheorais interview with Micho 'Carriga' McMahon, Kilrush, 14 July 1970 (Mathún Mac Fheorais Collection, Local Studies Centre, Ennis).

8 MA MSPC A24, Record of the 5th Battalion, West Clare Brigade, p. 15.

9 MA MSPC A24. Records of Activities of Battalion 1, West Clare Brigade, IRA, 1917–1923, p. 5.

10 Éamonn Gaynor, *Memoirs of a Tipperary Family: The Gaynors of Tyone 1887–2000* (Dublin 2003), p. 132.
11 MA MSPC A24, Records of Activities of the 5th Battalion, West Clare Brigade, IRA, 1917–1923, p. 24.

## The Indian mutiny

1 BMH WS 262 (Joseph Hawes), p. 3.
2 BMH WS 262 (Joseph Hawes), p. 5.
3 RTÉ Press Centre, 22–27 April 2006. Quote attributed to Oliver Hawes, grandson of Joseph Hawes (https://presspack.rte.ie/2006/04/23/black-sheep/, accessed 09 April 2019).
4 NAUK, WO 141 84. 1st Battalion The Connaught Rangers (88 Regiment of Foot): Mutiny in India: General court-martial, sentences and possible remission (www.findmypast.co.uk, accessed 09 April 2019).
5 MA MSPC, Con.Ran/116, (Joseph Hawes), Statement of Joseph Hawes.
6 BMH WS 262 (Joseph Hawes), pp 44–45.
7 MA MSPC, Con.Ran/116. (Joseph Hawes); statement of Joseph Hawes.
8 'Deaths', *Cork Examiner*, 4 December 1972, p. 2.

## Staying loyal to the Royal

1 'Items of Interest', *Irish Independent*, 28 October 1920, p. 6.
2 'No Sessions', *Cork Examiner*, 23 August 1920, p. 6.
3 BMH WS 1253 (Joe Daly), pp. 5–6.
4 BMH WS 1253 (Joe Daly), pp. 5–6.
5 Éamonn Gaynor, *Memoirs of a Tipperary Family: The Gaynors of Tyone 1887–2000* (Dublin 2003), p. 140.
6 BMH WS 1253 (Joe Daly), p. 8.
7 'A Magistrate's Experiences', *Clare Champion*, 21 January 1921, p. 3. This *Clare Champion* report had given conflicting dates for the attempt to arrest Kelly (24 and 29 June). However, Dr Hillery attended to Mrs Kelly after the event on 27 June, so the reference to 29 June must be incorrect; the date of 24 June is also given in NAUK, CO 905 15. Ireland, Criminal Injuries to Private Persons. County Clare.
8 BMH WS 1253 (Joe Daly), p. 8.
9 Author's interview with Gerry Neenan, August 2010.
10 Author's interview with John 'the soldier' Kelly, 13 November, 2010
Éamonn Gaynor, *Memoirs of a Tipperary Family: The Gaynors of Tyone 1887–2000* (Dublin 2003), p. 140.

11 Author's interview with John 'the soldier' Kelly, 13 November, 2010.
Éamonn Gaynor, *Memoirs of a Tipperary Family: The Gaynors of Tyone 1887–2000*
(Dublin 2003), p. 140.

12 'Boy kidnapped by Sinn Féiners', *The Observer*, 11 July 1920, p. 14.
'Clare Youth Kidnapped', *Irish Times*, 10 July 1920, p. 7.
'Co. Clare Sensation', *Cork Examiner*, 10 July 1920, p. 5.
'Clare Boy Kidnapped', *Ulster Herald*, 17 July 1920, p. 7.
BMH WS 1253 (Joe Daly), p. 8.

13 Éamonn Gaynor, *Memoirs of a Tipperary Family: The Gaynors of Tyone 1887–2000*
(Dublin 2003), p. 140.

14 Éamonn Gaynor, *Memoirs of a Tipperary Family: The Gaynors of Tyone 1887–2000*
(Dublin 2003), p. 140.
BMH WS 474 (Liam Haugh), p. 14.

15 'A Magistrate's Experiences', *Clare Champion*, 21 January 1921, p. 3.

16 Éamonn Gaynor, *Memoirs of a Tipperary Family: The Gaynors of Tyone 1887–2000*
(Dublin 2003), p. 141.
'A Magistrate's Experiences', *Clare Champion*, 21 January 1921, p. 3.

17 Éamonn Gaynor, *Memoirs of a Tipperary Family: The Gaynors of Tyone 1887–2000*
(Dublin 2003), p. 141.
'Volunteers' work in West Clare', *Freeman's Journal*, 1 July 1920, p. 3.

18 Éamonn Gaynor, *Memoirs of a Tipperary Family: The Gaynors of Tyone 1887–2000*
(Dublin 2003), p. 141.

19 NAUK, WO 141 99 199, Record of the Rebellion in Ireland, Vol IV, Part 2, Chapter
3; Intimidation of JPs (www.findmypast.co.uk, accessed 21 February 2019).

20 BMH WS 1253 (Joe Daly), pp. 8–9.
'Sergeants' Mess Notes', *Highland Light Infantry Chronicle, 1920–1921*, Vol. XX, No.
4, October 1920, p. 88.

21 '2nd Battalion Notes', *Highland Light Infantry Chronicle, 1920–1921*, Vol. XX, No. 4,
October 1920, p. 88.

22 'Daring Seizure in Clare. Mails and Military Equipment Taken', *Irish Times*, 19 July
1920.

23 'Train Held Up', *Clare Champion*, 24 July 1920.

24 '2nd Battalion Notes', *Highland Light Infantry Chronicle, 1920–1921*, Vol. XX, No. 4,
October 1920, p. 88.
'Exchange of Troops', *Freeman's Journal*, 26 July 1920, p. 3.

25 Éamonn Gaynor, *Memoirs of a Tipperary Family: The Gaynors of Tyone 1887–2000*
(Dublin 2003), p. 142. When Christy's postman spotted a postcard from Dublin
Castle, acknowledging receipt of both his resignation and his retraction, he showed it
to a local Volunteer.

26 'A Magistrate's Experiences', *Clare Champion*, 21 January 1921, p. 3.

27 Éamonn Gaynor, *Memoirs of a Tipperary Family: The Gaynors of Tyone 1887–2000* (Dublin 2003), p. 143.

28 MA MSP 34 REF 34241 (Teresa Dunleavy), Signed statement of Major Conor Whelan, Vice Commandant, West Clare Brigade, re Pension Application of Teresa Dunleavy.

29 Éamonn Gaynor, *Memoirs of a Tipperary Family: The Gaynors of Tyone 1887–2000* (Dublin 2003), p. 143.

30 NAUK, WO 35 148, Court of Inquiry in lieu of Inquest, Thomas Curtin, 9 December 1920, Testimony of Lieutenant A W Tuffield, 2nd Battalion, the Royal Scots.

31 Mathún Mac Fheorais interview with Jack Dunleavy, Kilrush, (Mathún Mac Fheorais Collection, Local Studies Centre, Ennis).
Éamonn Gaynor, *Memoirs of a Tipperary Family: The Gaynors of Tyone 1887–2000* (Dublin 2003), p. 144.

32 NAUK, WO 35 148, Court of Inquiry in lieu of Inquest, Thomas Curtin, 9 December 1920; testimony of Head-Constable James Treacy.

33 BMH WS 0993 (Mr. Justice Cahir Davitt), pp. 43–44.
Author's interview with Eddie Cotter, 2 August 2010. Judge Davitt mistakenly refers to Kelly as Ryan and he is in error in respect of Kelly's regiment and period of service. However, the accuracy of the remainder of his allusion to Kelly was verified by cross-reference to NAUK, WO 35 148, Court of Inquiry in lieu of Inquest, Thomas Curtin and supporting anecdotal account provided by Eddie Cotter.

34 NAUK, WO 35 148, Court of Inquiry in lieu of Inquest, Thomas Curtin, 9 December 1920; testimony of solicitor Michael Killeen.

35 MA MSP 34 Ref 34241 (Teresa Dunleavy).

36 NAUK, WO 35 148, Court of Inquiry in lieu of Inquest. Thomas Curtin, 9 December 1920.

37 Éamonn Gaynor, *Memoirs of a Tipperary Family: The Gaynors of Tyone 1887–2000* (Dublin 2003), p. 144.

38 NAUK, WO 35 148, Court of Inquiry in lieu of Inquest. Thomas Curtin, 9 December 1920; testimony of Dr Richard Counihan.

39 NAUK, WO 35 148, Court of Inquiry in lieu of Inquest. Thomas Curtin, 9 December 1920.

40 Éamonn Gaynor, *Memoirs of a Tipperary Family: The Gaynors of Tyone 1887–2000* (Dublin 2003), pp. 142–143.

41 'A Magistrate's Experiences', *Clare Champion*, 22 January 1921, p. 3.

42 'Appeals: West Clare Appeals', *Saturday Record*, 5 March 1921.

43 NAUK, CO 905 15, Ireland, Criminal Injuries to Private Persons. Fr Gaynor's account incorrectly gave the sum awarded to Christy as £1000.

44 'Priest Dropped From Car', *Irish Independent*, 24 May 1921, p. 5.
'The Catholic Clergy and the Independence Movement' by Tomás Ó Fiaic, *Capuchin Annual 1970*, p. 498.

45 Éamonn Gaynor, *Memoirs of a Tipperary Family: The Gaynors of Tyone 1887–2000* (Dublin 2003), pp. 145–146.

46 'Roman Catholic Clergymen Courtmartialled', *Irish Times*, 24 May 1921, p. 6. 'Crown forces Impugned. Priests' Remarkable Allegations', *Irish Independent*, 24 May 1921, p. 5.

47 NAUK, WO 135 136 127 (www.findmypast.co.uk, accessed 21 February 2019).

48 'Courtmartial Results', *Irish Times*, 8 June 1921, p. 7.

49 NAUK, WO 135 136 127 (www.findmypast.co.uk, accessed 21 February 2019).

50 Éamonn Gaynor, *Memoirs of a Tipperary Family: The Gaynors of Tyone 1887–2000* (Dublin 2003), pp. 148, 150.

## The Rob Roy Hotel

1 'On the run', *Clare Champion*, 3 December 1920.

2 Kieran Sheedy, *The Clare Elections* (Dublin 1993), pp. 625–626.

3 MA MSPC, MD/6954, evidence of D P Sheedy re P J Darcy, 26 June 1947, pp 185–186.

4 MA MSPC, MD/6954, evidence of D P Sheedy re P J Darcy, 26 June 1947, p. 186.

5 MA MSPC, MD/6954, signed statement of Daniel Sheedy, 25 November 1946.

6 MA MSPC, MD/6954, signed statement of Daniel Sheedy, 25 November 1946.

7 MA MSPC, MD/6954, sworn evidence given before the Referee and Advisory Committee by Chief Superintendent Liddy re P J Darcy, 20 May 1947, p. 14.

8 NAUK, WO 35 207 118, Sinn Féin Activists F–W, Castle File No. 5146, Liddy, John, Danganelly, Cooraclare, Co Clare.

9 MA MSP 34, Ref 34241 (Teresa Dunleavy), Signed statement of Commandant Seán Morrissey, 3rd Battalion, West Clare Brigade, 8 March 1943, re Pension application of Teresa Dunleavy.

10 Author's interview with John McCarthy, Ballinagun, 2 July 2010.

11 BMH WS 1251 (Martin Chambers), p. 10.

12 Author's interview with Liam Haugh, son of Bill Haugh, 14 July 2010.

13 BMH WS 1251 (Martin Chambers), p. 12.

14 BMH WS 474 (Liam Haugh), p. 16.

15 Author's interview with Paul Markham, 16 April 2019.

16 MA MSPC A24, Record of 4th Battalion, West Clare Brigade, 1918–1923/4, p. 10.

17 MA MSPC A24, Record of 4th Battalion, West Clare Brigade, 1918–1923/4, p. 10.

18 Author's interview with Mícheál Ó Catháin, 3 October 2011.

19 Author's interview with James Stephens, son of Walter Stephens, 16 April 2019.

20 Michael O'Brien, 'The Men Who Fought the Tans', *Kilmurry Ibrickane Magazine* 1993/94, pp. 25–26.

21 Author's interview with James Stephens, son of Walter Stephens, 16 April 2019.

22 Author's interview with Pádraig De Barra, 29 September 2009.
Mathún Mac Fheorais interview with Micko Tubridy, p. 7 (Mathún Mac Fheorais Collection, Local Studies Centre, Ennis).

23 BMH WS 474 (Liam Haugh), p. 35.
MA MSP, 34 REF 33488 (Bridget Honan).

24 BMH WS 883 (John M McCarthy), Appendix N. Weekly Intelligence Summary, 6th Division, 17 May 1921, p. 4. These documents were captured by the IRA in an operation in the Kilteely district of County Limerick, according to John McCarthy, p. 91.

## Hanley

1 Irving Crump, 'A Good Bad-Man – Wild Bill Hickok', in *Boys' Life*, August 1928.

2 Birth certificate of William Haugh (in author's possession). However, Haugh gave his birth date as 6 December 1892 in his 1916 and his 1920 passport applications.

3 www.libertyellisfoundation.org/passengerdetails/ (search criteria: *name*: William Haugh / *arrived*: 1909 / *ship name*: Baltic), accessed 16 August 2018.

4 Passport Application No 30705, William Haugh, (1916), www.findmypast.ie, British and Irish Roots Collection. United States. Bureau of Labor Statistics. Street Railway Employment in the United States.
Bulletin of the United States Bureau of Labor Statistics, No. 204, Washington DC, Government Printing Office, September 1916, https://fraser.stlouisfed.org/title/3846, accessed 24 August, 2018.

5 New York State Archives, Abstracts of World War 1 Military Service, 1917–1919 for William Haugh: www.ancestry.co.uk, accessed 5 May 2019.
BMH WS 474 (Liam Haugh), p. 11.

6 Author's interview with Liam Haugh, son of Bill Haugh, 14 July 2010.
Natasha Frost, *Bermuda Triangle Mystery: What Happened to the USS Cyclops?* www.history.com/news/bermuda-triangle-uss-cyclops-mystery-world-war-i, accessed 26 July 2019.

7 BMH WS 474 (Liam Haugh), p. 10.
www.ancestry.co.uk, UK Incoming Passenger Lists 1878–1960, (search criteria: *name:* William Haugh, Martha McEntee / *arrived:* 31 May 1920 / *ship name:* Baltic), accessed 16 August 2018.

8 Author's interview with Liam Haugh, son of Bill Haugh, 14 July 2010.

9 BMH WS 474 (Liam Haugh), pp. 10–11.

10 Mathún Mac Fheorais interview with Micho 'Carriga' McMahon, Kilrush, 14 July 1970 (Mathún Mac Fheorais Collection, Local Studies Centre, Ennis).

11 Author's interview with Michael Howard, 30 October 2009.

12 BMH WS 1316 (John Flanagan), pp. 14–15.

13 BMH WS 474 (Liam Haugh), p. 12.

14 Shanahan, E. (2016) 'Guns in the Water: Quilty's Car, Spindler's Aud, and the First Casualties of the Easter Rising of 1916', *Breac: A Digital Journal of Irish Studies* (University of Notre Dame), https://breac.nd.edu/articles/guns-in-the-water-quiltys-car-spindlers-aud-and-the-first-casualties-of-the-easter-rising-of-1916/, accessed 21 November 2017.

15 NAUK, WO 35 139 00547, List of Prisoners in Cork Men's Prison under GS 103 and GS 108, p. 2 (www.findmypast.co.uk, accessed 07 March 2019).
NAUK, WO 35 139 01171, Recommendation to release J J Quilty signed by General Strickland (www.findmypast.co.uk, accessed 7 March 2019).

16 MA MSPC A24 West Clare Brigade, 1 Western Division, 2nd Battalion, West Clare Brigade, pp. 4–5.

17 BMH WS 1316 (John Flanagan), p. 13.

18 *The Irish Press*, 1 April 1966, p. 5.

19 BMH WS 1322 (Art O'Donnell), p. 53.
BMH WS 1316 (John Flanagan), pp. 13–14.

20 NAI CSORP 19535, 'Armed Sinn Féiners watching out for Captain Lendrum MC, RM', Constable John Hanlon, 18 August 1920.

21 'Searches for Official Letters', *Irish Times*, 20 August 1920, p. 6.
NAUK, CO 904 112, RIC Confidential Report for August 1920.

22 Interview by Peg Bermingham with Jack Dunleavy, age 101, on 26 February 2011 (Mathún Mac Fheorais Collection, Local Studies Centre, Ennis).

23 BMH WS 474 (Liam Haugh), p. 14.
Cooralclare/Cree Historical Society, *Cooraclare & Cree, Parish of Kilmacduane: history & folklore* (Clare 2002), p. 415.

24 'Kilrush Shooting. Inquest on Constable', *Cork Examiner*, 25 August 1920, p. 5.

25 'Evidence of Dr J F Counihan at inquest into Const Hanlon's death held at Kilrush National School', *Irish Times*, 25 August 1920, p. 5. Many newspaper reports indicated that Hanlon had been shot through the eye, the bullet exiting through the back of the head.
Mathún Mac Fheorais interview with Martie Mulqueen, Ballykett, 13 March 1971 (Mathún Mac Fheorais Collection, Local Studies Centre, Ennis).

26 'Kilrush Shooting. Inquest on Constable', *Cork Examiner*, 25 August 1920, p. 5.

27 Author's interview with Liam Haugh, son of Bill Haugh, 14 July 2010.

28 'Shot Dead in Kilrush', *Clare Champion*, 28 August 1920.

29 'The Kilrush Tragedy', *Cork Examiner*, 24 August 1920, p. 5.

30 Michael Hopkinson, *The Irish War of Independence* (United States, Canada 2004).

31 'More Fires in Lisburn', *Manchester Guardian*, 24 August 1920, p. 9.

32 'Kilrush Shooting. Inquest on Constable', *Cork Examiner*, 25 August 1920, p. 5.

33 'Widow's Claim', *Clare Champion*, 25 September 1920.

34 Death certificate of James Brendan Hanlon (in author's possession). Some newspaper accounts state that the Hanlons had two children, but appear to omit Anna Frances, born 26 December 1916 (mother named as Joanna or Johanna Aguetha Nyhan); Godparents were Timothy Donovan and Kathleen Nagle. Ref. 1156; Frances married Michael John Murphy in St Andrew's Church, Westland Row, Dublin, 1 September 1946.

35 BMH WS 474 (Liam Haugh), p. 11.
   BMH WS 1251 (Martin Chambers), p. 8.

36 BMH Military Service Pensions Collection 24SP3896 (Conor Whelan).

37 *Police Gazette* or *Hue and Cry*, 28 December 1920.
   Bureau of Military History, Appendix to Contemporary Documents, Part 2, p. 169 Group 6.
   NAUK, WO 35 155B 35, *Police Gazette* or *Hue and Cry*, 12 April 1921.

38 Author's interview with Michael Howard, 30 October 2009. Howard claimed that Haugh had used Howard's father's gun to shoot Hanlon.


## Patrick (Sonny) Burke

1 'Clare Cattle-Driving Charge', *Weekly Irish Times*, 6 September 1919, p 2.
   ' A Catalogue of Outrage', *Irish Times*, 14 May 1920, p 5.

2 NAUK, Easter Rising & Ireland Under Martial Law 1916–1921: NAUK, WO 35, Patrick Burke, Ballinagun near Cooraclare: letter from W J Studdert to General Sir Neville Macready, Commander-in-Chief, Forces in Ireland, 28 August 1920 (www.findmypast.co.uk, accessed 29 January 2019).
   NAUK, CO 904/142, Summary of Police Reports, August 1920.

3 BMH WS 474 (Liam Haugh), p. 15.
   Cooralclare/Cree Historical Society, *Cooraclare & Cree, Parish of Kilmacduane: history & folklore* (Clare 2002), p 415. One account of this event states that the men were on a mission from Headquarters in relation to a disputed farm in Ballinagun.
   Maurice (Moss) Twomey (1930), The West Clare Brigade Papers, IE 2135, p. 45 (Pádraig Burke), University of Limerick Special Collections.

4 'A Martyr to Duty', *Saturday Record*, 14 April 1928.

5 BMH WS 474 (Liam Haugh), p. 15.
   *The Banner* Claremen and Women's Patriotic, Benevolent and Social Association of New York. (New York 1963), p. 183, Patrick Burke.
   'Arrest Near Cooraclare', *Cork Examiner*, 30 August 1920, p. 3.

6 Cooralclare/Cree Historical Society, *Cooraclare & Cree, Parish of Kilmacduane: history & folklore* (Clare 2002), p. 415.
   *The Banner* Claremen and Women's Patriotic, Benevolent and Social Association of New York. (New York 1963), p. 183, Patrick Burke. The Cooraclare & Cree history states that Hassett and O'Donnell were held for two months but, according to official documents, their release was ordered on 7 September 1920.

NAUK, Easter Rising & Ireland Under Martial Law 1916–1921; NAUK, WO 35, Patrick Burke, Ballinagun near Cooraclare, Handwritten memo indicating that the release of the two had been ordered (www.findmypast.co.uk, accessed 29 January 2019).

7   NAUK, Easter Rising & Ireland Under Martial Law 1916–1921. WO 35, Patrick Burke, Ballinagun near Cooraclare, Letter from W J Studdert to General Sir Neville Macready, Commander-in-Chief, Forces in Ireland, 28 August 1920 (www.findmypast. co.uk, accessed 29 January 2019).

8   'Two Years for Clare Man', *Clare Champion*, 25 September 1920.
    'Recent Courts-Martial Decisions', *Weekly Irish Times*, 25 September 1920, p. 2.

9   Irish Prison Registers 1790–1924. Cork County Gaol General Register 1915–1924. (Patrick Burke) (www.findmypast.co.uk, accessed 18 February 2019).

10  MA MSPC, 1D 285 (Patrick Burke).
    MA MSPC. 1D 285, death certificate, Patrick Burke.

11  'West Clare Celebrations', *Clare Champion*, 14 April 1928.
    '2 West Clare Volunteers', *Clare Champion*, 21 April 1928.

Ambush season

1   NAUK, CO 904 142, Summary of Police Reports, August 1920.
    *The Banner*. Claremen and Women's Patriotic, Benevolent and Social Association of New York. (New York 1963), p. 184.
    BMH WS 1316 (John Flanagan), p. 15.
    'Destruction of Military Waggon. Echo of Kilrush Hold Up' *Clare Champion*, 22 January 1921. The *Clare Champion* incorrectly reported the date of this ambush as 22 September.

2   NAUK, WO 35/115/12, Easter Rising & Ireland Under Martial Law 1916–1921, John Mulqueen, Moore Street, Kilrush, Co Clare, Ireland, (www.findmypast.co.uk, accessed 5 February 2019).

3   NAUK, CO 904 112, RIC Confidential Report for August 1920.

4   MA MSPC A24, West Clare Brigade, 1 Western Division, Record of 1st Battalion, p. 4.

5   MA MSPC A24, West Clare Brigade, Report on Drumdigus Ambush. (William Shannon).

6   MA MSPC A24, West Clare Brigade, Report on Drumdigus Ambush. (William Shannon),

7   BMH WS 474 (Liam Haugh), pp. 17–18
    *The Banner* Claremen and Women's Patriotic, Benevolent and Social Association of New York, (New York 1963), p. 184.
    BMH WS 1251 (Martin Chambers), p. 14.
    'Courtsmartial Results. Trench Trap on a County Clare road', *Irish Times*, 6 November 1920, p. 2.
    NAUK, WO 35/120, Easter Rising & Ireland Under Martial Law 1916–1921, William Shannon, Ireland. (www.findmypast.co.uk, accessed 05 February 2019).

8   'Claremen Courtmartialled', *Saturday Record*, 6 November 1920.
    NAUK, WO 35/116, Easter Rising & Ireland Under Martial Law 1916–1921, Irish
    Prison Registers 1790–1924, (Shannon Wm) (www.findmypast.co.uk, accessed 5
    February 2019).

## Conflict at Kilmore

1   'Kilrush, Petty Sessions. Light Business', *Clare Champion*, 24 July 1920.

2   NAUK, CO 904 112, RIC Confidential Report for August 1920.

3   NAUK, CO 762/81, Irish Grants Committee, Application of F W Gore-Hickman, 1
    January 1927.

4   NAUK, Easter Rising & Ireland Under Martial Law 1916–1921; NAUK, WO
    35/115/19, John Daly, Co Clare, Ireland (www.findmypast.co.uk, accessed 05 February
    2019).
    General Headquarters Ireland, Parkgate, Dublin, Press Report, 16 October 1920, Case
    of Patrick Daly and others.

5   NAUK, Easter Rising & Ireland Under Martial Law 1916–1921; NAUK, WO 35/114,
    John Daly, Co Clare, Ireland (www.findmypast.co.uk, accessed 05 February 2019).

6   NAUK, CO 762/81, Irish Grants Committee. Application of F W Gore-Hickman, 1
    January 1927.

7   BMH WS 474 (Liam Haugh), p. 9
    'West Clare Shooting, Land Agent Seriously Wounded', *Cork Examiner*, 15 July 1920,
    p. 5.
    'Agent Seriously Wounded, Crown Witness Kidnapped', *Cork Examiner*, 16 July 1920,
    p. 5.
    'Shooting in West Clare', *Clare Champion*, 21 August 1920.
    'Incidents in the Provinces' *Irish Times*, 13 October 1920, p. 3.
    MA MSPC A24, West Clare Brigade, 2nd Battalion, West Clare Brigade IRA Pre-Truce
    Activities.

8   NAUK, CO 762/81, Irish Grants Committee; application of F W Gore-Hickman, 1
    January 1927.

9   'Provincial News in Brief', *Freeman's Journal*, 3 November 1921, p. 5.
    Maurice (Moss) Twomey (1930), The West Clare Brigade Papers, IE 2135, p. 45
    (Pádraig Hassett), University of Limerick Special Collections.
    MA MSPC. DP 9914 (Patrick Hassett) and 3MSRB 26 (Patrick Hassett).
    BMH WS 474 (Liam Haugh), p. 10.

10  NAUK, Ireland, Petty Sessions Court Registers. Clare, Ireland. 15, 23, 31 July and 4,
    12, 18 August 1920, John Daly (www.findmypast.co.uk, accessed 08 February 2019).

11  Geoff Simmons Collection, letter from George Harris Noblett, former RIC District
    Inspector, Kilrush to Rex Taylor, 4 January 1961.

NAUK, Ireland, Petty Sessions Court Registers. Clare, Ireland. 18 August 1920, John Daly (www.findmypast.co.uk, accessed 08 February 2019).
NAUK, CO 904 112. RIC Confidential Report for August 1920.


## Captain Lendrum

1  NAI CSORP 17514, Alan Lendrum, letters from Alan Lendrum to Dublin Castle, 23 June and 8 July 1920. Lendrum sought permission to source petrol from Kilrush RIC. He argued that this option would represent savings for the Government in travel and subsistence allowances.
Letter from Alan Lendrum to American Oil Company, 27 June 1920.

2  'Correspondence', *Belfast Newsletter*, 10 July 1959.

3  BMH WS 474 (Liam Haugh), pp. 18–19.

4  NAUK, CAB 27 108, Cabinet, Irish Situation Committee, Reports received from Resident Magistrates, June 1920.

5  *The Banner* Claremen and Women's Patriotic, Benevolent and Social Association of New York (New York 1963), p. 185.

6  NAI CSORP 19535, Constable John Hanlon, 18 August 1920, Armed Sinn Féiners watching out for Captain Lendrum MC RM.

7  NAI CSORP 19535, Memo dated 15 September 1920 attached to Lendrum letter dated 9 September 1920.

8  NAI CSORP 19535, Minute from Chief Secretary's Office to Captain Lendrum RM granting permission for his move to Kilrush and Captain Lendrum's response.

9  'No Petty Sessions', *Clare Champion*, 25 September 1920.

10 It was customary for farmers to inform neighbours when they would be drawing in trams of hay from the meadow. Neighbours could then ensure that the narrow roads were kept clear of animals or of traffic and they may even offer to help with the making of a rick or a wind.

11 Author's interview with Nora Hayes (née Meade, born 1916 and formerly of Caherfeenick), December 2010.

12 Cooralclare/Cree Historical Society, *Cooraclare & Cree, Parish of Kilmacduane: history & folklore* (Clare 2002), p. 450, 'September 1920: Capture of British Officer'.

13 Author's interview with Paddy Killeen, 2 July 2010.

14 MA MSPC A24 West Clare Brigade, 1 Western Division, Battalion 3, West Clare Brigade, p. 4.
BMH WS 474 (Liam Haugh), p. 19. Anecdotal accounts suggest that Lendrum reached down into the car, either to get a gun or to pull the hand-brake and that this action precipitated a response from the ambush party.

15 'Malicious Damage Claims. The Kilkee Cases', *Irish Times* 14 January 1921, p. 5.
George Noblett, DI RIC Kilrush, in evidence at Ennis Quarter Sessions on 13 January 1921.

16 Interview with Aidan Carroll, son of Eddie Carroll, Willie Shanahan's double first cousin, July 2009. Shanahan confided in Eddie Carroll about the events of the day. BMH WS 474 (Liam Haugh), p. 18–19. Haugh may have been referring to Willie Shanahan when he wrote '... an officer who was supposed to be present had not yet arrived when Lendrum drove up ...The Volunteer officer concerned now came up. The car was driven ...'
Author's interview with Pat Sullivan, 22 August 2010.

17 MA MSPC A24 West Clare Brigade, 1 Western Division, Record of 4th Battalion, p. 7.

18 Author's interview with Danny Garry (born 1 January 1916), July 2010.

19 Author's interview with James Cahill, 18 April 2010.

20 Maureen Meaden's series of interviews with Suzanne Neylon, her grand-aunt and the sister of James Neylon, 27 December 1991–13 September 1996. Copy in author's possession.

21 Author's interview with Mikie Whelan, 24 July 2010. Mikie lived a short distance from the ambush site,

22 TG4 documentary, *My Fight for Irish Freedom: Scéal Dan Breen* (www.youtube.com/watch?v=F198jLoNVeY, accessed 4 April 2019).

23 Signed statement of Joe Daly Junior, 14 October 2010.
Author's interview with John Daly, 17 August 2109.

24 Author's interviews with Eddie Cotter, July 2010, Mikie Whelan November 2009 and John Kelly, 26 July 2010.

25 'Captain Lendrum's Fate', *Irish Independent*, 2 October 1920, p. 5.

26 Author's interview with Nora Hayes (née Meade), December 2010.
Author's interview with Paddy Killeen, 2 July 2010.

27 NAUK, CO 904 168, The Murders near Milltown Malby [*sic*].

28 NAUK, CO 904 168, The Murders near Milltown Malby [*sic*].

29 NAUK, WO 141 93 208, Record of the Rebellion in Ireland, Vol IV, Part 2, Chapter V. The Rebel Campaign From the Beginning of July, 1920, to the End of September, 1920. Ambush at Ennistymon (www.findmypast.co.uk, accessed 22 February 2019).

30 NAUK, CO 904 168 The Murders near Milltown Malby [*sic*], p. 3.
NAUK, CO 904 142, Summary of Police Reports September 1920. The Court of Inquiry into the deaths of the six policemen was held at Ennistymon Workhouse at 18.00hrs on 24 September 1920.

31 'Fate of RM in Clare. Missing and Reported Dead', *Irish Independent*, 24 September 1920, p. 5.
'Police Raids in Kilkee. Cabins and Hay Burned on Seaboard', *Cork Examiner*, 25 September 1920, p. 5.

32 'Mystery of Clare RM. Kidnapped or Shot: Reported Dead and Buried', *Freeman's Journal*, 24 September 1920, p. 5.

33 MA MSPC A24. Record of the 5th Battalion, West Clare Brigade, p. 14.

34 'The Clare Ambushes and Reprisals. Threat to Burn Towns', *Irish Independent*, 28 September 1920, p. 6.
'Reprisals for Captain Lendrum', *The Banner* Claremen and Women's Patriotic, Benevolent and Social Association of New York,(New York 1963), p. 177.

35 'Late Capt Lendrum', *Irish Independent*, 5 October 1920, p. 5.
'The Death of West Clare RM', *Saturday Record*, 22 January 1921,.

36 'Missing Resident Magistrate's Body Found in Clare', *Manchester Guardian*, 2 October 1920, p. 5.

37 MA MSPC A24, Record of 3rd Battalion, West Clare Brigade, 1918–1923/4, p. 4.

38 Pat O'Dwyer, 'The Black and Tans are Coming', *Kilmurry Ibrickane Parish Magazine*, 1979, 1980, pp. 32–34.
Éamonn Gaynor, *Memoirs of a Tipperary Family: The Gaynors of Tyone 1887–2000* (Dublin 2003), p. 127.

39 Murt McInerney Collection, Letter from Michael Killeen to his sister Mary, 6 August 1919.
'Obituary Notices. Mr Michael Killeen, Doonbeg', *Clare Champion*, 23 January 1937.

40 Author's interview with Eddie Cotter, 2 August 2010.
Author's email correspondence from Michael McCarthy, nephew of Johnny McCarthy, 21 August 2012.

41 Author's email correspondence from Michael McCarthy, 15 September 2012.

42 'Captain Lendrum's Death', *Irish Times*, 5 October 1920, p. 5.

43 PRONI T2569, Noblett (depositor) papers. Copy notice relating to the death of Capt. Lendrum.

44 'Ambushed and Shot', *Irish Times*, 2 October 1920, p. 5.

## Telling tales

1 Eoin Shanahan, 'Telling Tales: the story of the burial alive and drowning of a Clare RM in 1920', *History Ireland*, Vol 18, No 1 (2010), pp 36–37.

2 NLS MS 30193, Letter from Major Aubrey Waithman Long, Ballina House, Ballina, County Mayo to George Blackwood, Editor of *Blackwood's Magazine*, 8 April 1921.

3 NLS MS 30193, Letter from James H Blackwood to Major Aubrey Waithman Long, 15 June 1921.

4 NLS MS 30193, Letter from Major Aubrey Waithman Long, Ballina House, Ballina, Co Mayo to George Blackwood, Editor of *Blackwood's Magazine*, 11 June 1921.

5 Geoff Simmons Collection, Letter from retired judge to a niece of Alan Lendrum, 21 August 1989.

6 'Letters to the Editor. The Late Capt. Lendrum', *Impartial Reporter*, October 1920.

7 'Malicious Damage Claims', *Irish Times*, 14 January 1921, p. 5.
NAUK, CO 904 168, Memo from Basil Clarke to DIG 2 October 1920, Walsh response to Clarke, 3 October 1920.

## Mac and Shanahan

1 Geoff Simmons Collection, handwritten notes on a letter from County Inspector H F Munro to DI George Noblett, Kilrush RIC, 27 September 1920.

2 'The Late Capt. Lendrum R.M', *Irish Independent*, 17 January 1921, p. 6.

3 *The Banner* Claremen and Women's Patriotic, Benevolent and Social Association of New York, (New York 1963), p. 185.
   Author's interview with Pádraig De Barra, (son of Fred Barry who had been active in the War of Independence), 29 September 2009.

4 'Scenes in Kilkee', *Saturday Record*, 16 October 1920.

5 MA MSP 34 REF 34241 (Teresa Dunleavy), Letter of Appeal from Teresa Dunleavy to The Referee, Military Pensions Board in support of her pension application 1 November 1942.

6 'A Shocking Death. Echo of Black and Tan Times', *Saturday Record*, 21 July 1928.
   Tomás Mac Conmara, 'The Terry Alts', *Clare Champion*, 15 November 2002.
   Professor James F Donnelly Junior, 'The Terry Alt Movement, 1829–31', *History Ireland*, Vol 2 No 4, Vol 2 (Winter 1994). The Terry Alt movement had its origins in Clare, but later spread to parts of neighbouring counties Galway, Limerick and Tipperary. The organisation was suppressed when 21 of its activists were executed and up to 100 more were either deported or gaoled.

7 Murt McInerney, 'Willie Shanahan', *Kilrush CBS Centenary Souvenir 1874–1974*, p. 65.
   'Two Doonbeg Patriots', *Clare Champion*, 4 January 1964.

8 'Damage to Manchester Martyrs' Monument', *Saturday Record*, 21 January 1922.

9 Michael Killeen, Clifden House, Doonbeg, undated letter to Patrick Shanahan (brother of Willie Shanahan).

10 BMH WS 883 (John M McCarthy), p. 17. Statement re Patk Darcy made by Capt. Martin Chambers to Commandant Power, 2 May 1945.

11 Imperial War Museum [GB], Cat No 6327, Reel 1. Brenton Haliburton Ashmore (Interviewee), Conrad Wood (Recorder), 20 September 1982; retrieved from www.iwm.org.uk/collections/item/object/80006148.

12 'Two Doonbeg Patriots' *Clare Champion*, 4 January 1964.
   'Comrades' Capture and Death', *The Banner* Claremen and Women's Patriotic, Benevolent and Social Association of New York, (New York 1963), p. 186.

13 NAUK, WO 35/115/12, Easter Rising & Ireland Under Martial Law 1916–1921; John Mulqueen, Moore Street, Kilrush, County Clare, Ireland (www.findmypast.co.uk, accessed 5 February 2019).
   Maurice (Moss) Twomey (1930), The West Clare Brigade Papers, IE 2135, p. 45 (Michael McNamara), University of Limerick Special Collections.
   Maurice (Moss) Twomey (1930), The West Clare Brigade Papers, IE 2135, p. 45 (William Shanahan), University of Limerick Special Collections.
   'Two Doonbeg Patriots', *Clare Champion*, 4 January 1964.
   'Comdt Willie Shanahan', *An Phoblacht*, 28 July 1928.

BMH WS 474, (Liam Haugh), p. 26.

14 'Attempt to Escape. Clareman Shot Dead', *Irish Times*, 23 December 1920, p. 3.

15 NAUK, CO 904 127, Telegram from District Inspector, Ennis to Chief Secretary's Office, Dublin Castle, 23 December 1920, 12.36pm.

16 'Comrades' Capture and Death', *The Banner* Claremen and Women's Patriotic, Benevolent and Social Association of New York, (New York 1963), p. 186.

17 Author's email correspondence from Gerard Morrissey, grandnephew of Fr John Considine, 27 October 2010.

18 Maurice (Moss) Twomey (1930), The West Clare Brigade Papers, IE 2135, p. 45. (William Shanahan), University of Limerick Special Collections.

19 BMH WS 1226 (Michael Russell), p. 4.
BMH WS 1251 (Martin Chambers), p. 9.

20 MA MSP 34 REF 34241 (Teresa Dunleavy), Letter of Appeal from Teresa Dunleavy to The Referee, Military Pensions Board in support of her pension application, 1 November 1942.
MA MSPC 1D78 (Michael McNamara), letters from Teresa McNamara to Army Pensions Board, 4 December 1923 and 6 March 1924.

21 NAUK, WO 35 154, Report of proceedings of Court of Inquiry into the death of Michael McNamara.

22 NAUK, WO 35 159A, Report of proceedings of Court of Inquiry into the death of William Shanahan.

23 St Flannan's College Archive, undated statement of Professor Éamon Waldron concerning his arrest and treatment in Ennis Gaol at the hands of Company Sergeant Major William H Strath, 2nd Battalion, Royal Scots.

24 Friends of Irish Freedom. National Bureau of Information. (1920–1922), *Newsletter of the Friends of Irish Freedom*, Vol 2, 1920–21, p. 136.
National Bureau of Information, Washington, DC. Washington, DC: The Bureau; retrieved from https://babel.hathitrust.org, accessed 10 July 2019.

25 Author's email correspondence from Maureen Kelly, daughter of May Havekin (née Shanahan), 11 October 2010.

26 MA MSPC 1D78 (Michael McNamara), minute from S Ó Donnchadha to Mr O'Loughlin, 3 October 1961.

27 MA MSPC ID 109 (William Shanahan).

## Trench warfare

1 BMH WS 1251 (Martin Chambers), p. 5.

2 'Military Claims for Compensation', *Saturday Record*, 15 October 1921.

3 Éamonn Gaynor, *Memoirs of a Tipperary Family: The Gaynors of Tyone 1887–2000* (Dublin 2003), p. 139.

4   BMH WS 1251 (Martin Chambers), p. 10.

5   Pat Bermingham, transcribed by Mathún Mac Fheorais from voice recordings made on 24 August and 8 October 2006, with amendments and additions that were informed by subsequent conversations, (Mathún Mac Fheorais Collection, Local Studies Centre, Ennis).

6   'Cooraclare Tragedy', *Saturday Record*, 9 April 1921.

7   'Door as Stretcher', *Saturday Record*, 5 March 1921.

8   NAUK, CO 905 15. Ireland, Criminal Injuries to Private Persons. County Clare.

9   'Criminal Injuries: Payment of Southern Decrees', *Cork Examiner*, 13 September 1924, p. 7.

10  BMH WS 1251 (Martin Chambers), pp. 10–11.

11  'Clare Motor Smash', *Nenagh Guardian*, 17 September 1921, p. 4.

12  BMH WS 474 (Liam Haugh), p. 34.

13  'Clare Town Isolated', *Irish Independent*, 14 April 1921, p. 5.

14  'Co Clare Round Up', *Evening Echo*, 25 April 1921, p. 2.

## Secret murder

1   Nevil Macready, (1921), *Proclamation No. 2: By the general officer Commanding-in-Chief, the forces in Ireland.*
    'Martial Law Proclaimed', *Saturday Record*, 8 January 1921.

2   'Scenes in Kilkee', *Saturday Record*, 16 October 1920.

3   NAUK, HO 184, RIC Nominal Return of men serving in Co Clare on 1 January 1920 (www.findmypast.co.uk, accessed 07 February 2019).
    NAUK, HO 184, RIC Nominal Return of men serving in Co Clare on 1 January 1921 (www.findmypast.co.uk, accessed 07 February 2019).

4   Email communication from Martin Halpin, grandson of Michael McNamara, 28 June 2019.

5   BMH WS 883 (John M McCarthy), Appendix N.
    Weekly Intelligence Summary, 6th Division, 17 May 1921, p. 4. These documents were captured by the IRA in an operation in the Kilteely district, County Limerick, according to John McCarthy, p. 91.
    NAUK, WO 35 144, Prisoners & Internees – cases and nominal rolls (www.findmypast.co.uk, accessed 28 June 2019).
    NAUK, WO 35 138, Nominal roll of internment camp prisoners, 1 July 1921 (www.findmypast.co.uk, accessed 28 June 2019).

6   *Irish Times*, 7 April 1921, p. 5.
    *Cork Examiner*, 7 April 1921, p. 5.

7   NAUK, WO 35 159A 13, Report of proceedings of Court of Inquiry into the death of Thomas Shannon.
    *Cork Examiner*, 30 May 1921, p. 8.

8   Eoin Shanahan, 'The Blackened Tans', *Clare Association Yearbook* (2014).

9   NAUK, WO 35 159A, Report of proceedings of Court of Inquiry into the death of William Shanahan.
    NAUK, WO 35 154, Report of proceedings of Court of Inquiry into the death of Michael McNamara. The Medical Report on the bodies of Shanahan and McNamara was practically devoid of detail in respect of the nature and extent of their injuries.

10  'Mr. Thos Shannon's Death', *Clare Champion*, 26 March 1921.

11  Martin Staunton, 'Kilrush and the Munster Fusiliers: the experience of an Irish town in the First World War', *Old Limerick Journal*, Vol 35, Winter Edition, 1993.
    *Irish Times*, 7 April 1921, p. 5.
    *Cork Examiner*, 7 April 1921, p. 5.

12  'West Clare Farmer's Death. Widow's Claim for Compensation', *Saturday Record*, 28 May 1921.

13  *Cork Examiner*, 30 May 1921, p. 8.
    In December 1920/January 1921, the General Commander of British Forces in Ireland had decreed that courts in areas that were subject to Martial Law would not, until further notice, have jurisdiction over cases where damage or injury was alleged to have been inflicted by British Forces.

14  'West Clare Farmer's Death. Widow's Claim for Compensation', *Saturday Record*, 28 May 1921.
    NAUK, CO 905 15, Ireland, Criminal Injuries to Private Persons. County Clare.

15  '"Brutal" says Judge. Shooting of West Clare Farmer', *Irish Independent*, 31 May 1921, p. 6.

16  BMH WS 474 (Liam Haugh), p. 27.

17  Eoin Shanahan, 'The Blackened Tans', *Clare Association Yearbook* (2014).

18  David Fitzpatrick, *Politics and Irish Life 1913–1921: Provincial Experience of War and Revolution*, (Cork 1977), pp. 29–30.
    Gabriel Doherty and John Borgonovo, 'Smoking Gun? RIC Reprisals, Summer 1920', *History Ireland* Vol 17, No 2 (March–April, 2009), pp. 36–39.

19  'Sinn Féin Magistrate Shot', *The Banner* Claremen and Women's Patriotic, Benevolent and Social Association of New York (New York 1963), p. 182.

20  'City's murdered mayors: the real story', *Limerick Leader*, 23 June 2012, p. 20.

21  Author's interview with Matthew Bermingham, 27 July 2011.

22  NAUK, Ireland, Petty Sessions Court Registers. Clare, Ireland. 3 September 1920, Thomas Shannon (www.findmypast.co.uk, accessed 07 February 2019).

23  'Obituary, Mr PJ Shanahan, Doonbeg', *Clare Champion*, 11 October 1947.
    'Obituary, Mr PJ Shanahan', *Clare Champion*, 18 October 1947.
    *Irish Independent*, 8 October 1947, p. 5.
    *Irish Press*, 10 October 1947, p. 5. This report contained some factual inaccuracies.

24  *Cork Examiner*, 23 November 1953, p. 2.

## The siege of Kilrush

1  BMH WS 1316 (John Flanagan), p. 18.
2  BMH WS 1316 (John Flanagan).
   BMH WS 1078 (Seán Murnane), p. 14.
3  'The Kilrush Raid, April 1921', *The Banner* Claremen and Women's Patriotic,
   Benevolent and Social Association of New York (New York 1963) p. 180. Stephen
   Madigan's private memoirs indicate that he was the author of this article.
4  BMH WS 1316 (John Flanagan), p. 16.
5  BMH WS 1316 (John Flanagan), p. 16.
   BMH WS 1251 (Martin Chambers), p. 14.
   BMH WS 1685 (Michael McMahon), p. 6.
6  BMH WS 1068 (Michael Brennan), p. 76.
7  BMH WS 1316 (John Flanagan), p. 19.
   Mathún Mac Fheorais interview with Micho 'Carriga' McMahon, Kilrush, 14 July
   1970 (Mathún Mac Fheorais Collection, Local Studies Centre, Ennis).
8  Mathún Mac Fheorais interview with Micho Tubridy, p. 7 (Mathún Mac Fheorais
   Collection, Local Studies Centre, Ennis).
   BMH WS 1685 (Michael McMahon), p. 6.
9  Mathún Mac Fheorais interview with Micho 'Carriga' McMahon, Kilrush, 14 July
   1970, p. 5 (Mathún Mac Fheorais Collection, Local Studies Centre, Ennis).
10 BMH WS 1068 (Michael Brennan), p. 94.
11 BMH WS 1068 (Michael Brennan), p. 94.
   BMH WS 1316 (John Flanagan), pp. 15–16.
12 BMH WS 1068 (Michael Brennan), p. 93.
13 BMH WS 1316 (John Flanagan), p. 18.
14 BMH WS 474 (Liam Haugh), p. 29.
15 'The Kilrush Raid, April 1921', *The Banner* Claremen and Women's Patriotic,
   Benevolent and Social Association of New York (New York 1963) p. 180.
16 Matthew Bermingham Jnr; statement given to Mathún Mac Fheorais, p. 4 (Mathún
   Mac Fheorais Collection, Local Studies Centre, Ennis).
17 Matthew Bermingham Jnr; statement given to Mathún Mac Fheorais (Mathún Mac
   Fheorais Collection, Local Studies Centre, Ennis).
18 Pat Bermingham, transcribed by Mathún Mac Fheorais from voice recordings made on
   24 August and 8 October 2006, with amendments and additions that were informed
   by subsequent conversations (Mathún Mac Fheorais Collection, Local Studies Centre,
   Ennis).
19 BMH WS 1316 (John Flanagan), p. 19.
   Mathún Mac Fheorais interview with Micho 'Carriga' McMahon, Kilrush, 14 July
   1970, p. 6 (Mathún Mac Fheorais Collection, Local Studies Centre, Ennis).
   BMH WS 1685 (Michael McMahon). p. 6.

20 NAUK, WO 35 154/47, Court of Inquiry in lieu of Inquest, Sergeant John McFadden, 26 April 1921; testimony of Constable F J Fallon No. 69971.

21 BMH WS 1068 (Michael Brennan), p. 95.
BMH WS 1685 (Michael McMahon), p. 6.

22 Mathún Mac Fheorais interview with Micho 'Carriga' McMahon, Kilrush, 14 July 1970 (Mathún Mac Fheorais Collection, Local Studies Centre, Ennis).

23 Pat Bermingham, transcribed by Mathún Mac Fheorais from voice recordings made on 24 August and 8 October 2006, with amendments and additions that were informed by subsequent conversations (Mathún Mac Fheorais Collection, Local Studies Centre, Ennis).

24 Mathún Mac Fheorais interview with Micho 'Carriga' McMahon, Kilrush, 14 July 1970, p. 6 (Mathún Mac Fheorais Collection, Local Studies Centre, Ennis).
BMH WS 1316 (John Flanagan), p. 19.

25 BMH WS 1316 (John Flanagan), pp. 18–19.
BMH WS 1685 (Michael McMahon), p. 7.

26 Author's interview with Liam Haugh, son of Bill Haugh, 14 July 2010.
BMH WS 474 (Liam Haugh), pp. 30–31.

27 Pat Bermingham, transcribed by Mathún Mac Fheorais from voice recordings made on 24 August and 8 October 2006, with amendments and additions that were informed by subsequent conversations (Mathún Mac Fheorais collection, Local Studies Centre, Ennis).

28 BMH WS 474 (Liam Haugh), p. 30.
NAUK, WO 35/89, Army Incident Report, 25 April 1921.
'The Kilrush Raid, April 1921', *The Banner* Claremen and Women's Patriotic, Benevolent and Social Association of New York (New York 1963) p. 180.
'Wounded Kilrush Private's Claim', *Saturday Record*, 15 October 1921.

29 BMH WS 1068 (Michael Brennan), pp. 95–96.

30 NAUK, WO 35 154/47. Court of Inquiry in lieu of Inquest, Sergeant John McFadden, 26 April 1921; testimony of Constable F J Fallon No. 69971.

31 NAUK, WO 35 154/47. Court of Inquiry in lieu of Inquest, Sergeant John McFadden, 26 April 1921; testimony of Constable P Hopkins No. 67754.

32 BMH WS 1068 (Michael Brennan), p. 96.
'Fuller Details', *Cork Examiner*, 27 April 1921, p. 7.

33 BMH WS 1316 (John Flanagan), p. 19.
BMH WS 1068 (Michael Brennan), p. 98. According to Brennan, his guide brought the men circuitously around three sides of Market Square, before journeying north along Henry Street.

34 NAUK, WO 35 154/47. Court of Inquiry in lieu of Inquest, Sergeant John McFadden, 26 April 1921; testimony of Constable P Hopkins No. 67754.
BMH WS 1068 (Michael Brennan), p. 98.
In interviews given to Mathún Mac Fheorais in 2006 (Mathún Mac Fheorais Collection, Local Studies Centre, Ennis) Patrick Bermingham stated that Brennan

took McFadden's gun from his pocket and handed it to Patrick's father Matthew Bermingham.

35  BMH WS 1251 (Martin Chambers), p. 14.

36  NAUK, WO 35 89, Army Incident Report, 25 April 1921.

37  BMH WS 1068 (Michael Brennan), p. 98.

38  Pat Bermingham, transcribed by Mathún Mac Fheorais from voice recordings made on 24 August and 8 October 2006, with amendments and additions that were informed by subsequent conversations.
Mathún Mac Fheorais interview with Micko 'Carriga' McMahon, Kilrush, 14 July 1970 (Mathún Mac Fheorais Collection, Local Studies Centre, Ennis).

39  BMH WS 1316 (John Flanagan), p. 22.

40  Mathún Mac Fheorais interview with Micko 'Carriga' McMahon, Kilrush, 14 July 1970, pp. 5–6. (Mathún Mac Fheorais Collection, Local Studies Centre, Ennis).

41  NAUK, WO 35 154/47, Court of Inquiry in lieu of Inquest, Sergeant John McFadden, 26 April 1921; testimony of Dr Richard Counihan.

42  BMH WS 983 (Thomas Tuohy), p. 18.

43  BMH WS 1462 (Seán Moroney), p. 11.
'The Kilrush Raid, April 1921', *The Banner* Claremen and Women's Patriotic, Benevolent and Social Association of New York (New York 1963) p. 180.
Mathún Mac Fheorais interview with Martie Mulqueen, 13 March 1971, p. 6. (Mathún Mac Fheorais Collection, Local Studies Centre, Ennis). Martie Mulqueen claims that Brennan was actually seeking out Sergeant McFadden: 'The East Clare men had come looking for this Sgt. McFadden. He shot a lot of people over in East Clare. He had done a lot of bad things. He burned their houses. They came for him specially.' However, Brennan's account does not corroborate this version.
Éamonn Gaynor, *Memoirs of a Tipperary Family: The Gaynors of Tyone 1887–2000* (Dublin 2003) p. 100.

44  Author's interview with Michael Howard, 2009.

45  NAUK, CO 904 143, Summary of Police Reports, 24 December 1920.

46  BMH WS 1251 (Martin Chambers), p. 14.

47  BMH WS 1068 (Michael Brennan), p. 98. This is Brennan's third uncomplimentary reference to his guide, whom he does not name. While there is no suggestion that Matt Bermingham was his guide, it was unfortunate for Brennan, who had no knowledge of the area, that he and Bermingham became separated after the shooting of Sergeant McFadden. Brennan states that, having spent an hour wandering about the town in the hope of meeting up with somebody who knew the way to the rendezvous point, he and the East Clare men who were still with him headed out the country. He knew that the agreed meeting place was a quarry, so they stopped at houses along the way to ask directions. An old man directed them to a quarry on the road to Cooraclare/Cree. Brennan had a whistle, which he blew at regular intervals. Eventually somebody heard him and responded and he and his party were reunited with the main group. But,

according to Pat Bermingham, his father Matthew made three trips to Kilrush looking for Brennan after he had been informed that the East Clare OC had failed to turn up at Canny's. Brennan turned up later at the home of Murty Tubridy in nearby Ballykett and Bermingham took him from there to Canny's.

48 BMH WS 1316 (John Flanagan), p. 22.

49 BMH WS 1316 (John Flanagan), p. 21.

50 MA MSPC A24, Record of 3rd Battalion, West Clare Brigade, 1918–1923/4, p. 5.

51 'Fuller Details', *Cork Examiner*, 27 April 1921, p. 7.
'Fierce Fight in Clare. Simultaneous attacks on police and military' *Manchester Guardian*, 25 April 1921, p. 7.

52 BMH WS 1068 (Michael Brennan). p. 99. Brennan wore a grey-green coat that resembled a tunic, khaki breeches, collar and shirt, brown boots and leggings, Sam Brown belt, holstered revolver with field glasses slung over his shoulder.

53 'Sergeant McFadden's Funeral', *Saturday Record*, 7 May 1921.

54 'The Rest of the News. Ulster', *Freeman's Journal*, 29 April 1921, p. 7.

55 Captain Walter May, www.theauxiliaries.com/men-alphabetical/men-m/may-w/may.html, accessed 28 October 2018.

56 Author's interview with Liam Haugh, son of Bill Haugh, 14 July 2010.
BMH WS 474 (Liam Haugh), p. 30.

57 'Reprisals with a Difference', *Manchester Guardian*, 3 January 1921.

58 BMH WS 474 (Liam Haugh), p. 33.
'Reprisals', *Saturday Record*, 30 April 1921.

59 NAUK, WO 35 169, C.R., 6th Division, No. 4899/Q.

60 Author's interview with Matthew Bermingham, 27 July 2011.

61 Author's interview with Liam Haugh, son of Bill Haugh, 27 October 2010.
BMH WS 474 (Liam Haugh), p. 33.

62 NAUK, WO 35 169. Claims for Damages, Miscellaneous. Denis Haugh to The Secretary, Irish Land Commission, 22 July 1921.
The Irish Land Commission to Vandeleur Estate, Kilrush, 3 August 1921.

63 'Kilrush Market House Burned Down', *Cork Examiner*, 3 May 1921, p. 2.

64 'Damage to Manchester Martyrs' Monument', *Saturday Record*, 21 January 1922.
Mathún Mac Fheorais interview with Jack Dunleavy, Kilrush, 14 July 1970, p. 1. (Mathún Mac Fheorais Collection, Local Studies Centre, Ennis).
'The Kilrush Monument Partly Demolished', *Saturday Record*, 18 June 1921.

65 'Clare Dressmaker's Claim for Compensation. Dead Police Sergeant and a Marriage Promise', *Manchester Guardian*, 16 January 1922, p. 8.

66 Birth certificate of Maureen Joan Sheedy in author's possession.

67 'Clare Dressmaker's Claim for Compensation. Dead Police Sergeant and a Marriage Promise', *Manchester Guardian*, 16 January 1922, p. 8.

68 *Irish Independent*, 22 April 1922, p. 1.

69 'In Memoriam', *Irish Independent*, 24 April 1923, p. 1.
   'In Memoriam', *Irish Independent*, 22 April 1924, p. 2.
   'In Memoriam', *Irish Independent*, 23 April 1925, p. 1.
70 'Military Claims for Compensation, *Saturday Record*, 15 October 1920.
71 'Provincial News in Brief', *Freeman's Journal*, 11 October 1921, p. 4.
72 BMH WS 883 (John M McCarthy), Appendix N: Weekly Intelligence Summary, 6th Division, 17 May 1921. These documents were captured by the IRA in an operation in the Kilteely district, County Limerick, according to John McCarthy, p. 91.
73 BMH WS 1068 (Michael Brennan), p. 99.
74 BMH WS 1316 (John Flanagan), p. 21.
75 BMH WS 1068 (Michael Brennan), p. 99.
76 BMH WS 1068 (Michael Brennan), p. 76.
77 'Kilrush Curfew', *Saturday Record*, 14 May 1921.
78 'Orders to the Press', *Saturday Record*, 30 April 1921.

## Operation Frustration

1 'Martial Law Proclaimed', *Saturday Record*, 8 January 1921.
2 'Raid in Kilrush', *Saturday Record*, 22 January 1921.
3 BMH WS 474 (Liam Haugh), p. 34.
4 Author's interview with Liam Haugh, son of Bill Haugh, 14 July 2010.
5 NAUK, HO 184, Nominal List of RIC by Counties, 1 January 1921.
6 BMH WS 474 (Liam Haugh), pp. 26–27.
7 NAUK, WO 141 93 213, Record of the Rebellion in Ireland, Vol IV, Part 2, Chapter 7. Temporary Lull in Rebel Activity (www.findmypast.co.uk, accessed 21 February 2019).
8 MA MSPC A24, Records of Activities of the 5th Battalion, West Clare Brigade, IRA, 1917–1923, pp. 18–19.
9 MA MSPC A24, Records of Activities of the 5th Battalion, West Clare Brigade, IRA, 1917–1923, pp. 19–21.
   BMH WS 474 (Liam Haugh), p. 36.
10 MA MSPC A24, Records of Activities of the 5th Battalion, West Clare Brigade, IRA, 1917–1923, p. 21.
11 MA MSPC A24, Record of the 5th Battalion, West Clare Brigade, p. 1.
12 BMH WS 809 (David Conroy), p. 2.
13 BMH WS 1251 (Martin Chambers), pp. 2–3. Chambers's recollection that this happened in June 1918 is incorrect, since McCarthy was in gaol at that time.
14 BMH WS 1251 (Martin Chambers), pp. 3–4. Chambers gave the date of this proposed ambush as 15 August 1919 but Haugh was still in the United States at that time, so the correct year must be 1920. (The Truce was in place in August 1921.)

15 BMH WS 474 (Liam Haugh), p. 25.
   BMH WS 1251 (Martin Chambers), p. 8.

16 BMH WS 1251 (Martin Chambers), p. 8.

17 'Moyasta Bridge Blown Up', *Saturday Record*, 9 July 1921.
   BMH WS 474 (Liam Haugh), p. 35.

18 *The Banner* Claremen and Women's Patriotic, Benevolent and Social Association of New York (New York 1963), p. 187.

19 BMH WS 1253 (Joe Daly), pp. 4–5.

20 UCDA (Mulcahy Papers), P7/A/20, Michael Brennan's report on the Meelick ambush to IRA Headquarters, 1921.
   NAUK, WO 35 154 19, Court of Inquiry in Lieu of Inquest, Christopher McCarthy, 23 June 1921.
   BMH WS 1371 (John McCormack).

21 MA MSPC A24, Records of Activities of 1st Battalion, West Clare Brigade, IRA, 1917–1923, p. 4.

22 BMH WS 474 (Liam Haugh), p. 38
   'Constable's Death. Ear Shot Off', *Cork Examiner*, 5 July 1921.

23 NAUK, WO 35 89. Military Operations and Inquiries (www.findmypast.co.uk, accessed 12 March 2019).
   'More Clare Burnings', *Freeman's Journal*, 4 June 1921, p. 5.
   'Clare Houses Burned', *Saturday Record*, 11 June 1921.
   BMH WS 474 (Liam Haugh), p. 37.

## 'Traitors and cranks'

1 Éamonn Gaynor, *Memoirs of a Tipperary Family: The Gaynors of Tyone 1887–2000* (Dublin 2003), p. 127.

2 Éamonn Gaynor, *Memoirs of a Tipperary Family: The Gaynors of Tyone 1887–2000* (Dublin 2003), p. 150.

3 'Letters to the Editor', *Saturday Record*, 18 June 1921.

4 NAUK, CO 762, Irish Grants Committee, County Clare Extracts, p. 2587, (John Keane), Local Studies Centre, Ennis.

5 NAUK, CO 762, Irish Grants Committee, County Clare Extracts, pp. 567, 2174. (Patrick Keane), Local Studies Centre, Ennis.

6 NAUK, CO 904 143, Summary of Police Reports, 24 December 1920.

7 Author's interview with Siney Talty, Patricia McCarthy and Christy McCarthy, 31 December 2011

8 Author's interview with Mícheál Ó Catháin, 3 October 2011.

9 MA MSPC, MD/6954, Signed and witnessed statement of Laurence Nolan, 8 January 1946.

10 Author's interview with Patrick and Timothy Kelly, grandsons of John 'Sheldrake' Kelly, 2 August 2011.

11 Éamonn Gaynor, *Memoirs of a Tipperary Family: The Gaynors of Tyone 1887–2000* (Dublin 2003), p. 144.

12 Éamonn Gaynor, *Memoirs of a Tipperary Family: The Gaynors of Tyone 1887–2000* (Dublin 2003), p. 143.

13 BMH WS 474 (Liam Haugh), p. 26.
The 'Sinn Féin Court at Clohanes' was not held in Clohanes in September, as Haugh states, but in neighbouring Cloonagarnaun on 6 December 1920. Haugh's allusion to the '… second Burrane effort' probably refers to the first planned Burrane ambush which was cancelled after it became known that the military had knowledge of the impending attack.

14 Author's interviews with Michael Howard, 31 October 2009 and 22 August 2011.

15 Author's interview with Michael Howard, 22 August 2011.

16 NAUK, WO 35 151B, Court of Inquiry in lieu of Inquest, Joseph Greene, 14 January 1921; evidence of Patrick Synan.

17 NAUK, WO 35 151B, Court of Inquiry in lieu of Inquest, Joseph Greene, 14 January 1921; evidence of DI Captain Walter May, ADRIC.

18 Pádraig Ó Ruairc, *Truce. Murder, Myth and the Last Days of the Irish War of Independence* (Cork 2016).

19 'Farmer shot Dead', *Clare Champion*, 8 January 1921.
'Farmer Shot in Clare', *Freeman's Journal*, 10 January 1921, p. 5.
'Items of Interest', *Nenagh Guardian*, 15 January 1921, p. 4.
'Farmer Shot Dead in Clare, *Irish Independent*, 10 January 1921, p. 6.

20 BMH WS 474 (Liam Haugh), p. 26.

21 MA MSPC, MD/6954, Letter from Mrs Margaret Daly to the Referee, Military Pensions Board in support of an application for a service medal for her brother, Patrick Darcy, 25 May 1947.

22 MA MSPC 24 SP 389 (Liam Haugh), Handwritten list of his activities during the War of Independence.

23 Author's interview with Michael Howard, 22 August 2011.

24 NAUK, WO 35 151B, Lieut Colonel, Commanding 2nd Battalion, Royal Scots, Ennis, 24 January 1921, Memo to Headquarters, 18th Infantry Brigade, Limerick.

25 Author's interview with Michael Howard, 22 August 2011.

## Patrick Darcy

1 'School Teacher's Mysterious Death at Doonbeg', *Saturday Record*, 15 October 1921.

2 Paul O'Looney Collection, Diplomas and Certificates awarded to Patrick Darcy.

3 MA MSPC A24, Record of 3rd Battalion, West Clare Brigade, 1918–1923/4, p. 1.

MA MSPC, MD/6954, Sworn evidence given before the Referee and Advisory Committee by Chief Superintendent Seán Liddy in the case of Patrick Joseph Darcy (deceased), 20 May 1947; Liddy noted that the attack took place at dusk and that it was a spur-of-the-moment decision and could not be specific about Darcy's role in the disarming of the two policemen.

4   MA MSPC, MD/6954, Sworn evidence of D P Sheedy re P J Darcy, 26 June 1947, p. 183.

5   NAUK, Ireland, Petty Sessions Court Registers. Clare, Ireland, 4 December 1916. Denis Sheehan (www.findmypast.co.uk, accessed 07 February 2019).

6   MA MSPC, MD/6954, Sworn evidence of D P Sheedy re P J Darcy, 26 June 1947, pp 175–176.

7   MA MSPC, MD/6954, Sworn evidence of John Daly re P J Darcy, 21 May 1947, p. 36.
    MA MSPC, MD/6954, Signed statement of ex RIC sergeant Lawrence Nolan. Nolan was adamant that Darcy had never given any information of a sensitive nature to Constable Hurley. In fact Constable Hurley married in early June 1920 and, in line with RIC protocols, he would no longer have been stationed in County Clare from that time.

8   MA MSPC, MD/6954, Sworn evidence of John Daly re P J Darcy, 21 May 1947, pp. 36–37; Sworn evidence of Major Conor Whelan re P J Darcy, 27 May 1947, p. 58; Sworn evidence of Chief Superintendent Liddy re P J Darcy, 20 May 1947, p. 21.

9   MA MSPC. MD/6954, Sworn evidence of Major Conor Whelan re P J Darcy, 27 May 1947.

10  BMH WS 1226 (Michael Russell), pp. 3–4.

11  BMH WS 883 (John M McCarthy), p. 91.

12  BMH WS 883 (John M McCarthy), Appendix N: Weekly Intelligence Summary, 6th Division, 17 May 1921. These documents were captured by the IRA in an operation in the Kilteely, County Limerick, district according to John McCarthy, p. 91.

13  MA MSPC, MD/6954, Sworn evidence of Chief Superintendent Liddy re P J Darcy, 20 May 1947, p. 6.

14  MA MSPC, MD/6954, Sworn evidence of Commandant Liam Haugh re P J Darcy. 12 June 1947, pp. 111–119.
    BMH WS 1149, (John McCarthy), Memorandum in the handwriting of Colonel Dan Bryan of a statement by Captain Liam Haugh.

15  MA MSPC, MD/6954, Sworn evidence given before the Referee and Advisory Committee by Chief Superintendent Liddy re P J Darcy, 20 May 1947, p. 14.

16  BMH WS 1149 (John McCarthy), Memorandum in the handwriting of Colonel Dan Bryan of a statement by Captain Martin Chambers.

17  NAUK, WO 35 147B, Proceedings of a Court of Inquiry in lieu of Inquest in respect of Patrick Darcy, 27 June 1921.

18  NAUK, WO 35 89B, Telegram from Royal Scots, Ennis, to General Headquarters, Parkgate, Dublin, 17 June 1921.

19 NAUK, WO 35 147B, Proceedings of a Court of Inquiry in lieu of Inquest in respect of Patrick Darcy, 27 June 1921.

20 Author's interview with Paul O'Looney, great-grandson of Margaret Darcy, 30 July 2011.

21 Paul O'Looney Collection, Copy of letter from Margaret Darcy to An Taoiseach, Éamon de Valera, St Patrick's Day, 1945.

22 Paul O'Looney Collection, Handwritten copy of two documents found on the body of Patrick Darcy on 17 June 1921. This document was delivered to Darcy's mother by an RIC policeman after his death.

23 NAI Administration Papers in the Personal Estate of Patrick Darcy (in author's possession).

24 MA MSPC, MD/6954, Sworn evidence given before the Referee and Advisory Committee by Commandant Thomas Marrinan re P J Darcy, 5 June 1947, pp. 101–102.

25 NAI Administration Papers in the Personal Estate of Patrick Darcy (in author's possession).

26 MA MSPC, MD/6954, Sworn evidence given before the Referee and Advisory Committee by Chief Superintendent Liddy re P J Darcy, 20 May 1947, p. 24.

27 MA MSPC, MD/6954, late Patrick J Darcy NT, Signed statement of Commandant Joseph Barrett (retired), 8 June 1947.
MA MSPC, MD/6954, Appendix A. Patrick Darcy, Cooraclare, Co Clare. Statement taken from Commandant Thomas Marrinan, 20 April 1945.
Series of letters from Colonel Dan Bryan to Minister for Justice Gerald Boland, various dates in 1945 and 1946.

28 Paul O'Looney Collection, Signed statement of John Darcy, witnessed by Bernard Barrett, 14 August 1945.
MA MSPC, MD/6954, late Patrick J Darcy NT, copy of John Darcy's statement.

29 MA MSPC, MD/6954, Signed Statement of retired Commandant Joe Barrett in the case of Patrick Joseph Darcy (deceased), 6 June 1947.
BMH WS 1149 (John McCarthy), Letter from Commandant Joe Barrett to Colonel Dan Bryan, 24 April 1945.

30 'A Limerick Tragedy. Vindication of the Late Mr James Dalton', *Freeman's Journal*, 19 February 1921, p. 5.
'Sensational Story at Limerick', *Irish Independent*, 28 May 1920, p. 5.

31 MA MSPC, MD/6954, Sworn evidence given before the Referee and Advisory Committee by Commandant Joe Barrett re Patrick Joseph Darcy (deceased), 13 June 1947.

32 MA MSPC, W1 D467 (James Dalton).
MA MSPC, WC 68 (James Dalton).

33 'School Teacher's Mysterious Death at Doonbeg', *Saturday Record*, 15 October 1921.

34 NAUK, CO 905 15, Ireland, Criminal Injuries to Private Persons. County Clare (Margaret Darcy).

35 Pádraig Óg Ó Ruairc, *The Men Will Talk To Me: Clare Interviews by Ernie O'Malley* (Cork 2016), p. 202.

36 MA MSPC, MD/6954, Letters and memos from Colonel Dan Bryan to Minister Gerald Boland, 24 April 1945, 29 May 1945, 28 July 1945, 8 February 1946, 11 February 1946, 15 February 1946 and 8 March 1946.

37 MA MSPC, MD/6954, Letter from Col Dan Bryan to Minister Gerald Boland, 29 May 1945. The record in question is MA MSPC A24, Record of 3rd Battalion, West Clare Brigade, 1918–1923/4.

38 MA MSPC, MD/6954, handwritten memo from Colonel George P Hodnett to General McMahon, 5 March 1947.

39 MA MSPC, MD/6954, Copy of Affidavit by John Daly, 18 May 1945. John Daly recalled discussions that he had had with the late Commandant Seán O'Dea, OC of the 3rd Battalion. Daly claimed that on one occasion O'Dea had told him of a conversation he had with Seán Liddy after the execution of Patrick Darcy, during which Liddy said 'It's alright if the Brigade is yet free of the spy.' Undated letter from Mick Blake, Clohanes School, Doonbeg, to Patrick Shanahan, Blake wrote 'I know a person to whom the guilty party admitted giving the information which led to the arrest of Willie and Mikey Mac. There was no question of payment for the information; there were two motives: jealousy and revenge. Do you know if a soldier gave evidence at Pa Darcy's courtmartial? There was one lad "put up" to swear that Darcy gave him the information.'

40 MA MSPC, MD/6954, p. 49, Comments by the Referee during sworn evidence given before the Referee and Advisory Committee in the case of P J Darcy on 21 May 1947 by Mrs Margaret Daly, Mr John Daly, Mr John Darcy and Deputy P Shanaghan [*sic*].

41 MA MSPC, MD/6954, Letter from John Daly to An Taoiseach, Éamon de Valera, 16 November 1947. At this time, John Daly had been, for a number of years, the Chairman of West Clare Comhairle Ceanntair, Fianna Fáil.

42 MA MSPC, MD/6954, pp, 31, 48, 49, Comments by the Referee during sworn evidence given before the Referee and Advisory Committee in the case of P J Darcy on 21 May 1947 by Mrs Margaret Daly, Mr John Daly, Mr John Darcy and Deputy P Shanaghan [*sic*].

43 The Bureau of Military History Collection, 1913–1921, was compiled between the years 1947 and 1957. It contains primary source data in the form of statements from a small number of those who were involved in the War of Independence in west Clare.

44 MA MSPC, MD/6954, late Patrick J Darcy NT. Signed statement of Commandant Joseph Barrett (retired), 8 June 1947.

45 MA MSPC, MD/6954, Late Patrick J Darcy NT, Signed statement of Commandant Joseph Barrett (retired), 8 June 1947.
MA MSPC, MD/6954, Late Patrick J Darcy NT, Copy of Affidavit by John Daly, 18 May 1945. Hickman's home at Hazelwood, near Quin, had been burned down by the IRA on 4 July 1921 after he had alerted the authorities about a planned IRA ambush of a British Cavalry patrol.

46 MA MSPC. MD/6954, Copy of unsigned statement of Martin McCarthy, dated Christmas 1946.

47 MA MSPC. MD/6954, Signed and witnessed statement of Laurence Nolan, 8 January 1946.

48 Letter from ex-Sergeant E M Sullivan to John Daly, 2 May 1946.

49 MA MSPC, MD/6954, 'Some Facts Concerning the case of Patrick D'arcy, Deceased'. Unsigned document submitted by John and Margaret Daly to the Referee and Advisory Committee in respect of the application of Margaret Darcy for posthumous award of Service Medal with Bar for her late brother Patrick Darcy.

50 MA MSPC, MD/6954, Sworn evidence given before the Referee and Advisory Committee by Martin Chambers in the case of Patrick Joseph Darcy (deceased), 13 June 1947, pp. 131–135.

51 MA MSPC, MD/6954, Sworn evidence given before the Referee and Advisory Committee by Chief Superintendent Liddy re P J Darcy, 20 May 1947, p. 6.
MA MSPC, MD/6954, Sworn evidence given before the Referee and Advisory Committee by Major Conor Whelan re P J Darcy, 29 May 1947, p. 66.

52 BMH WS 0838 (Seán Moylan), p. 1.

53 BMH WS 1149 (John McCarthy), Memorandum in the handwriting of Colonel Dan Bryan of a statement by Captain Martin Chambers.

54 MA MSPC, 24 SP 592, Letter of appeal from Stephen Hanrahan to Secretary, Board of Assessors, Military Service Pensions.
MA MSPC, MD/6954, Sworn evidence given before the Referee and Advisory Committee by Stephen Hanrahan in the case of Patrick Joseph Darcy (deceased), 25 June 1947, pp. 166–168.

55 MA MSPC. MD/695, Copy statement of Stephen Hanrahan, ex Vice-Commandant, 2nd Battalion, West Clare Brigade.
MA MSPC. MD/6954, Sworn evidence given before the Referee and Advisory Committee by Stephen Hanrahan in the case of Patrick Joseph Darcy (deceased), 25 June 1947, pp. 166–168.

56 MA MSPC, MD/6954, Sworn evidence given before the Referee and Advisory Committee by Michael Melican in the case of Patrick Joseph Darcy (deceased), 25 June 1947, pp. 166–168.

57 MA MSPC. MD/6954. Sworn evidence given before the Referee and Advisory Committee by Commandant Thomas Martin [sic] in the case of P J Darcy, 4 June 1947, pp. 81–82.

58 MA MSPC, MD/6954, Sworn evidence of Chief Superintendent Liddy re P J Darcy, 20 May 1947, pp. 7, 11.

59 BMH WS 474 (Liam Haugh), p. 36.

60 MA MSPC, MD/6954, Sworn evidence given before the Referee and Advisory Committee by James Spellissy re Patrick Joseph (deceased), 17 June 1947, p. 150.
BMH WS 1540 (T. S. McDonagh), p. 13.

61 MA MSPC, MD/6954, Sworn evidence given before the Referee and Advisory Committee by James Spellissy re Patrick Joseph Darcy (deceased), 17 June 1947, p. 138.

62 BMH WS 1540 (T. S. McDonagh), p. 15, Certified copy of death certificate for David Findlay, 18 January 1922. No. 203; retrieved from https://civilrecords.irishgenealogy.ie.

63 Pádraig Óg Ó Ruairc, *Blood on the Banner: The Republican Struggle in Clare* (Cork 2009).
NAUK, WO 35 159A 11, Report of proceedings of Court of Inquiry into the death of William Shanahan.

64 Paul O'Looney Collection, Letter from War Office, Whitehall, to Messrs Michael Sellors & Co, Limerick, 31 July 1947.

65 MA MSPC, MD/6954, Letter from John Daly to the Office of the Referee, Military Pensions Board, 7 August 1947.

66 MA MSPC, MD/6954, Concluding signed statement of the Referee and Advisory Committee following the sworn inquiry re the application of Margaret Darcy for posthumous award of Service Medal with Bar for her late brother Patrick Darcy.

67 The Record of the 3rd Battalion, West Clare IRA, states that this attack took place in April 1918; see MA MSPC A24, Record of 3rd Battalion, West Clare Brigade, 1918-1923/4, p. 1.

68 MA MSPC, MD/6954, Letter from Referee Tadhg Forbes to the Minister (probably Gerald Boland, Minister for Justice), outlining the conclusions from the sworn inquiry re the application of Margaret Darcy for posthumous award of Service Medal with Bar for her late brother Patrick Darcy.

69 MA MSPC, MD/6954, Letter from John Daly to An Taoiseach, Éamon de Valera, 28 August 1947.

70 MA MSPC, MD/6954, Letter from R Ó Súilleabháin, Private Secretary to Minister for Defence, to Private Secretary to An Taoiseach, Éamon de Valera, 17 October 1947.

71 MA MSPC, MD/6954, Letter from John Daly to An Taoiseach, Éamon de Valera, 16 November 1947.

72 'I.R.A. Raids', *Sunday Press*, 13 November 1955; Letter from Margaret D'arcy Daly.

73 'I.R.A. Raids', *Sunday Press*, 13 November 1955; Letter from Patrick Shanahan.

74 MA MSPC, MD/6954, Sworn evidence given before the Referee and Advisory Committee by Michael Melican in the case of Patrick Joseph Darcy (deceased), 25 June 1947, pp. 163–164.

75 NAUK, WO 35 147B, Proceedings of a Court of Inquiry in lieu of Inquest in respect of Patrick Darcy, 27 June 1921.

76 BMH WS 1226 (Michael Russell), pp. 5–6.
MA MSPC, MD/6954, Copy of Affidavit by Margaret Daly, 19 May 1945.
Michael Fitzmartin, Handwritten summary of his role in the War of Independence which formed part of his pension application (in author's possession) courtesy of his brother Senan Fitzmartin; Russell's Witness Statement names this man as James Fitzmartin.

77 MA MSPC, MD/6954, Sworn evidence given before the Referee and Advisory

ENDNOTES

Committee by James Spellissy in the case of Patrick Joseph Darcy (deceased), 17 June 1947, pp. 136, 143.

78 MA MSPC, MD/6954, Sworn evidence given before the Referee and Advisory Committee by Michael Melican in the case of Patrick Joseph Darcy (deceased), 25 June 1947, pp. 153–154.
BMH WS 1226 (Michael Russell), p. 6.

79 'Ambush on Kilrush Road. Auxiliaries Fired On', Saturday Record, 18 June 1921.
MA MSPC A23, Record of the 2nd Battalion, Mid Clare Brigade. Attack on Auxiliaries at Darragh, 9 June 1921.

80 MA MSPC, MD/6954, Late Patrick J Darcy NT, signed statement of Commandant Joseph Barrett (retired), 8 June 1947.
MA MSPC, MD/6954, Sworn evidence given before the Referee and Advisory Committee by Commandant Joe Barrett in the case of Patrick Joseph Darcy (deceased), 13 June 1947, pp. 123–126.

81 BMH WS 1226 (Michael Russell), pp. 6–7.

82 NAUK, WO 35 147B, Proceedings of a Court of Inquiry in lieu of Inquest in respect of Patrick Darcy, 27 June 1921.

83 MA MSPC, MD/6954, Copy of Affidavit by Margaret Daly, 19 May 1945.

84 NAUK, WO 35 147B, Proceedings of a Court of Inquiry in lieu of Inquest in respect of Patrick Darcy, 27 June 1921.

85 MA MSPC, MD/6954, Copy of Affidavit by Margaret Daly, 19 May 1945.
BMH WS 1226 (Michael Russell), p. 7.

86 A number of witnesses at the 1947 sworn inquiry incorrectly stated or inferred that Darcy was taken to Dan Sheedy's house on the evening of 16 June 1921. It is likely that the house he was taken to belonged to the Kellys, who lived to the east of the Community Centre on the Doonbeg Road.

87 BMH WS 1226 (Michael Russell), p. 8.

88 Paul O'Looney Collection, Signed handwritten statement of Teresa Dunleavy, 16 May 1947.

89 BMH WS 1226 (Michael Russell), pp. 8–9.

## Cugadh na mBan

1 MA MSPC CMB 70, West Clare Brigade, 5th Battalion.

2 Author's interview with Mary Driver, 19 August 2019.

3 MA MSP, 34 REF 34241 (Teresa Dunleavy), Sworn affidavit of Teresa Dunleavy, 27 October 1943. Letter of appeal from Teresa Dunleavy to The Referee, Military Pensions Board in support of her pension application 1 November 1942.

4 MA MSP, 34 REF 32799 (Kathleen Bonfield).

5 MA MSPC A24, Record of 4th Battalion, West Clare Brigade, 1918-1923/4, p. 10.

6   MA MSP, 34 REF 48549 (Ellen McMahon).

7   MA MSP, 34 REF 48558 (Mary McMahon), Statement of Bill Haugh to Military Service Pensions Board, 20 June 1940.

8   MA MSP, 34 REF 32889 (Mary O'Dea).

9   MA MSP, 34 REF 33488 (Bridget Honan), Sworn statement given before the Advisory Committee by Bridget Honan (née Liddy), 21 June 1940.

10  MA MSP, 34 REF 33488 (Bridget Honan).
    Certified copy of Marriage Certificate for Michael Honan and Bridget Liddy, 24 June 1924; retrieved from https://civilrecords.irishgenealogy.ie.

11  Mathún Mac Fheorais interview with Jack Dunleavy, Kilrush, (Mathún Mac Fheorais Collection, Local Studies Centre, Ennis).

12  BMH WS 883 (John M McCarthy) p. 63; Certified copy of marriage certificate for Conor Whelan and Catherine McCreery, 19 September 1923. No. 118; retrieved from https://civilrecords.irishgenealogy.ie.

13  Author's interview with Liam Haugh, son of Bill Haugh, 14 July 2010.

14  BMH WS 474 (Liam Haugh) p. 10.
    www.ancestry.co.uk, UK Incoming Passenger Lists 1878–1960, (search criteria: *name:* William Haugh, Martha McEntee / *arrived:* 31 May 1920 / *ship name:* Baltic) (Accessed 16 August 2018).

15  Éamonn Gaynor. *Memoirs of a Tipperary Family: The Gaynors of Tyone 1887–2000* (Dublin 2003), pp. 131–132.

16  'Clare Girls' Hair Trimmed', *Irish Independent.* 22 November 1920, p. 6.
    'Girl's Hair Cut. Co Clare Dance Incident', *Cork Examiner*, 22 November 1920, p. 5.

17  'Girls' Hair Cut Off', *Freeman's Journal*, 15 April 1920, p. 4.
    'Girls' Hair Cut Off', *Saturday Record*, 17 April 1920.

18  'Girls' Hair Cut Off', *Belfast Newsletter*, 17 December 1920, p 10.

19  'Cutting a Girl's Hair off in West Clare', *Saturday Record*, 9 July 1921.
    'Cutting of Girl's Hair', *Cork Examiner*, 6 July 1921, p. 7.

20  NAUK, CO 905 15, Ireland, Criminal Injuries to Private Persons, County Clare.

21  'Clare Girl's Hair Cut', *Irish Independent*, 23 October 1920, p. 3.

22  'Crown forces and the Giving of Evidence', *Freeman's Journal*, 13 May 1921, p. 5.
    'The Clare Claims for Compensation', *Saturday Record*, 30 April 1921.
    NAUK, CO 905 15. Ireland, Criminal Injuries to Private Persons. County Clare.

## The blackened Tans

1   'The Black and Tans', *Weekly Irish Times*, 9 February 1929, p. 4.

2   'Balbriggan scenes. Man who Witnessed two Deaths', *Irish Independent,* 27 October 1920, p. 6.

3 'Balbriggan Victims. Military Inquiry Opens', *Manchester Guardian*, 23 September 1920, p. 7.

4 'Balbriggan, The Homeless and Destitute, Appeal for Funds', *Freeman's Journal*, 30 September 1920, p. 1.

5 Richard Bennett, *The Black and Tans*, (Barnsley 2010), pp. 94–95.

6 'Three men shot dead in Clare Reprisals', *Manchester Guardian*, 24 September 1920, p. 7.

7 Extract from a letter from an officer in Ireland, dated 28 September 1920; Papers of Andrew Bonar Law, House of Lords Record Office, 102/6/9, in John Ainsworth, 'The Black & Tans and Auxiliaries in Ireland, 1920–1921: their origins, roles and legacy', a paper presented to the Annual Conference of the Queensland History Teachers' Association in Brisbane, Saturday, 12 May 2001, p. 4.

8 Patrick Lynch, *With the IRA in the fight for freedom: the red path of glory*, (Cork 2010), pp. 142–147.
Charles Townshend, *The Republic: the fight for Irish Independence 1918–1923*, (London 2014), p. 187.
Ernie O'Malley, *Raids and Rallies*, (Cork 2011), pp. 109–113.
Richard Bennett, *The Black and Tans*, (Barnsley 2010), pp. 94–95.
Donal O'Sullivan, *The Irish Constabularies 1822–1922: a century of policing in Ireland*, (Dingle, 1999), p. 330.
W H Kautt, *Ambushes and Armour; the Irish Rebellion 1919–1921*, (Dublin 2010), p. 95.
Seán Spellissy, *A History of County Clare*, (Dublin 2003), p. 64.
Pádraig Óg Ó Ruairc, *Blood on the Banner: The Republican Struggle in Clare*, (Cork 2009), pp. 167–170.
Conor Kostik, *Revolution in Ireland: popular militancy 1917–1923*, (Cork 1996).
D M Leeson, *The Black & Tans: British Police and Auxiliaries in the Irish War of Independence*, (New York 2011), pp. 175–176.
BMH WS 1540 (T S McDonagh) p. 8.
John Ainsworth, 'The Black & Tans and Auxiliaries in Ireland, 1920–1921: their origins, roles and legacy', a paper presented to the Annual Conference of the Queensland History Teachers' Association in Brisbane, Saturday, 12 May 2001, p. 4,
James S Donnelly Jr, '"Unofficial" British Reprisals and IRA Provocations, 1919–20: the cases of three Cork towns', *Eire-Ireland*, Vol 45 no 1/2 (Spr/Summ, 2010) p. 185,
'Obituary. Matthias McD Bodkin, K.C.', *Irish Times*, 8 June 1933, p. 8.
'Who Controls the RIC?' *Manchester Guardian*, 25 September 1920, p. 9.
'The Struggle of the Irish People', Address to the Congress of the United States adopted at the January Session of Dáil Éireann (1921), p. 22, https://babel.hathitrust.org/cgi/pt?id=loc.ark:/13960/t2r50353t&view=1up&seq=3, accessed 30 July 2019.

9 'Ruins in Clare. Shocking Report of Young Man's Fate', *Manchester Guardian*, 25 September 1920, p. 9.

10 'The Scourge of Clare. A night of Horror', *Manchester Guardian*, 24 September 1920, p. 7.

11 'Thos Connole's Death', *Clare Champion*, 5 February 1921.

'How Tom Connole, Ennistymon, Was Killed', *Freeman's Journal*, 11 October 1920, p. 6.

12 'Sequel to Rineen Ambush', *Saturday Record*, 5 February 1921.

13 MA MSPC ID 470 A (Patrick Lehane) Application of Mrs Margaret Lehane under the Army Pensions Act 1923, Question 4.
NAUK, WO 35 153A, Courts of Inquiry in lieu of Inquest, Patrick Lehane, Daniel Lehane, Charles Lynch (Patrick Lehane is mistakenly confused with P J Linnane in one document in this file). Lehane's death certificate records that he was '… found burned due to reprisals. No medical attendant.' Both the application of Mrs Lehane and a British Army internal communication agree that Pake Lehane was shot and burned in Flanagan's Pub.
'Resident Magistrate's Motor Car', *Saturday Record*, 23 April 1921. Meldon's car was taken 'in the name of the Irish Republic' the following morning as he prepared to leave the town.

14 Archives of the Society of Jesus, Australia, 'Seven Years in Limerick', undated typescript, Hackett Papers.

15 'How Tom Connole, Ennistymon, Was Killed', *Freeman's Journal*, 11 October 1920, p. 6.

16 NAUK, WO 35 89, Army Incident Report, Ennistymon, 22 September 1920.

17 'Payment for Damage. Clare Reprisals Admissions', *Manchester Guardian*, 22 February 1921, p. 7.

18 BMH WS 474 (Liam Haugh), p. 22.
Pádraig Óg Ó Ruairc, *Blood on the Banner: The Republican Struggle in Clare*, (Cork 2009), p. 212.
*The Banner* Claremen and Women's Patriotic, Benevolent and Social Association of New York, (New York 1963), p. 185.

19 NAUK, WO 35 148, Court of Inquiry in lieu of Inquest, Thomas Curtin, 9 December 1920, Testimony of Lieutenant A W Tuffield, 2nd Btn, the Royal Scots.

20 'Crown forces Impugned', *Irish Independent*, 24 May 1921, p. 5.

21 'Courtsmartial Trials', *Irish Times*, 17 December 1920, p. 3.
NAUK, WO 35 133, Court-martial case registers (www.findmypast.co.uk, accessed 07 February 2019).

22 BMH WS 1226 (Michael Russell), p. 4.
BMH WS 1251 (Martin Chambers), p. 9.
MA MSP 34, REF 34241 (Teresa Dunleavy), Letter of appeal from Teresa Dunleavy to The Referee, Military Pensions Board in support of her pension application, 1 November 1942.
MA MSPC 1D78 (Michael McNamara); Letters from Teresa McNamara to Army Pensions Board, 4 December 1923 and 6 March 1924.
Friends of Irish Freedom. National Bureau of Information. (19201922). Newsletter of the Friends of Irish Freedom, Vol 2, 1920–21, p. 136.
National Bureau of Information, Washington DC. Washington DC: The Bureau; retrieved from https://babel.hathitrust.org, accessed 10 July 2019.
Joseph McKenna, *Guerilla Warfare in the Irish War of Independence 1919–1921*, (North Carolina 2011), p. 178.
'Election Contest in Clare', *Clare Champion*, 17 November 1945.

23  BMH WS 474 (Liam Haugh), p. 27.

24  'Sequel to Rineen Ambush', *Saturday Record*, 5 February 1921.

25  'Memorials Unveiled', *Connacht Tribune*, 27 September 1958, pp. 7–8. Here John Burke, who participated in the Rineen Ambush, attributes the killing of Dan Lehane and the burning of his house to Black and Tans.
MA MSPC ID 470 A (Patrick Lehane), Statement of Chief Superintendent Éamonn Ó Dubhthaig re application of Mrs Margaret Lehane under the Army Pensions Act 1923.

26  'Lahinch and Ennistymon Burnings,' *Saturday Record*, 5 February 1921.

27  D M Leeson, *The Black & Tans: British Police and Auxiliaries in the Irish War of Independence* (New York 2011), p. 193.

28  John Dorney, "Cowardly, Cunning and Contemptible'– the British campaign in Dublin, 1919–1921', *The Irish Story*, www.theirishstory.com/2017/02/16/cowardly-cunning-and-contemptible-the-british-campaign-in-dublin-1919-1921/#.XT2vFvLdupq.

29  'Big Expansion in Paperback', *Irish Independent*, 30 June 1965, p. 8.

30  Tomás Mac Conmara, *The Time of the Tans: an oral history of the War of Independence in County Clare*, (Cork 2019), p. 30.

31  D M Leeson, *The Black & Tans: British Police and Auxiliaries in the Irish War of Independence*, (New York 2011), p. 193.

32  Educational Company of Ireland, *A Basic History of Ireland From the earliest times to 1922*, (Dublin), p. 313.

## Reclaiming the streets

1  James T McGuane, *Kilrush From Olden Times*, (Galway 1984), p. 75.

2  Maurice (Moss) Twomey (1930), The West Clare Brigade Papers, IE 2135, p. 45 (Dan Crawford), University of Limerick Special Collections.

3  Maurice (Moss) Twomey (1930), The West Clare Brigade Papers, IE 2135, p. 45 (Thomas Keane), University of Limerick Special Collections. Both Keane's birth year and date of death are incorrect in the account in the Moss Twomey archive. Certified copy of death certificate for Thomas Keane, 5 March 1916; retrieved from https://civilrecords.irishgenealogy.ie.

4  Maurice (Moss) Twomey (1930), The West Clare Brigade Papers, IE 2135, p. 45 (Michael Keane), University of Limerick Special Collections.
*The Banner* Claremen and Women's Patriotic, Benevolent and Social Association of New York (New York 1963), p. 190.

5  Maurice (Moss) Twomey (1930), The West Clare Brigade Papers, IE 2135, p. 45 (Patrick O'Dea), University of Limerick Special Collections.

6  Maurice (Moss) Twomey (1930), The West Clare Brigade Papers, IE 2135, p. 45 (John O'Gorman), University of Limerick Special Collections.

7   Maurice (Moss) Twomey (1930), *The West Clare Brigade Papers*, IE 2135, p. 45
    (Patrick Keating), University of Limerick Special Collections.
    Certified copy of death certificate for Patrick Keating, 29 August 1922; retrieved from
    https://civilrecords.irishgenealogy.ie.

8   James T McGuane, *Kilrush From Olden Times*, (Galway 1984), p. 75.
    Valuation Office, Dublin, Index of Townlands and streets, Electoral Division of Kilrush
    Urban, 1937–1966. A number of Kilrush streets still bear the names of the west Clare
    men in whose honour they were renamed, including O'Dea's Road, Fahy's Road and
    O'Gorman Street.

## Calm before the storm

1   BMH WS 1068 (Michael Brennan), p. 116.

2   'Truce', *Nenagh Guardian*, 23 July 1921, p. 3.

3   'Alleged Breaches of the Truce', *Nenagh News*, 30 July 1921, p. 4.

4   BMH WS 474 (Liam Haugh), p. 34.

5   MA MSPC A24, Record of 2nd Battalion, West Clare Brigade, 1918–1923/4, pp. 8–9.
    MA MSPC A24. Record of 5th Battalion, West Clare Brigade, 1918–1923/4.

6   NAUK, CO 904 151, Summary of Police Reports (County Clare), October 1920.

7   NAUK, CO 904 151, Summary of Police Reports (County Clare), October 1920.
    NAUK, WO 35 207 118, Sinn Féin Activists F–W, Castle File No. 5146, Liddy, John,
    Danganelly, Cooraclare, Co Clare.

8   BMH WS 1068 (Michael Brennan), pp. 58, 86.

9   'The Flames of 1920. Farmers and the Black and Tans', *Clare Champion*, 8 May 1926.

10  Mathún Mac Fheorais interview with Pat Bermingham (Mathún Mac Fheorais
    Collection, Local Studies Centre, Ennis).

11  Author's interview with Siney Talty, 31 December 2011.

12  'Home from Prison Welcome To Clare Priests,' *Cork Examiner*, 28 October 1921, p. 4.

13  'Clare Rejoicings,' *Cork Examiner*, 9 December 1921, p. 5.

## Afterword

1   Éamonn Gaynor, *Memoirs of a Tipperary Family: The Gaynors of Tyone 1887–2000*
    (Dublin 2003), p. 178.

# Bibliography

Abbott, Richard, *Police Casualties in Ireland 1919–1922* (Cork 2000).

Bennett, Richard, *The Black and Tans* (London 1959).

Bennett, Richard, *The Black and Tans* (Barnsley 2010).

Bonsall, Penny, *The Irish RMs: The Resident Magistrates in the British Administration in Ireland* (Dublin 1997).

Breathnach, M, *A Basic History of Ireland from the Earliest Times to 1922* (Dublin undated).

Brennan, Michael, *The War in Clare 1911–1921: Personal Memories of the Irish War of Independence* (Dublin 1980).

Brown, Kevin J, *Éamon de Valera & The Banner County* (Dublin 1982).

Childers, Erskine, *The Constructive Work of Dáil* Éireann, *No.2* (Dublin 1921).

Claremen and Women's Patriotic Benevolent and Social Association of New York (eds), *The Banner,* (New York 1963).

Coogan, Tim Pat, *De Valera, Long Fellow, Long Shadow* (London 1993).

Coogan, Tim Pat, *Ireland Since the Rising* (USA 1966).

Cooraclare/Cree Historical Society (eds) *Cooraclare & Cree, Parish of Kilmacduane: history & folklore* (Clare 2002).

Crowley, John, Ó Drisceoil, Donal and Murphy, Mike (eds) *Atlas of the Irish Revolution* (Cork 2017).

Dinan, Brian, *Clare and its People: A Concise History* (Cork 1987)

*Evidence on Conditions in Ireland: Comprising the Complete Testimony: Affidavits and Exhibits Presented before the American Commission on Conditions in Ireland,* transcribed and annotated by Albert Coyle, Official Reporter to the Commission (Washington 1921).

Farrell, J G, *Troubles* (London 1970).

Fitzpatrick, David (ed), *Revolution? Ireland, 1917–23* (Dublin 1990).

Fitzpatrick, David (ed), *Politics and Irish Life: 1913–1921: Provincial Experience of War and Revolution,* (2nd edition, Cork 1998).

Gallagher, Frank, *The Four Glorious Years 1918–1921,* (2nd edition, Dublin 2005).

Gaynor, Éamonn, *Memoirs of a Tipperary Family: The Gaynors of Tyone 1887–2000* (Dublin 2003)

Henry, O F M Cap., Father (ed), *The Capuchin Annual 1970* (Dublin 1970)

Hezlet, Sir Arthur, *The 'B' Specials: A History of the Ulster Special Constabulary* (London 1972).

Hopkinson, Michael, *The Irish War of Independence* (Dublin 2002).

Kautt, William H, *Ambushes and Armour: The Irish Rebellion 1919–1921* (Dublin 2010).

Kostik, Conor, *Revolution in Ireland: Popular Militancy 1917–1923* (Cork 1996).

Kotsonouris, Mary, *Retreat from Revolution: The Dáil Courts, 1920 –1924* (Dublin 1994).

Leeson, David M, *The Black and Tans: British Police and Auxiliaries in the Irish War of Independence* (Oxford 2011).

Liddy, James, *Gold Set Dancing* (Clare 2000).

Long, A W, *Tales of the RIC,* Blackwood, William & Sons (eds), (Edinburgh and London 1921).

Lynch-Robinson, Sir Christopher, *The Last of the Irish RMs* (London 1951).

Mac Mathúna, Seosamh, *Kilfarboy, A History of a West Clare Parish* (Dublin 1976).

Mac Conmara, Tomás, *Time of the Tans: An Oral History of the War of Independence in County Clare* (Cork 2019).

McCarthy, Daniel, *Ireland's Banner County. Clare from the fall of Parnell to the Great War, 1890–1918* (Clare 2002).

McGuane, James, *Kilrush from Olden Times* (Indreabhán 1984).

Niall, Brenda, *The Riddle of Father Hackett: A Life in Ireland and Australia* (Canberra 2009).

Ó'Brion, Leon, *The Prime Informer: A Suppressed Scandal* (London 1971).

Ó Comhraí, Cormac & Stiofán, *Peadar Clancy: Easter Rising Hero, Bloody Sunday Martyr* (Athlone 2016).

O'Malley, Ernie, *Raids and Rallies* (Cork, 2011)

Ó Ruairc, Pádraig Óg, *Blood on the Banner: The Republican Struggle in Clare* (Cork 2009)

Ó Ruairc, Pádraig Óg, *Revolution: A Photographic History of Revolutionary Ireland 1913–23* (Cork, 2012).

Ó Ruairc, Pádraig Óg, 'The Difference is a Fine but a Real One: Sectarianism in Clare during the Irish War of Independence 1919–21', *The Other Clare: Journal of the Shannon Archaeological and Historical Society* (Shannon 2010).

Ó Ruairc, Pádraig Óg, *The Men Will Talk to Me: Clare Interviews by Ernie O'Malley* (Cork 2016).

Ó Ruairc, Pádraig Óg, *Truce: Murder, Myth and the Last Days of the Irish War of Independence* (Cork 2016).

# BIBLIOGRAPHY

O'Sullivan, Donal, *The Irish Constabularies 1822–1922: A Century of Policing in Ireland* (Kerry 1999).

Ryan, Canon Peter, *History of Kilmurry Ibrickane* (Clare 1969).

Shanahan, Eoin, 'Telling Tales: the story of the burial alive and drowning of a Clare RM in 1920', *History Ireland*, 18 (1), (Jan–Feb 2010).

Shanahan, Eoin, 'The Blackened Tans' in *The Clare Champion* (November 2013); also published in *The Royal Irish Constabulary Forum, Research Genealogy and History of the old Irish Police Forces* (2014).

Shanahan, Eoin, 'The Shooting of Tom Shannon, forgotten hero of the War of Independence in West Clare', *Clare Association Yearbook, 2016.*

Shanahan, Eoin, 'Guns in the Water: Quilty's Car, Spindler's Aud, and the First Casualties of the Easter Rising of 1916', *Breac: A Digital Journal of Irish Studies* (University of Notre Dame 2016)

Shanahan, Eoin, 'Kilmihil's Bloody Sunday', *Clare Association Yearbook, 2018.*

Sheedy, Keiran, *The Clare Elections* (Dublin 1993).

Somerset Fry, Peter & Fiona, *A History of Ireland* (London 1988).

Spellissy, Seán, *A History of County Clare* (Dublin 2003).

Townshend, Charles, *The Republic: The Fight for Irish Independence* (London 2013).

Various, *With the IRA in the Fight for Freedom 1919 to the Truce: The Red Path to Glory* (Tralee 1963).

Various, *Blackwood's Magazine Volume CCIC, January–June 1921*, Blackwood & Sons (eds) (London 1921).

## Digital Sources

www.ancestry.co.uk

www.breac.nd.edu

https://digitalcollections.tcd.ie/home/

www.findmypast.co.uk

https://hansard.parliament.uk/

www.hathitrust.org

www.history.com

www.historyireland.com

www.irishconstabulary.com

www.irishgenealogy.ie/en/

www.iwm.org.uk

www.libertyellisfoundation.org

www.presspack.rte.ie/press-pack-login/

www.rte.ie/centuryireland

www.theauxiliaries.com

www.theirishstory.com

www.youtube.ie

# Index abbreviations

| | |
|---|---|
| B&T | Black and Tan |
| Btn | Battalion |
| CI | County Inspector |
| DI | District Inspector |
| ECB | East Clare Brigade |
| ELB | East Limerick Brigade |
| F&FY | Fife & Forfarshire Yeomanry |
| HLI | Highland Light Infantry |
| IWM | Imperial War Museum |
| JP | Justice of the Peace |
| LV | Limerick Volunteer |
| RIC | Royal Irish Constabulary |
| RM | Resident Magistrate |
| RS | Royal Scots |

# Index

# INDEX

# M

Eoin Shanahan was born and reared in the parish of Doonbeg, in the heart of west Clare. He is a nephew of Willie Shanahan, one of the local heroes of the War of Independence.

Eoin is a graduate of Dublin City University, with a Masters Degree in Education and Training. He has conducted extensive historical research and he has published in a wide variety of journals including *History Ireland*, *Clare Association Yearbook*, *Breac: A Digital Journal of Irish Studies* (University of Notre Dame) and *The Old Limerick Journal*.

Prior to his retirement as a primary school teacher, he spent a number of years as an advisor with the Professional Development Service for Teachers (PDST) where he continues to work as an Associate. He has done some pioneering work in the areas of Phonological and Phonemic Awareness, as evidenced in his seminal work 'Towards an Inventory of the Phoneme-Grapheme Units of Standard Irish English', published in *Voices of Educators in 21st Century Ireland* (Hibernia College, 2018).

# CLAREBOOKS

ClareBooks is an 'umbrella' publisher, conceived in 2018 by Belfast-born writer and graphic designer, Niall Allsop, with the aim of enabling authors to publish their work.

Specifically the ClareBooks imprint focuses on facilitating the publication of non-fiction titles. Ideally these would be projects conceived by Clare-based authors or books with an obvious Clare theme such as ClareBooks' first title, Patricia Lysaght's *Welsh Óg: A Clare Storyteller*.

ClareBooks is especially delighted to have had the opportunity to work with Eoin Shanahan to enable the publication of his *The hand that held the gun: Untold stories of the War of Independence in west Clare*, the culmination of over a decade of meticulous research and the sourcing of many hitherto unpublished photographs.

*If you have a non-fiction book project that fits the ClareBooks criteria, especially in one of the follow genres—Clare interest, travel, biography & memoir, transport, crafts, humour or local history—then visit the ClareBooks website, www.clarebooks.ie, for further information.*

Printed in Great Britain
by Amazon